George Dickie

The botanist's guide to the counties of Aberdeen, Banff and Kincardine

George Dickie

The botanist's guide to the counties of Aberdeen, Banff and Kincardine

ISBN/EAN: 9783337273217

Printed in Europe, USA, Canada, Australia, Japan

Cover: Foto ©Andreas Hilbeck / pixelio.de

More available books at **www.hansebooks.com**

THE

BOTANIST'S GUIDE

TO THE COUNTIES OF

ABERDEEN, BANFF, AND KINCARDINE.

BY

G. DICKIE, A.M., M.D., &c.

PROFESSOR OF BOTANY IN THE UNIVERSITY OF ABERDEEN.

ABERDEEN:
A. BROWN & CO.
EDINBURGH: JOHN MENZIES, AND A. & C. BLACK.
LONDON: LONGMAN & CO.

1860.

FIS\91
DICKIE, G.
The botanist's guide
COZG1   aa

TO

A. THOMSON, Esq. OF BANCHORY,

IN TESTIMONY OF ENCOURAGEMENT GIVEN BY HIM TO THE STUDY
OF NATURAL SCIENCE, AND AS A MARK OF ESTEEM,

The following Pages

ARE DEDICATED BY

THE AUTHOR.

CONTENTS.

	Page
PREFACE,	vii
INTRODUCTORY REMARKS,	xiii
DICOTYLEDONOUS PLANTS,	1
MONOCOTYLEDONOUS PLANTS,	158
INTRODUCED PLANTS,	216
FERNS AND ALLIES,	226
MOSSES,	237
LIVERWORTS,	262
CHARACEAE,	267
LICHENS,	268
SEA-WEEDS, &c. &c.,	281
MUSHROOMS,	319
ADDENDA,	336
INDEX,	337

PREFACE.

THE BOTANY of Aberdeenshire and neighbouring Counties has at various periods occupied the attention of observers.

More than 100 years ago, Dr. David Skene, a contemporary and correspondent of Linnæus, studied the Zoology and Botany of his native district; his manuscript is still extant, and in possession of Mr. Thomson of Banchory. The genus *Skenea* of Malacologists stands on the records of science as a memorial of the merits of this accurate observer. Several important facts from the MSS. of Dr. Skene will be found in different parts of this work. The late Professor James Beattie, of Marischal College, was a contributor to Sir J. E. Smith's work on the "Flora of Britain." The late Rev. Dr. Smith, of Chapel of Garioch, studied the plants of that part of the country. Lectures on Botany were delivered in Aberdeen, in 1817 and 1818, by the late Rev. A. B. Mackay. The late Professor Knight, of Marischal College, did essential service in diffusing a taste for botanical pursuits; and, as a former pupil in his botanical class, I must bear testimony to his zeal in this department. Dr. Alexander Murray published in 1836 the first part of his "Northern Flora," in which it was his intention to embrace a complete account of the indigenous plants in a range embraced by a boundary stretching from the Forfarshire coast on the east to that of Sutherland on the west; consisting of that portion of the east and interior of Scotland which lies north of Montrose, in addition to the western part of the County of Sutherland. The lamented death of Dr. Murray in 1837 put a stop to this work.

My respected friend, the Rev. Mr. M'Millan, more than 30 years ago studied the plants of Aberdeen, and conducted classes which were attended by amateurs and students of the medical school. Mr. Morren, about the same period, also gave instructions in this department. Mr. Cow, surgeon, now of Crimond, began about 1836, to print a "Flora of Aberdeen," which, however, was never published, the sheets being left incomplete in the hands of the printer. The late Professor Graham, of Edinburgh, with his pupils, made frequent visits, chiefly to the interior of the country, a practice which has been continued by his successor, Dr. Balfour. Notes of species collected in these excursions have appeared in the *Edinburgh New Philosophical Journal*, and in the *Transactions of the Edin-*

burgh Botanical Society. Mr. Watson, author of "Cybele Britannica," has also examined some of the higher parts of the country, and the results appear in that work; the value of his inquiries is such as to require no eulogy from me. The late Mr. Gardiner, of Dundee, published, in 1845, "Rambles in Braemar," containing notices of the rarer plants. In 1836, I published a "Flora of Aberdeen," embracing a range of about 12 miles south-west and north, and therefore, comprehending part of the County of Kincardine. Subsequent to that date, facts were collected with the view of extending the work, and of comprehending the entire Flora, Phænogamic and Cryptogamic, of the three Counties of Kincardine, Aberdeen, and Banff. Removal to another part of the kingdom interrupted for a time my investigations. Portions of the materials thus accumulated have appeared in various publications. The "Aberdeen Flora" of Mr. P. Macgillivray, published in 1853, contains additional species and localities not recorded in the work already alluded to. My friend, the late Professor Macgillivray, had accumulated notes on the Botany of the County of Aberdeen, which, after his decease, were embodied in the "Natural History of Deeside," published after his death, and privately distributed through the liberality of His Royal Highness Prince Albert.

The following pages afford evidence that there are

not a few ardent cultivators of Botany who have carefully and very successfully studied the plants of the three Counties to which this work refers. To them my cordial thanks are specially due for the liberality with which they supplied information. The facts respecting latitudinal range of the species in Britain are taken from my friend Mr. Watson's " Cybele Britannica;" the range in altitude is to be understood as that of the respective species, for the most part in the County of Aberdeen, and the facts here recorded are in most cases derived from my own observations; where these were imperfect, I have quoted Mr. Watson's measurements made on the Braemar mountains. Where a ? follows the range in altitude, it will be understood that I consider this as still uncertain and not fully ascertained.

In a few instances, the altitudinal range has not been measured by any one; but so many fixed points are known that I have felt no hesitation in stating such range—an example may suffice. Arenaria *trinervis*, one of the rarest of our plants, occurs in Den of Gight, the elevation of which is certainly not above 200 feet, the only other station for it, known at present, is near the Linn of Dee, the height of which is 1190 feet more or less.

The work would have been incomplete without a notice of the "Cryptogamic" plants. To Mr. Croall, of Montrose, I am indebted for notes of *Mosses* and *Hepaticae* found in Braemar. The Rev. J. Yuill and Mr. Bell have contributed notes of Marine *Algae* from Peterhead ; and in this department of the subject I have also received aid from Miss Smith, who has successfully studied the species found on the coast of Kincardine. In some respects, however, this part of the work is not so perfect as could be desired, especially as regards the *Fungi or Mushrooms*, the species recorded being those in my own collection solely, these plants being often neglected by Botanists, though presenting a very interesting field for study. I believe Aberdeenshire to be peculiarly rich in Fungi; and it is to be hoped that the present attempt may stimulate others to study them. The fullest account of the *Lichens* is that given in Professor Macgillivray's "Natural History of Deeside;" and though my own collection is tolerably complete, there are several recorded in that work which have not been found by me, they are therefore quoted on the authority of my deceased friend. Doubtless more extended investigations will add much to the materials brought together here, which may be regarded as "Collectanea" for a Flora of a district which presents an interesting field for the Botanist.

INTRODUCTION.

A FEW remarks on the physical characters of the district may be necessary in the outset. The County of Aberdeen occupies a position between 56° 52′ and 57° 42′ north, and 1° 49′ to 3° 48′ west longitude; its greatest length is at least 80 miles, stretching between Cairn Eilar on the borders of Perth and Inverness, and the Buchan-ness near Peterhead. It presents an undulating coast line of more than fifty miles; which, from Aberdeen to Peterhead has a north-east direction; thence it runs almost due north to Cairnbulg Head, and then trends nearly due west to the borders of Banffshire. The county embraces a surface of 1950 English square miles.

A line from Peterculter, on the borders of Kincardine, to Pennan, on the borders of Banff, divides it into two portions which present very different physical aspects; the portion to the east of this line presents no elevation exceeding 900 feet, and no part is more than 20 miles distant from the German ocean. To the west of the line indicated, there is a gradual rise of the surface toward the south-west. This becomes obvious if we trace the levels of the two principal rivers—the Dee and the Don. The former has an elevation of 1640 feet at a distance of 70 miles from its mouth; the Don, about 55 miles inland, is 1240 feet above the sea. The river Muick in a course of 10 miles only, from its source at Loch Muick to its junction with the Dee at Ballater, presents a difference of level amounting to more than 500 feet.

These facts are singularly in contrast with observations made on the course of the river Ythan, which drains part of the more eastern district; at 22 miles from the German ocean it is only 124 feet above that sea. Some of the passes from one glen to another illustrate the same point; the highest level of the path on the east shoulder of Mount Battock, (28 miles west from Aberdeen,) is about 2000 feet; while that on the west shoulder of Mount Keen, 10 miles more inland, attains an elevation of 2400 feet. Again, if we take a general view of the heights of the mountains in sections of 10 miles from east to west, we observe a regular increase in elevation till we reach a zone in which few of the numerous mountains are lower than two or three thousand feet, and many exceed four thousand, the extreme summit being that of Ben Macdui, viz. :—about 4300 feet; and, therefore, in Britain, second only to Ben Nevis.

The County of Kincardine lies between 56° 43' and 57° 5' north latitude, and 1° 47' to 2° 30' west longitude; it is about 32 miles long from north to south, and 24 in breadth; ⅔ of the surface are estimated as arable, the remaining ⅓ being occupied by the eastern part of the Grampians, the highest of these in the county being Clochnaben, which attains an elevation of nearly 2000 feet.

The County of Banff is bounded on the north by the Moray Frith, on the south and east by Aberdeenshire, and on the west by Morayshire. It is in 58° north latitude, and 2° 13' to 3° 40' west longitude. It presents an area of 647 square miles, and about 120,000 acres are under cultivation. The surface gradually rises toward the south-west or interior, the culminating point being Cairngorm, the height of which is about 4100 feet.

The valuable list of altitudes published by Mr. Jamieson, renders any farther details unnecessary.*

A brief summary of the climatology of the district may find an appropriate place here.

Records of barometer, thermometer, and rain guage have been kept at Aberdeen, by the late Mr. G. Innes; by the late Professor Gray, now continued by his son in conjunction with Mr. A. Cruickshank. I also, for some years, made similar

---

* List of Altitudes in the Counties of Aberdeen, Banff, and Kincardine, by Thomas F. Jamieson. A. Brown & Co., Aberdeen, 1859.

observations, which were communicated weekly to one of the local newspapers. Observations have also been made at Peterhead; at Alford, by the late Rev. Dr. Farquharson; and by Dr. Gairden, at Balfluig; at Huntly Lodge, by Mr. Acheson; at Castle Newe, Strathdon, by Mr. Walker; and at Banchory House, by A. Thomson, Esq.

At Castleton of Braemar, Mr. Pearce has been for more than two years noticing the results shown by thermometer, barometer, and rain guage, in that elevated locality, 1180 feet above the sea. The results are sufficiently interesting to encourage perseverance. The instruments are of the best quality; and have been provided by the liberality of H. R. Highness, Prince Albert. Mr. Pearce also registers the force of Ozone, a branch of inquiry which, it is to be hoped, will become more general.

It is unnecessary here to give more than the general results at a few stations :—

ABERDEEN.—1823-1841 INCLUSIVE.
Means of the Seasons.

DEG.
Spring,..........March, April, May,............45·13
Summer,........June, July, August,............57·31
Autumn,........September, October, November, 47·92
Winter,........December, January, February,..37·93
Annual Mean Temperature, 1823 to 1841 inclusive,....47·07

DEG.
Extremes of Annual Mean { Highest, 49·65 in 1828.
Temperatures,........ { Lowest, 44·25 in 1838.

Average number of days on which Snow or Rain fell in each Month, from 1830 to 1841 inclusive.

	No. of days on which Snow fell.		No. of days on which Rain fell.
January,...............	6·25	......	7·91
February,.............	4·08	......	7·25
March,................	2·50	......	9·91
April,.................	2·83	......	10·16
May,..................	1·58	......	10·66
June,..................	0·16	......	12·91
July,...................	0·08	......	13·91
August,...............	0·00	......	12·91
September,...........	0·08	......	14·41
October,..............	0·508	......	12·91
November,...........	2·41	......	12·75
December,............	2·00	......	11·08

Amount of mean annual fall of Rain, 28·78 inches.

TABLES KEPT AT CASTLE NEWE, STRATHDON, ABERDEENSHIRE,

North lat. 57 deg. 11 min. 43 sec. West long. 3 deg. 3 min. 45 sec.—868 feet above Sea level, and 35 miles direct inland from the same.

By ALEXANDER WALKER, Gardner to Sir Charles Forbes, Bart. of Newe.

	SELF-REGISTERING THERMOMETERS (in open shade, and 5 feet above ground.)						RAIN GAUGE.					
	Mean average temperature during the last 26 years.	Extreme highest temperature during the last 26 years.	Year in which it happened.	Extreme lowest temperature during the last 26 years.	Year in which it happened.	Above mean average.	Below mean average.	Mean average depth during the last 24 years.	Greatest quantity of rain, &c. that fell in month during the last 24 years.	Year in which it happened.	Least quantity of rain, &c. that fell in month during last 24 years.	Year in which it happened.	Above mean average depth in 1859.	Below mean average depth in 1859.
January,.....	33·5	55	1833	1	1855	3·7	...	2·6	4·8	1857	0·7	1835	0·6	0·6
February,....	36·0	59	1835	*12	1838	1·2	...	2·4	5·6	1848	1·0	1839	0·6	...
March,.......	37·2	61	1858	8	1857	3·1	1·8	2·3	5·1	1857	0·9	1850	0·0	...
April,........	43·2	70	1840	12	1839	...	...	2·1	5·1	1856	0·5	1844	1·6	1·3
May,.........	46·8	78	1849	19	1839	3·8	...	2·4	4·0	1840	0·8	1841	...	...
June,.........	54·7	81	1857	24	1838	0·0	...	2·3	4·4	1848	0·8	1841	0·3	1·8
July,.........	57·1	87	1855	32	1854	0·3	1·3	3·3	7·8	1837	1·0	1857	...	1·8
August,......	56·8	84	1856	30	1856	...	2·1	2·8	4·9	1856	1·2	1857	...	0·9
September,...	50·2	82	1852	28	1838	...	7·5	3·1	8·9	1847	0·5	1855	3·5	1·6
October,.....	49·9	68	1841	15	1838	...	3·4	4·4	9·0	1844	1·1	1856	0·0	...
November,...	39·5	62	1850	7	1839	...	5·7	3·5	7·4	1839	0·9	1858	2·9	...
December,...	37·8	59	1850	11	1836	...	...	2·4	6·3	1836	0·0	1840	...	...
Sums,.......	...	...	...	...	...	...	...	34·054	73·570		9·79		8·490	6·997
Means,......	45·2	70·5	...	12·9	...	0·9	1·8	2·8	6·1		0·8		0·7	0·58

* 12° under Zero.

INTRODUCTION. xvii

METEOROLOGICAL TABLE, FOR THE YEAR 1859.
COMPILED FROM OBSERVATIONS TAKEN AT BRAEMAR, ABERDEENSHIRE, BY T. PEARCE, ESQ.
Lat. 57° N. Lon. 3° 24' W. Height above Sea Level, 1180 feet.

1859.	HYGROMETER		SELF-REGISTERING THERMOMETERS.												CLOUD.	OZONE.	RAIN.	
	Dry Bulb Mean of Daily Observations	Wet Bulb Mean of Daily Observations	Maximum in the Sun		Minimum on Grass		Maximum in Shade		Minimum in Shade		Mean of the Maximum and Minimum in Shade	Mean Daily Range	Greatest Daily Range	Range for the Month	Adopted Mean Temperature of Air	Adopted Mean Temperature of Evaporation	Amount, 0 to 10	Amount, 0 to 10	Number of Days on which Rain fell	Amount in Inches
	°	°	Highest in the Month °	Mean of Daily Observations °	Lowest in the Month °	Mean of Daily Observations °	Highest in the Month °	Mean of Daily Observations °	Lowest in the Month °	Mean of Daily Observations °	°	°	°	°	°	°				
Jan....	36·4	34·7	63·0	44·7	15·2	29·0	48·8	41·8	17·1	31·9	36·6	9·9	19·7	31·7	36·5	34·8	6·3	8·3	19	4·15
Feb....	37·1	35·2	62·1	47·1	11·0	30·4	51·2	41·8	11·0	33·1	37·0	8·7	24·5	40·2	37·0	35·1	7·1	8·1	22	2·63
March	39·4	37·0	66·2	53·2	18·8	32·3	55·0	44·7	22·1	35·1	38·9	9·6	19·1	32·9	39·1	36·7	7·6	7·6	29	2·83
April..	37·5	35·1	74·2	59·8	19·0	28·3	63·8	44·4	23·3	31·3	36·3	13·1	25·8	40·5	39·1	36·7	6·2	7·4	21	3·08
May...	50·6	46·7	98·2	78·2	23·5	33·1	74·5	61·3	29·3	38·5	48·2	23·8	40·0	45·2	49·4	45·5	4·9	6·9	4	0·26
June..	52·4	48·9	103·0	83·5	2·1	40·6	73·2	63·2	35·3	45·1	52·3	18·1	31·6	37·9	52·3	48·8	6·2	7·3	17	3·17
July...	55·9	52·4	96·2	82·7	29·0	45·7	73·2	65·7	33·3	46·7	55·3	16·9	32·4	39·9	55·6	52·1	6·4	6·9	17	1·97
Aug...	54·4	50·9	90·4	77·1	29·8	42·2	74·4	62·9	35·2	46·6	53·1	16·2	28·9	39·5	53·7	50·2	5·9	7·4	17	1·63
Sept...	48·4	45·4	85·0	66·0	25·7	38·8	63·3	54·9	29·2	42·4	47·4	12·5	26·5	34·1	47·9	44·9	6·5	7·5	24	2·50
Oct....	41·4	39·2	80·5	57·7	10·9	32·9	65·0	47·9	10·9	35·4	40·6	9·8	28·1	54·1	41·0	38·8	6·5	7·6	18	6·23
Nov....	35·1	33·6	58·0	45·4	10·0	28·3	49·3	40·0	20·8	30·6	35·5	9·8	22·2	28·5	35·3	33·8	6·6	8·1	23	4·73
Dec....	31·1	30·2	48·0	36·6	-7·0	23·8	46·0	35·1	0	27·1	31·1	8·0	28·0	46·0	31·1	30·2	7·7	8·4	23	2·69
Means	43·3	40·7	*	*	*	*	*	*	*	*	*	*	*	*	*	*	6·5	7·6	...	† 35·87
1858	43·1	40·5	103·0	61·0	-7·0	33·6	74·7	50·3	0	36·9	42·6	13·2	40·0	39·2	42·9	40·4	6·2	8·0	19	27·90
1857	45·3	42·7	96·0	61·4	6·5	33·9	77·0	50·3	9·0	37·0	42·6	13·3	36·4	39·2	42·8	40·2	6·1	8·0	15	32·71
1856	45·1	40·7	...	...	...	...	79·5	51·2	4·9	39·9	44·7	11·4	34·3	35·7	45·0	42·3	5·6	...	16	...
							80·1	...	...	...										

* Highest and Lowest in the Year. † Amount in the Year.

In estimating the native plants of any district, it is necessary to separate those not truly indigenous; but, which have escaped from gardens or been otherwise introduced. There has been too often a desire to present a long array of species, instead of giving a fair estimate of those which may be considered really wild. Here as elsewhere there are plants which certainly never formed part of the original Flora; such are placed by themselves, and will be found at pages 216 to 326 and Supplement. My own impression is, that the list might have been more numerous, since many of our common weeds were likely introduced; but, having now become thoroughly established, even at a distance from cultivated places, it would be difficult to make such distinction. Another formidable obstacle is the difference of opinion among botanists respecting species and their varieties; the standard adopted here, is the "British Flora," by Sir W. J. Hooker, and Professor Arnott. Excluding the species above alluded to, which are 91 in number, other Phænogamic plants amount to 650, consisting of 463 Dicotyledones, and 187 Monocotyledones; these are distributed among 53 natural orders of the former, and 11 of the latter.

The British *Dicotyledonous* families not represented in our Flora are, *Berberidaceæ*, *Frankeniaceæ*, *Tiliaceæ*, *Aceraceæ*, *Balsaminaceæ*, *Celastraceæ*, *Rhamnaceæ*, *Tamariscaceæ*, *Cucurbitaceæ*, *Loranthaceæ*, *Jasminaceæ*, *Orobanchaceæ*, *Amaranthaceæ*, *Eleagnaceæ*, *Thymeleaceæ*, *Santalaceæ*, and *Asaraceæ*; the *Monocotyledonous* orders not represented are, *Amaryllidaceæ*, *Tamaceæ*, *Hydrocharidaceæ*, and *Restiaceæ*. It may be worthy of remark, that these natural families contain but a small proportion of British species, and several of them have only one or two representatives in the United Kingdom.

A mere list of species, genera and orders, cannot afford any very precise idea of the characteristics of our Flora; some more definite method of comparison is necessary; and such is presented to us in the highly laborious and philosophical "Cybele Britannica," of my friend, Mr. H. C. Watson.

Mr. Watson refers every native species to one or other of the following types :—*

1. BRITISH.—Those more or less diffused through the length and breadth of our country; such as hazel, alder, chickweed, dandelion, &c.
2. ENGLISH.—Species which prevail in England, especially the south; or, are rare northwards in Scotland.
3. GERMANIC.—Such as are mainly confined to the south-eastern counties of England, or become rare westward and northward.
4. ATLANTIC.—Native species found chiefly in the western and south-western parts.
5. SCOTTISH.—Most prevalent in Scotland, reaching only the northern counties of England, or becoming rarer southwards.
6. HIGHLAND.—"Boreal in a more intense degree, as regards climate, than the Scottish." Some are entirely alpine; others descend to the sea level toward the north-west, north, and east.
7. LOCAL.—This type comprehends a very small number of species, so very limited in the range, as not to come under any of the preceding.

Taking then as our standard of comparison, the first six floral types of Mr. Watson, we shall be able to attain a definite idea of the characteristic features of the Aberdeenshire Flora.

1. BRITISH.—Most of these constitute our common plants, almost everywhere diffused, and many of them familiar to all as ordinary weeds. Some of this type, however, though abundant in more southern parts of Britain, become scarce here and may be ranked among our rare species; such are *Ranunculus auricomus, Arabis hirsuta, Arenaria trinervis, Bidens cernua, Lycopus Europæus, Listera ovata, Malaxis paludosa, Alisma ranunculoides,* &c. &c.

* The names of these types are to be understood as indicating, respecting our native plants, the district or districts where they predominate.

2. ENGLISH.—Of this type comparatively few reach us, and some of them, though now extensively spread, very probably may have been introduced along with seeds of agricultural plants.
3. SCOTTISH.—Plants of this division are well represented in this part of Scotland, being 58 in number, and, therefore, about five-sixths of the British species, so designated, occur here. Most of them are abundant, and several are species highly prized by southern collectors. A few examples may be mentioned, *Rubus saxatilis*, *Trientalis Europœa*, *Linnœa borealis*, *Pyrola media*, *Pyrola minor*, *Goodyera repens*, *Listera cordata*, &c. Three of them, *Linnœa*, *Trientalis*, and *Goodyera*, may be specially noted as very widely distributed and abundant here.
4. GERMANIC.—There are only eight examples of this type in our list, and they are mostly rare or local plants; the total number of such in the British Flora being estimated at more than 190.
5. ATLANTIC.—*Sedum Anglicum* and *Scilla verna* are the only representatives; the latter confined to the North-western part of our coast, on the borders of the Moray Frith.
6. HIGHLAND.—The plants belonging to this division are estimated at about 100 species in the whole British Flora; of these eight-tenths are found in our list. Many of these are very local, and entirely confined to the higher districts. A few of them reach the coast, and are found almost at the sea level, viz., *Sedum Rhodiola*, *Saxifraga oppositifolia*, *Saxifraga hypnoides*, and *Polygonum viviparum*. Some others appear at a lower altitude along the course of the Dee and Deveron, such have probably been transported by floods, viz., *Oxyria reniformis*, *Epilobium alpinum*, *Alchemilla alpina*, &c. Among the more interesting of this type, found in the interior and usually very local, may be mentioned *Astralagus alpinus*, *Mulgedium alpinum*, *Arbutus alpina*, and various species of *Saxifraga*, *Hieracium*, *Salix*, *Juncus*, *Carex*, and *Poa*.

We can now form some idea respecting the characteristic features of the Flora. The plants belonging to the English, Germanic, and Atlantic types, constitute but a very insignificant part of our native vegetation. In addition to the more common species, constituting the British type, there is a general intermixture of Scottish forms, and in particular localities the Highland type predominates.

In order to complete the review, it will be necessary to examine briefly the distribution of species in zones of altitude; for just as those of the English and Germanic types, and some of those belonging to the British, become rare, and finally disappear towards the north, so certain species are lost as we pass to the interior, and rise in elevation above the level of the sea, the Flora becoming finally entirely Arctic in its character.

The three Counties, owing to the physical peculiarities already pointed out, present an excellent field for studying the altitudinal distribution of plants.

Adopting as our standard the characteristics of the Agrarian region, or region of cultivation in Britain, as given by Mr. Watson, we find that, since certain species of indigenous plants, whose presence marks the Infer-agrarian and Mid-agrarian zones, are absent from this district, and, I believe, from Scotland, the Super-agrarian is the only one of the three which can apply to this part of Britain.

The upper limit of *Pteris aquilina* (the common Brake Fern), is considered as marking the upper limit of the Super-agrarian zone, and, therefore, also that of cultivation in Britain. The limit of this Fern varies here from 1600 to 1900 feet; *very rarely*, however, does it attain the latter. In several localities, on the bare stony sides of the hills, I have found the limit to be 1600 to 1700 feet. It may be worthy of notice, that even in places distant from any cultivation, the common Mole makes its tunnels at these altitudes. On Morven, this animal occurs at 1723 feet; near Ballater, at Brakely, it reaches 1642; at the Pulock moss, 1735; and on the Khoil, 1800 feet.

At various places, even more than forty miles from the sea-board, cultivation at high altitudes is frequent. The heights of the following places where oats, turnips, &c. are or have been grown, I have measured, with aid of the mountain Sympiesometer and Aneroid:—Near Ballater, the Line 1108, Corrybeg 1126, Lin Mui 1300, Easter Morven 1400; at Braemar, Castleton 1160, Tomintoul 1500; Gairnside, Glen Fenzie, 1500; Strathdon, Brasachiel 1383 feet; in Corgarff, cultivation far exceeds 1280 feet, which is the height of the Don at that place. At the farm of Lin Mui above-mentioned, there are several old ash trees, the two largest of these in 1843 I found to be at the base respectively, five feet and four feet two inches in girth; at present (September, 1859), their girths are five feet six and four feet four inches. At Altguisach, a hunting seat belonging to His Royal Highness Prince Albert, near Loch Muick, about 1400 feet above the sea, and fifty miles inland, most of the ordinary culinary plants are grown, also the smaller fruits, as red, white, and black currants, &c. Bay and Portugal laurels, standard roses, &c. also succeed. There are likewise thriving larches, the girths of four of the largest of which were recorded in 1843 (Dr. Dickie on the "Forest and other Trees of Aberdeenshire"—*Scottish Agricultural Journal.*) In that year they had each respectively a circumference, near the ground, equal to four feet nine, four feet five, four feet, and three feet six inches. These trees are now reported (September, 1859), as equal to five feet seven, five feet six, five feet four, and five feet; they have, therefore, grown more rapidly in proportion than the ash trees already alluded to.

A few records have been consulted with the view of ascertaining the average periods necessary for the maturing of oats, at different elevations, and at various distances from the sea; though not sufficiently numerous to afford satisfactory conclusions, it may be interesting for the present to state them. At elevations not exceeding five hundred feet, and about twenty miles from the coast, the mean time is 172 days; at places exceeding one thousand feet, and from forty to fifty-five miles inland, the result is 179 days.

In some of the inland and higher parts of this Super-agrarian zone, several plants of the Highland type constitute a prominent feature of the vegetation. Thus, behind the farm of Lin Mui, *Cerastium alpinum* and *Asplenium viride*, &c. are abundant; and *Polygonum viviparum*, *Arabis petræa*, &c. are frequent, even at lower altitudes.

The region above the limit of the Brake Fern is denominated by Mr. Watson "Arctic." In Aberdeenshire, all the zones of this region are fully represented. The lowest or Infer-arctic extends from the upper limit of *Pteris*, already mentioned, to the upper limit of *Erica tetralix* (cross-leaved heath), at 2100 feet; the next or Mid-arctic is comprehended between 2100 and 3000 feet, the latter constituting about the upper point attained by *Calluna vulgaris* (common heath or Ling); the last or Super-arctic zone extends from the limit of *Calluna* to about 4400 feet on Ben Nevis, the highest point in Scotland, and in Aberdeenshire to 4300, the top of Ben Macdui.

The Mid-arctic zone is peculiarly rich in the rare forms of the Highland type, for instance, *Astragalus alpinus*, *Carex rupestris*, *Carex leporina*, *Carex Vahlii*, *Erigeron alpinus*, &c. At the extreme part of the Super-arctic zone, the Highland forms alone occur. Thus, on the summit of Ben Macdui, only seven flowering plants are found (these grow beside the Cairn), viz., *Silene acaulis*, *Saxifraga stellaris*, *Salix herbacea*, belonging to the Dicotyledons; *Luzula spicata*, *Luzula arcuata*, *Carex rigida*, and *Festuca vivipara*, belonging to the Monocotyledonous division; the only other plant of any great size associated with these is a well-known Club-moss, *Lycopodium Salago*, which occurs also at Aberdeen near the sea level, all others are mosses and lichens.

The following table, compiled from my own observations, will afford an idea of the total number of species, and the prevailing types at different altitudes; the letters indicate the respective types, B. British; S. Scottish; H. Highland.

BENNACHIE, 1700 feet. { 10 B,..................... Dicotyledons.
                       { 4 B,..................... Monocotyledons.
LONACH, 1836 feet.   { 9 B, 2 S, 2 H,.. Total, 13 Dicotyledons.
                       { 8 B,..................... 8 Monocotyledons.

KHOIL,	}	8 B, 2 S, 4 H,..Total	14 Dicotyledons.
2000 feet.		4 B, 1 H,....... ,,	5 Monocotyledons.
BUCK OF CABRACH,	}	5 B, 1 S, 2 H,.. ,,	8 Dicotyledons.
2264 feet.		3 B, 1 H,....... ,,	4 Monocotyledons.
MOUNT BATTOCK,	}	3 B, 2 H, 1 S,.. ,,	6 Dicotyledons.
2563 feet.		1 B, 1 H,....... ,,	2 Monocotyledons.
MOUNT KEEN,	}	2 B, 2 H,........ ,,	4 Dicotyledons.
3125 feet.		1 B, 3 H,........ ,,	4 Monocotyledons.
LOCHNAGAR,	}	1 S, 3 H,........ ,,	4 Dicotyledons.
3800 feet.		1 B, 3 H,........ ,,	4 Monocotyledons.
BEN-A-BUIRD,	}	2 B, 4 H,........ ,,	6 Dicotyledons.
3900 feet.		1 B, 5 H,........ ,,	6 Monocotyledons.
BEN MUIC DHUI,	}	3 H,.................	3 Dicotyledons.
4300 feet.		4 H,.................	4 Monocotyledons.

The few instances selected are the very summits of the respective mountains; places where a complete list of species can be readily got. It will be obvious at a glance that there is a rapid decrease in the number of species belonging to the British type, the last to disappear being *Calluna vulgaris;* of the Scottish type, *Empetrum nigrum* ascends highest, viz. :— to 4100 feet. On the other hand, the Highland type increases steadily in numbers, till at last, species belonging to it constitute alone the scanty Flora. As Mr. Watson correctly remarks, "the Mid Arctic zone is, however, that in which there is the greatest development of Highland species, there all the rarer forms of that type are chiefly found." The proportion of *Monocotyledons* to *Dicotyledons* at different altitudes is also worthy of notice. In the entire Flora of the County of Aberdeen, the proportion is 1 to 2·4; at 3125, 3800, and 3900 feet, they are equal; and at the highest point they are 1·3 to 1. The *Monocotyledons*, therefore, increase in proportional numbers as we ascend. The Diagram given here, is intended to afford a general view of some of the facts discussed.

In the text, letters K, A, and B, indicate Counties.

For the following excellent Summary, I am indebted to
ALEXANDER CRUICKSHANK, A.M.

PHYSICAL AND GEOLOGICAL STRUCTURE

OF THE COUNTIES OF

ABERDEEN, BANFF, AND KINCARDINE.

THE Counties of Aberdeen, Banff, and Kincardine form a continuous quadrilateral tract of land, in the north-east part of the middle third of Scotland, of about 2960 square miles —Aberdeen occupying 1932, Banff 648, and Kincardine 380 square miles. This tract is bounded on the south by one of the main offshoots of the Grampians, and the North Esk, which separate it from Perthshire and Forfarshire; on the west by Inverness-shire, Elginshire, and the Spey; and on the north and east by the German Ocean. Aberdeenshire occupies the middle of the tract, and has Banffshire on the north-west and Kincardineshire on the south-east. The tract is 87 miles long, from Scarsock mountain in the south-west to Rattray Head in the north-east; and 65 miles broad, from the mouth of the North Esk in the south-east to the mouth of the Spey in the north-west. The length of coast line is 120 miles —60 in Aberdeenshire, 30 in Banffshire, and 30 in Kincardineshire.

The tract is formed of nine large river basins, (North Esk, Bervie, Dee, Don, Ythan, Ugie, Deveron, Avon, and Fiddich), separated by mountain ranges, which include the highest mass of land in the British Isles. The loftiest mountains are confined to the south-west or most inland fifth of the tract, and have generally rounded massive and dome-shaped forms, with corries or semi-circular hollows near their summits and usually facing the north-east. The corries have perpendicular walls, sometimes upwards of 1000 feet high, and are formed of rude prismatic blocks of granite piled on each other. There is often a tarn or small mountain lake at the bottom of the corries, at the height of 1000 to upwards of 3000 feet above the sea level.

From this high mountain tract, in the south-west portion of the three counties, many of the tops of which are 3000 to upwards of 4000 feet high, the country slopes towards the German Ocean in a north, north-east, and easterly direction, ending at the sea in low sandy tracts, or in cliffs 10 to 150 feet high, and at Gamrie reaching the height of 600 feet.

The basis of the three counties is formed by two main mountain ranges, which arise from the splitting of the great Grampian range of mountains of central Scotland, in the south-west corner of Aberdeenshire. The one range runs east for 70 miles, separating Aberdeenshire from the counties of Perth and Forfar; and after traversing the north part of Kincardineshire, it terminates in a bleak, high, and undulating tract and bold coast between Aberdeen and Stonehaven. The average height of this range is 1200 to 1500 feet. It contains 32 mountains varying in height from 1200 to 3800 feet, at which latter height it culminates in Lochnagar. The roads and footpaths across it vary from a height of 150 to about 2400 feet above the sea. The other main range runs northeast for 80 miles, separating Aberdeenshire from the counties of Inverness and Banff; while a little of the north-west portions of Aberdeenshire lies on its west side, and ends in the bold coast of Gamrie. The south-west portion of this range comprises a knot of mountains of 60 or 70 square miles in extent, the highest mass of land in the British Isles; and includes 12 mountains 3000 to 4295 feet high, culminating at the latter height in Ben Macdui. The rest of this range is comparatively low, rising in the Foudland hills about 1500 feet and in the Auchmeddan range about 750 feet, and sinking in Kinnethmont to 569 feet and in Auchterless to 162 feet above the sea.

These two main mountain ranges emit a variety of lateral ones of inferior height, which form the boundaries or watersheds between the great river basins of the three counties.

The North Esk and Bervie rise in the middle third of the south side of the east main branch of the Grampians, the North Esk being the longer and more westerly stream, and draining the south fourth of Kincardineshire and the north fourth of Forfarshire, while the Bervie drains the middle seventh of Kincardineshire. The upper parts of these contiguous basins are bounded by hills of which about a dozen are 1000 to 3180 feet high, culminating in Mount Keen at the latter height. The upper two-fifths of the basin of the North Esk consist of gneiss; the middle fifth is crossed by a band of mica-slate, succeeded on the east by a band of clay-slate; and the lower three-fifths consist of old red sandstone and conglomerate. The upper fourth of the basin of the Bervie is successively crossed by bands of gneiss, mica-slate, and clay-slate, the very sources being however in granite; and the lower three-fourths consist of old red sandstone and conglomerate.

The basins of the Dee, Don, Ythan, and Ugie, all lie in Aberdeenshire, on the east side of the second main mountain range running north-east from the south-west corner of that county to Gamrie, as previously described. The only exception is, that about the north third of Kincardineshire is included within the basin of the Dee.

The Dee rises in the Ben Macdui knot of mountains in the south-west of Aberdeenshire, at the height of 4060 feet above the sea level. Its basin is bounded on the south by the east main branch of the Grampians, and on the north by an offshoot of the Ben Macdui knot running east for 60 miles through the hills of Morven, Cushnie, Fare, and Brimmond, to the north-west side of the city of Aberdeen, and including these four and other four hills varying in height from 900 to 2880 feet, culminating at the latter height in Morven. Some of the roads across this range rise upwards of 2000 feet above the sea. The Dee drains the south half of Aberdeenshire. The basin of the Dee is pretty equally divided between alternating and irregular large tracts of granite and gneiss. The south side of the basin in Braemar contains a large tract of quartzite.

The Don rises in the west of Aberdeenshire, on the borders of the south-east end of Banffshire, at the height of 1740 feet above the sea. Its basin is bounded on the south by the north water-shed of the Dee, and on the north by a range about 70 miles long, first running north-east and forming part of the second main branch of the Grampians, which then emits a branch south-east ending in Scotston moor, north-west of Don-mouth. This range separates the basin of the Don from those of the Ythan and Upper Deveron, and rises in six hills from 800 to 2600 feet high. The middle of the basin of the Don is divided into the vales of Alford and the Garioch, by a prominent hill-ridge between Correan hill and Bennachie. The Don drains the middle fourth of Aberdeenshire. Its basin is formed of large irregular tracts of granite and gneiss, the former, in the basin of its tributary the Ury, often passing into syenite. The sources of the Don are in mica-slate, and those of the Ury are in clay-slate, which is also to be seen in Auchindoir and Kildrummy, where it is bordered on the west by an isolated patch of old red sandstone.

The Ythan and Ugie both rise in the comparatively low termination of the north-east main branch of the Grampians, which for about 30 miles between the Foudland hills and the

Gamrie coast does not exceed 746 feet above the sea (this being the height of the ridge south of Auchmeddan), and sinks as low as 162 feet in Auchterless. These two rivers drain about the north fifth of Aberdeenshire, the basin of the Ythan being twice the size of that of the Ugie. These basins chiefly consist of gneiss and granite. The upper third of the basin of the Ythan consists of clay-slate, and the sources of the Ugie are in the same rock. Mormond (an isolated hill in the north of Buchan, 743 feet, forming part of the north water-shed of the Ugie) consists of quartzite.

The remaining three large basins of the three counties, viz. the Deveron, Avon, and Fiddich, occupy the west slopes of the north-east main branch of the Grampians above described, which runs between the Ben Macdui knot of mountains and Gamrie. The Deveron drains about one-half of Banffshire and the north-west seventh of Aberdeenshire, while the Avon and Fiddich drain about the south-west fourth of Banffshire into the Spey.

The Deveron rises about the middle of the west side of Aberdeenshire, or about the middle of the west side of the north-east main branch of the Grampians. Its basin is bounded on the east by the north half of this branch, and on the west by an offshoot of this range, forming a very irregular line, running north and then east, and rising in about a dozen hills from 700 to 2568 feet, culminating at the latter height in Corryhabbie, and rising in the Knock to 1416 feet. The lower third of the basin of the Deveron consists of clay-slate and greywacke, with a little old red sandstone on the east. These are succeeded by tracts of syenite, mica-slate, quartzite, and clay-slate; while the sources of the river are in a tract of gneiss.

The Avon rises on the north side of the Ben Macdui knot of mountains. Its basin is bounded on the west by a branch from the west end of this knot running almost due north from the north Cairngorm through Cromdale hill to the Spey; and on the east by a portion of the main north-east range of the Grampians, and an offshoot running north-west through Corryhabbie and Ben Rinnes to the same river. The borders of the basin of the Avon consist of granite at the top, and mostly of quartzite along the sides; while the tracts in the vicinity of the stream itself consist of gneiss, mica-slate, clay-slate, and old red sandstone.

The Fiddich rises in Corryhabbie. Its basin is bounded on the south-west by the west part of the east water-shed of the Avon; and on the east by the south part of the west water-shed of the Deveron, ending in Ben Aigan. Its basin chiefly consists of mica-slate and quartzite.

The more important points regarding the nine chief river basins of the three counties may be arranged approximately in the following Table:—

	North Esk	Bervie	Dee	Don	Ythan	Ugie	Deveron	Avon	Fiddich
General direction of longitudinal axis of basins,	S.E.	S.E.	E.N.E.	E.	E.S.E.	E.S.E.	N.E.	N.	N.N.W.
Number of tributaries and their branches above 1 mile long,	121	30	212	188	78	36	97	65	22
Number of tributaries, 1 to 5 miles long, directly connected with	30	18	70	70	36	25	50	24	8
Number of tributaries, 5 to 20 miles long, connected with	12	0	36	16	18	10	14	8	1
Number of tributaries 10 to 20 miles long,	3	0	6	5	2	1	5	3	1
Length of basins in miles,	32	13	65	42	25	20	36	20	10
Greatest breadth of basins in miles,	15	8	15	20	15	7	16	12	6
Average breadth of basins in miles,	10	6	12	9	8	5	10	7	4
Length of rivers by their windings,	40	16	81	60	30	25	55	40	14
Number of square miles drained by	320	44	900	495	220	140	410	193	56
Number of parishes drained by....	10	4	21	33	10	6	22	2	1

While the drainage of by far the greater part of the three counties is performed by these nine great rivers and their numerous tributaries, there remains about a twenty-fifth of their surface, distributed around their coasts, between the sea terminations of these rivers, into about 50 small detached basins, drained by as many streams from 1 to 15 miles long. These 50 burns have about 140 branches upwards of a mile long.

The above table, in conjunction with the statement just made, shows into what a multitude of drainage troughs so minute a portion of the earth's surface as is comprised in these three counties is divided.

The north-east course of the main branch of the Grampians, from the south-west corner of Aberdeenshire to Gamrie, combined with the nearly north trend of the east coast of that county, causes the river basins on their east side to decrease in size as we proceed north. Thus, taking the basin of the Dee as unity, that of the Don is about a half, that of the Ythan a fourth, and that of the Ugie an eighth.

It is a curious fact with respect to these four rivers, that, if we prolong the major axes of their basins seaward, they will meet in the line of the major axis of the Dee basin, about 60 miles east-north-east of Aberdeen; whereas the major axis of the basin of the Deveron is parallel to those of the Spey and Findhorn, and the great rent of Scotland along the line of the Caledonian Canal.

On taking a general view of the geology of the three counties, we find that the north third of Kincardineshire, and nearly all Aberdeenshire, comprising the basins of the Dee, Don, Ythan, and Ugie, consist of large irregular tracts of granite and gneiss; that the rest of Kincardineshire, including the basins of the North Esk and Bervie, consists of old red sandstone with narrow bands of clay-slate and mica-slate; and that the basins of the Deveron, Avon, and Fiddich, occupying nearly all Banffshire, consist mostly of granite, mica-slate, clay-slate, and quartzite, with very little gneiss. Granite occupies a greater area in Aberdeenshire and Kincardineshire than in any other tract in the British Isles of like extent.

In the gneiss, mica-slate, and clay-slate tracts there occur small isolated and far-between patches of other rocks than those forming the bulk of the three counties. These consist of beds of primary limestone, and masses and veins of serpentine, felspar porphyry, compact felspar, trap including greenstone and basalt. These rocks do not occupy a five-hundredth of the surface, but they sometimes occur in lines over great tracts of country.

To complete the above outline of the geology of the three counties, it will be sufficient merely to enumerate the various accumulations of loose materials intervening between the surface of the fundamental hard rocks and the vegetable soil. The solid rocks of the tract are often immediately covered by shattered portions of their own substance, and, especially in granite districts, by considerable depths of the upper parts of the rock so disintegrated in situ as to be easily dug out by the spade in the form of angular gravel.

Above these untransported materials, and, in their absence, above the solid rock itself, in all parts of the three counties, the surface is covered by immense accumulations of loose drifted deposits, which have no small influence in determining the superficial outline of the country on the small scale; while the fundamental rocks, above enumerated, themselves determine the great features of mountain, valley, and glen. These deposits consist of boulder clay or till, a stiffish unstratified mixture of clay, sand, gravel, and boulders; very loose stratified shingles, gravels, and sands, with rolled pebbles and boulders; beach deposits above existing tides, brick clays and drift sand near the coasts; and gravels, sands, and silts deposited along the courses of the present rivers. Connected with these deposits are the boulder flints, containing chalk fossils in Buchan; the small patches of dark-blue clay enclosing greensand fossils in Cruden, and lias fossils near Turriff and Banff; and the sandstone and fossiliferous limestone boulders in the curious gravel knolls and ridges of Slains.

Above the solid rock and the more impervious of the loose deposits covering them are to be found, in most parts of the three counties, tracts of peat, often many square miles in area, and in a few places reaching to the depth of upwards of 40 feet.

It is in the upper parts of the basins of the Dee, Don, Avon, and North Esk, over an area of about 25 miles in diameter, or comprising about 370 square miles—an area every part of which is upwards of 600 feet above the sea level—that the rarer plants so interesting to the alpine botanist are to be found. These plants have to be searched for, often at the risk of life and limb, on the tops and sides of mountains, in mountain lochs, in bright green and wet grassy plots on the bottoms and perpendicular sides of often almost inaccessible corries, as well as amid heaps of fallen blocks, and the rough gravelly debris of mountain torrents. This alpine tract, the highest of like extent in these isles, exhibits scenery of the grandest description, in its numerous towering mountains, huge precipices, and deep glens. It has become an abode of royalty, and is visited every year by thousands of tourists from all quarters of the world. On no other tract in the kingdom does snow lie so long, or so deeply, as on this area; and on its highest mountains numerous patches of snow, some of them acres in extent, lie all the year round, though exposed to the direct rays of the sun.

The most interesting tracts for the lowland botanist are the rocky (often also almost inaccessible), sandy and benty shores of the three counties, and the deep, woody, moist and rocky dens occurring here and there over their lower tracts.

A. C.

THE BOTANIST'S GUIDE.

CLASS I.
DICOTYLEDONOUS, OR EXOGENOUS PLANTS.

Sub-Class I.—THALAMIFLORAE.

ORDER I.—RANUNCULACEAE.

1. THALICTRUM. MEADOW RUE.

1. *T. alpinum*, Linn. *(Alpine M.)*
Perennial. Flowers in June and July. Highland type. Range in Britain, 53°—61°; altitude, 1600 to 3500 feet.

Abundant in the interior; south and west margins of Loch Callater, Rev. J. Brichan; Corgarff, Donside, Mr. Barron; Braeriach, Dr. Murchison; Ben-Avon and Ben-a-Buird, Mr. R. Mackay. Also on Little Craigendall, Lochnagar, Callater Rocks, Rocks of Dhuloch, G. D.; Wells of Dee, Mr. Croall.

2. *T. minus*, Linn. *(Small M.)*
Perennial. Flowers in June and July. Scottish type. Range in Britain, 50°—59°; coast only.

Occasionally along the coast line.

K.—St. Cyrus Links south from Kirkside; plentiful on stony beach half a mile north from Johnshaven, Dr. Stephen.

A.—"In arenosis" Broadhill, Aberdeen Links, Dr. D. Skene; frequent in the sandy links from the Dee to the Ythan, G. D.; Cruden, Mr. A. Murray; Crimond, Mr. Cow.

B.—Scarce on the links at Buckie, but plentiful in the links at Cullen, Mr. Carmichael.

2. ANEMÓNE. ANEMONE.

1. A. *nemorosa*, Linn. *(Wood A.)*
Perennial. Flowers, March to June. British type. Range in Britain, 50°—58°; sea level to 2000 feet.
Moist woods and pastures. General.

3. RANUNCULUS. CROWFOOT.

1. R. *aquatilis*, Linn. *(Common water C.)*
Perennial. Flowers, May to July. British type. Range in Britain, 50°—60°; sea level to 1200 feet.
Of general occurrence in lakes, ponds, and ditches; rare at Castleton, Braemar.

2. R. *hederaceus*, Linn. *(Ivy C.)*
Perennial. Flowers, March to September. British type. Range in Britain, 50°—59°; coast to 1260 feet.
Wet places and shallow water. Generally diffused.

3. R. *Lingua*, Linn. *(Great Spearwort.)*
Perennial. Flowers, July to September. English type (or British?) Range in Britain, 50°—58°; coast to 500 feet.

Rare in this district.

A.—Occasionally along the course of the Ythan from Gight to Ellon, G. D. Loch of Strathbeg, in Crimond, Mr. A. Murray. Loch of Auchlossan, in Lumphanan, Professor Macgillivray.

4. R. *Flammula*, Linn. *(Small Spearwort.)*
Perennial. Flowers, June to August. British type.
Range in Britain, 50°—61°; coast to 2700 feet.
Margins of lakes and ditches. Common. Var. *reptans:* margins of Alpine lakes.

5. R. *Ficaria*, Linn. *(Pilewort C.)*
Perennial. Flowers, March to June. British type.
Range in Britain, 50°—61°; sea level to 500 feet.
Pastures, woods, &c. Common in the lower districts; rare in the more inland parts.

6. R. *auricomus*, Linn. *(Wood C.)*
Perennial. Flowers in April and May. British type.
Range in Britain, 50°—58°; coast to 1500 feet.
In moist woods. Rare.

K.—On the farm of Auchallan, Banchory-Ternan, Dr. Adams; Corbie Den, Kingcausie, G. D.; In Den below Blackness, Strachan, Dr. Stephen.

A.—North bank of the Don, above the old bridge, G. D. Wood below the "Lion's face" at Castleton, Dr. Ogilvie.

7. R. *sceleratus*, Linn. *(Celery-leaved C.)*
Perennial. Flowers, May to August. British type.
Range in Britain, 50°—59°; coast line.
Pools and ditches. Chiefly in the coast district.

K.—Marshes near mouth of the North Esk, Dr. Stephen; at the Cove, G. D.

A.—North side of Dee at Wellington Bridge, near

the brick-work in the Old-town Links, and between the old and new bridges of Don, G. D.; in a ditch on the east side of King Street, Mr. P. Macgillivray; at St. Fergus, Mr. A. Murray.

B.—Parish of Alvah, Rev. Dr. Todd.

8. R. *acris*, Linn. *(Upright meadow C.)*
Perennial. Flowers in June and July. British type.
Range in Britain, 50°—61°; coast to 2800 feet.
Common everywhere.

9. R. *repens*, Linn. *(Creeping C.)*
Perennial. Flowers, May to August. British type.
Range in Britain, 50°—61°; coast to 2000 feet.
Common everywhere in this district.

10. R. *bulbosus*, Linn. *(Bulbous C.)*
Perennial. Flowers in April and May. British type.
Range in Britain, 50°—58°; coast to 1500 feet.
In meadows and pastures. Local in the district.

K.—At Jackstone, St. Cyrus; and coast near Garron Point, Dr. Stephen; Banchory-Ternan, Dr. Adams.

A.—On the Broadhill and other places in the Links, and banks of Dee above the old bridge, G. D.; Cruden, Mr. A. Murray; Aberdour, Rev. G. Gairdner; about the Castle of Cluny, Mr. Barron; at the Bridge of Alford, Rev. J. Minto; at Castleton, Braemar, Mr. Watson.

B.—Parish of Alvah, but not common, Rev. Dr. Todd; links of Buckie and Portessie, Mr. Carmichael; in Mortlach, Dr. L. Stewart.

4. CALTHA. MARSH MARYGOLD.

1. C. *palustris*, Linn. *(Common M.)*
Perennial. Flowers, April to June. British type.
Range in Britain, 50°—61°; coast to 3500 feet.

Marshes. Everywhere ; at the above-mentioned altitude on Ben Macdui, Mr. R. Mackay.

5. TROLLIUS. GLOBE-FLOWER.

1. T. *Europaeus*, Linn. *(Mountain G.)*
Perennial. Flowers, June to August. Scottish type. Range in Britain, 52°—61° ; 50 to 3350 feet.
Moist woods and rocks. Chiefly in the interior.

K.—Parish of Garvock, Stat. Account ; Arbuthnot, Mr. Chrystal ; Banchory-Ternan, Dr. Adams ; Blackness, Strachan, Dr. Stephen ; Corbie Den and south bank of the Dee at Kingcausie, G. D.

A.—At Normandyke, Culter, Dr. J. Smith ; Aboyne, Statistical Account ; by the Don at Monymusk, and in Corgarff, Strathdon, Mr. Barron ; banks of the Dee at Ballater ; in Glen Callater, G. D. ; Binhill in Cairnie, Rev. J. Abel ; moor near Hillhead in Clatt, Dr. A. Fleming ; parish of Glass, Stat. Account.

B.—Parish of Alvah, rare, Mr. G. C. Smith.

ORDER II.—NYMPHAEACEAE.

1. NYMPHAEA. WHITE WATER-LILY.

1. N. *alba*, Linn. *(Great W. W. L.)*
Perennial. Flowers in July. British type. Range in Britain, 50°—61° ; 50 to 600 feet.
In lakes. Chiefly in the lower districts.

K.—Lochs of Park and Leys, Dr. Adams ; in a small lake at north side of the avenue leading to Maryculter House, G. D.

A.—Corbie Loch, parish of Old Machar ; in a small lake between Bieldside and the river Dee, G. D. ;

parish of St. Fergus, Stat. Account ; Loch of Dalhaiky, Cluny, Mr. Barron ; in parish of Longside, Stat. Account ; in a small loch two miles from Kincardine O'Neil, Prof. Macgillivray; "In lacubus, Kinnord," Dr. D. Skene, (this is Loch Cannor, a few miles west from the village of Aboyne.)

2. NUPHAR. YELLOW WATER-LILY.

1. N. *lutea*, Smith. *(Common Y. W. L.)*

Perennial. Flowers in July. English type. Range in Britain, 50°—58° ; 50 to 600 feet.

In lakes ; but rarer than Nymphaea.

K.—Loch of Leys, Dr. Adams.

A.—Corbie Loch, G. D. ; Loch Cannor, Mr. Sutherland.

2. N. *pumila*, De Cand. *(Small Y. W. L.)*

Perennial. Flowers in July and August. Scottish type. Range in Britain, 56°—58° ; 200 to 600 feet.

Rare in this district.

K.—Loch of Leys (along with the last) Dr. Adams.

A.—Abundant at the north-east end of Loch Cannor, near village of Aboyne, August 1836, G. D.[*]

---

[*] There is no mention of this species in the Skene M.SS., now nearly 100 years old; as already stated Dr. S. only records Nymphaea in Loch Cannor. Nuphar lutea is probably there an introduced plant as well as in other parts of this district, and N. pumila merely a stunted variety, an opinion also held by Dr. Adams.

ORDER III.—PAPAVERACEAE.

1. PAPAVER. POPPY.

1. P. *dubium*, Linn. *(Long smooth-headed P.)*
Annual. Flowers in June and July. British type. Range in Britain, 50°—61°; coast to 500 feet.
Fields and waste places. Not unfrequent.

2. P. *Rhaeas*, Linn. *(Common red P.)*
Annual. Flowers, May to August. British type. Range in Britain, 50°—58°.
Corn-fields; but rare, and uncertain in appearance.

3. P. *Argemone*, Linn. *(Prickly-headed P.)*
Annual. Flowers in June and July. British type (or English). Range in Britain, 50°—58°; coast only.
In fields. Very rare.
K.—At St. Cyrus and Dunnottar, Dr. Stephen.
A.—Found near Aberdeen by Dr. David Skene. I have never met with it in this quarter, G. D.

2. GLAUCIUM. HORNED POPPY.

1. G. *luteum*, Tourn. *(Yellow H.)*
Annual. Flowers, June to 1 September. English type. Range in Britain, 50°—57°; coast only.
Sandy sea-shore. Very rare.
K.—Beach north of Johnshaven, Dr. Stephen. In Bay of Nigg, 100 years ago, Dr. D. Skene; his description (in MSS.) is full, and leaves no doubt respecting the plant. It is now extirpated.

Order IV.—FUMARIACEAE.

1. FUMARIA. FUMITORY.

1. *F. capreolata*, Linn. *(Rampant F.)*
Annual. Flowers, June to September. British type.
Range in Britain, 50°—60°; coast to 500 feet.
Waste places. Very local in this district.

K.—Crathes, Banchory-Ternan, Dr. Adams.

A.—Formerly beside the hut at the old Bridge of Don; occasionally on the banks of the Dee near Aberdeen, G. D.; north bank of the Don, beside a hedge between the old and new bridges, Mr. P. Macgillivray; in parish of Premnay, Rev. J. Minto; in Strathdon, Stat. Account; parish of Cruden, Mr. A. Murray; at Aberdour, Rev. G. Gairdner; parish of Glass, Stat. Account.

B.—In Alvah, but rare, Rev. Dr. Todd; parish of Grange, Stat. Account.

2. *F. officinalis*, Linn. *(Common F.)*
Annual. Flowers, April to September. British type.
Range in Britain, 50°—61°; coast to 600 feet.
Waste places. Not uncommon.

2. CORYDALIS. CORYDALIS.

1. *C. claviculata*, De Cand. *(White climbing C.)*
Perennial. Flowers in June and July. British type.
Range in Britain, 50°—58°; 50 to 700 feet.

Bushy and shady places among stones and gravel.

K.—At Kingcausie, G. D.; Banchory-Ternan, Dr. Adams.

A.—"Den of Robslaw," Dr. D. Skene, where it still grows; abundant on the north bank of Dee above the old bridge, and beside the rivulet and dam half a mile north of Mill of Murtle, G. D. ; Gallowhill wood at Cluny, Mr. Barron ; Old Deer, Stat. Account ; at Tullynessle, Stat. Account ; wood at Candacraig, Strathdon, Rev. J. Minto.

B.—In parish of Mortlach, rare, Dr. L. Stewart.

Order V.—CRUCIFERAE.

1. BARBAREA. WINTER CRESS.

1. B. *vulgaris*, Brown. *(Yel. rocket or com. W. C.)*
Perennial. Flowers, May to August. British type.
Range in Britain, 50°—58° ; 50 to 450 feet.
Waste places, &c. ; but not common.

K.—Banchory-Ternan, rare, Dr. Adams.

A.—Occasionally about Aberdeen, as at Stocket, banks of Dee and Don, &c., G. D. ; at Cluny, Mr. Barron ; at Alford, Rev. Dr. Farquharson ; banks of the Bogie, in Rhynie, Rev. J. Minto.

B.—Very local in Alvah, Rev. Dr. Todd.

2. ARABIS. ROCK CRESS.

1. A. *petraea*, De Cand. *(Alpine R. C.)*
Perennial. Flowers, June to August. Highland type.
Range in Britain, 53°—61° ; 50 ? or 700 to 3000 feet.

Chiefly confined to the highland districts. "Island in the Dee opposite Banchory House, three miles west from Aberdeen, washed down from Braemar," Mr. P. Macgillivray ; abundant on the gravelly banks of the Dee at Ballater (700 feet); on the craig behind the farm of Linn Mui near Ballater, at 1450 feet ; abundant along the course of the river Quoich ; also on Ben Macdui and Ben-a-Buird, &c.

2. A. *hirsuta*, Brown. *(Hairy R. C.)*
Biennial. Flowers, June to August. British type. Range in Britain, 50°—58°; sea level to 1700 feet.

Rocks, &c.; but rare in this district.

K.—Cliffs of St. Cyrus, a quarter of a mile east from Kirkside, Dr. Stephen; Banchory-Ternan, Rev. J. Brichan.

A.—On the embankment, north side of Dee opposite to Nether Banchory Church; banks of the Dee at Ballater; on a bank by the Ballachbuie road between Balmoral and Bridge of Invercauld, G. D.; Craig Koynach and "Lion's face," at Castleton, Mr. Gardiner; Strathdon, Stat. Account.

Coast at Boyndie, near Banff, Dr. Shier.

3. CARDAMINE. BITTER CRESS.

1. C. *amara*, Linn. *(Large flowered B. C.)*
Perennial. Flowers, April to June. British type. Range in Britain, 50°—58°; sea level to 1000 feet.

K.—Kingcausie, G. D.; Banchory-Ternan, Rev. J. Brichan.

A.—Hab. in Den of Robslaw, Dr. D. Skene, where it still grows; banks of Dee, Don, Ury, and Burn of Culter, Mr. P. Macgillivray; Midmar, Mr. Barron; Alford, Rev. Dr. Farquharson; wood at Murtle, G. D.; Den of Knockespock, Rev. J. Minto; Strathdon, Stat. Account; Buchan District, Mr. A. Murray.

B.—Parish of Banff, Stat. Account; in Alvah, but local, Rev. Dr. Todd; Mortlach, rare, Dr. L. Stewart.

2. C. *pratensis*, Linn. *(Common B. C.)*
Perennial. Flowers, April to June. British type. Range in Britain, 50°—61°; coast to 2000 feet.

Common in moist meadows.

3. C. *hirsuta*, Linn. *(Hairy B. C.)*
Annual. Flowers, March to August. British type. Range in Britain, 50°—61°; sea level to 2400 feet. In moist and shady places. Common.

4. NASTURTIUM. WATER CRESS.

1. N. *officinale*, Brown. *(Common, W. C.)*
Perennial. Flowers, May to September. British type. Range in Britain, 50°—60°; coast to 1200 feet.

Streams and ditches. Frequent; more abundant in the lower parts of the district than in the interior; rare in Mortlach and Corgarff.

5. COCHLEARIA. SCURVY GRASS.

1. C. *officinalis*, Linn. *(Common S. G.)*
Annual or Perennial. Flowers, May to September. British type. Range in Britain, 50°—61°; coast to 3600 feet.

The ordinary form is common along the whole coast, and extends some distance into the interior along the course of rivers.

Var. C. *Groenlandica*, L, on the higher mountains, and on the serpentine tracts of the Don district.

Var. C. *Danica*, L, occasionally at the Cove, south from Aberdeen, and formerly on the Inch at Aberdeen.

6. DRABA. WHITLOW GRASS.

1. D. *verna*, Linn. *(Common W. G.)*
Annual. Flowers, March to June. British type. Range in Britain, 50°—60°; sea level to?

Frequent on walls, rocks, dry banks, &c. General along the coast, and found also, but very local, in the inland districts.

2. D. *incana*, L.   *(Twisted podded W. G.)*
Biennial. Flowers in June and July. Highland type. Range in Britain, 53°—61°; 2500 feet.
Dry Alpine rocks. Very rare.
A.—Head of Glen Callater, Mr. Croall.

3. D. *rupestris*, Brown.   *(Rock W.G.)*
Perennial. Flowers in July. Highland type. Range in Britain, 56°—59°; 3000 feet.
Alpine rocks.
B.—Known only upon Cairngorm in this district.

7. THLASPI.   PENNY CRESS.

1. T. *arvense*, Linn.   *(Field P. C.)*
Annual. Flowers, May to July. British type. Range in Britain, 50°—60°; sea level to 1100 feet.
Fields and waste places.
K.—Banchory-Ternan, Dr. Adams.
A.—Fields about King Street, Ferryhill, &c. G. D. Kildrummy and Corgarff, Mr. Barron; Doun of Invernochty and banks of Ernan, in Strathdon, Rev. J. Minto; Buchan district, Mr. A. Murray.
B.—Rare in Alvah, Rev. Dr Todd; Mortlach, Dr. L. Stewart.

8. TEESDALIA.   TEESDALIA.

1. T. *nudicaulis*, Brown.   *(Naked stalked N.)*
Annual. Flowers in May and June. English type. Range in Britain, 50°—58°; sea level to 300 feet.
Sandy and gravelly places. Rare.
K.—At Kingcausie, Rev. D. Milne; roadside near Crathes, Rev. J. Minto.
A.—"In arenosis," Old-town Links, Dr. D. Skene,

where it is still to be found ; north bank of the Dee, a mile above the old bridge, G. D. ; Skene Road, at the eleventh mile-stone, Mr. Barron ; frequent in parish of Drumoak, Dr. J. Smith ; Sands of Forvie, at Ythanmouth, Mr. Cow ; parish of Glass, Stat. Account.

9. CAKILE. SEA ROCKET.

1. C. *maritima*, Willd. *(Purple S. R.)*

Annual. Flowers, June to August. British type. Range in Britain, 50°—61° ; coast only.

Sandy sea-shores.

General in suitable localities from St. Cyrus to mouth of the Spey.

10. SISYMBRIUM. HEDGE MUSTARD.

1. S. *officinale*, Linn. *(Common H. M.)*

Annual. Flowers in June and July. British type. Range in Britain, 50°—60° ; sea level to 500 feet.

Waste places and by road-sides. Frequent in lower districts ; rare in the interior ; not in Corgarff list.

2. S. *Thalianum*, Hooker. *(Thale H. M.)*

Annual. Flowers, April to June. British type. Range in Britain, 50°—60° ; sea level to 1260 feet.

Dry banks and walls. Not common in this district.

K.—Frequent at St. Cyrus and Benholme, Dr. Stephen ; Banchory-Ternan, Dr. Adams.

A.—Near Aberdeen, in various places ; north bank of Dee, one mile above the old bridge ; tops of walls at Morningfield and Summerhill, G. D. ; Cluny, Mr. Barron ; Alford, Rev. J. Farquharson ; Cruden, Mr. A. Murray ; embankment formed in making the road opposite Balmoral, Mr. Croall ; Castleton, Braemar, Mr. Barron.

B.—Rocky banks covered with gravel at Bridge of Alvah, but rare, Rev. Dr. Todd.

3. S. *Sophia*, Linn. *(Fine leaved H.)*
Annual. Flowers, June to August. English type. Range in Britain, 50°—58°; coast only.
Very rare.
K.—St. Cyrus, Stat. Account.

11. ALLIARIA. GARLIC MUSTARD.

1. A. *officinalis*, De Cand. *(common G. M.)*
Biennial. Flowers in May and June. British type. Range in Britain, 50°—58°; sea level to 400 feet.
Waste places. Rare.

K.—Burn of Benholme, Dr. Stephen; Banchory-Ternan, Rev. J. Brichan; Den of Leggart, Dr. A. Fleming.

A.—Robslaw Den; formerly at old House of Robslaw; road-side north from Powis, G. D.; Drumnahoy, Cluny, Mr. Barron; Paradise, Monymusk, Mr. P. Macgillivray.

B.—Alvah, local, Rev. Dr. Todd; in parish of Mortlach, Dr. L. Stewart.

12. SUBULARIA. AWL-WORT.

1. S. *aquatica*, Linn. *(Water A. W.)*
Perennial. Flowers in July. Highland type. Range in Britain, 53°—59°; from 150 to 2200 feet.
Shallow margins of Lakes. Rare.

A.—East end of Loch of Park, G. D.; Lake at Pitfour, Rev. J. Minto; in parish of Old Deer, Stat. Account; in a small loch, a little east of Loch Builg, Mr. Barron; Lochs Muick and Callater, Professor Macgillivray; Loch Ceander, head of Glen Callater, G. D.

13. CAPSELLA. SHEPHERD'S PURSE.

1 C. *Bursa Pastoris*, De Cand. (*Common S. P.*)
Annual. Flowers, March to October. British type.
Range in Britain, 50°—61°; sea level to 1200 feet.
Common, everywhere. In Corgarff, at the above altitude.

14 LEPIDIUM. PEPPER WORT.

1. L. *Smithii*, Hooker. (*Mithridate P. W.**)
Annual. Flowers, May to August. British type.
Range in Britain, 50°—58°; sea level to 1000 feet.
Dry gravelly banks, &c. Not common.
K.—Banchory-Ternan, Dr. Adams.
A.—North bank of Dee, above the old bridge; banks of Don, at Kettock's Mill; beside the Preventive Station, at Don-mouth; in Belhelvie Links, G. D.; near Culter House, Dr. J. Smith; fields, &c. in Leochel, Mr. Sutherland; road-side at House of Newton, Rev. J. Minto; banks of Dee at Castleton, Mr. Watson.
B.—About Banff, Stat. Account; Haugh below Bridge of Alvah, and occasionally on the banks of the Deveron in other parts of the parish, Rev. Dr. Todd; Mortlach, but rare, Dr. L. Stewart.

15. SENEBIERA. WART CRESS.

1. S. *Coronopus*, De Cand. (*Common W. C.*)
Annual. Flowers, June to September. English type.
Range in Britain, 50°—58°.
Rare, and confined to certain parts of the coast line.

---

* L. *campestre* is mentioned in Skene MSS. as found at Gordon's Mill, near Aberdeen; I have never seen it in this district.—G. D.

A.—Fish-town at Colliston, Mr. Cow; abundant beside the lighthouse at Cairnbulg-head, Dr. Templeton and G. D.; and also along the coast northwards, at Fish-town of Pitullie, G. D.

17. SINAPIS. MUSTARD.

1. S. *arvensis*, Linn. *(Charlock Mustard.)*
Annual. Flowers in June and July. British type. Range in Britain, 50°—61°; sea level to 1260 feet.
Fields and waste places. Common. Corgarff at the above altitude.

18. RAPHANUS. RADISH.

1. R. *Raphanistrum*, Linn. *(Wild R. jointed charlock.)*
Annual. Flowers, May to October. British type. Range in Britain, 50°—61°; sea level to 1,200 feet.
In fields, &c. Common.

ORDER VI.—RESEDACEAE.

1. RESEDA. MIGNONETTE.

1. R. *Luteola*, Linn. *(Yellow Weed.)*
Annual. Flowers, June to August. British type. Range in Britain, 50°—58°; sea level to 600 feet.
Waste places. Rare.
K.—At Benholme, and in a field by the road half a mile north-west from Brotherton, Dr. Stephen.

At Banchory-Ternan, Dr. Adams.

A.—" On brae from hangman's house at Aberdeen, to Footdee Church," Skene, MSS. ; (now covered with houses); by the side of the road from King Street to the brick-work in the Old-town Links, Dr. A. Fleming; near Morrison's Suspension Bridge, Professor Macgillivray; by the mills above Manse of Dyce, Dr. A. Fleming; at Aboyne, and in parish of Coull, Stat. Account; at the old Castle of Kildrummy, Mr. Barron.

B.—Alvah, very rare and scarcely indigenous, Rev. Dr. Todd; parish of Mortlach, Dr. L. Stewart; on the gravelly banks of Tynet and Golochy burns, Mr. Carmichael.

ORDER VII.—CISTACEAE.

1. HELIANTHEMUM. ROCK ROSE.

1. H. *vulgare*, Gaertner. *(Common R. R.)*
Perennial. Flowers, July to September. British type. Range in Britain, 50°—58°; sea level to 1700 feet.

Dry rocks and banks. Not common.

K.—Banchory-Ternan, Dr. Adams; north side of Bay of Nigg, G. D.

A.—Den of Maidencraig, on the Skene road, four miles from Aberdeen; by the Don at the new bridge, G. D. ; Drumnahoy, Cluny, Mr. Barron ; moor at Cannor near Aboyne, Stat. Account; Alford, Rev. Dr. Farquharson ; Clatt, Rev. J. Minto ; Corgarff, Mr. Barron ; on Formanhill, Rev. J. Abel ; rocks behind the farm of Tomintoul at Castleton, Braemar ; and on the Craig of Lin Mui, near Ballater, G. D.

B.—" I have only met with a few specimens growing on rocks on Deveron side," Rev. Dr. Todd ; links of Buckie and Portessie, and on the Binhill at Cullen, Mr. Carmichael; in Mortlach, Dr. L. Stewart.

ORDER VIII.—VIOLACEAE.

1. VIOLA. VIOLET.

1. V. *palustris*, Linn. *(Marsh V.)*
Perennial. Flowers, March to July. British type. Range in Britain, 50°—60°; sea level to 4000 feet.
Bogs and marshes. Rather local.

K.—Frequent in Benholme; in Durris and Strachan, Dr. Stephen ; Banchory-Ternan, Dr. Adams ; formerly in Ferryhill moss ; bogs near Scotston and Denmore, &c., G. D. ; Aberdour, Rev. G. Gairdner ; Haughton woods in Alford, Dr. A. Murray ; in Clatt, Rev. J. Minto ; in Corgarff, Mr. Barron ; two-thirds up Lochnagar on the east side, and on Ben Macdui at 4000 feet, and on the summit of the Mourne at Castleton, G. D.

B.—Frequent along the streamlet flowing from Come's Well and in woods near the base of hill of Alvah, Rev. Dr. Todd ; Mortlach, Dr. L. Stewart.

2. V. *canina*, Linn. *(Dog's V.)*
Perennial. Flowers, April to August. British type. Range in Britain, 50°—61°; sea level to 2600 feet.
Woods, banks, rocks, &c. Common.

3. V. *pumila*, Vill. *(Dillenius' V.)*
(V. flavicornis, Smith.)

Perennial. Flowers, April to August. English ? type.
Range in Britain, 50°—57°; sea level to 100 feet.
Dry sandy places. Local.

K.—Bay of Nigg, G. D.; about St. Cyrus, Stat. Account.

A.—Links at Aberdeen, G. D.

B.—Parish of Alvah, Rev. Dr. Todd.

4. V. *tricolor*, Linn. *(Pansy V.)*
Biennial. Flowers, March to October. British type.
Range in Britain, 50°—61°; sea level to 1700 feet.
Banks, fields, waste places, &c. Common.

5. V. *lutea*, Hudson. *(Yellow mountain V.)*
Perennial. Flowers, May to September. Scottish type.
Range in Britain, 51°—59°; 400 to 2600 feet.
Inland banks, pastures, and rocks.

Chiefly in the interior. Abundant at Greystone, in Alford; in Towie and Glenbucket, Dr. A. Murray: parish of Glass, Stat. Account; plentiful about Ballater and Castleton; rocks in Glen Callater at the "break-neck fall," G. D.; very abundant in the old churchyard of Cushnie, Mr. Sutherland.

B.—At Tomintoul, "Flora of Moray."

ORDER IX.—DROSERACEAE.

1. DROSERA. SUN-DEW.

1. D. *rotundifolia*, Linn. *(Round-leaved S.)*
Perennial. Flowers in July and August. British type.
Range in Britain, 50°—61°; sea level to 2000 feet.

Bogs and moist heaths. Of general occurrence.

2. D. *Anglica*, Hudson. *(Great English S.)*
Perennial. Flowers in July and August. Scottish type. Range in Britain, 50°—61°; 50 to 1800 feet.

Bogs and marshes. Rather local.

A.—Marsh at south side of Corsehill, near Scotston and Denmore, G. D. ; moor near Tarbethill in Belhelvie, Professor Macgillivray ; bog in parish of Longside, Mr. Murray ; bog near Manse of Drumoak, Professor Macgillivray ; bog on the west side of Auchmenzie, in Clatt, Rev. J. Minto ; marsh by the north side of the Braemar road, a little west from Bridge of Gairden, G. D. ; Glen Callater, Mr. A. K. Clark ; base of Ben-a-Buird, Mr. R. Mackay ; near base of Ben Macdui, G. D.

2. PARNASSIA. GRASS OF PARNASSUS.

1. P. *palustris*, Linn. *(common G. of P.)*
Perennial. Flowers in August and September. British type. Range in Britain, 50°—61°; sea level to 2700 feet.

Bogs and marshes. Very local.

K.—In different parts of Kincardineshire, Stat. Account ; Banchory-Ternan, Rev. J. Brichan ; Kingcausie, G. D.

A.—Scotston moor, and Millden burn in Belhelvie, G. D. ; at Cruden, Mr. A. Murray, Hill of Fare, Mr. Barron ; rocks in Glen Callater, at 2600 feet, G. D.; top of the Mourne at Castleton, Mr. Croall.

B.—Coast at Gamrie, Rev. G. Gairdner ; bogs at Sandlaw, Rosyburn, Newton, Muiryhill, &c. parish of Alvah, Rev. Dr. Todd ; in Mortlach, Dr. L. Stewart.

ORDER X.—POLYGALACEAE.

1. POLYGALA. MILKWORT.

1. P. *vulgaris*, Linn. *(Common M.)*
Perennial. Flowers, May to August. British type.
 Range in Britain, 50°—60°; sea level to 2500
 feet.
Dry pastures, &c. Common.

ORDER XI.—ELATINACEAE.

1. ELATINE. WATER-WORT.

1. E. *hexandra*, De Cand. *(Hexandrous W.)*
Annual. Flowers in July and August. English type.
 Range in Britain, 50°—58°; at 200 feet.
Very rare.
K.—In shallow water at the east end of the Loch
of Park, where it was first observed by Dr. A. Fleming.

ORDER XII.—CARYOPHYLLACEAE.

1. DIANTHUS. PINK.

1. D. *deltoides*, Linn. *(Maiden P.)*
Perennial. Flowers, June to August. British type.
 Range in Britain, 50°—58°; coast line to 700
 feet ?
Banks, pastures, &c. in gravelly soil. Rare.
K.—Coast at St. Cyrus, Bervie, and bridge at Burn

of Benholme, Stat. Account; in parish of Arbuthnot, Mr. Chrystall; road-side above Gourdon; links east of Brotherton, Dr. Stephen.*

2. SILENE. CATCHFLY.

1. *S. acaulis*, Linn. *(Moss Campion.)*
Perennial. Flowers, June to August. Highland type.
Range in Britain, 53°—61°; 2300 ? to 4320 feet.
Confined to the higher ranges of mountains, but very abundant there.

A.—Mount Keen, Lochnagar, Little Craigendall, Callater Rocks, Ben-a-Buird, Ben Macdui, G. D.; on Braeriach and Cairntoul, Mr. R. Mackay.

B.—Cairngorm, Mr. R. Mackay.

2. *S. inflata*, Smith. *(Bladder Campion.)*
Perennial. Flowers in June and July. British type.
Range in Britain, 50°—58°; sea level to 800 feet.
Pastures and waste places. Not uncommon in the lower districts.

K.—St. Cyrus and Bervie, Dr. Stephen; at new Church of Nigg, G. D.; Banchory-Ternan, Rev. J. Brichan.

A.—About Aberdeen, at Wellington Bridge, Powder Magazine, Footdee, banks of Dee and Don, &c. G. D.; in Buchan, Mr. A. Murray; Aberdour, Rev. J. Gairdner; Rhynie and Auchindoir, but rare in Clatt, Rev. J. Minto; Forgue, and near Glack, Rev. J Abel.

B.—Dunlugas, rare, Rev. Dr. Todd; Mortlach, rare, Dr. L. Stewart.

3. *S. maritima*, Withering. *(Sea Campion.)*

---

* Rev. A. Beverly has found it on the bank of the Dee near Ballater, " apparently washed down from a garden."

Perennial. Flowers, June to August. British type. Range in Britain, 50°—61°; sea level to 2000 feet.

Sandy and stony places, &c. General.

By the coast, common; and occasionally in the interior, along the courses of the Dee, the Don, the Deveron. Frequent on some of the higher mountains —Khoil, Lochnagar, &c. &c.

4. S. *nutans*, Linn. *(Drooping C.)*
Perennial. Flowers, May to July. English type. Range in Britain, 50°—57°; coast only.
Very rare.

K.—Coast at St Cyrus, and Kineff, Stat. Account.

3. LYCHNIS. LYCHNIS.

1. L. *Flos-cuculi*, Linn. *(Ragged Robin.)*
Perennial. Flowers in May and June. British type. Range in Britain, 50°—61°; coast to 1300 feet.
Moist meadows and pastures. Common.

2. L. *vespertina*, Sibthorp. *(White L.)*
Biennial. Flowers, June to September. British type. Range in Britain, 50°—61°; coast to 500 feet?

In fields, &c. Rather scarce in the interior, more frequent in the lower parts; but nowhere a common plant.

K.—St. Cyrus, Benholme, Dunnottar, Muchalls, Nigg, Dr. Stephen.

A.—About Robslaw, Deeside at Cults, &c. &c. G. D.; Forgue, Rev. J. Abel.

B.—Local in Alvah, Rev. Dr. Todd; in Mortlach, rare, Dr. L. Stewart.

3. L. *diurna*, Sibthorp. *(Red Campion.)*

Perennial. Flowers in June and July. British type. Range in Britain, 50°—61°; coast to 2500 feet.

Moist shady places; frequent and general. At the above altitude on Lochnagar.

4. SAGINA. PEARL-WORT.

1. *S. maritima*, Don. *(Sea P.)*

Annual. Flowers, May to July. British type. Range in Britain, 50°—61°; coast only.

Moist places along the coast line.

K.—St. Cyrus, south from Kirkside; coast at Gourdon; Garron Point, Dr. Stephen. Near Girdleness Lighthouse; also at the south pier, G. D.

A.—Fissures of stones, north pier; the Inch; tidal line at railway viaduct; and Old-town Links, G. D.; Buchanness, Mr. A. Murray; Ythan-mouth, Mr. Cow.

B.—Coast at Banff, Mr. G. C. Smith. *

2.—*S. procumbens*, Linn. *(Procumbent P.)*

Perennial. Flowers, May to September. British type. Range in Britain, 50°—61°; sea level to 2700 feet.

Waste places, pastures, &c. Common.

3. *S. saxatilis*, Wimm. *(Alpine P.)*

Perennial. Flowers, June to August. Highland type. Range in Britain, 56°—59°; 2000 to 2500 feet?

Rare. At high elevations, by streams, and on wet

---

* *S. apetala*, Linn. Mentioned in Prof. Macgillivray's Nat. History of Deeside, as found "about Aberdeen, and along the rocky shore;" is also reported at St. Cyrus. The true plant does not occur in the district; it and *S. maritima*, are, however, considered by some as identical.

rocks. The true plant is far from common, but occurs on Ben-a-Buird, and others of the Braemar range.

4. S. *subulata*, Wimm. *(Awl-leaved P.)*
Perennial. Flowers, June to August. Scottish type. Range in Britain, 50°—61°; sea level to 1800 feet?
Dry places about rocks, &c. Local.

K.—At St. Cyrus; Cloch Hill, Benholme, Dr. Stephen. At Girdleness Lighthouse, &c. G. D.; Banchory-Ternan, Dr. Adams.

A.—Robslaw Quarry; banks of the Dee; serpentine rocks, by the Udny road, near Meadowbank, G. D.; Hill of Fare, Mr. Barron; Normandyke, Culter, Dr. J. Smith.

B.—Speyside, parish of Aberlour, Dr. L. Stewart.

5.—S. *nodosa*, Linn. *(Knotted P.)*
Perennial. Flowers in July and August. British type. Range in Britain, 50°—60°; coast to 1200 feet.
Wet places. Frequent, but not a common plant.

K.—Den of Jackstone; and on St. Cyrus' Sands, in marshy places; Annie's dam, Benholme; Sootywells, Garvock, Dr. Stephen.

A.—Near Aberdeen, on Stocket moor; in Old-town Links; Belhelvie Links, &c. G. D.; Dalhaiky, Cluny, but rare, Mr. Barron; Alford, Rev. Dr. Farquharson; Clatt, Rev. J. Minto; Corgarff, Mr. Barron; Cruden, Mr. A. Murray; Castleton, Braemar, Mr. Sutherland.

B.—Among chingle, by Deveronside, in Alvah, rare, Rev. Dr. Todd; Mortlach, Dr. L. Stewart.

5. HONCKENYA. SEA PURSLANE.

1. H. *peploides*, Ehrh. *(Ovate-leaved S. P.)*
Perennial. Flowers, May to July. British type. Range in Britain, 50°—61°. Coast only.

Sandy shores, along the entire coast.

6. ARENARIA. SANDWORT.

1. *A. verna*, Linn. *(Vernal S.)*
Perennial. Flowers, May to July. Scottish type?
Range in Britain, 50°—58°; 600 to 1500 feet.
Rocks in the interior.

Confined to the serpentine tracts in Leslie; Clatt; at Noth; Knockespock, Rev. J. Minto. Towanrieffe, (serpentine), Auchindoir, Mr. Sutherland. On rocks of same composition at Den of Craig; and on the Greenhill of Strathdon, G. D.

2. *A. serpyllifolia*, Linn. *(Thyme-leaved S.)*
Annual. Flowers, June to August. British type.
Range in Britain, 50°—60°; sea level to 900 feet.
Walls; and dry waste places. Rather local.

A.—Tops of walls at Ferryhill; road-side at Broomhill; Raeden; Kittybrewster, G. D. On the Deeside road, at the third mile-stone, Dr. J. Smith; Drumnahoy, in Cluny, Mr. Barron; parish of Coull, Stat. Account; in Rhynie, Rev. J. Minto; upon the bridge over the Dee, at Invercauld, Mr. Croall.

3. *A. trinervis*, Linn. *(Three-nerved S.)*
Annual. Flowers, June to July. British type. Range in Britain, 50°—58°; 200 to 1000 feet.
Shady woods. Very rare in this district.

A.—In the wood at Den of Gight, parish of Methlick, G. D; in a small ravine, west from Linn of Dee, Mr. Croall.

B.—Wood of Shaws, parish of Alvah, Rev. Dr. Todd.

7. STELLARIA. STITCHWORT.

1. S. *media*, Withering. *(Common Chickweed.)*
Annual. Flowers, nearly all the year. British type. Range in Britain, 50°—61°; sea level to 1800 feet?
Common everywhere.

2. S. *holostea*, Linn. *(Greater S.)*
Perennial. Flowers, April to June. British type. Range in Britain, 50°—60°; sea level to 1300 feet.
Woods and hedges. Generally diffused in all parts of the district.

3. S. *graminea*, L. *(Narrow-leaved S.)*
Perennial. Flowers, April to August. British type. Range in Britain, 50°—61°; sea level to 1400 feet.
Dry pastures, heaths, &c. Frequent.

4. S. *uliginosa*, Murr. *(Bog S.)*
Annual. Flowers, May to June. British type. Range in Britain, 50°—61°; sea level to 2800 feet.
Ditches and streams. Generally diffused.

8. CERASTIUM. MOUSE-EAR CHICKWEED.

1. C. *vulgatum*, Linn. *(Broad-leaved M.)*
Annual. Flowers, April to September. British type. Range in Britain, 50°—61°; sea level to 900 feet.
Road-sides and waste places. Common.

2. C. *viscosum*, Linn. *(Narrow-leaved M.)*
Annual. Flowers, March to September. British type. Range in Britain, 50°—61°; sea level to 2397 feet.

Waste places, &c. Common.

3. *C. semidecandrum*, Linn. *(Small M.)*

Annual. Flowers, March to May. British type. Range in Britain, 50°—61°; sea level to 500 feet.

Wall tops and dry sandy places. Frequent.

K.—Coast at St. Cyrus, Dr. Stephen; near Aberdeen, at the south pier; Old-town Links; Inch, &c., G. D.; in Buchan, Mr. A. Murray; Aberdour, Rev. G. Gairdner; Clatt and Grange, Rev. J. Minto.

B.—Parish of Alvah, but local, Rev. Dr. Todd.

4. *C. tetrandrum*, Curtis. *(Four-cleft M.)*

Annual. Flowers, May to August. British type. Range in Britain, 50°—61°; coast line.

Dry sandy places. Local.

K.—At the Cove, Dr. Stephen.

A.—At Aberdeen, links at the Broadhill and northwards.

5. *C. arvense*, Linn. *(Field C.)*

Perennial. Flowers, April to September. British type. Range in Britain, 50°—58°; 50 to 500 feet.

Dry gravelly places. Very local

K.—Near the mill on Burn of Shevoch, at Kirk of Durris, Rev. A. Beverly; banks of Dee behind Nether-Banchory Church, and between the Mill Inn at Maryculter and the river Dee, Professor Macgillivray; at farm of Bankhead, Maryculter, Dr. A. Fleming.

A.—In a field near the north end of the old Bridge of Dee; and on north bank of the Dee, a mile above the old bridge, G. D.; about Drumoak, &c., Dr. J. Smith; Upper Drumnahoy, Cluny, Mr. Barron; in parishes of Rhynie, Clatt, and Leslie, not common, but plentiful where it does grow, Rev. J. Minto.

B.—In parish of Alvah, Rev. Dr. Todd. ; in Mortlach, Dr. L. Stewart.

6. C. *alpinum*, Linn. *(Hairy alpine C.)*

Perennial. Flowers, June to August. Highland type. Range in Britain, 53°—59°; 1480 to 3000 feet? Confined to the higher and inland districts.

Craig behind the farm of Lin Mui, west from Ballater, at the low elevation above mentioned, in this locality it is abundant, G. D. ; also on Lochnagar, Callater Rocks, Ben Macdui, and other parts of the same range.

7. C. *latifolium*, Linn. *(Broad-leaved alpine C.)*

Perennial. Flowers, June to September. Highland type. Range in Britain, 53°—59°; 1800 to 3000 feet.

This is a rarer plant than the last.

A.—On Little Craigendall, Mr. Croall ; Ben Macdui ; Cairntoul.

B.—At head of Loch Avon ; on Cairngorm ; in Glen Avon, " Flora of Moray."

8. C. *trigynum*, Fries. *(Stitchwort C.)*

Perennial. Flowers in July and August. Highland type. Range in Britain, 56°—58°; 2400 to 4000 feet.

Very rare.

A.—Rocks on the north and south sides of Ben Macdui, Mr. R. Mackay ; Little Craigendall, and Wells of Dee, Mr. Sutherland.

B.—On Cairngorm, Mr. H. C. Watson.

ORDER XIII.—LINACEAE.

1. LINUM. FLAX.

1. L. *catharticum*, Linn. *(Purging F.)*
Annual. Flowers, June to September. British type. Range in Britain, 50°—61°; sea level to 1700 feet.
Pastures and heaths. Generally diffused.

2. RADIOLA. FLAX SEED.

1. R. *millegrana*, Smith. *(Thyme-leaved F.)*
Annual. Flowers in July and August. British type. Range in Britain, 50°—60°; sea level to 650 feet.
Bogs and wet gravelly places. Rather local.

K.—Moor of Benholme, Mr. Chrystall; near new Church of Nigg, and in Bay of Nigg, G. D.; west side of embankment a little above Nether-Banchory Church, Dr. Stephen; marshes at Feuch bridge, and Loch of Park, Dr. Adams.

A.—Links at Aberdeen, Dr. R. Harvey; Fyfe moss, Belhelvie, and road-side at Scotston moor, in marshy spots, G. D.; Upper Drumnahoy, Cluny, Mr. Barron; Loch of Auchlossan, Lumphanan, Dr. A. Murray; road-side above Kincardine O'Neil, Mr. Sutherland; at west end of Loch Cannor, G. D.; Heugh of Crimond, and elsewhere in Buchan, Mr. Cow; on the hill, a mile west of Aberdour manse, Mr. A. Cruickshank.

B.—At hill of Maunderlea, Alvah, Mr. G. C. Smith.

Order XIV—MALVACEAE.

1. MALVA. MALLOW.

1. M. *rotundifolia*, Linn. *(Dwarf M.)* Perennial. Flowers, July to September. English type. Range in Britain, 50°—58°; coast only.

Very rare. This is the only wild species of mallow in the district.

K.—St. Cyrus, at Milton of Mathers, Mr. Sutherland and Mr. Croall; south end of the Wellington Suspension Bridge, Mr. Smith.

A.—Formerly at the south end of the fish-town of Footdee, G. D.; at Ravenscraig, parish of Peterhead, Mr. A. Murray.

Order XV.—HYPERICACEAE.

1. HYPERICUM. ST. JOHN'S WORT.

1. H. *quadrangulum*, Linn. *(Square-stalked St. J.)* Perennial. Flowers in July. British type (or English). Range in Britain, 50°—58°; coast to 450 feet.

By ditches, and in wet pastures. Local.

K.—St. Cyrus cliffs, and north from Den Fenella, and in Den of Morphie, Dr. Stephen; marshes about Muchals; by the dam at south end of Den of Leggart; Corbie Den, Maryculter, G. D.

A.—Beside Gilcomston dam; by rivulets in the links of Belhelvie; banks of Dee and Don, &c., G. D.; by the sides of the burn at Robslaw Bleachfield, Mr. Sutherland; beside the avenue to Culter House, Dr. J. Smith; Wanton Wells, Insch, Mr. M'Donald; Alford,

Rev. Dr. Farquharson; Burn of Forgue near Cobairdy, Rev. J. Abel.

B.—Denmill, Alvah, rare; more abundant in some of the neighbouring parishes, Rev. Dr. Todd.

2. H. *humifusum*, Linn. *(Trailing St. J.)*

Perennial. Flowers in July. British type (or English). Range in Britain, 50°—58°; sea level to 400 feet.

Dry pastures and waste places. Frequent.

K.—South bank of Dee, above the old bridge, G. D.

A.—North bank of Dee; frequent in Belhelvie; abundant about Drumoak, &c. &c.

B.—Frequent in pastures in parish of Alvah, Rev. Dr. Todd; Mortlach, Dr. L. Stewart.

3. H. *pulchrum*, Linn. *(Small upright St. J.)*

Perennial. Flowers in June and July. British type. Range in Britain, 50°—61°; sea level to 2000 feet.

Banks, moors, woods, &c. Frequent. General in this district.

4. H. *hirsutum*, Linn. *(Hairy St. J.)*

Perennial. Flowers in July and August. British type, (or English.) Range in Britain, 50°—58°; sea level to 700 feet.

Banks and rocky places. Rather local.

K.—Den Fenella; St. Cyrus' cliffs; Arbuthnot; Stonehaven to Muchalls, Dr. Stephen; near the old Church of Nigg, G. D.; north bank of Dee below Maryfield Cottage, Banchory-Ternan, Dr. Adams; near Maryculter House, Dr. J. Smith.

A.—North bank of Dee above the old bridge; north bank of the Don above the old bridge, where it grew 100 years ago "in rupibus Don, prope pontem," Skene, MSS.; foot of Glen Gairden, Mr. Croall; banks of Dee at Ballater, Rev. A. Beverly; in Alford, on Don braes opposite Kirktown of Forbes, Rev. J. Minto; banks of Don at Breda, Mr. Sutherland; parish of Glass, Stat. Account; Deveron-side at Huntly Lodge, Rev. J. Abel.

B.—Braes of Montcoffer, and occasionally on Deveron-side above and below Bridge of Alvah, Rev. Dr. Todd; woods at Duff House, "Flora of Moray;" Fiddoch-side, rare, Dr. Stewart.

5. H. *perforatum*, Linn. *(Perforated St. J.)*
Perennial. Flowers in July and August. British type. Range in Britain, 50°—61°; coast line to 380 feet?
Shady places. Very rare.
K.—Den Fenella; Kirkside, St. Cyrus; and below North Esk bridge, Dr. Stephen.
A.—Den of Robslaw, G. D.; parish of Glass, Stat. Account.

ORDER XVI.—GERANIACEAE.

1. GERANIUM. CRANE'S BILL.

1. G. *sanguineum*, Linn. *(Bloody C.)*
Perennial. Flowers in July. British type (or Intermediate). Range in Britain, 50°—58°; sea level to 1200 feet.
Banks and rocks. Rather local; appears to be more abundant in the southern parts of this district.
K.—Coast at St. Cyrus, Garvock, Benholme, and Johnshaven, Dr. Stephen; Kineff, Stat. Account;

abundant on the cliffs at the Cove and southwards, G. D.

A.—Banks of Don; and at Castleton, Braemar, G. D. Not in lists of plants at Corgarff, Alvah, nor Mortlach.

2. G. sylvaticum, Linn. *(Wood C.)*

Perennial. Flowers in June and July. Scottish type (or Intermediate). Range in Britain, 52°—60°; 100 to 2600 feet.

Woods and river banks. Rather local.

K.—Den of Davo; below Blackness, Strachan; Burn of Benholme, Dr. Stephen; parish of Arbuthnot, Mr. Chrystall; Corbie Den, G. D.; Banchory-Ternan, Dr. Adams.

A.—Robslaw Den; banks of Dee and Don, along the course of both; Craig of Lin Mui, near Ballater; Corrymulzie, Braemar; Callater Rocks, and Ben Macdui, G. D.; Clatt, Den of Craig, &c. Rev. J. Minto; woods of Avochie, Rev. J. Abel; Laithers, near Turiff, Mr. A. Murray.

B.—Along Deveron-side, and near Bridge of Alvah, Rev. Dr. Todd; common in Mortlach, Dr. L. Stewart.

3. G. pratense, Linn. *(Blue Meadow C.)*

Perennial. Flowers, June to August. British type (or English). Range in Britain, 50°—58°; coast to 1747 feet.

Moist shady places, rocks, &c. Local.

K—Coast at St. Cyrus, Stat. Account; Arbuthnot, Mr. Chrystall; beach between Gourdon and Johnshaven, Dr. Stephen; Finnan and Portlethen, G. D.

A.—Donside at Dyce; Kintore and Kemnay, Mr. P. Macgillivray; banks of Don at Castle Forbes, Dr. A. Fleming; Drumnahoy in Cluny, Mr. Barron; Khoil at Ballater, at 1747 feet, G. D.; a little above

Balmoral, Mr. Croall ; ruins of Castle of Lismore in Rhynie, Rev. J. Minto ; Den of Wardhouse, Mr. M'Donald. Reported as scarce in the higher parts of the Garioch district. Banks of the Deveron opposite Mayen House, Rev. J. Abel.

B.—Deveron-side, and near Bridge of Alvah, Rev. Dr. Todd ; Delnabo and Campdalmore, near Tomintoul, " Flora of Moray."

4. G. *Robertianum*, Linn. *(Herb-Robert.)*
Annual. Flowers, May to September. British type. Range in Britain, 50°—60° ; sea level to 1500 feet.
Woods, waste places, &c. Frequent, and general.

5. G. *molle*, Linn. *(Dove's-foot C.)*
Annual. Flowers, April to September. British type. Range in Britain, 50°—61° ; sea level to 1000 feet.
Dry pastures, &c. &c. Common.

6. G. *dissectum*, Linn. *(Jagged-leaved C.)*
Annual. Flowers, May to August. British type. Range in Britain, 50°—59° ; sea level to 1250 feet.
Pastures and waste places. Frequent.

The highest and most inland locality known to me, is at Castleton, Braemar, where it was observed by Mr. Croall ; Corgarff, Mr. Barron.

2. ERODIUM. STORK'S BILL.

1. E. *cicutarium*, Smith. *(Hemlock S.)*
Annual. Flowers, June to August. British type. Range in Britain, 50°—59° ; sea level to 300 feet ?
Dry sandy places, and waste ground. Frequent.

Order XVII.—OXALIDACEAE.

1. Oxalis. Wood-Sorrel.

1. O. *Acetosella*, Linn. *(Common W.)*
Annual. Flowers, April to August. British type. Range in Britain, 50°—60°; sea level to 3800 feet.
Woods, and shady crevices about stones and rocks. General.

Sub-Class II.—CALYCIFLORAE.

Order XVIII.—LEGUMINOSAE.

1. Ulex. Furze.

1. U. *Europaeus*, Linn. *(Furze, Whin, or Gorse.)* Perennial. Flowers, February to August. British type. Range in Britain, 50°—59°; sea level to 1200 feet.
Of general occurrence in the lower districts, thinning out towards the interior. It is plentiful, but rather small, about Ballater. Between Castleton and Crathie it is rarely seen; at the former place, it is one of the rarest of plants. In Glen Muick, the last whin bush is seen half a mile east of Acholzie. It occurs in Mortlach.

2. Genista. Greenwood.

1. G. *Anglica*, Linn. *(Needle Gorse, Petty-whin.)* Perennial. Flowers in May and June. British type, (or English.) Range in Britain, 50°—58°; near sea level, 2200 feet.

Heaths and moors. Very general; and on the whole, more abundant in the interior.

Hills at Nigg; Stocket and Scotston moors; Garlogie moor; Hill of Fare; Aboyne; Ballater; Crathie; Castleton.

3. SPARTIUM. BROOM.

1. S. *scoparium*, Linn. *(Common Broom.)*
Perennial. Flowers, April to June. British type. Range in Britain, 50°—59°; sea level to 2000 feet.

Dry waste places. Common.

Like the whin, this plant becomes rarer in passing to the more inland districts. It is, however, very luxuriant about Aboyne, and also at Ballater. From Crathie to Castleton it is scarce, but occurs, though rare, a few miles west from the latter. In Glen Muick it ceases with the whin. On Donside it is still luxuriant some distance west of Inverernan, the whin having disappeared several miles lower.* On the cliffs in Glen Callater, Mr. Croall found "a few plants, 10 or 12 inches in length, closely appressed to the rock, and in full flower."

4. ONONIS. REST-HARROW.

1. O. *arvensis*, Linn. *(Common R.)*
Perennial. Flowers, June to August. British type. Range in Britain, 50°—59°; sea level to 400 feet.

* In the severe winter of 1855, when the temperature fell to minus 1° F. (at Aberdeen), the whin and broom in all exposed places were killed to the ground. This effect was most conspicuous along the coast, probably because these plants attain larger size, and the shelter afforded by the snow is less. The plants were pushing vigorous shoots from the under-ground part, in the following season.

Old pastures and waste places. Very local.

K.—At St. Cyrus; Den of Morphie; and north from Stonehaven, Dr. Stephen.

A.—Old-town Links near the brick-work, and on a bank opposite Fintray House, Dr. A. Fleming; links, north of Don-mouth, Mr. P. Macgillivray; Milltown of Kemnay, and bank of Ury at Inverury, Mr. Burnet; at Aboyne, Deeside, Stat. Account; Dungarvan, parish of Leslie, Mr. M'Donald; near the mouth of the river Ugie, on the north side, G. D.; links of St. Fergus, Mr. A. Murray.

B.—Occasionally on Deveron-side, and Bridge of Banff, Rev. Dr. Todd; in Mortlach, but rare, Dr. L. Stewart.

5. ANTHYLLIS. KIDNEY-VETCH.

1. A. *Vulneraria*, Linn. *(Common K. V.)*
Perennial. Flowers, July to September. British type.
Range in Britain, 50°—61°; sea level to 2450 feet.
Dry pastures and rocks. General in the district.

6. MEDICAGO. MEDICK.

1. M. *lupulina*, Linn. *(Black M.)*
Annual. Flowers, May to August. British type.
Range in Britain, 50°—58°; sea level to 1200 feet.
Fields and waste places. Frequent. Is abundant in Corgarff, at the height above mentioned

7. TRIFOLIUM. TREFOIL-CLOVER.

1. T. *repens*, Linn. *(White T. or Dutch C.)*
Perennial. Flowers, May to September. British type.
Range in Britain, 50°—61°; sea level to 2000 feet.

Meadows, pastures, &c. Frequent and widely diffused; attains the elevation above mentioned on Morven.

2. T. *pratense*, Linn. *(Purple C.)*

Perennial. Flowers, May to August. British type. Range in Britain, 50°—61°; sea level to 1250 feet.

Meadows and pastures. Frequent.

3. T. *medium*, Linn. *(Zigzag T.)*

Perennial. Flowers, June to August. British type. Range in Britain, 50°—61°; sea level to 1000 feet.

Dry banks and rocky places. Frequent, but rather local.

K.—Blackness, Strachan; Dens of Jackstone, St. Cyrus; Morphie and Davo, Dr. Stephen; coast north from Stonehaven, and at Girdleness, G. D.

A.—Banks of Dee at Aberdeen; Den of Maidencraig, &c. G. D.; Cluny, Mr. Barron; Clatt, Rev. J. Minto; Alford, Rev. Dr. Farquharson; on the ascent to the Lin Mui, near Ballater, G. D. Not in Corgarff nor Mortlach lists.

B.—In parish of Alvah, Rev. Dr. Todd.

4. T. *arvense*, Linn. *(Hare's-foot T.)*

Annual. Flowers in July and August. British type, (or English.) Range in Britain, 50°—58°; coast line to 400 feet.

Fields, &c. Rare.

K.—On ruins of Dunnottar Castle, G. D.

A.—Tillenhilt, and Upper Drumnahoy, Cluny, Mr. Barron; in Buchan district, Mr. A. Murray.

B.—In parish of Alvah, Rev. Dr. Todd.

5. T. *scabrum*, Linn. *(Rough T.)*

Annual. Flowers, May to July. English type. Range in Britain, 50°—57°; coast only.

Maritime pastures. Very rare.

K.—Coast at Kaim of Mathers, St. Cyrus; at Dunnottar, by the footpath to the castle, Dr. Stephen.

6. T. *procumbens*, Linn. *(Hop T.)*
Annual. Flowers in July and August. British type. Range in Britain, 50°—60°; sea level to 500 feet.

Dry pastures, &c. Frequent; especially in the lower parts of the district.

7. T. *filiforme*, Linn. *(Slender yellow T.)*
Annual. Flowers in June and July. British type, (or English.) Range in Britain, 50°—58°; sea level to 500 feet?

Pastures and waste places. Frequent; scarcer in inland parts. Rare in Mortlach, Dr. L. Stewart

8. LOTUS. BIRD'S-FOOT TREFOIL.

1. L. *corniculatus*, Linn. *(Common B.)*
Perennial. Flowers in July and August. British type. Range in Britain, 50°—60°; sea level to 1900 feet?

Pastures and banks. General, and frequent.

2. L. *major*, Scop. *(Large B.)*
Perennial. Flowers in July and August. British type, (or English.) Range in Britain, 50°—58°; sea level to 500 feet.

Sides of streams, ditches, &c. Frequent, but not common.

K.—At Cove, Nigg, &c., &c., G. D.

A.—Banks of Dee and Don; Stocket and Scotston moors, &c., &c., G. D.; Alford, Rev. J. Minto. Not in Corgarff list.

B.—Below the Den at Linhead, in Alvah, rare, Rev. Dr. Todd. Not in list of Mortlach plants.

9. ASTRAGALUS. MILK-VETCH.

1. A. *glycyphyllus*, Linn. *(Sweet M. V.)*
Perennial. Flowers in July and August. Germanic type, (or British.) Range in Britain, 50°—58°; coast chiefly.
Woods and bushy places. Very rare in this district.
K.—Cliffs at St. Cyrus, Dr. Stephen; Thornyhive, near Dunnottar Castle, Dr. A. Fleming, where it grew 100 years ago, "Solummodo inveni in rupibus Thornyhive, prope Dunnottar," Skene MSS.
A.—Den of Boyne, Mr. A. Murray.

2. A. *hypoglottis*, Linn. *(Purple Mountain M. V.)*
Perennial. Flowers in June and July. Germanic type, (or British.) Range in Britain, 51°—58°; coast line only.
Dry grassy banks. Very local.
K.—Coast at Benholme, Stat. Account. Abundant at the Cove; Burnbanks; and north end of Bay of Nigg, G. D.
A.—"South-east corner of the Broadhill in links at Aberdeen," Dr. D. Skene. It is still there in small quantity.

3. A. *alpinus*, Linn. *(Alpine M. V.)*
Perennial. Flowers in July and August. Highland type. Range in Britain, 56°—58°; 2400 to 2600 feet.
A. Upon the face of a hill called Little Craigendal, north-west of the House of Invercauld in Braemar. This interesting addition to the Flora of our county was made some years ago by Professor Balfour.

10. VICIA. VETCH. TARE.

1. V. *lathyroides*, Linn. *(Spring V.)*
Annual. Flowers, April to June. British type? Range in Britain, 50°—58°; coast line.
Sandy pastures. Very local.

K.—Coast at St. Cyrus, Stat. Account.

A.—Formerly on the Inch at Aberdeen, G. D. "Solummodo inveni in campis nostris maritimis," Skene MSS.; it is still very plentiful in the links north of the Broadhill, G. D. Links at Cruden, Mr. A. Murray.

B.—In Alvah, but not common, Rev. Dr. Todd.

2. V. *sativa*, Linn. *(Common V.)*
Annual. Flowers in May and June. British type, (or English.) Range in Britain, 50°—59°; sea level to 500 feet.

Pastures and waste places. Frequent, but not common.

Var. β, *angustifolia* is found on the coast at St. Cyrus; north of the Dee, a mile above the old bridge; sandhills east of the Preventive Station at Don-mouth; at Aberdour. In Alvah, and in Mortlach.

3. V. *sepium*, Linn. *(Bush V.)*
Perennial. Flowers, June to August. British type. Range in Britain, 50°—60°; sea level to 1800 feet.
Woods and shady places. General and common.

4. V. *lutea*, Linn. *(Rough-podded yellow V.)*
Perennial. Flowers in June and July. English type? Range in Britain, 50°—57°; coast only.
Stony and rocky banks. Very rare.

K.—On the north bank of the river North Esk, near the sea, Dr. A. Murray; St. Cyrus cliffs, near the cave at Nether Warburton, and at the base of the cliffs, Dr. Stephen.

5. V. *Cracca*, Linn. *(Tufted V.)*
Perennial. Flowers, June to September. British type. Range in Britain, 50°—61°; sea level to 2000 feet?

Bushy places and banks. General in this district.

6. V. *sylvatica*, Linn. *(Wood V.)*
Perennial. Flowers, June to August. British type? Range in Britain, 50°—58°; sea level to 1500 feet.

In woods and upon shady rocks. Widely diffused, but not a common plant.

K.—Abundant on the Cliffs at St. Cyrus, Dr. Stephen. Coast at Johnshaven; Dunnottar; Muchalls; the Cove, &c., G. D.

A.—Strathdon, Mr. Barron. Falls of the Glassilt, head of Loch Muick; in the wood south-west from Balmoral Castle; Braemar, G. D. Cruden, Mr. A. Murray; Aberdour, Rev. G. Gairdner.

B.—Coast at Gamrie, Rev. G. Gairdner.

7. V. *hirsuta*, Koch. *(Hairy V.)*
Annual. Flowers, June to August. British type. Range in Britain, 50°—60°; 50 to 500 feet.

Waste places. Not common.

K.—Stony beach at Den Fenella, &c. Dr. Stephen.

A.—Near Aberdeen, at Robslaw Quarry; north side of the Don, near the sea, &c. G. D. Reported as growing in Cluny, Alford, Aberdour, &c.

B.—In Alvah, Rev. Dr. Todd; in Mortlach, Dr. L. Stewart.

11. ORNITHOPUS. BIRD'S-FOOT.

1. O. *perpusillus*, Linn. *(Common B. F.)*

Annual. Flowers in June and July. British type.
Range in Britain, 50°—58°; local.
Dry sandy and gravelly soil. Very rare.

B.—Formerly on dry pastures, farm of Boghead, lying between the mill-dam of Nether Mindon, and the public road, parish of Alvah, Rev. Dr. Todd.

12. LATHYRUS. VETCHLING. EVERLASTING-PEA.

1. L. *pratensis*, Linn. *(Meadow Vetchling.)*
Perennial. Flowers in July and August. British type.
Range in Britain, 60°—61°; sea level to 1200 feet.
Meadows and pastures. Common.*
Attains the above elevation in Corgarff.

13. OROBUS. BITTER-VETCH.

1. O. *tuberosus*, Linn. *(Tuberous B. V.)*
Perennial. Flowers in May and June. British type.
Range in Britain, 50°—61°; sea level to 2000 feet.
Moors and mountain pastures. General.

ORDER XIX.—ROSACEAE.

1. PRUNUS. PLUM AND CHERRY.

1. P. *communis*, Hudson. *(Common P.)*
Var. a, *spinosa*, (P. *spinosa*, Linn.) (The Sloe.)

* L. *sylvestris*, Linn. is reported as found by the late Dr. Stephen, at St. Cyrus' cliffs, on the west side of the cave at North Warburton, with Vicia lutea. The Scottish localities for this plant are all rather suspicious, and therefore the plant is for the present excluded from the list.

Perennial. Flowers in April and May. British type. Range in Britain, 50°—59°; coast line to 700 feet.

Rocky places, &c. Widely diffused, but not common.

K.—Kincardineshire coast, at the Cove, &c.

A.—North bank of Don at the old bridge, G. D. : steep bank at Church of Peterculter, Dr. J. Smith : woods of Cordach at Kincardine O'Neil, Mr. Barron ; near Dee Castle, and at Ballater, G. D. ; in Rhynie, Rev. J. Minto ; Den of Gight, G. D. ; coast at Aberdour, Rev. G. Gairdner.

B.—Deveron-side, Rev. J. Abel ; braes of Mountcoffer and Inverkeithny, Rev. Dr. Todd ; in Mortlach, Dr. L. Stewart.

2. P. *Padus*, Linn. *(Bird-Cherry.)*

Perennial. Flowers in May. British type. Range in Britain, 51°—59° ; from 50 to 1000 feet.

Woods, &c. Very local.

K.—Road-side near Kingcausie, and in the Corbie Den, G. D.

A.—At Parkhill, G. D. ; Craibstone, Mr. P. Macgillivray ; about Ballater, and banks of Dee at Castleton, G. D. ; in Strathdon, Mr. Barron.

B.—Den at Linhead, Alvah, Rev. Dr. Todd ; in Mortlach, Dr. L. Stewart.

2. SPIRAEA. MEADOW-SWEET.

1. S. *Ulmaria*, Linn.

Perennial. Flowers, June to August. British type. Range in Britain, 50°—61°; coast line to 2400 feet ?

Meadows and moist banks. Generally diffused.

3. DRYAS. DRYAS.

1. D. *octopetala*, Linn. *(White D.)*

Perennial. Flowers in June and July. Highland type. Range in Britain, 54°—60°; 2400 to 2700 feet.

High inland pastures and rocks. Rare.

A.—On Lochnagar, Mr. R. Mackay; Little Craigendall, G. D.; on Ben Avon, Ben-a-Buird, and Ben Macdui, Mr. R. Mackay.

4. GEUM. AVENS.

1. G. *urbanum*, Linn. *(Common A.)*

Perennial. Flowers in June and July. British type, (or English.) Range in Britain, 50°—58°; 50 to 500 feet.

Woods and hedges. Rather general here, but far from common.

K.—Road-side, near Kingcausie, G. D.

A.—Formerly at the Stocket, G. D.; woods of Lairney, Mr. Barron; in Alford, Rev. Dr. Farquharson; more plentiful in Alford than the next species; Den of Craig, Rev. J. Minto; Cobairdy, Frendraught, and Avochie woods, Rev. J. Abel; Aberdour, Rev. G. Gairdner.

B.—Abundant in parish of Alvah, Rev. Dr. Todd; in Mortlach, Dr. L. Stewart; in Rothiemay, Rev. J. Abel.

2. G. *rivale*, Linn. *(Water A.)*

Perennial. Flowers, May to July. British type, (or Scottish.) Range in Britain, 50°—60°; 50 to 2000 feet ?

By sides of rivers and in wet places. General, but not common.

K.—Corbie Den, Maryculter, G. D.

A.—Wood at the old Bridge of Don, and occasionally along the courses of both Dee and Don, G. D.; woods of Midmar, and in Corgarff, Mr. Barron; banks of Dee at Ballater, G. D.; Alford, Rev. J. Minto; frequent on Deveron-side, Rev. J. Abel; Aberdour, Rev. G. Gairdner.

B.—Near Bridge of Alvah, but rare, Rev. Dr. Todd; not common in Mortlach, Dr. L. Stewart.

5. RUBUS. BRAMBLE, RASPBERRY.*

1. R. *Idaeus*, Linn. *(Common R.)*

Perennial. Flowers in June and July. British type. Range in Britain, 50°—60°; coast to 1800 feet.

Woods and waste places. Frequent; and general. In the Ballater district is often met with at the above altitude; as in Corry Rath, opposite Mount Keen; Fall of the Glassilt, head of Loch Muick, &c.

2. R. *suberectus*, And. *(Upright B.)*

Perennial. Flowers in July and August. Scottish type. Range in Britain, 53°—59°; coast line to 1300 feet.

Thickets and waste places. So far as yet known, a local species.

A.—North bank of the Dee, a mile above the old bridge, G. D.; Castleton, Braemar, Prof. Macgillivray; parish of Aberdour, Rev. G. Gairdner.

3. R. *corylifolius*, Smith. *(Hazel-leaved B.)*

---

* The species of this genus have given rise to much difference of opinion among our authorities. It is to be feared that many varieties have been ranked as species. We regret the impossibility, at present, of giving a more satisfactory account of those in this district.

Perennial. Flowers in July and August. English type ?
Range in Britain, 50°—60°; coast line to 1000
feet ?

Hedges and waste places. General. A species under this name, reported from most parts of the district.

4. R. *fruticosus*, Linn. *(Common B.)*

Perennial. Flowers in July and August. English type.
Range in Britain, 50°—57°; coast line to 500
feet ?

Thickets and wastes. General. A species under this name reported from most parts of the district.

5. R. *rhamnifolius*, W. & H. *(Black-leaved B.)*

Perennial. Flowers in May and June. English type ?
Range in Britain, 50°—60°; coast line to 1200
feet ?

Hedges and thickets. Rare.

Var. β, *nitidus*. Braemar, Prof. Macgillivray.

6. R. *saxatilis*, Linn. *(Stone B.)*

Perennial. Flowers in July and August. Scottish type, (or Highland.) Range in Britain, 51°—61°; 200 to 1800 feet.

Shady rocks, &c. General, but not a common plant.

K.—Corbie Den, Kingcausie, G. D.; parish of Strachan, Stat. Account; Den between Durris and Maryculter, Mr. P. Macgillivray.

A.—Den of Maidencraig, G. D.; woods of Midmar, Mr. Barron; Linn of Muick; Craigendarrch at Ballater; Falls of the Glassilt, Mr. Mackay and G. D.; near Castleton on Craig Koynach, Mr. Gardiner; Corrymulzie, G. D.; Burn of Caw at the water-fall, Corgarff, Mr. Barron; woods of Auchindoir, Rev. J. Minto; Tullynessle, Mr. Sutherland; in the Buchan district, Mr. A. Murray.

B.—Rocks at Bridge of Stonley, parish of Alvah. Rev. Dr. Todd; in Mortlach, Dr. L. Stewart. *

6. R. *Chamaemorus*, Linn. *(Mountain B. or cloudberry.)*
Perennial. Flowers in June and July. Highland type. Range in Britain, 53°—59°; 1000 to 3700 feet.

Alpine bogs; often concealed among long heath. Confined to the more inland and higher districts, but there in the greatest profusion.

K.—Parish of Fordoun, Dr. A. Murray.

A.—Hill of Fare, at 1200 feet, 15-16 miles west from Aberdeen, the station nearest the coast line, in this county, G. D. Near the east and west tops of Benachie, Mr. A. Cruickshank; on this hill—20 miles from the coast—I have seen it much lower than at the places indicated by Mr. Cruickshank, and certainly not much exceeding 1000 feet; in Clatt and Tullynessle, Rev. J. Minto; abundant on Morven, Mount Keen, Lochnagar, Glen Callater, Mourne, Ben Avon, Ben-a-Buird, Ben Macdui, &c. &c.; and on Donside, in Corgarff.

B.—Abundant also in the higher inland parts of Banffshire; on the Bin Hill at Cullen, north side only, Mr. Carmichael; the extreme point of which hill does not exceed 1060 feet above the sea.

6. FRAGARIA. STRAWBERRY.

1. F. *vesca*, Linn. *(Wood S.)*
Perennial. Flowers, May to August. British type. Range in Britain, 50°—61°; sea level to 1700 feet.

Woods, dry banks, &c. Frequent.

* R. *caesius*, Linn. Has been reported as found in Kincardineshire, and in Midmar; I have never seen the plant in this district, and consider its existence here as very doubtful.

This plant, though rather general in the district, is not common, and appears to be on the whole equally frequent in the inland as in the lower parts.

K.—Corbie Den, &c. G. D.

A.—Den of Robslaw; banks of Dee; Robslaw quarry; Den of Leggart; Hillton quarry, &c. &c. G. D. Alford, Rev. Dr. Farquharson; Corgarff, Mr. Barron; Falls of the Glassilt, Mr. Mackay and G. D.; Carr Rocks at Castleton, Braemar.

B.—At Hill of Alvah and Bridge of Alvah, rare, Rev. Dr. Todd; Mortlach, Dr. L. Stewart.

7. COMARUM. MARSH CINQUE-FOIL.

1. *C. palustre*, Linn. *(Purple M. F.)*
Perennial. Flowers, May to July. British type.
Range in Britain, 50°—61°; coast line to 1300 feet?
Marshes and peat bogs. Frequent.

8. POTENTILLA. CINQUE-FOIL.

1. *P. anserina*, Linn. *(Silver-weed C.)*
Perennial. Flowers in June and July. British type.
Range in Britain, 60°—61°; coast line to 1300 feet.

Meadows, sandy and stony places. Frequent and general in the district; occurs near Castleton, at the elevation above mentioned.

2. *P. alpestris*, Hal. Fil. *(Orange alpine C.)*
Perennial. Flowers in June and July. Highland type.
Range in Britain, 52°—57°; 1300 to 2600 feet.
Confined to the higher and inland parts.

A.—At Braemar, in the following localities :—near Corrymulzie, Mr. Croall; top of Craig Koynach, Mr.

Gardiner ; Carr Rocks, Mr. Sutherland ; Glen Callater, Mr. A. K. Clark ; Rocks of Dhuloch, Mr. Mackay and G. D. ; Lochnagar, Little Craigendall, and Ben Macdui, Mr. R. Mackay.

3. P. *reptans*, Linn. *(Creeping C.)*

Perennial. Flowers, June to August. English type. Range in Britain, 50°—58° ; 200 to 400 feet ?

Shady places, &c. Very rare in this district.

A.—Den of Robslaw, Dr. J. Henderson ; where I also gathered it in 1837, G. D.

B.—At Loch Park, in Mortlach, Dr. L. Stewart.

4. P. *Tormentilla*, Sibth. *(Tormentil.)*

Perennial. Flowers, June to August. British type. Range in Britain, 50°—61° ; coast to 3300 feet.

Moors and heaths. General in the district.

It is one of the few plants on the summit of Morven, and occurs on Ben-a-Buird at the height above mentioned.

Var. β, *reptans*, is not uncommon.

5. P. *Fragariastrum*, Eprh. *(Strawberry-leaved C.)*

Perennial. Flowers in March and April. British type (or English.) Range in Britain, 50°—58° ; 200 to 1400 feet ?

Woods and banks. Not very frequent.

K.—In Den of Leggart, and Corbie Den ; south bank of Dee at Craiglug, G. D.

A.—Wood at old Bridge of Don, G. D.; at Aboyne, Stat. Account ; dry bank at Church of Forgue, Rev. J. Abel. Not in the Corgarff list.

B.—In Alvah, rare, Rev. Dr. Todd.

9. SIBBALDIA. SIBBALDIA.

1. S. *procumbens*, Linn. *(Procumbent S.)*

Perennial. Flowers in July. Highland type. Range in Britain, 56°—61°; 1600 to 4200 feet.

Confined to the higher mountain ranges in the interior, where it occurs in great profusion.

A.—Upon Morven, from 1800 feet to near the summit it forms a perfect carpet of vegetation, G.D.; Lochnagar, Mr. R. Mackay; on the Callater Rocks, G. D.; Corry of Loch Kander, Professor Macgillivray; on the south brow of Ben Macdui, not 200 feet from the summit, Mr. Mackay and G. D.

B.—On Belrinnes, Dr. L. Stewart.

10. ALCHEMILLA. LADY'S MANTLE.

1. *A. vulgaris*, Linn. *(Common L. M.)*
Perennial. Flowers, June to August. British type (or Scottish.) Range in Britain, 50°—60°; sea level to 2500 feet.

Way-sides, pastures, &c. Frequent.

2. *A. alpina*, Linn. *(Alpine L. M.)*
Perennial. Flowers, June to August. Highland type. Range in Britain, 54°—60°; 50 to 4170 feet.

Inland pastures and mountains. Chiefly in the interior, but descending very low along the course of the Dee, &c. The *lowest natural limit* of this plant is probably about 400 to 600 feet, in lower stations being chiefly along the course of the Dee, owing to transportation of seeds. In natural pastures along the level of the road at Ballater, Abergeldie, and Crathie, this species takes the place of *A. vulgaris* which almost disappears.

A.—North bank of the Dee, beside the hut at the old bridge, (1836,) G. D.; banks of Dee near Manse of Drumoak, Dr. J. Smith. "Ad summitatem montis, Morven; ad ripas Dee, Tullich; et in arena ad ripas inter Durris et Drumoak," Dr. D. Skene, MSS. Common about Ballater, and upwards to Castleton, &c., &c., G. D. ; abundant in Corgarff, Mr. Barron ; Inchmore, near the source of the Don, "Northern Flora."

B.—Den at Linhead, and at Craigs of Alvah, Rev. Dr. Todd ; near Keith, Rev. Mr. Cowie ; Mortlach, Dr. L. Stewart.

3. A. *arvensis*, Smith. *(Field L. M.)*
Annual. Flowers, May to August. British type. Range in Britain, 50°—60° ; coast line to 1700 feet.

Gravelly places, fields, walls. Frequent, but more abundant in the lower than in the higher inland parts. On top of Bennachie.

11. AGRIMONIA. LINN. AGRIMONY.

1. A. *Eupatoria*, Linn. *(Common A.)*
Perennial. Flowers in June and July. British type, (or English.) Range in Britain, 50°—58°; coast line to 700 feet.

Banks and rocks, &c. Very local.

K.—Coast at St. Cyrus and Arbuthnot, Mr. Chrystall. Coast at Muchalls, Dr. J. Henderson ; where I have also gathered it.

A.—North bank of Don between the bridges, and in the wood above the old bridge, Mr. P. Macgillivray ; where it was found nearly 100 years ago, by Dr. D. Skene, who writes "in rupibus, Don, prope pontem." Den of Gight, G. D. ; north bank of Don, above the bridge at Inverury, Mr. Sutherland ; banks of the Gairden, near Ballater, Rev. A. Beverly ; in Cruden, Mr. A. Murray, ; frequent between Haddo and Inverkeithny Church, Rev. J. Abel ; coast at Aberdour, Rev. G. Gairdner.

B.—Coast at Gamrie, Rev. G. Gairdner ; braes of Mountcoffer, and below King-Edward manse, near the burn, Rev. Dr. Todd.

12. ROSA. ROSE, &c.

1. R. *spinosissima*, Linn. *(Burnet-leaved R.)* *
Perennial. Flowers in May and June. British type. Range in Britain, 50°—60°; coast line to 1800 feet.

Heaths and rocks. Very general.

K.—Abundant on rocks and grassy banks along the Kincardineshire coast, G. D.; Banchory-Ternan, Rev. J. Brichan.

A.—Aberdeen Links; banks of Dee and Don; in the interior about Ballater; summit of Khoil, &c. G. D.

B.—Banks of Deveron; rocks at Bridge of Alvah, Rev. Dr. Todd; in Mortlach, but rare, Dr. L. Stewart.

3. R. *Sabini*, Woods. *(Sabine's R.)*
Perennial. Flowers in June. British type. Range in Britain, 51°—58°; 300 to 1400 feet.

Very local and rare?

A.—Buchan district, Mr. A. Murray; about Castleton in Glen Clunie, &c.

Var. β, *Doniana*. Linn of Quoich, Professor Macgillivray.

4. *Rosa villosa*, Linn. *(Villous R.)*
Perennial. Flowers in June and July. British type.
Range in Britain, 50°—61°; 50 to 1200 feet.

Waste places, &c., &c. Generally diffused.

About Aberdeen, Ballater, &c., G. D.; Corgarff, Mr. Barron; in Alvah, Rev. Dr. Todd. Not in Mortlach list.

5. R. *tomentosa*, Smith. *(Downy-leaved R.)*

---

* R. *rubella*, Smith. Reported as found on the banks of Dee at Abergeldie, is considered by many a mere variety of R. *spinosissima*.

Perennial. Flowers in June and July. British type. Range in Britain? Coast line to 1200 feet? Woods and waste places.

Its range in this district is uncertain; it is by many, considered a mere variety of the last. Occurs in Alvah; not in Mortlach list.

6. R. *inodora*, Fries. *(Slightly scented R.)*
Perennial. Flowers in June and July. British type. ? Range in Britain, 50°—57°; 150 to 1200 feet? Hedges, &c. Local? in this district.

"Banchory to Castleton," Macgillivray, Natural History of Deeside.

7. R. *canina*, Linn. *(Dog R.)*
Perennial. Flowers in June and July. British type. Range in Britain, 50°—61°; 50 to 1450 feet.

K.—Not uncommon along the Kincardineshire coast, G. D.

A.—Banks of Dee and Don; Robslaw quarry; Stocket, &c., &c. "A nearly spineless variety, with long trailing branches, occurs in the wood above the old Bridge of Don," Mr. P. Macgillivray; also in the interior, as at Ballater; in Glen Muick, &c. G. D.; Corgarff, Mr. Barron; less common than R. *villosa* in Clatt and Auchindoir, Rev. J. Minto.

B.—Alvah, Rev. Dr. Todd; Mortlach, Dr. L. Stewart.

8. R. *caesia*, Smith. *(Glaucous Dog R.)*
Perennial. Flowers in June and July.

This species is probably a mere variety of R. *canina*; I cannot distinguish it, and place it here on the authority of Professor Macgillivray, "Ballater to Castleton," Nat. Hist. of Deeside.

13. Pyrus. Pear, &c.

1. P. *aucuparia*, Gaertner. *(Rowan-tree.)*
Perennial. Flowers in May and June. British type. Range in Britain, 50°—61°; sea level to 2100 feet.
Woods and rocks. Frequent.

This species is of general occurrence, and undoubtedly wild in many parts of the district; it is a frequent denizen of precipitous cliffs in the interior; Mr. Watson observed examples of it 2 feet in girth, on Lochnagar at an elevation of 1800 feet.

Order XX.—ONAGRACEAE.

1. Epilobium. Willow-herb.

1. E. *angustifolium*, Linn. *(Rose-bay W.)*
Perennial. Flowers in July. British type. Range in Britain, 50°—61°; coast line to 2000 feet.
Woods and moist rocks. Not common.

K.—Den Fenella, Dr. Stephen; parish of Arbuthnot, Mr. Chrystall; occasionally along the coast from Stonehaven to Aberdeen; Corbie Den, Maryculter, G. D.

A.—Near the top of Benachie; Pannanich cliffs; Bridge of Gairden; Linn of Muick; Linn of Dee; Falls of the Glassilt, head of Loch Muick, G. D.; Den of Knockespock; west side of the Hill of Lonach, and north side of the Hill of Knockley, in Strathdon, Rev. J. Minto; Burn of the "Caw," in Corgarff, Mr. Barron; coast at Aberdour, Rev. G. Gairdner.

B.—Rocks at Bridge of Alvah, Rev. Dr. Todd; Delnabo, Tomintoul, "Flora of Moray."

2. E. *hirsutum*, Linn. *(Great hairy W.)*
Perennial. Flowers in July and August. English type (or British.) Range in Britain, 50°—58°; coast line only.

Sides of ditches, &c. Very rare in this district.

K.—At Nether-Warburton, St. Cyrus, Dr. Stephen; " In rupes maritimas, *Thornyhive*, ultra *Dunnottar*," Dr. D. Skene.

A.—Near Ellon, Dr. Murray; by the side of a stream below Manse of Slains, Mr. Cow.

3. E. *parviflorum*, Schreb. *(Small-flow. hairy W.)*
Perennial. Flowers in July and August. British type (or English.) Range in Britain, 50°—59°; coast line to 500 feet.

Marshes and sides of lakes and streams. Not common.

K.—Jackstone, St. Cyrus, and Den of Morphie, Dr. Stephen; coast at Muchalls, Finnan, &c., Rev. J. Farquharson; Loch of Leys, Dr. Adams.

A.—Loch of Skene, and banks of the Ury near Inverury, Mr. Burnett; Alford, Rev. Dr. Farquharson; banks of the Ythan, at Ellon, Mr. Thom; banks of the Ugie, near Peterhead, Dr. Shier; links of St. Fergus, Mr. A. Murray.

B.—Mortlach, Dr. L. Stewart. Not in the Alvah list.

4. E. *montanum*, Linn. *(Mountain W.)*
Perennial. Flowers in June and July. British type. Range in Britain, 50°—61°; coast line to 1800 feet.

Banks and waste places. Frequent.

General in the three counties; attaining the elevation above mentioned near the Falls of the Glassilt, head of Loch Muick, G. D.

5. E. *tetragonum*, Linn. *(Square-stalked W.)*
Perennial. Flowers in July and August. British type.
   Range in Britain, 50°—60°; coast line to 1800 feet?

Wet places. Frequent and widely diffused in the district.

6. E. *palustre*, Linn. *(Marsh W.)*
Perennial. Flowers in July and August. British type.
   Range in Britain, 50°—61°; coast to 1800 feet.

Sides of lakes and ditches, &c. Not common, but found in most parts of the district.

7. E. *alsinifolium*, Vill. *(Chickweed-leaved W.)*
Perennial. Flowers in July. Highland type. Range in Britain, 50°—59°; 1800 to 3000 feet.

Sides of alpine streams. Frequent.

A.—About streams on the Mourne at Castleton, G. D.; on the Carr Rocks, Castleton, Mr. Croall; on Lochnagar, Loch Kander, and Ben Macdui, Mr. R. Mackay; on the ascent to Ben Avon, from Little Craigendall, Mr. Gardiner; at the source of the Don, Dr. A. Murray.

B.—Delnabo, Tomintoul, "Flora of Moray."

8. E. *alpinum*, Linn. *(Alpine W.)*
Perennial. Flowers in July. Highland type. Range in Britain, 53°—59°; 1300 to 3800 feet.

At spring-heads and by streams. Confined to the higher parts of the interior, but there in the greatest profusion. More common than the last.

K.—Parish of Fordoun, Dr. A. Murray.

A.—In 1836, I found a few straggling plants among the wet gravel and stones upon the north bank of the Dee, above the old bridge, not 50 feet above the sea level; the seeds or plants had doubtless been transported by floods. On the hills at Ballater, Mr. R. Mackay; abundant about the base of Morven, Lochnagar, Little Craigendall, the Mourne at Castleton, Glen Callater, Ben Macdui, G. D.; in parish of Alford, Rev. Dr. Farquharson; in Corgarff, not unfrequent, G. D.; in Clatt, Rev. J. Minto.

B.—On Belrinnes, Dr. L. Stewart.

2. CIRCAEA. ENCHANTER'S NIGHTSHADE.

1. C. *Lutetiana*, Linn. *(Common E.)*
Perennial. Flowers in July and August. British type (or English.) Range in Britain, 50°—59°; 80 to 200 feet.
Woods. Very rare in this district.

K.—Banchory-Ternan, "Northern Flora."

A.—Banks of the Dee, and banks of the Don at the old bridge, "Northern Flora;" Den of Gight, Stat. Account; Buchan district, Mr. A. Murray.

2. C. *alpina*, Linn. *(Alpine E.)*
Perennial. Flowers in July and August. Scottish type (or Highland.) Range in Britain, 51°—60°; 200 to 1200 feet.
Widely diffused, but not common.

K.—Drumtochty, Dr. D. Lyall; Banchory-Ternan, Rev. J. Brichan. Var. *intermedia*, near Drumtochty, Fordoun, Rev. A. Beverly.

A.—Den of Robslaw, G. D. At Castleton, Braemar; Paradise, Monymusk, Mr. Barron. Glenkindy in Strathdon, Mr. Proctor.

B.—Den at Linhead, and also at Deveron-side, half a-mile below Bridge of Alvah, Rev. Dr. Todd; at Cullen, Mr. Carmichael; in Mortlach, several stations, Dr. L. Stewart.

ORDER XXI.—HALORAGACEAE.

1. HIPPURIS.   MARE'S-TAIL.

1. H. *vulgaris*, Linn.   *(Common M.)*
Perennial.   Flowers in June and July.   British type.
   Range in Britain, 50°—61° ; 50 to 1200 feet.
Ditches and bogs.   Rather rare.

K.—Pitready, Strachan ; Jackstone, St. Cyrus, Dr. Stephen ; pool by the avenue to Maryculter House, Mr. Sutherland ; marsh above Bay of Nigg, Mr. P. Macgillivray.

A.—Formerly in Ferryhill moss ; Braediach moss in Skene ; bogs at Corsehill near Scotston, G. D. Upper Drumnahoy, in Cluny, Mr. Barron ; Alford, Rev. Dr. Farquharson; Turnerhall moss, Dr. D. Skene; Corgarff, Mr. Barron ; Clatt, Rev. J. Minto ; Old Deer, Stat. Account ; Cruden, Mr. A. Murray ; Aberdour, Rev. G. Gairdner.

B.—Gamrie parish, Stat. Account ; moss at Muiryhill, Alvah, Rev. Dr. Todd ; several stations in Mortlach, Dr. L. Stewart.

2. MYRIOPHYLLUM.   WATER-MILFOIL.

1. M. *spicatum*, Linn.   *(Spiked W. M.)*
Perennial.   Flowers in June and July.   British type.
   Range in Britain, 50°—60° ; coast line to 1600 feet.
Stagnant waters.   Abundant.

A plant under the above name is reported from all parts of the district, and at the height above mentioned in Loch Callater. It is probable that M. *alterniflorum* may be the species in some of the localities, the two being often confounded ; I possess, however, no note of having seen it, G. D.

Order XXII.—LYTHRACEAE.

1. PEPLIS. WATER-PURSLANE.

1. *P. Portula*, Linn. *(Common P.)*

Annual. Flowers in July and August. British type. Range in Britain, 50°—60°; 100 to 500 feet.
Marshy places. Rather rare.

K.—Lochs of Park and Leys, Rev. J. Brichan.

A.—In a little marsh at the north end of the road bounding Summerhill (near Aberdeen) on the west, also at Stocket moor, G. D.; ditch at the 12th milestone, Deeside turnpike, Dr. J. Smith; frequent in wet bogs in Cluny, Mr. Barron; Leochel, Mr. Sutherland; Alford, Rev. Dr. Farquharson; Old Deer, Stat. Account; Cruden, Mr. A. Murray.

B.—In Alvah, not common, Rev. Dr. Todd.

Order XXIII.—PORTULACEAE.

1. MONTIA. BLINKS.

1. *M. fontana*, L. *(Water B.)*

Annual. Flowers, April to September. British type. Range in Britain, 50°—60°; coast to 3300 feet.
Ditches and wet places. Common.

It is abundant in all parts, and is one of those species which grow at springs and about rills on our mountains, associated with *Epilobium alpinum*, *Saxifraga stellaris* &c., &c.

ORDER XXIV.—PARONYCHIACEAE.

1. SPERGULARIA. SANDWORT-SPURREY.

1. S. *rubra*, St. Hil. *(Field S.)*
Annual. Flowers, June to September. British type.
Range in Britain, 50°—58°; coast line to 1250 feet.
Gravelly and sandy places. Not uncommon. Reported from most parts of the district; occurs at Castleton, Braemar.

2. S. *marina*, Camb. *(Sea-side S.)*
Biennial? Flowers, June to August. British type.
Range in Britain, 50°—61°; coast line only.
On sand, clay, and in fissures of rocks along our coast line.

2. SPERGULA. SPURREY.

1. S. *arvensis*, Linn. *(Corn S.)*
Annual. Flowers, June to August. British type.
Range in Britain, 50°—61°; coast line to 1386 feet.
Light soil, in fields, &c. Common.

ORDER XXV.—CRASSULACEAE.

1. SEDUM. STONECROP.

1. S. *Rhodiola*, De Cand. *(Rose-root S.)*
Perennial. Flowers in June and July. Highland type.
Range in Britain, 52°—61°; coast line to 3500 feet.

Sea cliffs and alpine rocks. Local on the coast; and on the higher ranges in the interior.

A.—On the rocks at "Bullers of Buchan," near Slains Castle, Dr. A. Murray. Cliffs on Lochnagar, and Callater Rocks, &c., &c., G. D.

2. S. *villosum*, Linn. *(Hairy S.)*

Biennial. Flowers in July and August. Scottish type. Range in Britain, 54°—58°; 50 to 1250 feet?

Marshy places. Generally diffused in the district; but not common.

K.—Bogs about Drumtochty; ditches, Hill of Garvock, and Hill of Woodstone, Mr. Croall. Marshes, near new Church of Nigg, G. D.

A.—Road-side at Stocket moor, close by the bridge; bog at Scotston and Denmore; marshes in Belhelvic Links, G. D. Reported as growing in Cluny, Alford, Corgarff, Fyvie, Clatt, Delgaty, and Laithers at Turriff.

B.—Bogbraes and Blackburn moors of Dunlugas, Alvah, Rev. Dr. Todd; in Mortlach, Dr. L. Stewart.

3. S. *acre*, Linn. *(Biting S. or Wall-pepper.)*

Perennial. Flowers in June and July. British type. Range in Britain, 50°—60°; coast line to 500 feet.

Sandy places, wall-tops, &c. Common in the lower districts; rarer in the interior.

K.—Not uncommon on the coast.

A.—Coast and wall-tops. Balfluig, in Alford; ruins of Castle of Lismore, in Rhynie, but rare, Rev. J. Minto. Walls of Huntly Castle, Rev. J. Abel.

B.—" Rare in Alvah, almost extinct," Rev. Dr. Todd; Mortlach, rare, Dr. L. Stewart; scarce in links of Buckie and Portessie, Mr. Carmichael.

4. S. *Anglicum*, Hudson. *(English S.)*

Annual. Flowers, June to August. Atlantic type (or British.) Range in Britain, 50°—61°; at 300 to 400 feet ?

Rocks, &c. A very rare plant on the east coast; of which I have never seen a trace in this district. It is peculiarly a western species, and I insert it here on the authority of Mr. P. Macgillivray's "Aberdeen Flora;" though I cannot help thinking there is some mistake.

A.—"On a sand bank near the mill, and one or two other elevations, mostly near the Don, in parish of Kemnay, Mr. Burnett."

ORDER XXVI.—SAXIFRAGACEAE.

1. SAXIFRAGA. SAXIFRAGE.

1. *S. stellaris*, Linn. *(Starry S.)*
Perennial. Flowers in July and August. Highland type. Range in Britain, 52°—59°; 1000 to 4320 feet.

Alpine rivulets, marshes, and wet rocks. Abundant in the interior.

A.—Springs near top of Mount Battock; abundant on Morven, Mount Keen, Lochnagar, banks of Loch Muick, Mourne at Castleton, Glen Callater, Ben-a-Buird, Ben Macdui &c. G. D. Waterfall on Burn of Cachantesin, in Strathdon, Mr. Barron.

B.—On Belrinnes, Dr. L. Stewart.

2. *S. nivalis*, Linn. *(Alpine-clustered S.)*
Perennial. Flowers in July and August. Highland type. Range in Britain, 53°—58°; 2400 to 3800 feet.

Alpine cliffs. Rare. Confined to rocks at high elevations.

A.—Upon the rocks at head of Glen Callater, Mr. Mackay and G. D.

3. S. *oppositifolia*, Linn. *(Purple Mountain S.)* Perennial. Flowers in April and May. Highland type. Range in Britain, 52°—61°; coast line to 3000 feet?

Upon moist sea cliffs and alpine rocks. Rare on the coast, but abundant on the higher hills.

A.—Coast at Aberdour, where it was first observed by Rev. G. Gairdner many years ago; the same station is more particularly described by Mr. A. Cruickshank, "on rocks on Aberdour coast, near Dundargue Castle ruins." In the interior it occurs on Lochnagar; margin of Loch Callater, and on the Callater Rocks; Little Craigendall, Ben Macdui, &c., &c., G. D.

4. S. *aizoides*, Linn. *(Yellow Mountain S.)* Perennial. Flowers, June to August. Highland type. Range in Britain, 54°—60°; 50 to 3000 feet.

About springs, rills, and rivers. Abundant in the interior.

K.—By Strachan and Potarch roads, Dr. Stephen.

A.—North bank of the Dee, one mile above the old bridge, Mr. J. Cadenhead; I saw it there in 1836. Not unfrequent along the course of the Dee; Hill of Fare at 500 feet, Mr. Barron; with solitary flowers near the house of Findrac, Mr. R. Fraser; frequent at rills by road-sides, Ballater and Castleton; Glen Callater, &c., &c., G. D.; Den of Chapelton, parish of Leslie, Mr. M'Donald; Buck of the Cabrach, Mr. Sutherland.

B.—By the Deveron, at Bridge of Alvah, Dr. Shier; in Mortlach, near the Spey, Dr. L. Stewart; at Tomintoul, "Flora of Moray."

F

5. S. *granulata*, Linn. *(White Meadow S.)*
Perennial. Flowers in May and June. British type, (or Intermediate). Range in Britain, 50°—58°; coast line to 875 feet.

Grassy banks, &c. Very local; not in more inland districts.

K.—In parishes of Bervie, Benholme, and Arbuthnot, Stat. Account; abundant at the Cove and elsewhere southwards, G. D.

A.—At Millden and Tarbathie, in Belhelvie, G. D.; top of Hill of Dunideer, parish of Insch, Rev. J. Minto; coast near Colliston in Slains, Mr. Cow; in Buchan, Mr. A. Murray.

B.—Near Portessie, on the coast, Mr. Carmichael.

6. S. *rivularis*, Linn. *(Alpine, Brook S.)*
Perennial. Flowers in July and August. Highland type. Range in Britain, 56°—58°; 3000 to 3600 feet.

Moist alpine cliffs. Confined to the higher parts, and rare.

A.—On the eastern precipice of Lochnagar, and on the west side where *Carex leporina* grows, G. D.; on Ben-a-Buird, Professor Balfour; on Cairntoul, Mr. R. Mackay.

7. S. *tridactylites*, Linn. *(Rue-leaved S.)*
Annual. Flowers, April to June. British type, (or English). Range in Britain, 50°—58°; coast only.

Dry sandy places. Very rare.

A.—Sparingly in links of Belhelvie, Mr. Cow; north bank of Ugie, near Peterhead, Mr. A. Murray; links at Strathbeg, Mr. Cow.

8. S. *hypnoides*, L. *(Mossy S.)*

Perennial. Flowers, May to July. Scottish type, (or Highland). Range in Britain, 51°—60°; coast line to 3000 feet?

In rocky places. Very local; on coast and inland.

A.—On the Khoil near Ballater; rocks in Glen Callater, G. D.; Den of Auchmedden, and coast at Aberdour, Rev. G. Gairdner.

B.—At Gamrie, Rev. G. Gairdner.

9. S. *caespitosa*, Linn. *(Tufted alpine S.)*
Perennial. Flowers in May and June. Highland type. Range in Britain, 56°—58°.

Alpine rocks, &c. Very rare.

A.—On Ben Avon, Dr. M. Barry; on Ben-a-Buird, 1830, Mr. M'Nab; "In August, 1830, Mr. M'Nab of the Edinburgh Botanic Garden, found at the base of the precipice, (east side of Ben-a-Buird,) a tuft of S. *caespitosa*, portions of which he gave to me, as I was near him when he happened to find it." Professor Macgillivray's Nat. History of Deeside, p. 127.

2. CHRYSOSPLENIUM. GOLDEN-SAXIFRAGE.

1. C. *alternifolium*, Linn. *(Alternate-leaved G.)*
Perennial. Flowers in April and May. British type, (or Intermediate). Range in Britain, 50°—58°; coast line to 600 feet?

Moist shady places. Very local.

K.—Wood by the turnpike opposite Kingcausie, G. D.

A.—South bank of the Don above the old bridge; banks of the Ythan at Ellon, G. D.; woods at Paradise, Monymusk, Mr. Barron; banks of Don at Breda, Alford, Mr. Sutherland; Den of Knockespock in Clatt, Rev. J. Minto; in Buchan district, Mr. A. Murray; parish of Glass, Stat. Account.

B.—Rare in Alvah, Rev. Dr. Todd; Mill of Eden,

parish of King Edward, Stat. Account; at Gamrie, Rev. G. Gairdner.

2. C. *oppositifolium*, Linn. *(Common G.)*
Perennial. Flowers, April to July. British type, (or Highland). Range in Britain, 50°—60°; coast line to ?
Sides of streams and shady places. Common.

ORDER XXVII.—UMBELLIFERAE.

1. HYDROCOTYLE. WHITE-ROT.

1. H. *vulgaris*, Linn. *(Common W.; or Marsh-pennywort.)*
Perennial. Flowers in July and August. British type. Range in Britain, 50°—61°; coast line to 500 feet ?
Bogs and marshes. Common in the lower districts; rarer in the interior.

2. SANICULA. SANICLE.

1. S. *Europaea*, Linn. *(Wood S.)*
Perennial. Flowers in June and July. British type. Range in Britain, 50°—59; 50 to 1200 feet.
Moist woods. General in the district, but not common.

K.—Wood at Corbie Den, Kingcausie, G. D.; Banchory-Ternan, Rev. J. Brichan.

A.—Near village of Aboyne, Stat. Account; at Coull, Mr. P. Macgillivray; wood at Castle of Midmar, Mr. Barron; birch wood between Corrymulzie and the Mourne, Mr. Croall; at Keig, Stat. Account; Mungo wood, near Huntly Castle, Rev. J. Abel; in Buchan, Mr. A. Murray; Den of Auchmedden, Rev. G. Gairdner.

B.—In a small wood at Tipperty, Alvah, rare, Rev. Dr. Todd; at Gamrie, Stat. Account; in Mortlach, Dr. L. Stewart.

3. ERYNGIUM. ERYNGO.

1. E. *maritimum*, Linn. *(Sea E. or Sea holly.)*
Perennial. Flowers in July and August. British type. Range in Britain, 50°—61°; coast only.
Sandy sea-shores. Very rare.
K.—Coast at St. Cyrus, Stat. Account.
A.—Links at Crimond, Mr. Cow.

4. CICUTA. WATER-HEMLOCK.

1. C. *virosa*, Linn. *(W. H.)*
Perennial. Flowers in June and July. British type. Range in Britain, 51°—58°? 400 feet.
Watery places. Very rare.
"Grounds of Castle Fraser and Fetternear," Mr. Burnett; Mr. P. Macgillivray's Flora. I have never seen it in the district, G. D.

5. HELOSCIADIUM. MARSH-WORT.

1. H. *inundatum*, Koch. *(Least M. W.)*
Perennial. Flowers in June and July. British type. Range in Britain, 50°—60°; 50 to 300 feet.
Lakes and pools. Is on the whole a scarce plant; perhaps often overlooked.
K.—Marsh above Bay of Nigg, G. D.; Banchory-Ternan, Rev. J. Brichan.
A.—Marshes at Stocket near Summerhill, G. D. at Loch of Skene, Mr. Barron.

6. BUNIUM. EARTH-NUT.

1. B. *flexuosum*, With. *(Common E. N.)*

Perennial. Flowers in May and June. British type. Range in Britain, 50°—60°; coast line to 1600 feet.

Woods and pastures. Frequent; and generally diffused through the district. Attains the above altitude in Braemar.

7. PIMPINELLA. BURNET-SAXIFRAGE.

1. P. *Saxifraga*, Linn. *(Common B. S.)*
Perennial. Flowers in July and August. British type. Range in Britain, 50°—59°; coast line to 1700 feet.

Dry pastures. Rather local.

K.—Coast north from Stonehaven, Dr. A. Fleming; Banchory-Ternan, Rev. J. Brichan; on a bank at the north end of Bay of Nigg, G. D.

A.—Banks of the Dee above and below the old bridge, and in the Old-town Links at the north end, G. D.; Upper Drumnahoy, Cluny, Mr. Barron; banks of Dee at Ballater, Mr. R. Mackay; top of Craig Koynach at Castleton, Mr. Watson; in Alford, Rev. Dr. Farquharson; in Clatt, Rev. J. Minto; in Cruden, Mr. A. Murray.

B.—Rare in Alvah, Rev. Dr. Todd.

8. ŒNANTHE. WATER-DROPWORT.

1. Œ. *crocata*, Linn. *(Hemlock W. D.)*
Perennial. Flowers in July. British type, (or English). Range in Britain, 50°—58°; coast line to 600 feet.

Watery places. Very rare.

K.—Marshy ditch close by Dunnottar, Dr. A. Fleming; farm of Ley, near Crathes Castle, Dr. Adams.

A.—Banks of the Ythan near Ellon, G. D.; Den of Kildrummy, in Strathdon, Rev. J. Minto.

9. LIGUSTICUM. LOVAGE.

1. L. *Scoticum*, Linn. *(Scottish L.)*
Perennial. Flowers in July. Scottish type. Range in Britain, 55°—61°; coast line.
Rocky sea coast. General along the rocky parts of the coasts of Kincardine, Aberdeen, and Banff.

10. MEUM. SPIGNEL, &C.

1. M. *Athamanticum*, Jacq. *(Bald-Money, &c.*)*
Perennial. Flowers in June and July. Scottish type, (or Intermediate.) Range in Britain, 52°—58°; 20 to 1500 feet.
Dry pastures. Chiefly in the interior.
K.—Banchory-Ternan, Dr. Adams.
A.—North bank of the Dee above the old bridge, G. D.; at the north end of Morrison's Suspension Bridge, Mr. P. Macgillivray; banks of the Dee at Drumoak, Dr. J. Smith; at Aboyne, Stat. Account; at Ballater; very abundant about Castleton, G. D.; in Strathdon, Mr. Barron. Not recorded as in Alvah nor Mortlach.

11. ANGELICA. ANGELICA.

1. A. *sylvestris*, Linn. *(Wild A.)*
Perennial. Flowers in July and August. British type. Range in Britain, 50°—61°; coast line to 2500 feet.
Moist woods and wet rocks. Frequent. Attains the above altitude in Glen Callater.

12. HERACLEUM. COW-PARSNIP.

1. H. *Sphondylium*, Linn. *(Common C. P.)*

* Called in this district *Highland Micken*.

Perennial. Flowers in July. British type. Range in Britain, 50°—61°; coast to 1300 feet? Rocks, waste places, &c., &c. Common.

13. CONIUM. HEMLOCK.

1. *C. maculatum*, Linn. *(Common H.)*
Biennial. Flowers in June and July. British type. Range in Britain, 50°—60°; coast to 400 feet?
Waste places. Frequent. Chiefly along the coast line; rare in the interior, but grows in Oldmeldrum; also in Mortlach.

14. SCANDIX. (SHEPHERD'S NEEDLE.)

1. *S. Pecten*, Linn. *(Common S; or Venus' comb.)*
Annual. Flowers, June to August. British type, (or English). Range in Britain, 50°—58°; coast line to 460 feet.
Fields, &c. Rare in this district.

K.—At Bervie, Stat. Account; frequently in St. Cyrus, Dr. Stephen; coast about Stonehaven, where it grew 100 years ago, " Inter segetes, ultra Stonehive," Skene MSS.

A.— Fields in Belhelvie, Mr. A. K. Clark and G. D.; Upper Drumnahoy, Mr. Barron; at St. Fergus, in Buchan, Mr. A. Murray.

B.—Near the School-house, parish of Alvah, Rev. Dr. Todd; in Mortlach, Dr. L. Stewart.

15. ANTHRISCUS. BEAKED-PARSLEY.

1. *A. sylvestris*, Koch. *(Wild B. P.)*
Perennial. Flowers, April to June. British type. Range in Britain, 50°—61°; sea level to 1260 feet.
Banks, waste places, &c. Found in most parts of the district.

2. A. *vulgaris*, Pers. *(Common B. P.)*
Annual. Flowers in May and June. British type.
Range in Britain, 50°—61°; 100 to 460 feet.
Waste places; road-sides. Rather rare, and not known to me in the more inland parts.

K.—Banchory-Ternan, rare, Dr. Adams.

A.—Road-side near Gilcomston Dam, G. D.; on the old Deeside road, between Ferryhill and the bridge, Mr. P. Macgillivray; at Drumnahoy in Cluny, Mr. Barron; in the Buchan district, Mr. Murray.

16. CHAEROPHYLLUM. CHERVIL.

1. C. *temulentum*, L. *(Rough C.)*
Biennial. Flowers in June and July. British type, (or English). Range in Britain, 50°—58°; 100 to 460 feet.
By hedges and roads. Rare.

K.—Banchory-Ternan, Rev. J. Brichan.

A.—Near Aberdeen by the side of a hedge a few hundred yards north-west from the toll-bar at Kittybrewster, G. D.; Upper Drumnahoy, Cluny, Mr. Barron; in parish of Aberdour, Rev. G. Gairdner.

B.—Rare in Alvah, "doubtfully indigenous," Rev. Dr. Todd.

17. DAUCUS. CARROT.

1. D. *Carota*, Linn. *(Wild C.)*
Biennial. Flowers in July and August. British type. Range in Britain, 50°—61°; coast to 500 feet.
Pastures and road-sides. Not common.

K.— Fields, St. Cyrus, Dr. Stephen; parish of Arbuthnot, Mr. Chrystall; Banchory-Ternan, Dr. Adams.

A.—Occasionally on the Inch at Aberdeen; Deeside road at Middleton and Cults ; by the Dee above the old bridge, G. D. Mains of Drum, Dr. J. Smith ; in Tullynessle and Towie, Rev. J. Minto ; common in Cromar, Mr. Sutherland; parish of Aberdour, Rev. G. Gairdner.

18. TORILIS. HEDGE-PARSLEY.

1. T. *Anthriscus*, Gaertner. *(Upright H. P.)*
Annual. Flowers in July and August. British type, (or English). Range in Britain, 50°—58° ; coast line to 500 feet.

Hedges and banks. Rather local.

K.—Dens of Fenella and Morphie, Dr. Stephen ; at Arbuthnot, Mr. Chrystall ; about Stonehaven, and along the coast northwards, at Portlethen, Cove, &c., close by the sea, G. D.

A.—North bank of the Dee, below Manse of Drumoak, G. D. ; near new Church of Peterculter, Professor Macgillivray ; north bank of Don, above the bridge at Inverury, Mr. Sutherland ; near Peterhead, Rev. J. Minto ; at St. Fergus, in Buchan district, Mr. A. Murray.

B.—In Alvah, Rev. Dr. Todd ; in Mortlach, Dr. L. Stewart.

ORDER XXVIII.—ARALIACEAE.

1. ADOXA. MOSCHATELL.

1. A. *moschatellina*, Linn. *(Tuberous M.)*
Perennial. Flowers in April and May. British type. Range in Britain, 50°—58° ; 40 to 1200 feet ?*

Shady banks and woods. Rather local.

* In Perthshire, it has been found at a much higher elevation. I have no record of it at any great height in this district, G. D.

K.—Dens of Morphie and Fenella, Dr. Stephen; parish of Arbuthnot, Mr. Chrystall; bank by the south Deeside road, nearly opposite Morrison's Suspension Bridge, Dr. A. Fleming; in a wood by the road-side at Kingcausie, and in the Corbie Den, G. D.

A.—In Den of Robslaw, G. D.; by the side of a stream, among alders, &c. at the north end of Morrison's Bridge over the Dee, Mr. P. Macgillivray; Fetternear grounds, and Paradise at Monymusk, Mr. Burnett; in a small corry at Tyrebagger hill, Mr. A. Cruickshank; in Strathdon, Stat. Account; at Asloon, Alford, Mr. Sutherland; near the old bridge at Avochie, Deveron-side, Rev. J. Abel.

B.—Den at Linhead; near Bridge of Alvah, east side, and occasionally by the river-side, from the bridge to the Cruive dyke, Rev. Dr. Todd. At the base of the Binhill, Cullen, Mr. Carmichael; in Mortlach, Dr. L. Stewart.

2. HEDERA. IVY.

1. *H. Helix*, Linn. *(Common I.)*
Perennial. Flowers in October and November. British type. Range in Britain, $50°-61°$; coast line to 500 feet?

Walls, rocks, &c. &c. General in all lower, and several of the inland parts of the district; but not a common plant. It is recorded in the interior at Rhynie and Mortlach.

ORDER XXIX.—CORNACEAE.

1. CORNUS. CORNEL.

1. *C. Suecica*, Linn. *(Dwarf C.)*
Perennial. Flowers in July and August. Highland type. Range in Britain, $54°-59°$; 1000 to 2700 feet.

Moist banks and hollows in the higher districts.

A.—Mount Keen, between the footpath on the shoulder and the summit, G. D. ; on Morven, where it was also found by Dr. D. Skene 100 years ago ; on Lochnagar, and Little Craigendall, G. D. It also occurs on other parts of the Braemar range, Ben Avon, Ben-a-Buird, Cairntoul, Braeriach, &c. &c. In Strathdon it has been found in Glen Carvy, Rev. J. Minto ; Glen Bucket, Dr. A. Murray ; Tornahaish, Mr. Barron.

B.—In Moitlach, on Belrinnes, Dr. L. Stewart.

ORDER XXX.—CAPRIFOLIACEAE.

1. SAMBUCUS. ELDER.

1. S. *Ebulus*, Linn. *(Dwarf E. or Dane-wort.)* Perennial. Flowers in July and August. English type. Range in Britain, 50°—58° ; 50 to 800 feet.

Waste places. Very local and rare, and chiefly inland.

K.—By the Burn of Benholme, above the Turnpike road bridge, Dr. Stephen ; parish of Arbuthnot, rare, Mr. Chrystall.

A.—At Charleston of Aboyne, Stat. Account ; at Doun of Invernochty, Strathdon, Mr. Mackay and G. D. ; near Manse of Rhynie and ruins of old Castle of Leslie, Rev. J. Minto.

B.—At Scatterty in Alvah, Rev. Dr. Todd ; Mortlach, Dr. L. Stewart.

2. VIBURNUM. GUELDER-ROSE.

1. V. *Opulus*, Linn. *(Common G.)*

Perennial. Flowers in June and July. British type (or English). Range in Britain, 50°—58°; 140 to 400 feet?

Woods, &c. Very rare in this district.

K.—Banks of the Dee at Banchory-Ternan, Dr. Adams.

A.—At Drum, Dr. J. Smith; Rushpot, Culter, Dr. Duncan.

B.—Den at Linhead, Alvah, Rev. Dr. Todd.

3. LONICERA. HONEYSUCKLE.

1. L. *Periclymenum*, Linn. *(Common H. or Woodbine.)*

Perennial. Flowers, June to September. British type. Range in Britain, 50°—61°; coast line to 1500 feet.

Rocks and woods. Frequent, but not a common plant. Frequent in the lower districts; found also in the interior, at a considerable elevation on the Hill of Fare, on the cliffs at Pannanich near Ballater, and on Craig Koynach at Castleton, &c.

4. LINNAEA. LINNAEA.

1. L. *borealis*, Gronov. *(Two-flowered L.)*

Perennial. Flowers in July. Scottish type. Range in Britain, 55°—58°; 100 to 2400 feet.

Woods and heaths. Very general in this district.

K.—Woods of Inglesmaldie, parish of Fettercairn, where it was first discovered as a native of Scotland, in 1795, by Professor J. Beattie, Jun. of Aberdeen. Dr. Simpson of Marykirk says it is now extinct there, owing to change of conditions of growth, consequent on the thinning of the woods. On the south border of Marykirk parish, in one of the Balmakewan fir plantations, 500 or 600 yards due south from the Free Church at the cross roads, Dr. Simpson. Woods in parish of Fordoun, Stat. Account; at Arbuthnot, Mr. Carmichael; woods at Banchory House, A. Thomson, Esq.; at Kingcausie, Mrs. Boswell; at Durris, Mr. P. Macgillivray; Tilchilly, near Banchory-Ternan, Dr. Adams.

A.—In a narrow plantation on the east side of the avenue to Scotston House; in a wood by the road near Countesswells, two miles west from Craigiebuckler, near Aberdeen, G. D. Woods at Park and Drum, Mr. P. Macgillivray. In a fir wood, west from the House of Craibston, where it was found about the end of the last century by the late Rev. Dr. Smith, Chapel of Garioch. Fir wood by the Great North Railway, and a little west of the House of Pitmedden, 8 miles from Aberdeen, Professor Macgillivray. On the north face of the Hill of Fare, above Midmar Castle; and in woods of Kebbaty, Mr. Barron. Among long heather, on the face of the hill, south of Pannanich Wells, about the level of the top of Pannanich cliffs, Mr. A. Cruickshank. A short way up the east side of Morven, and in woods in Cromar, Mr. Sutherland; on the banks of Loch Muick, Dr. A. Murray; on the Carr Rocks at Castleton, Mr. Croall; among birches, half up the hill of Ben Beck at Castleton, Mr. Gardiner; in parish of Alford, Rev. Dr. Farquharson; in Tullynessle, near the top of the hill opposite to Terpersie, Rev. J. Minto. Two large patches on the Hill of Moneybattock, in Tullynessle; and one beside the avenue to the House of Haughton, in Alford, Dr. A. Fleming. Craigston woods near Turriff, Mr. A. Murray; Craigston woods, parish of King Edward, Rev. Dr. Todd.

B.—Two stations in Hill of Alvah; several in Hill of Mountcoffer, and woods of Forglen, Rev. Dr. Todd. In woods at Gordon Castle, Fochabers, where it was discovered by the late Mr. Hoy; near an avenue on the Hill of Whiterash, at Fochabers, Mr. Carmichael. In a wood behind Pittyvaich, (in Mortlach); and near Beechmount, Dr. L. Stewart.

Order XXXI.—RUBIACEAE.

1. GALIUM. BED-STRAW.

1. G. *verum*, Linn. *(Yellow B. S.)*
Perennial. Flowers, June to August. British type. Range in Britain, 50°—61°; sea level to 1800 feet.
Sea-shores and dry places. Frequent, and generally diffused in the district.

2. G. *cruciatum*, Linn. *(Cross-wort B. S.)*
Perennial. Flowers, April to July. British type, (or English). Range in Britain, 50°—59°; coast line to 350 feet.
Banks and hedges. Very rare in this district.
A.—In Buchan, "Northern Flora;" in a hedge at the Manse of Keith, Rev. Mr. Cowie.

3. G. *saxatile*, Linn. *(Smooth Heath B.)*
Perennial. Flowers, June to August. British type. Range in Britain, 50°—61°; sea level to 3300 feet.
Waste places, heaths, rocks, wall-tops. Common. *

4. G. *uliginosum*, Linn. *(Rough Marsh B.)*
Perennial. Flowers in July and August. British type, (or English). Range in Britain, 50°—61°; coast line to 400 feet.
Moist meadows and sides of ditches. Rather local.
K.—Marsh above south end of Bay of Nigg, G. D.; Banchory-Ternan, Dr. Adams.
A.—At Stocket and Scotston moors, &c., G. D.;

---

* G. *pusillum*, Linn. probably occurs in this district, since it has been found in Forfarshire. I, however, possess no record of its presence. It is perhaps often overlooked or confounded with G. *saxatile*, G. D.

in parish of Alford, Rev. Dr. Farquharson ; in Clatt, Rev. J. Minto ; about Huntly, Drumblade, and Forgue, Rev. J. Abel ; Aberdour, Rev. G. Gairdner.

B.—Alvah, Rev. Dr. Todd ; Mortlach, Dr. L. Stewart.

5. G. *palustre*, Linn. *(White Water B.)*

Perennial. Flowers in July and August. British type. Range in Britain, 50°—61° ; coast line to 1500 feet.

About marshes, lakes, &c. Generally diffused.

K.—Arbuthnot parish, Mr. Chrystall ; Banchory-Ternan, Rev. J. Brichan ; marshes at Nigg, G. D.

A.—Banks of Dee above the old bridge, Stocket moor, &c., &c., G. D. ; Loch Muick, G. D. ; common in Cluny, Mr. Barron ; Alford, Rev. J. Farquharson ; Clatt, Rev. J. Minto ; Corgarff, Mr. Barron ; Forgue, &c., Rev. J. Abel ; Cruden, Mr. A. Murray ; Aberdour, Rev. G. Gairdner.

B.—Alvah, abundant, Rev. Dr. Todd ; Mortlach, Dr. L Stewart.

Var. β, *Witheringii* is also rather general in the district.

6. G. *Mollugo*, Linn. *(Great Hedge B.)*

Perennial. Flowers, June to August. English ? type, (or British). Range in Britain, 50°—58° ; coast line to 1200 feet.

Hedges, pastures, &c. Rare.

K.—Road-side at Rickarton, near Stonehaven, Dr. A. Fleming ; Banchory-Ternan, Rev. J. Brichan.

A.—Near the manse at Castleton, Braemar, Mr. Sutherland ; at the Printfield, near Aberdeen, Dr. A. Fleming.

B.—Near Dunlugas, the only locality in Alvah, Rev. Dr. Todd.

Galium.]

7. **G. boreale, Linn.** *(Cross-leaved B.)*
Perennial. Flowers in June and July. Highland type. Range in Britain, 53°—61°; coast line to 2500 feet.

Moist banks and rocks. Rather generally diffused, but not common.

K.—Dens of Morphy and Fenella, Stat. Account; Banchory-Ternan, Rev. J. Brichan, where it grew 100 years ago, "In ripis siccis et arenosis fluviorum, Dee, &c., Banchory-Ternan," Skene MSS.

A.—Banks of the Dee at the old bridge and upwards; not uncommon along the whole course of that river; Ballater, Castleton, Glen Callater, &c., G. D.; Glen Gairden, Rev. J. Abel; Corgarff, Mr. Barron; Auchindoir, Mr. Sutherland; Buchan district, Mr. A. Murray.

B.—Deveron-side at Bridge of Alvah, rare, Rev. Dr. Todd; rare in Mortlach, Dr. L. Stewart; Avon-side, Rev. J. Abel.

8. **G. Aparine, Linn.** *(Goose-grass or Cleavers.)*
Annual. Flowers in June and July. British type. Range in Britain, 50°—60°; coast line to 500 feet.

Waste places, hedges, &c. Common in the lower parts of the district; becoming less so in the interior.

2. SHERARDIA. FIELD-MADDER.

1. **S. arvensis, Linn.** *(Blue F. M.)*
Annual. Flowers, May to August. British type, (or English). Range in Britain, 50°—58°; coast line to 1200 feet.

Gravelly places and dry pastures. Frequent. Attains the above elevation in the Don district, at Corgarff.

3. ASPERULA. WOODRUFF.

1. **A. odorata**, Linn. *(Sweet W.)*
Perennial. Flowers in May and June. British type.
Range in Britain, 50°—61°; 100 to 1300 feet.
Woods and shady places. Rather local.

K.—Dens of Morphy and Fenella, Stat. Account; rocks and ravines in different parts of Kincardine, Mr. Chrystall; Corbie Den, Kingcausie, G. D.; den between Maryculter and Durris, Mr. P. Macgillivray.

A.—Vale of Alford, on the banks of the Burn of Linturk; Loch Muick, Dr. A. Murray. Corrymulzie, Braemar, G. D.; abundant among juniper, between Inchrory and Loch Builg, Mr. Proctor; Carr Rocks at Castleton, Mr. Sutherland; Ardo, near Oldmeldrum, Dr. A. Murray; near Haddo House, Earl of Aberdeen (N. Flora); Stretinnon wood, parish of Glass, Rev. Mr. Cowie; Den of Auchmedden, Rev. G. Gairdner.

B.—Millowood, Rev. Mr. Cowie; near Turriff, Dr. Shier; rocky banks below Bridge of Alvah, Rev. Dr. Todd; Mortlach, Dr. L. Stewart.

ORDER XXXII.—VALERIANACEAE.

1. VALERIANA. VALERIAN.

1. **V. officinalis**, Linn. *(Great wild V.)*
Perennial. Flowers in July and August. British type.
Range in Britain, 50°—60°; coast line to 1200 feet.

Woods and moist banks. Frequent; and generally diffused.

Var. β, sambucifolia, I have seen about Ballater and elsewhere; it is often overlooked.

2. FEDIA. CORN-SALAD.

1. F. *olitoria*, Vahl. *(Common C. S., or Lamb's Lettuce.)*

Annual. Flowers, April to June. British type. Range in Britain, 50°—60°; coast line to 400 feet.

Sandy places and dry banks. Very local.

K.—South parts of Kincardineshire, Mr. G. Don. Den Fenella; cliffs at North Warburton, St. Cyrus; Brotherton, in Benholm, Dr. Stephen. "An undoubted native of several spots on the coast, between Stonehaven and Muchalls," Dr. Murray (in Northern Flora).

A.—North bank of the Dee, one mile above the old bridge, G. D.; sandhills in Old-town Links, opposite the brick-work, Dr. Fleming; fields at the Printfield, Mr. A. Smith; Balfluig in Alford, Rev. Dr. Farquharson; Crimond, Mr. A. Murray.

B.—In Alvah, "doubtfully indigenous," Rev. Dr. Todd; near Castle Oliphant, at Keith, Rev. Mr. Cowie.

ORDER XXXIII.—DIPSACEAE.

1. SCABIOSA. SCABIOUS.

1. S. *succisa*, Linn. *(Devil's-bit S.)*

Perennial. Flowers, July to September. British type. Range in Britain, 50°—61°; coast line to 2400 feet.

Meadows, pastures, and heaths. Common.

2. KNAUTIA. KNAUTIA.

1. K. *arvensis*, Coult. *(Field K.)*

Perennial. Flowers, June to August. British type. Range in Britain, 50°—60°; 100 to 450 feet.

Pastures and fields. Very local ; decreasing northwards and inland.

K.—Near North Esk bridge, and St. Cyrus, Dr. Stephen. About Marykirk, G. D. Not uncommon in Kincardineshire, Mr. Chrystall.

A.—At Craiglug, near Aberdeen, Mr. A. Smith ; fields near Scotston, G. D. ; in Alford, but rare, Rev. J. Minto ; Buchan district, " N. Flora ;" road-side, near Balcairn, Meldrum, Rev. J. Abel.

ORDER XXXIV.—COMPOSITAE.

1. TRAGOPOGON. GOAT'S-BEARD.

1. T. *pratensis*, Linn. *(Yellow G. B.)*
Biennial. Flowers in June and July. British type (or English). Range in Britain, 50°—59° ; coast line to 400 feet.
Meadows and pastures. Very rare.

K.—Coast at St. Cyrus, Dr. Stephen.

A.—Sandhills in the links at Aberdeen, north-east from the Broadhill ; formerly on the south bank of the Canal, at east end of the bridge at Nelson Street, G. D. Quarry in wood of Lochshangie, Kemnay, Mr. Burnett ; parish of Insch, rare, Mr. M'Donald.

2. APARGIA. HAWKBIT.

1. A. *autumnalis*, Willd. *(Autumnal H.)*
Perennial. Flowers in August. British type. Range in Britain, 50°—60° ; coast line to 2900 feet (Macdui).

Meadows and pastures. In one or other of its forms, this species is not unfrequent in different parts of the district.

3. HYPOCHAERIS. CAT'S-EAR.

1. H. glabra, Linn. *(Smooth C.)*
Annual. Flowers, July to September. Germanic type, (or British). Range in Britain, 50°—58°; local at 200 feet?
Fields and gravelly places. Very rare.
K.—In a corn-field, half-a-mile south from Bridge of Feugh, Dr. Stephen.

2. H. radicata, Linn. *(Long-rooted C.)*
Perennial. Flowers in July and August. British type. Range in Britain, 50°—60°; coast line to 1300 feet?
Pastures and waste places. Frequent, and general.

4. MULGEDIUM. BLUE SOW-THISTLE.

1. M. alpinum, Less. *(Alpine B.)*
Perennial. Flowers in July and August. Highland type. Range in Britain, 56°—57°; 2100 to 2700 feet (Watson).
Moist alpine rocks. Very rare.
Cliffs, east side of Lochnagar, by the side of a ravine leading to the top; first found here by Mr. Don many years ago; gathered there by Mr. R. Mackay, 15 years ago. In August last (1859), Professor Balfour informed me that it is still there.

5. SONCHUS. SOW-THISTLE.

1. S. arvensis, Linn. *(Corn S.)*
Perennial. Flowers in August and September. British type. Range in Britain, 50°—61°; coast line to 900 feet.
Fields, &c. Frequent, chiefly in the lower parts of the district.

2. S. *oleraceus*, Linn. *(Common S.)*
Annual. Flowers, June to August. British type.
Range in Britain, 50°—61°; coast to 1000 feet.
Waste places. Common.

(S. *asper*, Hoffm. is not mentioned as distinct in any notes in my possession; it is probably often confounded with the last. It is doubtful if it be really a good species.)

6. CREPIS. HAWK'S BEARD.

1. C. *virens*, Linn. *(Smooth H.)*
Annual. Flowers, June to August. British type.
Range in Britain, 50°—60°; sea level to 500 feet.
Dry pastures, walls, &c. A rare plant in this district.

K.—Brigton, St. Cyrus, Dr. Stephen; village of Banchory, Dr. Adams.

A.—Near Aberdeen, in a hollow half-a-mile northwest from Morison's Suspension Bridge, Rev. J. Farquharson; road-side between Scotston moor and the Ellon turnpike, Mr. P. Macgillivray; Drumnahoy in Cluny, Mr. Barron; on Donside, at Mill of Kemnay, Mr. Burnett; at Alford, Rev. Dr. Farquharson; in Cruden, Mr. A. Murray.

B.—In Mortlach, Dr. L. Stewart.

2. C. *succisæfolia*, Tausch. *(Succory-leaved H.)*
Perennial. Flowers in July and August. Intermediate, (or Highland). Range in Britain, 54°—57°; local at 150 feet?
In woods. Very rare.

K.—Banks of Dee at Banchory-Ternan, Professor Macgillivray.

3. C. *paludosa*, Moench. *(Marsh H.)*
Perennial. Flowers in July and August. Scottish

type (or Highland). Range in Britain, 51°—58°: 100 to 1700 feet.

Moist woods and rocks. Rather local.

K.—At Arbuthnot, Mr. Chrystall; Corbie Den, Kingcausie, G. D.

A.—Wood at the old bridge of Don; Robslaw Den, G. D; wood at Midmar Castle, north side of the Hill of Fare, Mr. Barron; on Craig Koynach at Castleton, Mr. Gardiner; Corrymulzie, G. D.; at the Cachintesin fall, Corgarff, Mr. Barron; Den of Auchmedden, Rev. G. Gairdner; Corryhaugh, south side of Deveron, Rev. J. Abel.

B.—In parish of Alvah, Rev. Dr. Todd.

7. LEONTODON. DANDELION.

1. L. *Taraxacum*, Linn. *(Common D.)*
Perennial. Flowers, March to October. British type. Range in Britain, 50°—61°; coast to 4000 feet.
(Var. β, palustre.)
Pastures, waste places, &c. Very common.

Var. β, *palustre* is abundant in the higher parts of the district; it occurs also in Alvah, "in a damp grassy avenue in the woods behind Rackmill Cottage, near the gate of the deer park," Rev. Dr. Todd.

8. HIERACIUM. HAWK-WEED.*

1. H. *Pilosella*, Linn *(Common Mouse-ear H.)*
Perennial. Flowers, May to August. British type. Range in Britain, 50°—60°; sea level to 2100 feet.

---

* The differences of opinion respecting the species of this genus, render an accurate record, in a local Flora, very difficult. It is much to be feared that there has been an unwarrantable multiplication of species. The distribution in Britain is imperfectly known.

Dry banks and pastures. Frequent.*

2. H. *Iricum*, Fries. *(Irish H.)*
Perennial. Flowers in July and August. Highland type. Range in Britain, 54°—55°; 1200 to ?
Upland rocks. Rare.

A.—Castleton, Braemar, Mr. Backhouse; rocks at Linn of Dee, and ruins of Mar Castle, Mr. Croall.

3. H. *cerinthoides*, Linn. *(Honey-wort H.)*
Perennial. Flowers in July and August. Highland type. Range in Britain, 54°—59°; 200 to 2300 feet.

Shady banks and rocks. Rather local.

K.—Den of Canterland, Mr. Croall.

A.—North bank of the Dee a mile above Ballater, G. D.; Craig Koynach at Castleton, Mr. Croall; Callater Rocks, Mr. R. Mackay.

4. H. *alpinum*, Linn. *(Alpine H.)*
Perennial. Flowers in July and August. Highland type. Range in Britain, 53°—59°; 1880 to 3000 feet.

Rocks, &c. in the interior, where it is abundant.

A.—Rocks in Glen Callater, G. D.; rocks of the Dhuloch, Mr. Mackay and G. D.; Lochnagar and Ben-a-Buird, Mr. R. Mackay.

5. H. *melanocephalum*, Backhouse. *(Bl.-headed H.)*
Perennial. Flowers in July and August. Highland type. Range in Britain, 53°— 59°; 1600 to 3300 feet.

Alpine pastures and rocks. Confined to the higher district.

* H. *villosum*, Linn, reported as found in Glen Callater and Lochnagar, is supposed to be an error, see Hooker and Arnott's *British Flora*, p. 218, 7th Edition.

A.—In Glen Derry, G. D. Abundant in the glens at the base of Ben Macdui, Mr. Croall; rocks in Glen Callater, G. D.; Little Craigendall, and slopes near the summit of Lochnagar, Mr. Croall.

6. **H. nigrescens, Willd.** *(Black-haired H.)*
Perennial. Flowers in July and August. Highland type. Range in Britain, 56°—58°. Range?
Alpine pastures and rocks. Confined to the higher districts.

A.—Cairntoul, Mr. Backhouse.
B.—About the base of Cairngorm, Mr. R. Mackay.

7. **H. Chrysanthum, Backh.** *(Golden-flowered H.)*
Perennial. Flowers in July and August. Highland type. Range in Britain, 55°—57°; 2000 to 3500 feet?

A.—Lochnagar and Glen Callater, Mr. Croall; Cairntoul, Mr. Backhouse.

8. **H. argenteum, Fries.** *(Silvery H.)*
Perennial. Flowers in July and August. Highland type. Range in Britain, 53°—58°? 2400 to 3200 feet?

A.—Little Craigendall, Mr. Croall; Craig Dhuloch, Mr. Backhouse.

9. **H. murorum, Linn.** *(Wall H.)*
Perennial. Flowers, June to August. British type. Range in Britain, 50°—61°; coast line to 2400 feet?
Walls, rocks, &c. &c. Frequent in different parts of the district.

10. **H. sylvaticum, Smith.** *(Wood H.)*
Perennial. Flowers in July and August. British type. Range in Britain, 50°—59°; coast line to 1800 feet?

Woods, banks, &c. Frequent, but not common.

K.—Coast at Muchalls, G. D.; Banchory-Ternan, Rev. J. Brichan.

A. Wood at the old Bridge of Don, and in the Old-town Links, G. D.; Craig Koynach at Castleton, Mr. Gardiner; about Ballater, G. D.

B.—In Alvah, Rev. Dr. Todd.

11. H. *Prenanthoides*, Vill. *(Rough-bordered H.)*
Perennial. Flowers in July and August. Highland type. Range in Britain, 54°—58°; 100 to 1200 feet?
Sides of streams, &c. Rather local.

K.—Woods of the Burn, parish of Fettercairn, Mr. Croall.

A.—North bank of the Dee at Slievanachie, near Ballater; and Corrymulzie, Braemar, G. D.

12. H. *strictum*, Fries. *(Straight-branched H.)*
Perennial. Flowers in July and August. Scottish type? Range in Britain? Range in altitude?
Mountain glens. Rare?

K.—In Kincardineshire, "Hooker's British Flora."

13. H. *Inuloides*, Tausch. *(Inula-like H.)*
Perennial. Flowers in August. Scottish? type. Range in Britain, 54°—58°; 700 to 1200 feet?
Shady places. Rare.

A.—At Ballater and Castleton, Mr. R. Mackay.

14. H. *Crocatum*, Fries. *(Saffron-coloured H.)*
Perennial. Flowers in July and August. Scottish? type. Range in Britain, 54°—58°? Altitude?
Shady rocks. Rare.

K.—Den of Canterland, Mr. Croall.

15. H. *boreale*, Fries. *(Shrubby broad-leaved H.)*

Perennial. Flowers in July and August. British type. Range in Britain, 50°—58°; coast line to 1200 feet.

Moist rocks and banks. Not common, yet widely diffused in the district.

K.—Arbuthnot, Mr. Chrystall; Banchory-Ternan, Rev. J. Brichan.

A.—Banks of the Dee above the old bridge; and also near the Manse of Drumoak; and occasionally along the whole course of the Dee from Castleton to Aberdeen, G. D. In parish of Alford, Rev. Dr. Farquharson.

B.—At Deveron-side, in Alvah, Rev. Dr. Todd.

The following species of Mr. Backhouse, reported as found in the upper part of this district, are unknown to me; and some of them are considered by authorities as undecided species, and have not as yet been inserted in all works on the British Flora. In reference to those mentioned on the authority of Mr. Croall, he informs me that they were authenticated by Mr. Baker of York :—

H. eximium. Rocks Little Craigendall, and at Wells of Dee, Mr. Croall.

H. holosericeum. Lochnagar and Glen Callater, Mr. Croall.

H. insigne. Loch Kander (head of Glen Callater), Mr. Backhouse.

H. affine. Loch Avon, Mr. Backhouse.

H. alpestre. Ben-a-Buird, Mr. Backhouse.

H. globosum. Cairntoul, Mr. Backhouse; Little Craigendall, Mr. Croall.

H. saxifragum (Fries). Cairntoul, Mr. Backhouse.

9. LAPSANA. NIPPLE-WORT.

1. *L. communis,* Linn. *(Common N.)*

Annual. Flowers, July to September. British type. Range in Britain, 50°—60°; coast line to 1200 feet.

Waste ground, &c. Common, but less so in the interior.

2. L. *pusilla*, Willd. *(Common N.)*

Annual. Flowers in July and August. Germanic type. Range in Britain, 50°—58°; 60 to 460 feet.

Gravelly fields. Very rare.

K.—On the south bank of the Dee by the side of the road to the Drumoak ferry, Mr. R. Mackay.

A.—Fields on the farm of Upper Drumnahoy in Cluny, and Craigiedarg, in this locality, I have seen it abundant; it was discovered by Mr. Barron.

10. ARCTIUM. BURDOCK.

1. A. *Lappa*, Linn. *(Common B.)*

Biennial. Flowers in July and August. British type. Range in Britain, 50°—61°; coast line to 800 feet.

Waste places, &c. Frequent, but not common, along the coast line. Rare inland.

K.—South parts of Kincardine, Mr. M'Farlane; St. Cyrus, Dr. Stephen; in Arbuthnot, Mr. Chrystall; at the Cove, &c., G. D.; Banchory-Ternan, Rev. J. Brichan.

A.—About Footdee and Old Aberdeen, &c., G. D.; at Peterculter and Drumoak, Mr. P. Macgillivray; at Aboyne, Stat. Account; road-side at Bridge of Muick, near Ballater, G. D.; near Huntly Castle, Rev. J. Abel; Peterhead, Rev. J. Minto; Aberdour, Rev. G. Gairdner.

B.—In parish of Alvah, Rev. Dr. Todd; at Mortlach, Dr. L. Stewart.

11. SAUSSUREA. SAUSSUREA.

1. *S. alpina*, De Cand. *(Alpine S.)*
Perennial. Flowers in July and August. Highland type. Range in Britain, 53°—61°; 2400 to 3800 feet.
Moist alpine rocks. Very local. On the higher ranges only.
A.—Near the summit of Lochnagar, on Little Craigendall, Corry of Loch Kander, and Callater rocks, G. D.; on Ben Macdui, Mr. R. Mackay.

12. CARDUUS. THISTLE.

1. *C. acanthoides*, Linn. *(Welted Thistle.)*
Annual. Flowers in July and August. British type, (or English). Range in Britain, 50°—60°; coast line to 1150 feet.
Waste places. Rather local, and rare inland.
K.—South parts of Kincardine, Mr. M'Farlane; at Arbuthnot, Mr. Chrystall.
A.—On the Inch at Aberdeen; near the Powder Magazine; at Robslaw quarry; by the side of the road, near avenue to Scotston House, G. D. Kildrummy Castle, Dr. A. Fleming; at Aboyne, Stat. Account; at Castleton, Braemar, Mr. Watson; at Clatt, but very rare, Rev. J. Minto.

2. *C. tenuiflorus*, Curtis. *(Slender-flowered T.)*
Biennial. Flowers in June and July. English type, (or British). Range in Britain, 50°—57°; coast only.
Dry sandy wastes. Very rare. North limit in County of Kincardine.
K.—Coast at Bervie, Mr. Chrystall.

13. CNICUS. PLUME THISTLE.

1. *C. lanceolatus*, Willd. *(Spear P.)*
Biennial. Flowers in July and August. British type. Range in Britain, 50°—61°; coast line to 1200 feet.

Pastures and waste places. Frequent in most parts of the district.

2. *C. palustris*, Willd. *(Marsh P.)*
Biennial. Flowers in July and August. British type. Range in Britain, 50°—61°; coast line to 1850 feet.

Moist places. Frequent; generally diffused.

3. *C. arvensis*, Hoffm. *(Creeping P.)*
Perennial. Flowers in July. British type. Range in Britain, 50°—61°; coast line to 1200 feet.

Waste places, &c. &c. Common.

4. *C. heterophyllus*, Willd. *(Melancholy P.)*
Perennial. Flowers in July and August. Scottish type (or Highland). Range in Britain, 51°—59°; 100 to 1200 feet.

Woods, moist rocks, and pastures. Chiefly inland.

K.—Parish of Arbuthnot, Mr. Chrystall; Corbie Den, Kingcausie, and bank of the Dee near the same, G. D.; Banchory-Ternan, Rev. J. Brichan.

A.—North bank of the Dee, above the old bridge, and near the Manse of Drumoak, G. D.; at Aboyne, Stat. Account; abundant on the banks of Dee and Muick at Ballater, also at Abergeldie, Balmoral, and Castleton, G. D. Banks of the Bogie, below the village of Rhynie, and in Den of Craig, Rev. J. Minto.

B.—In Mortlach, Dr. L. Stewart.

14. CARLINA. CARLINE THISTLE.

1. *C. vulgaris*, Linn. *(Common C.)*

Biennial. Flowers in July and August. English type (or British). Range in Britain, 50°—58°; coast line only.

Dry pastures and banks. Very rare.

K.—Cliffs of St. Cyrus, Dr. Stephen; occasionally on the coast between Stonehaven and Portlethen, G. D.

15. CENTAUREA. BLUE-BOTTLE; KNAP-WEED.

1. C. *nigra*, Linn. *(Black-discoid K.)*
Perennial. Flowers in July and August. British type. Range in Britain, 50°—61°; coast line to 1200 feet.

Meadows, grassy banks, &c. Frequent.

2. C. *Cyanus*, Linn. *(Corn B. B.)*
Annual. Flowers in June and July. British type. Range in Britain, 50°—61°; coast line to 1386 feet.

Fields and waste places. Frequent, but not a common plant.

K. South parts of Kincardine, Mr. M'Farlane; Arbuthnot, Mr. Chrystall; Banchory-Ternan, Rev. J. Brichan.

A.—Frequent about Aberdeen; also at Skene, Cluny, Meldrum, Forgue, Alford, Clatt, Corgarff, Ballater, Castleton.

B.—Alvah; Mortlach.

16. BIDENS. BUR-MARIGOLD.

1. B. *cernua*, Linn. *(Nodding B. M.)*
Annual. Flowers, July to September. English type, (or British). Range in Britain, 50°—58°; coast line to 300 feet?

In marshy places. Very rare.

K.—Bogs in parish of Arbuthnot, nearly extirpated,

Mr. Chrystall. Formerly in Loch of Leys, Banchory-Ternan, Dr. Adams.

B.—Bog at North Sandlaw in Alvah, Rev. Dr. Todd.

17. ARTEMISIA. MUGWORT.

1. A. *vulgaris*, Linn. *(Common M.)*
Perennial. Flowers in July and August. British type. Range in Britain, 50°—61°; coast line to 1380 feet.

Waste places and fields. Frequent in most parts of the district.

2. A. *maritima*, Linn. *(Sea M.)*
Perennial. Flowers in August. English type. Range in Britain, 50°—57°; coast only.

Sea-shores. Very rare.

K.—Coast at St. Cyrus, Rev. Dr. Keith; Garron Point, a few miles north from Stonehaven, Mr. Sutherland.

18. EUPATORIUM. HEMP-AGRIMONY.

1. E. *cannabinum*, Linn. *(Common H. A.)*
Perennial. Flowers in July and August. British type, (or English). Range in Britain, 50°—59°; coast line only.

Moist banks and rocks. Rare.

K.—Coast at St. Cyrus and Bervie, Stat. Account; "in rupes maritimas, *Thornyhive*, ultra *Dunnottar Castle*," Dr. D. Skene; rocks on the coast, a little south of Portlethen, G. D.

19. ANTENNARIA. EVERLASTING.

1. A. *dioica*, Gaertner. *(Mountain E.)*
Perennial. Flowers in June and July. Scottish type, (or British). Range in Britain, 50°—61°; coast line to 2000 feet.

Natural Pastures and heaths. Frequent; widely diffused in this district.

K.—South parts of Kincardine; Arbuthnot; at Girdleness Lighthouse; hills at Nigg; Banchory-Ternan.

A.—Stocket moor; Scotston moor; Brimman hill; Hill of Fare; Corgarff; Ballater; Abergeldie, &c. &c. Coast line at Cruden and Aberdour.

B.—Alvah; Mortlach.

Var. β, *hyperborea*, Glen Callater, &c.

20. GNAPHALIUM. CUDWEED.

1. G. *sylvaticum*, Linn. *(Highland C.)*
Perennial. Flowers in July and August. British type. Range in Britain, 50°—60°; coast line to 1300 feet.

Pastures, &c. Frequent in the district.

K.—South parts of Kincardine; Arbuthnot; Banchory-Ternan.

A.—Near Aberdeen at Stocket; Scotston; Drumoak, &c., &c. In Clatt and Corgarff; about Ballater, Abergeldie, Balmoral, Crathie, Castleton.

B.—Alvah; Mortlach.

Var. β, *Norvegicum*, Lochnagar, Mr. R. Mackay; base of North Gully cliffs, Braemar, Mr. Sutherland; on Morven, G. D.

2. G. *uliginosum*, Linn. *(Marsh C.)*
Annual. Flowers in July and August. British type. Range in Britain, 50°—61°; coast line to 500 feet.

Sides of ditches. Frequent, but not common.

K.—Arbuthnot, Mr. Chrystall; Banchory-Ternan, Rev. J. Brichan; road-side ditches about Nigg, &c., G. D.

A.—Ditches by Belhelvie turnpike; road-side at

H

Stocket, &c., G. D. Alford, Rev. Dr. Farquharson; Clatt, Rev. J. Minto; Cruden, Mr. A. Murray; Aberdour, Rev. G. Gairdner. (Not in list of Corgarff plants).

B.—Not common in Alvah, Rev. Dr. Todd; Mortlach, Dr. L. Stewart.

3. G. *supinum*, Linn. *(Dwarf C.)*
Perennial. Flowers in July and August. Highland type. Range in Britain, 56°—60°; 1382 to 4250 feet.

In gravelly and moist places at high altitudes in the interior, where it is abundant.

K.—South-east shoulder of Mount Battock, at an elevation of 1582 feet, and thence upwards, August, 1859; this is a locality nearer to the coast—a distance of 15 miles—than any known to me in the district, G. D.

A.—In the Corry Rath by the Tanner river, at the north base of Mount Keen, at an elevation of 1350 feet, the lowest station known to me in the district, August, 1859, G. D. Frequent by the sides of the road through Glen Gairden to Corgarff on Donside; a common plant on all the higher mountains in the upper parts of Aberdeenshire. On Morven, Mount Keen, Lochnagar, Little Craigendall, Ben-a-Buird, Ben Avon, Ben Macdui, &c., G. D.

B.—Belrinnes, Dr. L. Stewart; Cairngorm, Mr. R. Mackay.

21. FILAGO. FILAGO.

1. F. *minima*, Pers. *(Least F.)*
Annual. Flowers, June to August. British type. Range in Britain, 50°—58°; coast line to 900 feet.
Tops of walls and dry sandy places. Not common.
K.—Cliffs of St. Cyrus, Dr. Stephen; Arbuthnot, Mr. Chrystall; Durris, Dr. Stephen; Banchory-Ternan, Rev. J. Brichan.

A.—Near Aberdeen on wall-tops at Stocket; Robslaw quarry; Scotston, &c., G. D. Drumnahoy in Cluny, Mr. Barron; Burn of the Vat near Ballater, G. D.; road-side at Balmoral, Mr. Croall, (this station cannot be under 900 feet); Clatt, Rev. J. Minto; Forgue, Rev. J. Abel; Sands of Forvie, Mr. Cow.

B.—Mortlach, Dr. L. Stewart.

2. F. *Germanica*, Linn. *(Common F.)*

Annual. Flowers in July and August. British type. Range in Britain, 50°—58°; coast line to 500 feet.

Tops of walls and gravelly wastes. Rather uncommon.

K.—Near an old churchyard, St. Cyrus, Dr. Stephen.

A.—Near Aberdeen; tops of walls by the road, south side of Raeden; at the Stocket, and about Manse of Belhelvie, G. D. Alford, Rev. Dr. Farquharson; fields in Cromar, Mr. Sutherland.

B.—Rare in parish of Alvah, Rev. Dr. Todd.

22. PETASITES. BUTTER-BUR.

1. P. *vulgaris*, Desf. *(Common B.)*

Perennial. Flowers in March and April. British type, (or English). Range in Britain, 50°—58°; coast line to 1250 feet.

Moist shady places. Frequent, but less so in the interior.

It occurs near Ballater at the elevation above mentioned; it is also in the Mortlach list.

23. TUSSILAGO. COLT'S-FOOT.

1. T. *Farfara*, Linn. *(Colt's-foot.)*

Perennial. Flowers in March and April. British type. Range in Britain, 50°—61°; coast line to 1500 feet.

Moist pastures and banks. Very general in the district.

24. ERIGERON. FLEA-BANE.

1. E. *alpinus*, Linn. *(Alpine F.)*
Perennial. Flowers in July and August. Highland type. Range in Britain, 56°—57°; 2500 to 2700 feet ?
Alpine rocks. Very rare and local.

A.—Cairntoul, and Corry of Loch Kander, Professor Macgillivray; on Glas Mheal, at head of Glen Callater, Mr. R. Mackay; on the Ben-a-Buird range, Mr. Watson.

25. ASTER. STARWORT.

1. A. *Tripolium*, Linn. *(Sea S.)*
Perennial. Flowers in August and September. British type. Range in Britain, 50°—58°; coast only.
Marshes by the sea. Very rare.

K. — Coast at St. Cyrus and Benholme, Stat. Account.

A.—Formerly on the Inch at Aberdeen, G. D.

26. SOLIDAGO. GOLDEN-ROD.

1. S. *Virgaurea*, L. *(Common G.)*
Perennial. Flowers in July and August. British type. Range in Britain, 50°—61°; coast line to 1300 feet.
Natural pastures, rocks, &c. Rather uncommon, especially in the lower districts.

K.—South parts of Kincardine, Mr. M'Farlane; on the more northern parts of the same coast, as at the Cove, &c., G. D.

A.—Banks of the Dee above the old bridge, and along the whole course of the river inland; frequent about Pannanich, Ballater, Glen Muick, &c. &c., G. D. ; in Clatt, Tullynessle, Auchindoir, Rev. J. Minto.

B.—Rocks at Bridge of Alvah, Rev. Dr. Todd ; in Mortlach, Dr. L. Stewart.

Var. β, about Ballater and in Glen Callater, Mr. R. Mackay.

27. SENECIO. GROUNDSEL, RAGWORT.

1. S. *vulgaris*, Linn. *(Common G.)*
Annual. Flowers, February to December. British type.
Range in Britain, 50°—61° ; coast line to 1200 feet.
Waste ground, &c. Common.

2. S. *sylvaticus*, Linn. *(Wood G.)*
Annual. Flowers, June to September. British type.
Range in Britain, 50°—59° ; coast line to 1180 feet.
Gravelly banks and wastes, &c. Frequent, but not very common.

K.—South parts of Kincardine, Mr. M'Farlane ; Arbuthnot, Mr. Chrystall ; Banchory-Ternan, Rev. J. Brichan.

A.—At Robslaw quarry, Stocket, Old-town Links, &c., G. D. ; Gallowhill, Cluny, Mr. Barron ; Alford, Rev. Dr. Farquharson ; about Castleton, Braemar, Mr. Croall ; in Clatt, Rev. J. Minto.

B.—Common in Alvah, Rev. Dr. Todd.

3. S. *Jacobaea*, Linn. *(Common R.)*
Perennial. Flowers in July and August. British type.
Range in Britain, 50°—61° ; sea level to 2000 feet.
Pastures and wastes. Common.

4. S. *aquaticus*, Hudson. *(Marsh R.)*

Perennial. Flowers in July and August. British type. Range in Britain, 50°—61°; coast line to 1180 feet.

Wet pastures, &c. &c. Frequent in most parts of the district.

28. BELLIS. DAISY.

1. B. *perennis*, Linn. *(Common Daisy.)*
Perennial. Flowers, February to November. British type. Range in Britain, 50°—61°; coast to 2500 feet.

Pastures, &c. &c. Very common. At the above altitude on Morven.

29. CHRYSANTHEMUM. OX-EYE.

1. C. *Leucanthemum*, Linn. *(Great white O.)*
Perennial. Flowers in June and July. British type. Range in Britain, 50°—61°; coast line to 1500 feet.

Pastures, &c. Frequent; less so inland.

2. C. *segetum*, Linn. *(Corn Marigold, yellow O.)*
Annual. Flowers, July to September. British type. Range in Britain, 50°—61°; coast line to 900 feet.

Fields and waste places. Frequent in most parts of the district; but not in the Corgarff list, and stated as rare in Forgue.

30. MATRICARIA. WILD CHAMOMILE, FEVERFEW.

1. M. *inodora*, Linn. *(Scentless F.)*
Annual. Flowers, June to October. British type. Range in Britain, 50°—61°; coast line to 1300 feet.

Fields and wastes. Common.

Var. β, *maritima*. Abundant along the coast.

31. ACHILLAEA. YARROW, MILFOIL.

1. A. *Ptarmica*, Linn. *(Sneeze-wort Y.)*
Perennial. Flowers in July and August. British type. Range in Britain, 50°—61°; coast to 1500 feet ? Moist meadows, &c. General in the district.

2. A. *Millefolium*, Linn. *(Common Y.)*
Perennial. Flowers, June to September. British type. Range in Britain, 50°—60°; coast to 1700 feet ? Pastures and waste places. Common.

ORDER XXXV.—CAMPANULACEAE.

1. CAMPANULA. BELL-FLOWER.

1. C. *rotundifolia*, Linn. *(Hairbell.)*
Perennial. Flowers in July and August. British type. Range in Britain, 50°—61°; coast to 3000 feet. Natural pastures, wastes, &c. &c. Common.
In the interior it often has only a single flower on a stem, thus resembling the Arctic C. *uniflora*.

2. C. *latifolia*, Linn. *(Giant B. F.)*
Annual. Flowers in July and August. Scottish type, (or Intermediate). Range in Britain, 51°—58°; 50 to 1100 feet.
Shady rocks and woods. Very local.

A.—Robslaw Den; banks of the Don at Monymusk; rocks at Bridge of Gairden, near Ballater, G. D.; Corrymulzie, Professor Macgillivray; Alford, Rev. Dr. Farquharson; Tullynessle, on the banks of the Don at Pond-dash, Rev. J. Minto; Laithers, near Turriff, Dr. Shier; banks of Deveron near Huntly, Mr. Sutherland.

B.—Millowood, near Keith, Rev. Mr. Cowie; shady

wood below Rockmill, Alvah, Rev. Dr. Todd; on the Binhill at Cullen, Mr. Carmichael.

3. *C. glomerata*, Linn. *(Clustered B.)*
Perennial. Flowers in July and August. Germanic type, (or English). Range in Britain, 50°—57°; coast line only.
Dry pastures, &c. Very rare.
K.—Coast at St. Cyrus, Dr. Stephen; Arbuthnot, rare, Mr. Chrystall. Coast at Dunnottar; very rare north from Stonehaven, as at Garron Point, G. D.

2. JASIONE. SHEEP'S-BIT.

1. *J. montana*, Linn. *(Annual S.)*
Biennial. Flowers, June to August. British? type, (or English). Range in Britain, 50°—61°.
Dry gravelly places. Very rare.
K.—Dry banks at Drumtochty, Mr. Croall. I have no note of its presence in Aberdeen or Banffshires; it occurs in Moray, but is very local.

ORDER XXXVI.—LOBELIACEAE.

LOBELIA. LOBELIA.

1. *L. Dortmanna*, Linn. *(Water L.)*
Perennial. Flowers in July and August. Scottish type, (or Highland). Range in Britain, 51°—59°; 150 to 1600 feet.
Lakes. Very local.
K.—Loch of Park, Dr. Adams.
A.—Loch of Skene, at the east end, G. D.; Loch Daven, north-west from Aboyne, Professor Macgillivray; "In lacu Kinnord," Dr. D. Skene; this locality

is Loch Cannor, on the road-side between Aboyne and Ballater; the plant still grows there. In Loch Muick, Professor Macgillivray; in Loch Callater, G. D.; in a small lake east of Loch Builg, Mr. Barron.

ORDER XXXVII.—VACCINIACEAE.

VACCINIUM. WHORTLEBERRY.

1. *V. Myrtillus*, Linn. *(Blaeberry, in this district.)*
Perennial. Flowers, April to June. British type, (or Highland). Range in Britain, 50°—61°; coast line to 4200 feet.

Woods and heaths. Abundant and general.

2. *V. uliginosum*, Linn. *(Bog W.)*
Perennial. Flowers in June and July. Highland type. Range in Britain, 54°—61°; 1800 ? to 3500 feet.

Alpine bogs. Confined to the most inland and highest mountains.

A.—Corgarff, abundant, Mr. Barron; Rocks of the Dhuloch, Mr. Mackay and G. D.; ascent to Lochnagar from Altguisach; Glen Callater, G. D.; ascent from west to Little Craigendall, in both flower and fruit, (1857), Mr. Sutherland.

3. *V. Vitis Idaea*, Linn. *(Red W., Cranberry of this district.)*
Perennial. Flowers in May and June. Highland type, (or Scottish). Range in Britain, 51°—59°; 200 to 3300 feet.

Heaths and woods. Less abundant in the lower districts.

K.— Parish of Arbuthnot, rare, Mr. Chrystall; Banchory-Ternan, Dr. Adams.

A.—Rare at Aberdeen; Den of Maidencraig, on the Skene road, three miles west from town; and upon a moor south from Garlogie, in Skene, G. D. In Cluny, Mr. Barron ; Alford, Rev. Dr. Farquharson ; Clatt, &c. Rev. J. Minto ; Whitehill, Cobairdy, Rev. J. Abel. Not reported from Cruden nor Aberdour.

B.—Small patches only, in the Hill of Alvah, Rev. Dr. Todd ; in Mortlach, chiefly on the higher hills, Dr. L. Stewart ; on the Binhill, Cullen—north side only, Mr. Carmichael.

4. V. *Oxycoccos*, Linn. *(Marsh W. ; Cranberry.)*
Perennial. Flowers in July and August. British type, (or Intermediate). Range in Britain, 50°—58° ; 200 to 2000 feet.

Boggy places. Rare, especially in the lower districts ; more frequent inland.

K.—Parish of Arbuthnot, rare, Mr. Chrystall.

A.—Aboyne and Coull, Stat. Account ; banks of Loch Muick, Dr. A. Murray ; on the ascent to Lochnagar from the Garrawalt Linn, G. D. ; "in monte Morven," Dr. D. Skene ; east face of the Mourne at Castleton, Mr. Gardiner ; in Glen Callater, Mr. Croall ; near the Dhuloch, Mr. Mackay and G. D.

B.—In the Cabrach, Dr. L. Stewart ; sides of the Binhill at Cullen, Mr. Carmichael.

Sub-Class III.—COROLLIFLORAE.

ORDER XXXVIII.—ERICACEAE.

1. ERICA. HEATH.

1. E. *Tetralix*, Linn. *(Cross-leaved H.)*
Perennial. Flowers in July and August. British type. Range in Britain, 50°—61° ; coast line to 2100 feet.

Heaths and moors. Abundant.

2. E. cinerea, Linn (*Fine-leaved H.*)
Perennial. Flowers, July to September. British type.
Range in Britain, 50°—61°; coast to 2000 feet.
Heaths. General and abundant.

2. CALLUNA. (LING; Cat-heather of this district.)

1. C. vulgaris, Salisb. (*Common L.*)
Perennial. Flowers in July and August. British type.
Range in Britain, 50°—61°; coast to 3300 feet.
Heaths and moors. Everywhere abundant.

The presence of this plant without *Erica tetralix* marks the Mid-Arctic zone of Mr. Watson. The highest point which it reaches in this district is that indicated above, and measured by Mr. Watson. On the rather extensive table top of Mount Battock, (2600 feet) there are but a *few stunted* plants of this species. On Mount Keen—highest point, 3180 feet, (Dr. S. Keith)—*, the *calluna* ceases at 2877 feet, I was unable to trace it higher. It is plentiful on the top of Morven, about 3000 feet, G. D.

3. AZALEA. AZALEA.

1. A. procumbens, Linn. (*Trailing Azalea.*)
Perennial. Flowers in May and June. Highland type.
Range in Britain, 56°—61°; 2100 to 3550 feet.
Dry gravelly places. Confined to the higher districts.

A.—Abundant on Lochnagar, Little Craigendall, Glen Callater, Ben Avon, Ben Macdui, &c. &c.

B.—Cairngorm, Mr. R. Mackay; Belrinnes, in Mortlach, Dr. L. Stewart.

---

* My own measurement (1859), gives 3125 feet, the height stated in *Penny Cyclopædia*.

4. ARCTOSTAPHYLOS.   BEAR-BERRY.

1. A. *alpina*, Sprengel. *(Black B.)*
Perennial. Flowers in May. Highland type. Range in Britain, 50°—61°; Range in altitude doubtful.
Dry alpine pastures. Very rare.

A.—Near the top of Hill of Corbuie, 'in Corgarff (head of Don), beside the Cairn, and in a line with it and a hill to the west, Mr. Barron. I have seen a specimen, but have not visited the place, and can find no measurement of the hill on record, G. D.

2. A. *Uva-ursi*, Sprengel. *(Red B.)*
Perennial. Flowers in May and June. Highland type.
Range in Britain, 54°—61° ; 200 to 2400 feet.
Dry heaths. Rather uncommon in the coast district ; in great profusion in the interior on moors, by road-sides, and at high altitudes.

K.—Parish of Arbuthnot, but not common, Mr. Chrystall ; Banchory-Ternan, Rev. J. Brichan.

A.—Not in the immediate vicinity of Aberdeen ; the nearest locality known to me is a moor at Garlogie, ten miles inland. Too plentiful inland to require any special details.

ORDER XXXIX.—PYROLACEAE.

1. MONESES. MONESES.

1. M. *grandiflora*, Salisb. *(Large-flowered M.)*
Perennial. Flowers in July. Scottish type. Range in Britain, 56°—58° ; range in altitude doubtful.
In woods. Very rare.

B.—Woods in parish of Mortlach, Rev. T. B. Bell ; woods in parish of Rothiemay, Dr. A. Murray.
I possess a specimen from this last locality, but have

never gathered the plant. It will doubtless be met with in other parts of the district.

2. PYROLA. WINTER-GREEN.

1. P. *secunda*, Linn. *(Serrated W.)*
Perennial. Flowers in July. Scottish type. Range in Britain, 54°—58°; 120 to 2000 feet.

Woods and shady rocks. Widely diffused, but not frequent in the lower parts.

K.—Banchory-Ternan, Rev. J. Brichan.

A.—Howe of Corrichie, Hill of Fare, Mr. Mackay and G. D.; Craigievar, parish of Leochel Cushnie, Stat. Account. "In Monte, *Morven*, Dr. Campbell;" Skene, MSS. Rocks of the Dhuloch, Mr. Mackay and G. D.; near the top of Craig Koynach, at Castleton, Mr. Gardiner; on the east face of the hill (Craig Vallich?) west from Linn of Quoich, G. D.; on Little Craigendall, Mr. R. Mackay; on Ben Beck, at Castleton, Mr. Gardiner. North bank of the Don, at Dyce, a few miles west from Aberdeen; and plantation near the Farm of Breda, in Alford, Dr. A. Fleming. In Strathdon, Rev. J. Minto; near the limestone quarry, west of the monument, in Corgarff, Mr. Barron; Laithers near Turriff, Dr. Shier.

B.—Wood of Tarrybreck in parish of Rothiemay, Rev. Dr. Todd; in Mortlach, but rare, Dr. L. Stewart.

2. P. *rotundifolia*, Linn. *(Round-leaved W.)*
Perennial. Flowers in July and August. Germanic type ? Range in Britain, 52°—58°; 300 ? to 2300 feet ?

Moist rocks and woods. Rare.*

---

* P. *media* is so often confounded with this species, that I feel some doubt about the stations given. The plant is certainly rare in this district; I have only once found it, viz. :—on the ascent to Lochnagar from Linn of Garrawalt, G. D.

A.—Woods of Kebbaty, Mr. Barron; head of Loch Muick, Prof. Macgillivray; Lochnagar, on the ascent from Linn of Garrawalt, G. D.; base of the Mourne above Castleton, Mr. Sutherland; in parish of Alford, Rev. Dr. Farquharson; parish of Coull, Stat. Account; in Tullynessle, Rev. J. Minto; Laithers near Turriff, Dr. Shier.

3. P. *media*, Swartz. *(Intermediate W.)*
Perennial. Flowers in July and August. Scottish type. Range in Britain, 52°—61°; 200 to 2000 feet.

Woods, and on moors among heather. Frequent, both in the lower districts and inland.

K.—Balmakewan woods, a few hundred yards south from Free Church at the cross-roads, Dr. Simpson; Brigton in St. Cyrus, Dr. Stephen; woods in parish of Fordoun, Dr. A. Murray. On a steep bank, south side of the road, at east end of Kingcausie demesne; and beside Loch of Park, G. D.

A.—Woods by the Skene road between the second and third mile-stones; Den of Maidencraig, four miles west from Aberdeen; on the hill at Scotston moor, G. D. Upon Benachie, Mr. Cruickshank; woods at Culter House, Dr. J. Smith; Hill of Fare, Mr. Mackay and G. D. Wood of Craigendarroch, by the roadside, at Ballater, and plentiful on the hill (1716 feet) behind the Farm of Line, east from the Free Manse at Ballater; and about Loch Muick, G. D.; Cairn-a-Drochet, (at Castleton,) south side, Mr. Gardiner; near the Linn of Quoich, and in Glen Callater, G. D.; on Ben Beck, Craig Koynach, &c., at Castleton, Mr. Gardiner; in Cluny, Mr. Barron; Alford, Rev. Dr. Farquharson; Strathdon, Rev. J. Minto; Den of Dungarvan, parish of Leslie, Mr. M'Donald; Laithers at Turriff, Dr. Shier; Cobairdy and Frendraught woods, Rev. J. Abel; in the Buchan district, Mr. Murray; about Ellon, Mr. Thom.

B.—Top of the Hill of Alvah, also along the walk encircling the hill, especially on the north and west sides, Rev. Dr. Todd ; in Mortlach, Dr. L. Stewart.

4. P. *minor*, Linn. *(Less W.)*
Perennial. Flowers in June and July. Scottish type, (or Germanic). Range in Britain, 51°—58°; 100 to 1600 feet.

Woods. Frequent ; but on the whole not so general and frequent as the last species.

K.—Woods of Fordoun, Dr. A. Murray ; abundant in the Corbie Den, Kingcausie, G. D. ; at Banchory-Ternan, Rev. J. Brichan.

A.—Wood at the old Castle of Drum, Dr. J. Smith; woods at Scotston, Denmore, Parkhill, &c. G. D. ; near Ballater, Mr. R. Mackay ; base of the Mourne, west from Castleton, Mr. Croall ; Craig Koynach, at Castleton, Mr. Gardiner. Woods at Auchindoir; and in Strathdon, Rev. J. Minto.

B.—Not unfrequent in the woods between the Mill of Alvah and the Dry Bridge ; also in the lower parts of the Hill of Alvah, Rev. Dr. Todd. In Mortlach woods, Dr. L. Stewart.

Order XL.—AQUIFOLIACEAE.

1. Ilex. Holly.

1. I. *Aquifolium*, Linn. *(Common H.)*
Perennial. Flowers in May and June. British type. Range in Britain, 50°—59°; 200 to 1500 feet.

Hedges and woods, &c. Often planted ; probably rare as a wild plant.

K.—Parish of Arbuthnot, Mr. Chrystall; Banchory-Ternan, Rev. J. Brichan. Dr. Adams informed me that in the woods of Glassel thousands of young plants spring up naturally.

A.—Near Whiteside in Tullynessle, and in other places occasionally, Rev. J. Minto. I have seen several stunted bushes almost concealed by grass and heath near the head of Corry Rath, north side of Mount Keen, at an elevation of 1500 feet.

B.—" Not indigenous in Alvah," Rev. Dr. Todd; wild in the parish of Cullen, Mr. Carmichael.

It is with much doubt that I admit this plant into the list of indigenous species. It was certainly never planted in such a wild place as the Corry Rath; at the same time, it is easy to understand how it may have been introduced there by the agency of birds.

ORDER XLI.—GENTIANACEAE.

1. ERYTHRAEA. CENTAURY.

1. *E. linarifolia*, Pers. *(Dwarf-tufted C.)*
Annual. Flowers in June and July. British type. Range in Britain, 50°—61°; coast only.

Pastures near the sea. Very rare.

K.—On a sloping grassy bank at the edge of a cliff, between Dounie Well and the Altons, Mr. P. Grant; coast at Bay of Nigg, Dr. Murray in "Northern Flora." In the spot first mentioned I have twice gathered it; I possess no other record of it in the district.

2. *E. Centaurium*, Pers. *(Common C.)*
Annual. Flowers, June to September. British type. Range in Britain, 50°—61°; at 260 feet.

Dry pastures. Very rare.

A.—Near Church of Kemnay, Alford Valley Line, Mr. Burnett (in Mr. P. Macgillivray's Aberdeen Flora).

2. GENTIANA. GENTIAN.*

1. G. Amarella, Linn. *(Small-flowered G.)*
Annual. Flowers, May to September. British type, (or Germanic). Range in Britain, 50°—61°; 50 to 300 feet.

Dry pastures. Rare; its distribution in this district seems peculiar; perhaps it may be often noted, on superficial examination, as G. campestris.

A.—By the Skene road, six and a-half miles from Aberdeen, Mr. Cow; in great profusion in links of St. Fergus, north from Peterhead—more abundant there than the next, Dr. Templeton and G. D.

2. G. campestris, Linn. *(Field G.)*
Annual. Flowers in August and September. British type, (or Scottish). Range in Britain, 50°—61°; coast to 1742 feet.

Natural pastures. Very general.

3. MENYANTHES. BUCKBEAN.

1. M. trifoliata, Linn. *(Buckbean.)*
Perennial. Flowers in May and June. British type. Range in Britain, 50°—61°; coast line to 1600 feet.

Bogs and marshes. General in the district, but not ascending high; it grows on Morven at the height above noted.

* G. nivalis, Linn. *(Small Alpine G.)*
Annual. Flowers in August. Highland type. Range in Britain, 56°—57°; in altitude?
Alpine rocks. Very rare.
A.—On the south-east face of Glas Mheal Mountain, head of Glen Callater, Rev. James Farquharson and Mr. R. Mackay.
Part of Glas Mheal is in County of Aberdeen; the face of it at head of Canlochan Glen is considered as belonging to Forfarshire. Being so near the borders of our district, this interesting plant is deserving of notice here.

ORDER XLII.—CONVOLVULACEAE.

1. CONVOLVULUS. BINDWEED.

1. C. *arvensis*, Linn. *(Field B.)*
Perennial. Flowers in June and July. English type (or British). Range in Britain, 50°—60°; coast only.
Waste places. Very rare.
K.—South Kincardine, Mr. M'Farlane; Arbuthnot, Mr. Chrystall; in a field and by the road-side near old Kirk of Nigg, G. D.
A.—Formerly in a field at the links, south of Bannermill, G. D.; where it was also known to Dr. D. Skene, 100 years ago.*

ORDER XLIII.—BORAGINACEAE.

1. ECHIUM. VIPER'S BUGLOSS.

1. E. *vulgare*, Linn. *(Common V.)*
Biennial. Flowers in June and July. British type, (or English). Range in Britain, 50°—58°; coast line to 1200 feet.
Gravelly wastes. Rather local in the district.
K.—Abundant on the cliffs of St. Cyrus, Dr. Stephen; Arbuthnot, Mr. Chrystall; Banchory-Ternan, Rev. J. Brichan.
A.—Rare about Aberdeen; at the Fyfe hills in Belhelvie; at Middleton, Deeside turnpike, G. D. At Drumoak, Rev. J. Abel; at Auchallater, near Castleton, Mr. A. K. Clark; at Tullynessle and in Strathdon,

---

* *Calystegia sepium*, and *C. Soldanella*, occur on the north-east border of Forfarshire. I possess no note of these species in this district

Rev. J. Minto; occasionally in fields, parish of Leochel, Mr. Sutherland; at Cobairdy, Rev. J. Abel; at Old Leslie, parish of Leslie, Mr. M'Donald.

B.—Occasionally in fields, and on the Hill of Stoneley, in Alvah, Rev. Dr. Todd; rare in Mortlach, Dr. L. Stewart.

2. LITHOSPERMUM. GROMWELL.

1. L. *arvense*, Linn. *(Corn G.)*
Annual. Flowers in May and June. British type. Range in Britain, 50°—59°; coast line to 500 feet.
Fields and waste places. Very local.

K.—Fields at Kirkside in St. Cyrus, Dr. Stephen; at Arbuthnot, Mr. Chrystall.

A.—Rare at Aberdeen and uncertain in its growth: formerly on the Inch; and in fields at Cardens and Robslaw; beside the mill at new Bridge of Don, G. D. Road-side near Manse of Alford, Dr. A. Murray; at Crimond, Mr. Cow.

B.—Fields in Alvah, Rev. Dr. Todd; Mortlach, Dr. L. Stewart.

3. MERTENSIA. SMOOTH GROMWELL.

1. M. *maritima*, Don. *(Sea-side G.)*
Perennial. Flowers in May and June. Scottish type. Range in Britain, 53°—61°; coast only.
Sandy and stony shores. Frequent.

K.—St. Cyrus, Stat. Account; Bervie and Johnshaven, Dr. Stephen; Arbuthnot and Benholme sands, Mr. Chrystall. Garron Point, north from Stonehaven; and abundant in Bay of Nigg, G. D.

A.—Occasionally on the Belhelvie shore, G. D.; Ugie mouth, "Northern Flora"; elsewhere near Peterhead, Dr. Shier; Aberdour, Rev. G. Gairdner.

B.—Gamrie shore, Rev. G. Gairdner; at "Banff, towards Doun, among sand at the sea-shore," Dr. D. Skene; mouth of the burn of Boyne, Rev. Mr. Cowie.

4. MYOSOTIS. SCORPION-GRASS.

1. *M. repens*, Don. *(Creeping Water S.)*
Perennial. Flowers, June to August. British type.
    Range in Britain, 50°—59°; coast line to 1200 feet.
    Bogs and ditches. Frequent and general.

I am inclined to agree with Mr. Watson that this is the plant of our district, though reported under the name of M. *palustris*.* In such belief it may be sufficient to state that the plant is reported as frequent in all parts.

2. M. *caespitosa*, Schultz. *(Tufted Water S.)*
Perennial? Flowers in June and July. British type.
    Range in Britain, 50°—61°; coast line to 1200 feet.
    Bogs and ditches. Frequent, but not so much so as the last.

K.—In marshes and ditches at Nigg, G. D.

A.—Near Aberdeen, at the Stocket and Scotston moors; also at Castleton, Braemar, G. D. In Alford, Rev. Dr. Farquharson; in Clatt, Rev. J. Minto.

My suspicion is that under the common name M. *palustris*, the M. *repens*, and M. *caespitosa* are frequently noted without careful examination.

3. M. *arvensis*, Hoffm. *(Field S.)*
Biennial. Flowers, June to August. British type.
    Range in Britain, 50°—61°; coast to 1200 feet?
    Fields and wastes. Common.

---

* Some authorities, however, consider them as scarcely distinct from each other.

4. **M. collina**, Hoffm. *(Early Field S.)*
Annual. Flowers in April and May. British type. Range in Britain, 50°—61°; coast chiefly.
Sandy places, &c. Local, but abundant where it does grow.

K.—St. Cyrus, Dr. Stephen.

A.—Abundant on the sand hills in the Old-town Links, north from the Broadhill; and formerly near the Lunatic Asylum, G. D. Buchan coast, Mr. Cow.

B.—Parish of Alvah, and Colleonard in Banff parish, Dr. Shier.

5. **M. versicolor**, Lehm. *(Yellow and blue S.)*
Annual. Flowers, May to July. British type. Range in Britain, 50°—61°; coast line to 1200 feet.
Fields and waste places. Common.*

5. LYCOPSIS. BUGLOSS.

1. **L. arvensis**, Linn. *(Small B.)*
Annual. Flowers in June and July. British type. Range in Britain, 50°—61°; coast line to 1380 feet.
Fields and wastes. Common. Occurs at the height above mentioned at Lin Mui, near Ballater.

6. SYMPHYTUM. COMFREY.

1. **S. tuberosum**, Linn. *(Tuberous C.)*
Perennial. Flowers in June and July. Scottish type. Range in Britain, 51°—58°; coast line to 500 feet.
Moist and shady places, &c. Frequent in the district.

---

* M. *sylvatica* is said to have been found in Corbie Den, Kingcausie, and in Robslaw Den; I have never seen the true plant in this district. Luxuriant specimens of M. *arvensis* are sometimes mistaken for it.

K.—Common at St. Cyrus, Dr. Stephen; Banchory-Ternan, Dr. Adams.

A.—Not unfrequent about Aberdeen and Old-town, as near Gilcomston Dam; road opposite Fountainhall; at Stocket; Den of Robslaw; Deeside road at Middleton, &c., G. D. Near the Church of Midmar, Mr. Barron; at Alford, Rev. Dr. Farquharson. Abundant at Tullynessle; at Lessendrum, Rev. J. Abel. In Clatt, Rev. J. Minto; in Buchan, Mr. A. Murray; Aberdour, Rev. G. Gairdner.

B.—Abundant on Deveron-side, Alvah, Rev. Dr. Todd; in the vicinity of Banff, "Northern Flora."

ORDER XLIV.—SCROPHULARIACEAE.

1. VERONICA. SPEEDWELL.

1. V. *serpyllifolia*, Linn. *(Thyme-leaved S.)*
Perennial. Flowers, June to August. British type. Range in Britain, 50°—61°; coast line to 2500 feet?

Pastures and waste places. Abundant.

Var. β, *humifusa*, Dickson, is frequent on all the higher ranges in the interior, as Lochnagar, &c. &c.

2. V. *alpina*, Linn. *(Alpine S.)*
Perennial. Flowers in July and August. Highland type. Range in Britain, 56°—58°; 2000 to 3000 feet.

Moist rocks and pastures. At high altitudes in the interior.

A.—Lochnagar, Glen Callater, Ben Macdui, Ben-a-Buird, Ben Avon, &c., &c.

3. V. *scutellata*, Linn. *(Marsh S.)*

Perennial. Flowers in July and August. British type.
Range in Britain, 50°—60°; coast line to 1300 feet.

Moist places. Generally diffused, but not common.

K.—Jackstone, St. Cyrus; Pitready, Strachan, Dr. Stephen. Arbuthnot, Mr. Chrystall; about Loch of Loirston, &c. G. D. Banchory-Ternan, Rev. J. Brichan.

A.—Near Aberdeen at Stocket and Scotston moors; and a marsh a little north-west of Summerhill, &c.; and in the interior at Loch Cannor and Castleton, G. D. At Dyce, Dr. A. Fleming; west end of Loch Park, Dr. Stephen; moss at Coalford, Norman Dyke, Peterculter, Dr. J. Smith; Drumnahoy, Mr. Barron; in Clatt, Rev. J. Minto; district of Kinore, Huntly, Rev. J. Abel; at Cruden, Mr. A. Murray; Aberdour, Rev. G. Gairdner.

B.—A hairy variety in Hill of Tipperty, Alvah, Rev. Dr. Todd; Mortlach, Dr. L. Stewart.

4. V. *Anagallis*, Linn. *(Water S.)*
Perennial. Flowers in July and August. British type.
Range in Britain, 50°—60°; coast line to 300 feet?

Slow streams and ditches. A rare plant in this district.

K.—Abundant and luxuriant at Arbuthnot, Mr. Chrystall.

A.—Side of Powis burn, near the Old-town Links, Mr. Cow; in the canal at St. Fergus, Mr. A. Murray; ditch in the woods near Craigston, parish of King Edward, Rev. Dr. Todd.

5. V. *Beccabunga*, Linn. *(Brooklime.)*
Perennial. Flowers, May to August. British type.
Range in Britain, 50°—61°; coast line to 1300 feet.

Ditches, &c. Frequent in the district.

6. V. *officinalis*, Linn.   *(Common S.)*
Perennial.   Flowers in June and July.   British type.
   Range in Britain, 50°—60°; coast to 1900 feet?
   Woods and pastures.   General.

7. V. *montana*, Linn.   *(Mountain S.)*
Perennial.   Flowers, April to July.   British type, (or
   English).   Range in Britain, 50°—58°.
Moist woods.   Rare.
   B.—Deskford, in a wood near the Church, Rev.
Mr. Cowie; between Gordon Castle and Deskford, Mr.
Craigie; Hollybank, near Gordon Castle, Mr. R. Bremner; in "Northern Flora."

8. V. *Chamaedrys*, Linn.   *(Germander S.)*
Perennial.   Flowers in May and June.   British type.
   Range in Britain, 50°—61; coast line to 1900
   feet.
Woods, pastures, &c.   Generally diffused.

9. V. *hederifolia*, Linn.   *(Ivy-leaved S.)*
Annual.   Flowers, April to August.   British type.
   Range in Britain, 50°—61°; coast line to 1200
   feet.
Fields and wastes.   Frequent, but not common.
Occurs in Corgarff at the height above mentioned.

10. V. *agrestis*, Linn.   *(Field S.)*
Annual.   Flowers, April to October.   British type.
   Range in Britain, 50°—60°; coast to 1200 feet.
Fields and wastes.   General.

11. V. *arvensis*, Linn.   *(Wall S.)*
Annual.   Flowers, April to August.   British type.
   Range in Britain, 50°—60°; coast line to 1200
   feet.
Walls and wastes.   Reported with the last from

different parts of the district; both are plentiful in Corgarff, and therefore attain, at least, the height above mentioned.

2. BARTSIA. BARTSIA.

1. B. *Odontites*, Hudson. *(Red B.)*
Annual. Flowers in July and August. British type.
Range in Britain, 50°—60°; coast line to 500 feet.

Moist waste places. Generally diffused, but not common.

K.—South parts of Kincardine, Mr. M'Farlane; Arbuthnot, Mr. Chrystall; near the Free Church, Banchory-Devenick, Mr. A. Cruickshank.

A.—Rather scarce about Aberdeen; marsh by the bridge at Stocket moor; by the road-side near the lodge at Scotston House, G. D. Road-side near Castle of Balfluig, Alford, Dr. A. Fleming; Clatt and Kinnethmont, Rev. J. Minto; Cobairdy, Drumblade, Rev. J. Abel; Rhynie and Huntly, Mr. Sutherland; beside the Manse of Old Deer, Mr. A. Cruickshank; abundant about Ellon, G. D.; at Cruden, Mr. A. Murray; Aberdour, Rev. G. Gairdner.

B.—In Alvah, Rev. Dr. Todd; at Mortlach, Dr. L. Stewart.

3. EUPHRASIA. EYEBRIGHT.

1. E. *officinalis*, Linn. *(Common E.)*
Annual. Flowers, May to October. British type.
Range in Britain, 50°—61°; coast to 3400 feet.

Natural pastures. Abundant in all parts of the district.

4. RHINANTHUS. YELLOW-RATTLE.

1. R. *Crista-Galli*, Linn. *(Common Y.)*
Annual. Flowers, May to August. British type.
Range in Britain, 50°—61°; coast to 1300 feet?

Pastures and wastes. Generally diffused.*

5. MELAMPYRUM. COW-WHEAT.

1. M. *pratense*, Linn. *(Common yellow C.)*
Annual. Flowers, June to August. British type.
Range in Britain, 50°—60°; 100 to 3000 feet.
Generally in moist woods. Frequent, but not common.

K.—South parts of Kincardine, Mr. M'Farlane; Banchory-Ternan, Rev. J. Brichan; in the woods at Kingcausie, G. D.; Gellan woods and Bridge of Dye, and by streams in Caerloch, parish of Strachan, Dr. Stephen.

A.—Woods of Drum, Dr. J. Smith; Glentanner, among birches, Dr. D. Skene. Abundant about Ballater, as at Slievanachie, &c.; and near the summit of Morven, G. D. Woods at Midmar Castle, Mr. Barron; side of the road through Tillyfour woods, Monymusk, Dr. A. Fleming; woods of Knockespock, Rev. J. Minto; in Corgarff, Mr. Barron; in Buchan, Mr. A. Murray; woods of Laithers, near Turriff, Dr. Shier; wood west of Mayen House, Deveron-side, Rev. J. Abel.

B.—Near a quarry in the wood of Shaws, Alvah, Rev. Dr. Todd; Mortlach woods, Dr. L. Stewart.

Var. β, about Castleton, Corrymulzie, and on the higher ranges, G. D.

2. M. *sylvaticum*, Linn. *(Lesser-flowered Yellow C.)*
Annual. Flowers in July. Scottish type. Range in Britain, 54°—58°; 200 to 1300 feet.
Woods. Rare, and chiefly inland.

---

* R. *major* (R. *angustifolius* of some), has been found in Forfarshire. I have gathered it in Moray, but I have never seen it in this district, and have no report from others of its occurrence.

K.—In parish of Arbuthnot, rare, Mr. Chrystall; woods at Blackhall, Banchory-Ternan, Dr. Adams; woods in parish of Strachan, Stat. Account.

A.—At Altguisach, head of Glen Muick, G. D.; in Corgarff, Mr. Barron.

6. PEDICULARIS. LOUSE-WORT.

1. P. *palustris*, Linn. *(Marsh L.)*
Perennial. Flowers in July and August. British type. Range in Britain, 50°—61°; coast line to 1667 feet.
Wet pastures. Frequent in almost all parts of the district.

2. P. *sylvatica*, Linn. *(Pasture L.)*
Perennial. Flowers, April to July. British type. Range in Britain, 50°—61°; coast to 1900 feet.
Moist pastures and heaths. More common than the last.

7. SCROPHULARIA. FIGWORT.

1. S. *nodosa*, Linn. *(Knotted F.)*
Perennial. Flowers, June to August. British type. Range in Britain, 50°—58°; coast to 500 feet.
Woods and wastes. Frequent.
Recorded as growing in most parts of the district; seems to thin out toward the interior; stated to be scarce in Mortlach. Not in the Corgarff list.

8. DIGITALIS. FOXGLOVE.

1. D. *purpurea*, Linn. *(Purple F.)*
Perennial. Flowers, June to August. British type. Range in Britain, 50°—60°; coast to 1800 feet.
Pastures and wastes. Very frequent.

9. LIMOSELLA. MUDWORT.

1. L. aquatica, Linn. *(Common M.)*
Annual. Flowers in July and August. Germanic type, (or English). Range in Britain, 50°—57°; coast only.
Muddy places. Very rare.
K.—North corner of the mill dam below the Free Manse at St. Cyrus, Dr. Stephen, in whose possession I saw living plants. This is the only locality known to me in this district; being inconspicuous the plant may be often overlooked.

ORDER XLV.—LABIATAE.

1. LYCOPUS. GIPSY-WORT.

1. L. Europaeus, Linn. *(Common G.)*
Perennial. Flowers in July and August. British type, (or English). Range in Britain, 50°—58°; about 200 feet only.
Marshy places. Very rare.
K.—Ury, Rev. A. Smith; formerly at east end of Loch Leys, Banchory-Ternan, Dr. Adams.

2. MENTHA. MINT.

1. M. aquatica, Linn. *(Water M.)*
Perennial. Flowers in July and August. British type. Range in Britain, 50°—60°; coast line to 500 feet.
Marshy places. Rather general, but not a common plant. Is reported from most parts of the district, but seems to become scarcer toward the interior.

2. M. arvensis, Linn. *(Field M.)*

Perennial. Flowers in July and August. British type. Range in Britain, 50°—60°; coast line to 1200 feet.

Fields and dry wastes. Not uncommon. Like the last, becoming scarcer inland; occurs, however, at Castleton, Braemar.

These are the only species of *Mentha* truly indigenous here, records of others—doubtless introduced—will be found elsewhere.

3. THYMUS. THYME.

1. T. *Serpyllum*, Linn. *(Wild T.)*
Perennial. Flowers, June to August. British type. Range in Britain, 50°—61°; coast to 2000 feet.
Dry pastures and wastes. Common and general.

4. ORIGANUM. MARJORAM.

1. O. *vulgare*, Linn. *(Common M.)*
Perennial. Flowers in July and August. British type, (or English). Range in Britain, 51°—58°; coast line to 900 feet?
Dry banks. Rare in this district.

K.—At St. Cyrus, by the North Esk river, Dr. Stephen; at Arbuthnot, Mr. Chrystall.

A.—North bank of the Dee, east from the Manse of Drumoak, where it was first pointed out to me by Dr. A. Murray; in Strathdon, Stat. Account.

B.—Near Craigellachie, Dr. L. Stewart.

5. TEUCRIUM. GERMANDER.

1. T. *Scorodonia*, Linn. *(Wood G.)*
Perennial. Flowers in July and August. British type. Range in Britain, 50°—60°; coast to 1300 feet.
Dry stony places, &c. Frequent and widely dif-

fused; appears to be less so in more inland parts, but is still plentiful at Ballater, and grows also at Castleton.

6. AJUGA. BUGLE.

1. A. *reptans*, Linn. *(Common B.)*
Perennial. Flowers in May and June. British type. Range in Britain, 50°—60°; coast line to 1600 feet.

Moist woods and pastures. Frequent in the lower parts; apparently less so in the interior and higher parts.

7. GALEOPSIS. HEMP-NETTLE.

1. G. *Tetrahit*, Linn. *(Common H.)*
Annual. Flowers, July to September. British type. Range in Britain, 50°—61°; coast to 1264 feet.

Fields and dry waste places. Reported from all parts of the district wherever cultivation extends.

2. G. *versicolor*, Curtis. *(Large-flowered H.)*
Annual. Flowers in July and August. Scottish type, (or British). Range in Britain, 51°—58°; coast line to 1200 feet.

Fields and wastes. Not so common as the last, though reported from most parts of the three counties.

K.—Arbuthnot, Mr. Chrystall; Banchory-Ternan, Rev. J. Brichan.

A.—Fields in King Street, and other places round Aberdeen, but rather uncertain in appearance, G. D.; fields about Castleton, Braemar, Mr. Croall; Alford, Rev. Dr. Farquharson; Clatt, Rev. J. Minto; rather common at Cobairdy, Rev. J. Abel.

B.—Abundant on the east side of Deveron, but very sparingly on the west side, in Alvah, Rev. Dr. Todd; in Mortlach, Dr. L. Stewart.

8. LAMIUM.   DEAD-NETTLE.

1. L. *purpureum*, Linn. *(Purple D.)*
Annual. Flowers, April to October. British type.
Range in Britain, 50°—61°; coast to 1200 feet.
Fields and wastes. Common in the lower parts; scarcer where cultivation is less general.

2. L. *incisum*, Willd. *(Cut-leaved D.)*
Annual. Flowers, April to August. British type.
Range in Britain, 50°—61°; coast to ?
Fields and waste places. Less common and not so widely diffused as the last. Not reported from several parts where the L. *purpureum* is common; it may have perhaps been confounded with it, and is indeed, by some, considered identical.

Another species, L. *intermedium*, Fries, is not reported from any part of the three counties, and probably for the same reason that L. *incisum* is omitted in some instances.

3. L. *amplexicaule*, Linn. *(Henbit N.)* [*]
Annual. Flowers, April to September. British type.
Range in Britain, 50°—59°; coast line to 500 feet.
Dry fields and waste places. Frequent.

K.—Arbuthnot, Mr. Chrystall; Banchory-Ternan, Rev. J. Brichan; frequent at St. Cyrus and in Strachan, Dr. Stephen.

A.—About Aberdeen occasionally, but rather uncertain in appearance. Reported as in Cluny, Alford, Clatt, Cruden, Forgue, Aberdour, Alvah. Not in lists

---

[*] It is difficult to reconcile the opinions of authorities respecting the British species of *Lamium*; one considers L. *amplexicaule* and L. *intermedium* as scarcely to be distinguished; another thinks L. *amplexicaule* distinct, but L. *incisum* and L. *intermedium* as nearly allied, and as very probably only varieties of L. *purpureum*.

from Corgarff and Mortlach. I have no note of its presence in the more inland parts.

9. STACHYS. WOUNDWORT.

1. S. *sylvatica*, Linn. *(Wood W.)*
Perennial. Flowers in July and August. British type. Range in Britain, 50°—61°; 100 to 1200 feet.

Woods and shady places. Frequent. Reported from most parts of the district. Occurs at Corrymulzie, Castleton; and also in Mortlach.

2. S. *palustris*, Linn. *(Marsh W.)*
Perennial. Flowers in July and August. British type. Range in Britain, 50°—61°; coast line to 1180 feet.

Moist fields, &c. Very general in the district.

Var. β, *ambigua*, at Arbuthnot and elsewhere; and seen at Invercauld, which would give a range of 200 to 1080 feet.

3. S. *arvensis*, Linn. *(Corn W.)*
Annual. Flowers, May to August. British type. Range in Britain, 50°—59°; coast line to 400 feet.

Dry fields and wastes. Rather local, and not so generally diffused as the first and second species.

K.—South parts of Kincardine, Mr. M'Farlane; Arbuthnot, Mr. Chrystall; Banchory-Ternan, Rev. J. Brichan; village of Cowie, near Stonehaven, Dr. A. Fleming.

A.—Occasionally in fields about Aberdeen, but rather uncertain in its growth. Fields near Muir of Rhynie, Rev. J. Minto; Aberdour, Rev. G. Gairdner.

B.—Common in the upper parts of the parish of Alvah, rarer in the lower, Rev. Dr. Todd; rare in Mortlach, Dr. L. Stewart.

10. NEPETA. GROUND-IVY.

1. N. *Glechoma*, Benth. *(Common G. I.)*
Perennial. Flowers in April and May. British type. Range in Britain, 50°—60°; coast line to 500 feet.

Hedges and wastes. Rather generally diffused, but not a common plant.

K.—In south, north, and north-west parts of Kincardine.

A.—Aberdeen, Cluny, Alford, Rhynie, Huntly, Clatt, Drumblade, Forgue, Cruden, Aberdour. Reported as rare at Alford, and not noted as in Corgarff.

B.—Alvah, Mortlach.

11. CALAMINTHA. CALAMINTH, &c.

1. C. *Acinos*, Clairv. *(Common C.)*
Annual. Flowers in August. British type, (or English). Range in Britain, 50°—58°; 100 to 460 feet.

Dry fields and wastes. Very local and rare. It is with some hesitation I admit it here.

K.—Banchory-Ternan, Rev. J. Brichan.

A.—Near the Manse of Drumoak, in fields, Dr. J. Smith; Upper Drumnahoy, Cluny, Mr. J. Barron, in which locality I have seen it; near Glenmillan, in Lumphanan, Rev. A. Beverly.

2. C. *Clinopodium*, Benth. *(Com. Wild-Basil.)*
Perennial. Flowers in July and August. British type, (or English). Range in Britain, 50°—58°; coast line to 800 feet.

Dry banks. Very local. Not reported from the northern parts of the district.

K.—"Ad ripas Dee, Banchory-Ternan," Dr. D. Skene, where it still grows.

A.—Rare near Aberdeen; has been found on the Inch, at the Craiglug, and about the old Bridge of Dee, G. D. North bank of the Dee at Drumoak, Dr. J. Smith; banks of the Muick and Dee at Ballater, G. D.; at Craig, Auchindoir, Mr. Sutherland.

12. PRUNELLA. SELF-HEAL.

1. P. *vulgaris*, Linn. *(Common S.)*
Perennial. Flowers in July and August. British type. Range in Britain, 50°—60°; coast to 2000 feet.
Moist pastures. Common and generally diffused.

13. SCUTELLARIA. SKULL-CAP.

1. S. *galericulata*, Linn. *(Common S.)*
Perennial. Flowers in July and August. British type. Range in Britain, 50°—58°; coast to 400 feet?
By lakes and in marshes. Rare in the district.

K.—Marshy places among Iris, along the shore at Muchalls, Dr. A. Murray; I have seen specimens collected there.

A.—In parish of Longside, Stat. Account.

B.—At Loch Park, in Mortlach, rare, Dr. L. Stewart.

ORDER XLVI.—LENTIBULARIACEAE.

1. PINGUICULA. BUTTERWORT.

1. P. *vulgaris*, Linn. *(Common B.)*
Perennial. Flowers, May to July. Scottish type, (or British). Range in Britain, 50°—61°; coast to 2800 feet.
Moist heaths and bogs. Generally diffused. A variety with white flowers has been found at the south

part of the base of Morven; on the same mountain the plant attains the elevation above mentioned.

2. UTRICULARIA. BLADDERWORT.

1. U. *vulgaris*, Linn. *(Greater B.)*
Perennial. Flowers in June and July. British type. Range in Britain, 50°—61°; coast line to 1600 feet.
Ditches and lakes. Widely diffused, but scarce.

K.—Moss of Forth, parish of Garvock, Dr. Stephen; marsh above Bay of Nigg, to the south-west, G. D.; near Kingcausie, Rev. D. Milne; Banchory-Ternan, Dr. Adams.

A.—Formerly in Ferryhill moss; mosses of Fyfe, in Belhelvie, and of Braediach in Skene; also at Loch of Skene, G. D. Loch Cannor, Mr. Sutherland; very fine at the west end of Loch Muick, G. D.; in Loch Callater, Rev. J. Brichan; marshes near the Lyne, Upper Drumnahoy, Mr. Barron; moss of Balfluig, in Alford, Rev. J. Minto; mosses in Hinder Kinnethmont, Mr. M'Donald.

B.—Moss holes about Muiryhill, Alvah, Rev. Dr. Todd.

2. U. *intermedia*, Hayne. *(Intermediate B.)*
Perennial. Flowers in June and July. Local type, (or Scottish). Range in Britain, 50°—59°; 200 to 600 feet.
Pools and ditches. Very rare; perhaps often overlooked.

K.—In shallow water at the east end of Loch of Park, 12 miles west from Aberdeen, G. D.

A.—At Loch Cannor (between Aboyne and Ballater), Mr. Sutherland.

3. U. *minor*, Linn. *(Less B.)*

Perennial. Flowers in July and August. British type. Range in Britain, 50°—59°; 100 to 600 feet.

Bogs and ditches. Rare.

K.—Marsh, half-a-mile north from Kirk of Garvock, Dr. Stephen; near Kingcausie, Rev. D. Milne; Banchory-Ternan, Rev. J. Brichan.

A.—Moss at the south side of Corsehill, opposite to Scotston, near Aberdeen, and marsh at the west end of Loch of Skene, G. D.; Loch Cannor, Professor Macgillivray; Moss of Balfluig, in Alford, also in Auchindoir, Rev. J. Minto.

ORDER XLVII.—PRIMULACEAE.

1. PRIMULA. PRIMROSE, &c.

1. *P. vulgaris*, Huds. *(Common P.)*

Perennial. Flowers in April and May. British type. Range in Britain, 50°—61°; coast to 1500 feet.

Pastures, &c. Frequent in all parts.

Var. β. *elatior*. Rather local in the district.

K.—At St. Cyrus; Kineff; Arbuthnot, Stat. Account. Banchory-Ternan, Rev. J. Brichan.

A.—Rare at Aberdeen, on the north bank of the Dee, west from Morison's Suspension Bridge, G. D.; at Tillenhilt, in Midmar, Mr. Barron; at Cruden, Mr. A. Murray.

B.—In parish of Alvah, Rev. Dr. Todd.

2. *P. veris*, Linn. *(Common Cowslip.)*

Perennial. Flowers in April and May. British type, (or English). Range in Britain, 50°—60°; coast line to 1500 feet.

Banks and natural pastures. It is less common in the maritime parts of the district, and increases in frequency toward the interior.

K.—St. Cyrus; Kineff, Stat. Account. Coast at Whistleberry, Dr. D. Lyall. On banks at the Cove.

A.—Den of Maidencraig, by the Skene road, Mr. P. Grant. "In pascuis inter Tullich et ripam Dee," Dr. D. Skene. Abundant by the Dee, above and below Ballater; and about the base of the Mourne at Castleton, G. D. Craig Koynach at Castleton, Mr. Croall. Micras; Abergeldie; Carr Rocks at Castleton, Mr. Sutherland. Den of Craig, near Rhynie; Bridge of Poldullie, Strathdon; Nochty-side, Inchrory, "Northern Flora." At Cruden, Mr. A. Murray; at Aberdour, Rev. G. Gairdner.

B.—At Gamrie, Rev. G. Gairdner; in Alvah, Rev. Dr. Todd.

2. GLAUX. SEA MILKWORT.

1. G. *maritima*, Linn. *(Sea M.)*
Perennial. Flowers in June and July. British type. Range in Britain, 50°—61°; coast only.

Marshy spots by the sea. Common along the coast.

3. TRIENTALIS. CHICKWEED WINTER-GREEN.

1. T. *Europaea*, Linn. *(European C.)*
Perennial. Flowers in June. Scottish type, (or Highland.) Range in Britain, 53°—61°; coast line to 2000 feet.

Woods and heaths. This interesting plant is abundant in most parts of the district, and is one of our most characteristic species; still it may be necessary to record a few of the *many* places where it grows.

K.—In different parts of Kincardine—Arbuthnot; Fordoun; Nigg; Banchory-Ternan, &c.

A.—In great abundance in almost every fir wood, and on the moors round Aberdeen; Stocket moor; woods by the Skene road; Parkhill, Scotston, Denmore, Hazelhead, &c. &c. About Ballater; ascent to

Lin Mui; round Loch Muick; on the ascent to Lochnagar; on the Hill of Fare; in Midmar woods; Clatt and Alford; Strathdon. Cobairdy woods and Deveronside. Old Deer. In Buchan district. Aberdour.

B.—In Banff parish; abundant in Alvah; on the Binhill, Cullen. In Mortlach. The Rev. J. Abel, who reports it as at Cobairdy, &c. states, that the earliest plants have the number *six* prevailing in the parts of the flower, while on those which flower at a later period, the number *seven* predominates.

4. LYSIMACHIA. LOOSE-STRIFE.

1. L. *nemorum*, Linn. *(Wood L.)*
Perennial. Flowers, May to August. British type.
   Range in Britain, 50°—58°; coast to 1860 feet.
Moist shady places. Very generally diffused.

2. L. *vulgaris*, Linn. *(Great yellow L.)*
Perennial. Flowers in July and August. English type, (or British). Range in Britain, 50°—58°; local at 50 feet ?
Wet shady places. Very rare.

A. (or K.)—On an island in the river Dee, (Powberry island), opposite Kingcausie, where it was first observed by Mr. Gammie. I have gathered it abundantly there.

5. ANAGALLIS. PIMPERNEL.

1. A. *arvensis*, Linn. *(Scarlet P.)*
Annual. Flowers, June to August. British type, (or English). Range in Britain, 50°—58°; coast line to 800 feet.

Dry fields and wastes. Rare in this district, and probably introduced with cereals, &c.

K.—Milton of Mathers, St. Cyrus, Dr. Stephen; Arbuthnot, Mr. Chrystall. Occasionally about Stonehaven; in a field south-west from Girdleness Lighthouse, Dr. A Fleming ; Banchory-Ternan, Rev. J. Minto.

A.—Fields about Ferryhill, &c., "Northern Flora." Upper Drumnahoy, Mr. Barron ; in Strathdon, Mr. Proctor.

B.—Fields about Dunlugas, in Alvah, Rev. Dr. Todd.

2. A. *tenella*, Linn. *(Bog P.)*
Perennial. Flowers in July and August. British type. Range in Britain, 50°—61° ; coast line to 500 feet ?

In marshy places. Rare in this district.

K.—Inland parts of St. Cyrus, Stat. Account ; at Arbuthnot, rare, Mr. Chrystall ; at Bervie, Stat. Account.

A.—"Moist banks of the Don in more than one place," Northern Flora. At Peterhead, south of the Lighthouse, Rev. J. Minto. Banks of the Ugie at Collyburn ; Rattray Head ; and Loch of Strathbeg, Mr. Cow ; at this last place I have gathered the plant. At St. Fergus, Mr. A. Murray ; in parish of Aberdour, Rev. G. Gairdner.

B.—Formerly in a bog near Mill of Alvah, Rev. Dr. Todd ; in Mortlach, but rare, Dr. L. Stewart.

ORDER XLVIII.—PLUMBAGINACEAE.

1. ARMERIA. SEA-PINK.

1. A. *maritima*, Willd. *(Common Sea P.)*
Perennial. Flowers, April to September. British type. Range in Britain, 50°—61°; coast to 3600 feet.

In various habitats on the whole coast ; along the course of the larger rivers from their source downwards; on serpentine tracts, very general; occurs also at different elevations on the higher ranges. A very variable plant, out of which some have proposed to institute several species. In some cases the calyx is entirely pilose, *Holotrichae;* in others there are lines of hairs on all or on some of the ribs, *Pleurotrichae.* Specimens from twenty different stations in the district gave the following results—in four the calyx all hairy, *Holotrichae,* these were gathered on the coast; in three, there were ten lines of hairs, with *scattered* hairs in the intervening spaces; in eleven, there were ten lines of hairs, the intervening spaces glabrous; in one, there were five lines densely pilose, and five with scattered hairs only; in one there were only five lines of hairs. The first seven might be called *Holotrichae,* these were coast specimens; among the remaining thirteen, *Pleurotrichae,* all the inland specimens were included, and part of those from the coast. Finally, it may be worthy of notice that specimens, which had been thirty years in cultivation had the calyx all hairy; and others, seven years cultivated had ten lines of hairs.

ORDER XLIX.—PLANTAGINACEAE.

1. PLANTAGO. PLANTAIN.

1. P. *major,* Linn. *(Greater P.)*

Perennial. Flowers, June to August. British type. Range in Britain, 50°—61°; coast to 1500 feet.

Pastures and wastes. Common.

2. P. *media,* Linn. *(Hoary P.)*

Perennial. Flowers, June to September. English type, (or British). Range in Britain, 50°—61°; 200 feet.

Pastures. Very rare in the district.

K.—Arbuthnot, rare, Mr. Chrystall; Kingcausie, "Northern Flora."

A.—Formerly in a field near Marine Terrace, Aberdeen, Dr. A. Fleming; at Haddo House, "Northern Flora."

3. P. *lanceolata*, Linn. *(Ribwort P.)*
Perennial. Flowers in June and July. British type. Range in Britain, 50°—61°; coast to 1900 feet.
Pastures and wastes. Common.

4. P. *maritima*, Linn. *(Sea-side P.)*
Perennial. Flowers, June to September. British type. Range in Britain, 50°—61°; coast to 1000 feet.
Waste places and rocks. Abundant along the coast line; less so in the interior.

K.—Banchory-Ternan.

A.—Hill of Fare, Alford, Clatt, Rayne, Turriff, Tullynessle, Forgue, Drumblade.

B.—Alvah; Mortlach, but rare.

5. P. *Coronopus*, Linn. *(Buck's-horn P.)*
Annual. Flowers in June and July. British type. Range in Britain, 50°—61°; coast to 60 feet.
Gravelly wastes. Frequent in the maritime districts; I have no note of its occurrence farther from the sea than 12 miles, viz. in parish of Methlic.

2. LITTORELLA. SHORE-WEED.

1. L. *lacustris*, Linn. *(Plantain S.)*
Perennial. Flowers in June. British type. Range in Britain, 50°—61°; coast line to 800 feet.
Margins of lakes and in marshes. Though widely diffused still not a common plant.

K.—Garvock and Muchalls, Dr. Stephen; abundant at Loch of Loirston, G. D.

A.—Near Aberdeen, at Stocket moor, Corbie Loch, Bishop's Loch, margin of the Dee, &c. G. D. Cluny, Mr. Barron; rare in Alford, Rev. Dr. Farquharson; marshes above Ballater, Mr. Croall; Cruden, Mr. A. Murray; parish of Longside, Stat. Account. Not in Corgarff.

B.—In Alvah, but rare, Rev. Dr. Todd. Not in Mortlach list.

Sub-Class IV.—MONOCHLAMYDEAE.

ORDER L.—CHENOPODIACEAE.

1. CHENOPODIUM. GOOSE-FOOT.

1. C. *album*, Linn. *(White G.)*
Annual. Flowers in July and August. British type. Range in Britain, 50°—61°; coast line to 500 feet.

Fields and wastes. Frequent. Noted as in different parts of Kincardine. In Aberdeenshire, along the coast line, and also in the interior at Alford. In Banffshire it occurs in Mortlach.

2. C. *Bonus-Henricus*, Linn. *(Mercury G.)*
Perennial. Flowers in June and July. British type, (or English). Range in Britain, 50°—61°; coast line to 500 feet.

Waste places. Rather local.

K.—In the south parts of Kincardine, Mr. M'Farlane; in Garvock and Strachan, Dr. Stephen; Arbuthnot, Mr. Chrystall; Banchory-Ternan, Rev. J. Brichan.

A.—Road-side at Mile-end, Stocket, G. D.; in Alford, Rev. Dr. Farquharson; in Clatt, Rev. J. Minto; Inverkeithny, near the manse, Rev. J. Abel; in Buchan, Mr. A. Murray.

B.—In Alvah, but doubtfully indigenous, Rev. Dr. Todd; in Mortlach, Dr. L. Stewart.

2. ATRIPLEX. ORACHE.

1. A. *Babingtonii*, Woods. *(Spreading-fruited O.)*
Annual. Flowers, July to September. British type. Range in Britain, 50°—60°; coast line.
Sea-shore. Frequent, and perhaps along the whole coast line. There has been so much confusion respecting species of this genus that reports are not always to be depended on.

2. A. *patula*, Linn. *(Halberd-leaved S.)*
Annual. Flowers, June to September. British type. Range in Britain, 50°—60°; coast line to 500 feet.
Fields and wastes. Frequent, but less so in the more inland parts.

3. SALICORNIA. GLASSWORT.

1. S. *herbacea*, Linn. *(Jointed G.)*
Annual. Flowers in August and September. British type. Range in Britain, 50°—61°; coast line.
Salt marshes. Rare, and very local.
K.—At Brotherton, near Johnshaven, "Northern Flora."
A.—Edges of the salt marsh at the mouth of the Ythan, G. D.

4. SUAEDA. SEA-BLITE.

1. S. *maritima*, Dumort. *(Annual S.)*
Annual. Flowers in July and August. British type. Range in Britain, 50°—61°; coast only.
Salt marshes by the sea. Very rare and local.
K.—Kincardineshire coast, Mr. Chrystall.
A.—Mud banks at the mouth of the Ythan, G. D.

5. SALSOLA. SALTWORT.

1. S. *Kali*, Linn. *(Prickly S.)*
Annual. Flowers in July. British type, (or English). Range in Britain, 50°—58°; coast line.

Sandy sea-shore. Along all our coast line, but not very plentiful anywhere.

K.—Sandy beach at St. Cyrus, and near the mouth of the North Esk, Dr. Stephen.

A.—Occasionally from Aberdeen to Don-mouth; between the Preventive Station at Don-mouth and the sea, and along the coast to the Ythan, G. D. Mouth of the Ugie at Peterhead, Mr. A. Murray; also along the coast northwards.

B.—Shore at Cullen, Mr. Carmichael.

ORDER LI.—SCLERANTHACEAE.

SCLERANTHUS. KNAWEL.

1. S. *annuus*, Linn. *(Annual K.)*
Annual or Biennial. Flowers in July. British type. Range in Britain, 50°—58°; coast line to 1200 feet.

Fields and dry walls. Generally diffused, but not common.

K.—Arbuthnot; Banchory-Ternan.
A.—Tops of walls, &c. at Robslaw and Stocket; Robslaw quarry; road-side at Scotston; in dry pastures and edges of fields in Alford, Corgarff, Clatt, Buchan.
B.—Alvah; Mortlach.

ORDER LII.—POLYGONACEAE.

1. POLYGONUM. PERSICARIA, &c. &c.

1. P. *Bistorta*, Linn. *(Snakeweed.)*

Perennial. Flowers in June and July. British type.
Range in Britain, 50°—58°; coast line to 500 feet.

Moist pastures and woods. Rather local; sometimes growing in places where it might have escaped from cultivation, but so frequently in localities where it was not likely to have been introduced, that I do not hesitate to place it in the list.

K.—In south parts of Kincardine, Mr. M'Farlane; Arbuthnot, Mr. Chrystall; side of a stream opposite Ardo, Mr. P. Macgillivray.

A.—Near Aberdeen, in Den of Robslaw; wood above the old Bridge of Don, G. D. Seaton woods, Mr. P. Macgillivray; Monymusk and Kemnay, Mr. Burnett; Asloon, in Alford, Rev. J. Minto; abundant at Cobairdy, Rev. J. Abel; in the Buchan district, Mr. A. Murray.

B.—Duff-House Park, probably introduced, Rev. Dr. Todd.

2. P. *viviparum*, Linn. *(Viviparous alpine Bistort.)*
Perennial. Flowers in June and July. Highland type.
Range in Britain, 53°—61°; coast line to 2500 feet.

Natural pastures. Very general in the district; growing almost at the sea level. A few of the many stations may be here recorded.

K.—Arbuthnot, Mr. Chrystall; since 1836, on a grassy bank east side of the road half-way between Wellington Bridge and new Church of Nigg, where it still grows, (1859); in a meadow at the head of Corbie Den, Maryculter, G. D.; Banchory-Ternan, Rev. J. Brichan.

A.—Pastures east of Garlogie Mill, west from Aberdeen, Mr. P. Macgillivray; Normandyke, at Peterculter, Dr. J. Smith. Abundant about Ballater; very luxuriant by the Dee at Castleton; in alpine pastures,

Glen Callater, &c. &c., G. D. Alford, Rev. Dr. Farquharson; Corgarff, Mr. Barron; very abundant in Clatt and neighbouring parishes, Rev. J. Minto; Hill of Barra, Bourtie, Rev. J. Abel; Laithers at Turriff, Dr. Shier.

B.—About Banff, Stat. Account; parish of Alvah, but rare, Rev. Dr. Todd; in Mortlach, Dr. L. Stewart.

3. P. *aviculare*, Linn. *(Common Knot-grass.)*

Annual. Flowers, May to September. British type. Range in Britain, 50°—61°; coast to 1200 feet.

Waste places. Common in most parts of the district.

4. P. *Convolvulus*, Linn. *(Climbing P.)*

Annual. Flowers in July and August. British type. Range in Britain, 50°—60°; coast line to 1200 feet.

In fields. Frequent, and in all parts of the district, coast and inland, where cultivation extends. At Castleton; Corgarff; and Mortlach.

5. P. *amphibium*, Linn. *(Amphibious P.)*

Perennial. Flowers in July and August. British type. Range in Britain, 50°—61°; coast line to 500 feet.

Marshes, lakes, &c. Frequent in the lower districts, less common in the interior, but grows in Alford, and occurs also in Mortlach; in Clatt, var β, *terrestre*, is much more common than the aquatic form.

6. P. *Persicaria*, Linn. *(Spotted P.)*

Annual. Flowers, July to September. British type. Range in Britain, 50°—61°; coast line to 1350 feet.

Waste places. Frequent in the lower districts, less so in the interior, but found at Lin Mui, &c., near

Ballater; by the side of Loch Muick; in Clatt; and in Mortlach.

7. *P. lapathifolium*, Linn. *(Pale flowered P.)*

Annual. Flowers in July and August. British type, (or English). Range in Britain, 50°—58°; coast to 500 feet.

Fields and wastes. Seems to be rare in this district, I have seldom met with it.

K.—Banchory-Ternan, Dr. Adams.

A.—Near Aberdeen, upon the Inch at the harbour, and at the west end of the garden at the Links, near Bannermill, G. D.; Monymusk, Mr. Sutherland; at Alford, but rare, Rev. Dr. Farquharson; at Meldrum, Rev. J. Abel.

8. *P. Hydropiper*, Linn. *(Biting P.)*

Annual. Flowers in August and September. British type. Range in Britain, 50°—61°; coast line to 600 feet.

By lakes, &c., and in marshes. Rather uncommon, yet widely diffused in this district.

K.—Half-a-mile west of the Church of Strachan, Dr. Stephen; south bank of the Dee, at the bend below Morison's Bridge, Mr. P. Macgillivray; Banchory-Ternan, rare, Dr. Adams.

A.—Near Aberdeen, at Gilcomston Dam; Den of Robslaw; was very abundant at Justice Mill Dam, which being now filled up, the plant is extirpated, G. D. Drumnahoy in Cluny, Mr. Barron. By the margin of Loch Cannor, between Aboyne and Ballater, G. D.

B.—Haugh below Bridge of Alvah, Rev. Dr. Todd.

2. RUMEX. DOCK AND SORREL.

1. *R. crispus*, Linn. *(Curled D.)*

Perennial. Flowers, June to August. British type. Range in Britain, 50°—61°; coast line to 1200 feet.

Pastures and wastes. Common in the lower districts, but occurs also in the interior, as in Corgarff, at the height above stated.

2. R. *obtusifolius*, Linn. *(Blunt-leaved D.)*

Perennial. Flowers in July and August. British type. Range in Britain, 50°—60°; coast line to 1200 feet.

Way-sides and wastes. Frequent, occurs in Corgarff and other parts of the interior.

3. R. *aquaticus*, Linn. *(Grainless water D.)*

Perennial. Flowers in July and August. Scottish type. Range in Britain, 54°—61°; coast line to 1300 feet.

Moist places. Frequent in most parts of the district.

K.—Banchory-Ternan, Dr. Adams.

A.—Rather plentiful about Robslaw quarry, &c., G. D.; very general in the Braemar district, Mr. R. Mackay; in Clatt, Rev. J. Minto; Laithers, near Turriff, Dr. Shier; in Buchan district, Dr. A. Murray.

B.—At Gamrie, Rev. G. Gairdner; in Alvah, Rev. Dr. Todd.

4. R. *conglomeratus*, Murr. *(Sharp-leaved D.)*

Perennial. Flowers, June to August. British type, Range in Britain, 50°—61°; coast line to 500 feet.

Moist places. I believe this to be frequent in the district.

5. R. *Acetosa*, Linn. *(Common S.)*

Perennial. Flowers, May to August. British type. Range in Britain, 50°—61°; coast line to 3559 feet.*

Natural pastures. Frequent and generally diffused.

6. R. *Acetosella*, Linn. *(Sheep's S.)*
Perennial. Flowers, May to July. British type. Range in Britain, 50°—61°; coast line to 2100 feet.

Pastures. Abundant and general.

OXYRIA. MOUNTAIN-SORREL.

1. O. *reniformis*, Hooker. *(Kidney-leaved M.)*
Perennial. Flowers in July and August. Highland type. Range in Britain, 52°—60°; 50 to 3800 feet.

Moist rocks, &c. In the higher and inland parts abundant, descending also almost to the sea level along the course of the Dee.

K.—Banchory-Ternan, Dr. Adams; south bank of Dee at Nether-Banchory, G. D.

A.—On the margin of the Dee, north side, half a-mile above the old Bridge; and near the Manse of Drumoak, in this last place it was found by Dr. Skene, nearly 100 years ago, "In ripa arenosa, Dee, east of Drumoak," Skene MSS. At Ballater; Gairnside; Abergeldie; Castleton, &c., and abundant in Glen Callater, and on all the higher mountains, Lochnagar; Ben Avon; Ben-a-Buird; Little Craigendall; Ben Macdui, &c. &c.

* In a paper on altitudinal range of species in Aberdeenshire, (*London Journal of Botany*, Vol. II. 1843), I assigned to this species a very low altitude, and to the R. *Acetosella* one much higher. This being the very opposite of Mr. Watson's statements, he suspects that I may have, in making a note, substituted the one species for the other. Trusting to his great accuracy, I adopt his opinion. G. D.

B.—Cairngorm, Mr. R. Mackay ; in Mortlach, upon Corryhabbie, Dr. L. Stewart.

ORDER LIII.—EMPETRACEAE.

1. EMPETRUM. CROWBERRY.

1. E. *nigrum*, Linn. *(Black C.)*
Perennial. Flowers, April to June. Scottish type, (or Highland). Range in Britain, 51°—60°; coast to 4100 feet.

Pastures and heaths. In great profusion throughout the district ; on the coast, close by the sea, associated with the common plants which grow there, and at high elevations along with strictly alpine species.

ORDER LIV.—EUPHORBIACEAE.

1. MERCURIALIS. MERCURY.

1. M. *perennis*, Linn. *(Perennial or Dog M.)*
Perennial. Flowers, March to May. British type. Range in Britain, 50°—58° ; coast line to 1720 feet.

Woods and shady rocks. Frequent, but not a common plant, though widely diffused.

K.—Banks of the North Esk, Stat. Account. Burn of Benholme ; Shevoch, Durris, Dr. Stephen. Banchory-Ternan, Dr. Adams ; Corbie Den, Maryculter, G. D.

A.—Near Aberdeen, on the banks of the Dee above the old bridge : wood at the old Bridge of Don ; woods at Pitmedden, G. D. On the serpentine rocks at Ballater ; at Linn of Muick ; at Castleton and Corrymulzie, G. D. Woods on the ascent to Lochnagar, at the altitude above mentioned, Mr. Watson; in Alford, Rev. Dr. Farquharson; wood at toll-bar of Colnabaichan, Strathdon, Mr. Barron; banks of the Bogie, Rev. J. Minto; Mungo wood, Huntly Castle, Rev. J. Abel; in Den of Gight, G. D.; at Aberdour, Rev. G. Gairdner.

B.—Shady places along Deveron-side, Rev. Dr. Todd; in Mortlach, Dr. L. Stewart.

2. EUPHORBIA. SPURGE.

1. E. *helioscopia*, Linn. *(Sun S.)*

Annual. Flowers, June to September. British type. Range in Britain, 50°—61°; coast line to 1300 feet.

Fields and wastes. Frequent, wherever cultivation extends. Occurs in lower parts of the district, as well as in the more inland. Grows at Castleton; Corgarff; Clatt; Mortlach.

2. E. *Peplus*, Linn. *(Petty S.)*

Annual. Flowers, June to October. British type, (or English). Range in Britain, 50°—59°; coast line to 1100 feet.

Fields and waste ground. Though frequent and widely diffused, this species I believe to be less so than the first. It occurs at Castleton; in Clatt, but very scarce; is omitted from the list of Corgarff species; grows in Mortlach.

3. E. *exigua*, Linn. *(Dwarf S.)*

Annual. Flowers, July to September. English type, (or British). Range in Britain, 50°—58°; altitude?

Usually in fields. Very rare; it is probably often overlooked, and may yet be found more abundant in this district. It has possibly been introduced with agricultural seeds.

B.—In corn fields, near the old Castle of the Boyne, Rev. Andrew Wilson. I possess a specimen from this locality.

ORDER LV.—CALLITRICHACEAE.

1. CALLITRICHE. WATER STARWORT.

1. *C. verna*, Linn. *(Vernal W.)*
Annual. Flowers, April to September. British type.
Range in Britain, 50°—61°; coast line to 1250 feet.
Pools and streams. Abundant; and found in all parts of the district.

Var. β, *platycarpa*, occurs occasionally in different places near Aberdeen; it may have been overlooked in other places.

2. *C. autumnalis*, Linn. *(Water W.)*
Annual. Flowers, June to August. Scottish type.
Range in Britain, 53°—60°; at 200 feet.
In ditches and lakes. Very rare.
K.—Loch of Park, east end, G. D.

3. *C. pedunculata*, De Cand. *(Pedunculated W.)*
Annual. Flowers in July and August. British type.
Range in Britain, 50°—59°; at 2200 feet.
In lakes, &c. Very rare, perhaps like the last, often overlooked.

A.—Loch Kander, at the head of Glen Callater, Mr. Watson, where the plant has also been gathered by others.

ORDER LVI.—URTICACEAE.

1. URTICA. NETTLE.

1. U. *urens*, Linn. *(Small N.)*
Annual. Flowers, June to August. British type.
Range in Britain, 50°—61°; coast to 1200 feet.
Waste places. Frequent in the lower parts; occurs also in inland localities. Banchory-Ternan, Aboyne, Castleton, Alford, Clatt, Mortlach.

2. U. *dioica*, Linn. *(Great N.)*
Perennial. Flowers, June to September. British type.
Range in Britain, 50°—61°; coast to 1300 feet.
Waste places. General.

ORDER LVII.—MYRICACEAE.

1. MYRICA. GALE.

1. M. *Gale*, Linn. *(Sweet G. Bog Myrtle.)*
Perennial. Flowers, May to July. British type. Range in Britain, 50°—59°; coast line to 1400 feet.
In bogs and on marshy heaths. Frequent, formerly more so; extirpated in many localities by draining and reclaiming of land.

K.—South Kincardine, Arbuthnot, Kingcausie, Durris, Banchory-Ternan.

A.—Scotston, Belhelvie, Aboyne, Ballater, Castleton, Skene, Drumnahoy, Alford, Kinnethmont, &c. &c.

B.—Rare in parish of Alvah; abundant in mosses of Marnoch, Rev. Dr. Todd. Mortlach, Dr. L. Stewart.

ORDER LVIII.—BETULACEAE.

1. BETULA. BIRCH.

1. B. *alba*, Linn. *(Common B.)*

Perennial. Flowers in April and May. British type.
  Range in Britain, 50°—60°; 300 to 1900 feet.

Heathy and stony places. Wild only in the more inland districts, but abundant there. In the higher parts it is often in the form of a mere bush, where, along with Juniper, it occupies the place of the whin and broom, which have disappeared. In 1842 there existed on the estate of Invercauld a tree of this species 13 feet in girth at the soil. On the summit of the ridge north from Mount Keen, and at an elevation of 2200 feet, I have seen the dead remains of birches, far larger than any growing at lower altitudes on other mountains in the district.*

2. B. *nana*, Linn. *(Dwarf B.)*
Perennial. Flowers in May. Highland type. Range in Britain, 55°—58°; 1600 to 2100 feet.

Alpine heaths. Confined to the inland and higher portions of the district. Though rather local, yet very abundant where it grows.

A.—With Catkins, at the head of Loch Muick, Mr. Croall. On the ascent to Lochnagar, both from Garrawalt and head of Glen Callater; very fine and abundant about Loch Phadrig, east side of Glen Callater, G. D. On Little Craigendall, Mr. Sutherland; on Ben-a-Buird, Mr. R. Mackay.

B.—In Glen Avon, "Flora of Moray."

2. ALNUS. ALDER.

1. A. *glutinosa*, Gaertn. *(Common Alder.)*
Perennial. Flowers in March and April. British type.
  Range in Britain, 50°—59°; 200 to 1300 feet.

Wet meadows and river-sides. Rarely wild in the lower parts; often truly so in the interior. Large trees

---

* I cannot agree with those who admit another species, B. *glutinosa*; distinct gradations occur from one to the other.

of this species occur along the river Muick. I have seen very large stems of it taken from a depth of 20 feet, in a moss at Loirston, near Aberdeen.

ORDER LIX.—SALICACEAE

1. SALIX. WILLOW, &c.

1. S. *pentandra*, Linn. *(Bay-leaved W.)*
Perennial. Flowers in May and June. Scottish type. Range in Britain, 51°—58°; coast line to 500 feet.
Sides of rivers. Rare. Seldom wild in the lower, generally so in some of the inland parts of the district.
K.—Arbuthnot, Mr. Chrystall; Banchory-Ternan, Dr. Stephen.
A.—Near Aberdeen by the stream north-west from Robslaw quarry; west end of the Loch of Skene, G. D. Alford, and Tullynessle near Bridge of Alford, Rev. J. Minto; "In prato humido ad ripas *Don*, inter Newe et Glenbucket," Skene MSS.
B.—Alvah, Rev. Dr. Todd.

2. S. *angustifolia*, Wulf. *(Little tree W.)*
Perennial. Flowers in April. Highland type. Range in Britain, 55°—60°; 1300 to 1500 feet?
Moist places. Confined to the interior.
A.—Shores of Loch Muick, Mr. Croall.

3. S. *fusca*, Linn. *(Dwarf silky W.)*
Perennial. Flowers in April and May. British type. Range in Britain, 50°—61°; coast to 1900 feet.
Heaths and wastes. Frequent in one or other of its forms in all parts of the district.

4. S. *reticulata*, Linn. *(Reticulated W.)*
Perennial. Flowers in June and July. Highland type. Range in Britain, 56°—59°; 2000 to 3000 feet.

Moist rocks. Confined to the interior, and on the higher ranges only, and there rather local, yet abundant where it occurs.

A.—In great abundance on the rocks at the waterfall, head of Glen Callater, G. D.

5. S. *arenaria*, Linn. *(Downy Mountain W.)*

Perennial. Flowers in June and July. Highland type.

Range in Britain, 54°—60°; 2000 to 3700 feet.

Crevices of rocks. Confined to the interior, but there general and abundant.

A.—Rocks at the head of Glen Callater; upon Lochnagar, and ascending nearly to its summit; Ben Macdui, G. D. Ben-a-Buird and Ben Avon, Mr. R. Mackay.

6. S. *cinerea*, Linn. *(Grey Sallow.)*

Perennial. Flowers in March and April. British type.

Range in Britain, 50°—61°; 200 to 500 feet?

Banks of rivers. Very local.

K.—Woods of the Burn; Den of Canterland, &c., Mr. Croall.

A.—Near Aberdeen, at Den of Robslaw, and banks of Don; and on Bennachie, G. D. In Alford, Rev. Dr. Farquharson.

B.—In Alvah, Rev. Dr. Todd.

7. S. *aurita*, Linn. *(Round-eared S.)*

Perennial. Flowers in April and May. British type.

Range in Britain, 50°—61°; coast line to 2100 feet.

Moist woods, &c. Frequent and widely diffused.

K.—Frequent on the coast south from Aberdeen; Den of Leggart, &c., G. D. Banchory-Ternan, Rev. J. Brichan.

A.—Den of Maidencraig, G. D.; banks of the Dee at Murtle, Dr. A. Fleming; in Alford, Rev. Dr. Farquharson; Ballater, G. D.; Glen Clunie, and banks of Dee at Castleton, Mr. Croall.

B.—In Alvah, Rev. Dr. Todd.

8. S. *caprea*, Linn. *(Great round-leaved S.)*
Perennial. Flowers in April and May. British type.
Range in Britain, 50°—58°; coast line to 1600 feet.
Woods, &c. Occurs in different parts of the district, but is rather local.

A.—Ferryhill; banks of Dee and Don; Robslaw quarry; Alford; Clatt; Castleton, Braemar.

9. S. *nigricans*, Smith. *(Dark-leaved S.)*
Perennial. Flowers, April to June. Scottish type.
Range in Britain, 53°—58°; 100 to 2300 feet.
By streams and on moist rocks. Rather local.

A.—North bank of the Dee, at Nether-Banchory, G. D.

Var. γ, *rupestris*; Glen Callater, Mr. R. Mackay.
Var. ε, *hirta*; Corry of Loch Kander, Professor Macgillivray.

10. S. *phylicifolia*, Linn. *(Tea-leaved W.)*
Perennial. Flowers in April and May. Scottish type.
Range in Britain, 53°—58°; 1100 to 2200 feet?
By streams. Local; confined to the interior.

A.—Glen Callater, Professor Balfour; at Linn of Quoich, and by streams on the west side of Cairn Drochet, near Castleton, Mr. Gardiner.

11. S. *Arbuscula*, Linn. *(Small Tree W.)*
Perennial. Flowers in June and July. Highland type.
Range in Britain, 55°—60°; 1400 to 2400 feet?
In different habitats and localities, under one or other of its forms.

A.—Var. *Myrsinites*, Lightf.; shores of Loch

Muick, and frequent on the higher mountains, G. D.; head of Glen Callater, Mr. R. Mackay.

12. S. *Myrsinites*, Linn. *(Gt. Whortle-leaved W.)*

Perennial. Flowers in June. Highland type. Range in Britain, 56°—58°; 2200 to 2500 feet?
Confined to the inland and higher parts.
Little Craigendall, Mr. Croall.

Var. γ, *arbutifolia*, Glen Callater, Mr. R. Mackay; Corry of Loch Kander, Professor Macgillivray.

13. S. *herbacea*, Linn. *(Least W.)*

Perennial. Flowers in June. Highland type. Range in Britain, 52°—60°; 2100 to 4300 feet.

In gravelly and stony places on the higher mountains. The lowest altitude at which I have seen the plant in this district is that above mentioned, viz. below the top of the Buck of the Cabrach. It is one of the few species which attain the summit of Ben Macdui. Although very abundant on Lochnagar and others of the Braemar range, there are several mountains bordering on 3000 feet where I have searched for it in vain, viz. Mount Battock, Morven, and Mount Keen. The Buck of the Cabrach, lower than either of those mentioned, in common with them, is comparatively isolated, and distant from any of the higher ranges.

14. S. *lanata*, Linn. *(Woolly broad-leaved W.)*

Perennial. Flowers in June and July. Highland type. Range in Britain, 56°—57°; 2400 to 2700 feet.

Alpine rocks in the interior. Very rare. The only locality in the district where I have seen this—the most beautiful of our native species—is on rocks at the head of Glen Callater. It occurs also in the Corry of Loch Kander, at the head of a branch of the main glen to the west.

2. POPULUS. POPLAR.

1. P. tremula, Linn. *(Trembling Poplar or Aspen.)* Perennial. Flowers in March and April. British type. Range in Britain, 50°—60°; coast line to 1600 feet.

In woods and on rocks. Widely diffused in the district; often planted; rather local in the wild state.

K.—Den of Davo, Garvock; Glen Dye, Strachan, Dr. Stephen. Cliffs at Muchalls, G. D.; Banchory-Ternan, Rev. J. Brichan.

A.—Near Aberdeen, in Den of Maidencraig, and near Loch of Skene, G. D.; Howe of Corrichie, Hill of Fare, Mr. Barron; Craigs of Pannanich, and other places near Ballater; also at Castleton. In 1842 there was a tree of this species at Invercauld, having a girth of 10 feet 6 inches at the soil, G. D. Alford, Rev. Dr. Farquharson; Corgarff, Mr. Barron.

B.—Rocks at Bridge of Alvah, and at Den of Linhead, Rev. Dr. Todd; in Mortlach, Dr. L. Stewart.

ORDER LX.—CUPULIFERAE.

1. QUERCUS. OAK.

1. Q. Robur, Linn. *(Common British O.)* *
Perennial. Flowers in April and May. British type. Range in Britain, 50°—59°; coast line to 1500 feet

On rocks and in woods. It occurs in a wild state in various parts of the district.

K.— On the coast at Muchalls, in the form of stunted bushes, G. D.

* It is now generally admitted that there is only one British species.

A.—On the Buchan coast; about Ballater and Castleton; on the Pannanich cliffs, at the altitude above mentioned, G. D.

B.—Den at Linhead, Alvah, Rev. Dr. Todd.

2. CORYLUS. HAZEL.

1. C. *Avellana*, Linn. *(Common Hazel.)*

Perennial. Flowers, February to April. British type. Range in Britain, 50°—60°; coast to 1400 feet.

Woods and rocks. Generally diffused; more frequent in some parts of the interior. It is unnecessary to specify localities for this well known plant. At Corrymulzie Linn, near Castleton, I measured a trunk of it, cut near the base, and found it 26 inches in circumference; the concentric layers were sixty in number, which were mostly of uniform thickness, the first six and the ten last were, however, rather thinner than the others. The remains of this species are often met with in bogs, the nuts being found entire, along with the roots and branches of the parent trees on which they grew.

ORDER LXI.—CONIFERAE.

1. PINUS. FIR.

1. P. *sylvestris*, Linn. *(Scotch F.)*

Perennial. Flowers in May and June. Scottish type. Range in Britain, 56°—59°; 1500 to 2200 feet.

Truly wild examples of this tree are at present only found in the interior of the district; the numerous remains found in peat bogs in many parts where it does not now grow, indicate a more general distribution of it in a former epoch. This remark applies not merely to the lower parts, but also to the higher and more inland localities. The stems of the plant are to be seen in peat mosses at high altitudes, where such trees cannot grow at the present day. Mr. Watson (*Cybele Britannica*, Vol. II. p. 410), alludes to a trunk with a girth of 8 feet, at 550 yards of elevation, in Aberdeenshire, the upper limit of *fir woods* being at present about 1950 feet, where the trees attain far less size. In 1842, there existed in Mar Forest an example of this tree, measuring in girth at the base, 22 feet 4 inches; the age unknown. In the same year I found that some stumps of this species in the forest of Balachbuie, having 120 annual zones, measured 8 feet in circumference at the base; taking such as a standard, the patriarch of the Mar Forest must have been more than 300 years old. The results of numerous observations [*] lead to the conclusion, that the rate of growth of this valuable tree continues steady up to 70 years, diminishing from that period to 90 and upwards. In very aged trees the annual zones near the outside of the trunk are very thin, and not easily counted. A remarkable distortion of the trunks of the Scotch Fir occurs in some localities; the stems present the most fantastic shapes, and the letter S represents a form frequently assumed. Such effect is usually supposed to be produced by the drifting of snow upon the trees when young, and while their stems are still slender and flexible. In the upper parts of Glen Quoich, the numerous dead and bleached stems of the Scotch Fir have a very remarkable spiral twist in the wood; it is probable that this is owing merely to the continued action of eddy winds upon the trees during their whole life. Such spiral arrangement of the wood is not a natural structure. It has been observed also in the forests of North-eastern Europe, and I believe the same explanation given.

---

[*] For details the reader is referred to a paper "On the Forest Trees of Aberdeenshire," published in the *Scottish Quarterly Journal of Agriculture*, March, 1843.

2. JUNIPERUS. JUNIPER.

1. J. *communis*, Linn. *(Common J.)*
Perennial. Flowers in May. British type. Range in Britain, 50°—61°; coast to 2600 feet.

Woods, heaths, rocks. Generally diffused, but rather local along the coast.

K.—South parts of Kincardine, Mr. M'Farlane; Arbuthnot, Mr. Chrystall; Banchory-Ternan, Rev. J. Brichan.

A.—Near Aberdeen, in Hazlehead woods, G. D; Normandyke, Culter, Dr. J. Smith; Midmar woods, Mr. Barron. Abundant about Ballater and Castleton. Clatt, Rev. J. Minto; Forman Hill, Rev. J. Abel.

Var. β, *nana*. On the Khoil at Ballater; abundant on Morven; also in Braemar, G. D. Wells of Dee, Mr. Croall.

B.—Rocks at Bridge of Alvah, and about Dunlugas, sparingly, Rev. Dr. Todd; at Cullen, Mr. Carmichael; Mortlach, Dr. L. Stewart.

CLASS II.

MONOCOTYLEDONOUS, OR ENDOGENOUS FLOWERING PLANTS.

Sub-Class I.—PETALOIDEAE.

ORDER LXII.—ORCHIDACEAE.

1. MALAXIS. BOG-ORCHIS.

1. M. *paludosa*, Sw. *(Bog O.)*
Perennial. Flowers in July and August. British? type. Range in Britain, 56°—59°; 200 to 1600 feet.

Boggy places. Very rare; perhaps often overlooked owing to its small size.

K.—By the Burn of Bingley, Strachan, a little below the high road, Dr. Stephen; more abundant in a large marsh half-a-mile south of the above station, Mr. Sutherland.

A.—In boggy places by the side of the foot-path leading from Altguisach Cottage to Lochnagar, Mr. Barron. I possess specimens from this locality, the estimated height of which is that above mentioned. The measured height of Altguisach is about 1360 feet; the station of this plant is at least 200 feet higher. At Linn of Dee, Dr. S. Ogilvie.

2. EPIPACTIS. HELLEBORINE.

1. E. *latifolia*, Sw. *(Broad-leaved H.)*
Perennial. Flowers in July and August. British type, (or English). Range in Britain, 50°—59°; 300 to 800 feet?

Woods and shady places. Very rare in this district.

A.— In a wood west from Loch of Skene, and woods at Cluny, Mr. Cow.

B.—Craighalkie, Tomintoul, "Flora of Moray"; banks of the river at Inchrory, parish of Kirkmichael, Mr. Mackay and G. D.

3. LISTERA. TWAY-BLADE.

1. L. *ovata*, Brown. *(Common T.)*
Perennial. Flowers, May to July. British type. Range in Britain, 50°—59°; 50 to 1000 feet.

Woods and moist pastures. Rare.

K.—In a wood at Balmakewan, 600 yards south from the Free Church at Cross-roads, Dr. Simpson; in a small wood a little west from the house of Heathcot, in Banchory-Devenick, G. D.; at Kingcausie, Mr. Gammie.

A.—On the ascent to the farm of Lin Mui from the saw-mill in Glen Muick, Mr. Mackay and G. D. Very rare in Cromar; and near Huntly, Mr. Sutherland.

B.—Craighalkie, near Tomintoul, "Flora of Moray."

2. L. *cordata*, Brown. *Heart-leaved T.)*

Perennial. Flowers, June to August. Scottish type, (or Highland). Range in Britain, 51°—60°; coast line to 1700 feet.

In woods and among heath. Very general and abundant, so much so that it will be necessary to indicate but a few of the many stations.

K.—South parts of Kincardine, Mr. M'Farlane; with L. *ovata* at Balmakewan, Dr. Simpson; Banchory-Ternan, Rev. J. Brichan; about Caerloch, in Strachan, Dr. Stephen; among long heather on the hills at Nigg, G. D.

A.—Near Aberdeen, on Scotston moor; wood at Denmore; woods by the Skene road, west from Robslaw quarry, &c. G. D. Hill of Fare, Mr. Barron. In the interior at Pannanich; and on the Craig of Lin Mui, near Ballater; at Castleton, Braemar, G. D. Alford, Rev. Dr. Farquharson; Corgarff, Mr. Barron; woods of Knockespock, in great profusion, Rev. J. Minto; in woods at foot of Forman Hill, in Forgue, Rev. J. Abel; Cruden, Mr. A. Murray; parish of King Edward, Stat. Account.

B.—Frequent in fir woods in parish of Alvah, Rev. Dr. Todd; abundant in Mortlach, Dr. L. Stewart.

4. GOODYERA. GOODYERA.

1. G. *repens*, Brown. *(Creeping G.)*

Perennial. Flowers in August and September. Scottish type. Range in Britain, 56°—58°; 50 to 1000 feet.

Old fir woods. Abundant, and like *Trientalis* and

Linnaea, very generally diffused; the three species are often associated.

K.—Fir woods of Balmakewan, parish of Marykirk, Dr. Simpson; woods of Inglismaldie, Mr. Croall; woods at Nether-Banchory and Kingcausie, G. D.; Banchory-Ternan, Rev. J. Brichan.

A.—Near Aberdeen, woods at Scotston; Denmore; Parkhill; Hazlehead; by the Skene road, west from Robslaw quarry; and near Loch of Skene, G. D. In the forest of Ballachbuie, west from Balmoral, Mr. Croall; Gallowhill wood, Cluny, Mr. Barron; Monymusk, Mr. Cow; Alford, Rev. Dr. Farquharson; woods of Knockespock, Rev. J. Minto; Bourtie woods, Rev. J. Abel; parish of King Edward, Stat. Account.

B.—In Alvah, Rev. Dr. Todd; abundant in Mortlach, Dr. L. Stewart.

5. ORCHIS. ORCHIS.

1. O. *mascula*, Linn. *(Early purple O.)*
Perennial. Flowers in April and May. British type.
Range in Britain, 50°—61°; coast to 300 feet?
Woods and pastures. Very local in this district, and apparently confined to the lower parts.

K.—South parts of Kincardine, Mr. M'Farlane; Den Fenella; St. Cyrus cliffs; and moor between the Feugh and Blackness, Strachan, Dr. Stephen. Above the quarry at Stonehaven, and on the coast northward, G. D.; at Kingcausie, Mr. Gammie; birch wood at Durris, Mr. P. Macgillivray.

A.—In the wood at the old Bridge of Don, G. D.: at Peterculter, Professor Macgillivray; in Leochel Cushnie, Mr. Sutherland; at Cruden, Mr. A. Murray.

B.—In Alvah, but not common, Rev. Dr. Todd.

2. O. *latifolia*, Linn. *(Marsh O.)*
Perennial. Flowers in June and July. British type.
Range in Britain, 50°—61°; coast line to 600 feet.

Marshy places. Frequent and general in different parts of the district, from the coast line to the interior.

3. O. *maculata*, Linn. *(Spotted palmate O.)*
Perennial. Flowers in June and July. British type. Range in Britain, 50°—61°; coast to 3000 feet.
Natural pastures and heaths. Very frequent, and in all parts of the district.

6. GYMNADENIA. GYMNADENIA.

1. G. *conopsea*, Brown. *(Fragrant G.)*
Perennial. Flowers in June and July. British type. Range in Britain, 50°—61°; coast line to 2000 feet.
Natural pastures and heaths. Frequent in most parts of the three counties.

7. HABENARIA. HABENARIA.

1. H. *viridis*, Brown. *(Green H.)*
Perennial. Flowers in July and August. British type, (or Scottish). Range in Britain, 50°—61°; coast to 2500 feet.
Natural pastures and rocks. Frequent in the district, yet far from common.

K.—St. Cyrus' sands, plentiful, Mr. Croall; on moor of Benholme, and near Kirk of Garvock, Dr. Stephen; Banchory-Ternan, Dr. Adams; upper part of Den of Kingcausie, G. D.

A.—Near Aberdeen, in the links, north from the Coast-guard station at Don-mouth; on serpentine rocks by the Udny road, near Meadowbank, G. D. About Ballater, Mr. R. Mackay. Near the top of the hill, west from Linn of Quoich, at Castleton; and on the rocks in Glen Callater, G. D. On Little Craigendall, Mr. R. Mackay. In Clatt; Strathdon; and Rhynie, Rev. J. Minto. Sands of Forvie; and links of Foveran, Mr.

Cow. In Cruden; links of St. Fergus and Strathbeg, Mr. A. Murray.

B.—At Rosyburn, in Alvah, Rev. Dr. Todd; rare in Mortlach, Dr. L. Stewart.

2. H. *albida*, Brown. *(Small white H.)*
Perennial. Flowers in June and July. Scottish type. Range in Britain, 52°—61°; coast line to 1900 feet?

Natural pastures. Very local.

K.—Plentiful on the moor below Blackness, Strachan; coast one and a-half miles south of Muchalls, Dr. Stephen. Upper part of the Den of Kingcausie, G. D.; Banchory-Ternan, Rev. J. Brichan.

A.—Den of Maidencraig, on the Skene road, four miles west from Aberdeen, Mr. P. Grant; about Ballater, Mr. Croall; at the base of Ben Macdui, Mr. R. Mackay; in Alford, Rev. Dr. Farquharson; Auchindoir, Rev. J. Minto; Cruden, Mr. A. Murray.

B.—In Alvah, Rev. Dr. Todd.

3. H. *bifolia*, Brown. *(Lesser H.)*
Perennial. Flowers in July and August. British type. Range in Britain, 50°—59°; coast line to 1200 feet.

Moist pastures, &c. Generally diffused, but becoming less frequent in the most inland parts. The highest locality known to me is at Castleton, Braemar, in the birch wood at the Manse, where it was observed by Mr. Croall.

4. H. *chlorantha*, Babington. *(Great H.)*
Perennial. Flowers in June and July. English type, (or British). Range in Britain, 50°—59°; 80 feet above sea level.

Pastures and woods. Very rare.

K.—In the wood on north side of the avenue to Maryculter House, G. D.

ORDER LXIII.—IRIDACEAE.

1. IRIS.   IRIS.

1. I. *Pseudacorus*, Linn.   *(Yellow water I.)*
Perennial. Flowers in May and June. British type. Range in Britain, 50°—61°; coast to 500 feet.
Wet meadows. Frequent in the lower parts of the district, less so toward the interior; grows in Premnay, Alford, and Rhynie, but is not in the lists of Corgarff and Mortlach plants.

ORDER LXIV.—TRILLIACEAE.

1. PARIS.   HERB-PARIS.

1. P. *quadrifolia*, Linn.   *(Common H.)*
Perennial. Flowers in May and June. British type, (or English). Range in Britain, 50°—58°; 50 to 300 feet.
Moist woods. Very local and rare.

K.—Dens of Morphy and Fenella, Stat. Account; Corbie Den, Kingcausie, where it was first found by Dr. D. Skene, in 1767.

A.—Woods at Craibstone, near Aberdeen, Rev. Dr. Smith, late of Chapel of Garioch; woods of Kemnay, east of the house, Rev. J. Abel.

ORDER LXV.—LILIACEAE.

1. AGRAPHIS.   HYACINTH.

1. A. *nutans*, Link.   *(Wild H.)*
Perennial. Flowers, April to June. British type. Range in Britain, 50°—58°; coast to 200 feet.

Shady places. Very local, and chiefly confined to the lower parts of the district.

K.—Banchory-Ternan, Rev. J. Brichan; Hazel thicket at Collie's Heugh, Glen of Dye, Strachan, Dr. Stephen.

A.—Near Aberdeen, in Den of Robslaw; banks of the Dee; wood beside the old Bridge of Don, G. D. Aberdour, Rev. G. Gairdner.

B.—Among the rocks and steep banks below Bridge of Alvah, Rev. Dr. Todd.

2. ALLIUM. GARLIC.

1. A. *vineale*, Linn. *(Crow G.)*

Perennial. Flowers in June. English type, (or British). Range in Britain, 50°—58°; 20 to 150 feet.

Shady places. Very rare.

K.—St. Cyrus' cliffs, and Den Fenella, Dr. Stephen.

A.—Near Aberdeen, in the wood at the old Bridge of Don, where it was found by Dr. D. Skene nearly 100 years ago.

2. A. *ursinum*, Linn. *(Broad-leaved G.)*

Perennial. Flowers in May and June. British type. Range in Britain, 50°—58°; coast line.

Moist and shady places. Very local.

K.—South Kincardine, Mr. M'Farlane; Den Fenella, at the foot of the stair below the water-fall, Dr. Stephen; Corbie Den, Kingcausie, G. D.

A.—Den of Robslaw; wood at the old Bridge of Don, G. D. Den of Auchmedden, Rev. G. Gairdner, where it was also found by Dr. D. Skene.

B.—Formerly near Rannas; also at Woodside, Mr. Carmichael.

3. SCILLA. SQUILL.

1. S. *verna*, Huds. *(Vernal S.)*

Perennial. Flowers in April and May. Atlantic type. Range in Britain, 50°—61°; coast line.
Maritime pastures. Very local.

A.—Coast near Fraserburgh, G. D.

B.—Cliffs at Gamrie, Rev. G. Gairdner; sea-braes at Banff, Mr. G. C. Smith.

ORDER LXVI.—MELANTHACEAE.

1. TOFIELDIA. SCOTTISH ASPHODEL.

1. T. *palustris*, Hudson. *(Mountain S. A.)*
Perennial. Flowers in July and August. Highland type. Range in Britain, 54°—59°; 1300 to 2400 feet.

Alpine marshes. Rather local, and confined to the inland and higher parts.

A.—About the south margin of Loch Callater, Rev. J. Brichan; wet rocks, head of Glen Callater, G. D.; at a considerable elevation on Cairn Drochet, near Castleton, Mr. Gardiner; Ben-a-Buird and Ben Macdui, Mr. R. Mackay; in Corgarff, Mr. Barron.

ORDER LXVII.—JUNCACEAE,

1. JUNCUS. RUSH.

1. J. *effusus*, Linn. *(Soft R.)*
Perennial. Flowers in July. British type. Range in Britain, 50°—61°; coast to 1950 feet.
Marshy places. Frequent and general.

2. J. *conglomeratus*, Linn. *(Common R.)*
Perennial. Flowers in July. British type. Range in Britain, 50°—61°; coast to 1900 feet.

Marshy ground. Frequent; I have seen both upon Morven at 1900 feet.

3. *J. glaucus*, Ehrh. *(Hard R.)* *
Perennial. Flowers in July. English type, (or British). Range in Britain, 50°—57°; coast line.
Wet and shady places. Very rare.

K.—Den of Canterland, abundant, Mr. Croall : at Arbuthnot, Mr. Chrystall.

A.—At Aberdour, Rev. G. Gairdner.

4. *J. Balticus*, Willd. *(Baltic R.)*
Perennial. Flowers in July. Scottish type. Range in Britain, 56°—59°; coast to 100 feet.
Marshy shores, &c. Rare and local.

A.—Margin of the Loch of Park, south side, Dr. Adams; marsh upon the coast, a mile north of Donmouth, Mr. Cow; Mr. C. also discovered it in the Cruden links. Coast near Fraserburgh, G. D.; links at Rattray head, Mr. A. Murray.

5. *J. filiformis*, Linn. *(Thread R.)*
Perennial. Flowers in July and August. Intermediate type, (or Scottish). Range in Britain, 54°—55°; coast line.
Stony margins of lakes. Very rare.

K.—Stony margin of Loch Loirston, three miles south of Aberdeen; two miles from the sea, and 250 feet above its level, 1850, G. D.

6. *J. maritimus*, Smith. *(Lesser Sea R.)*
Perennial. Flowers in July and August. British type, (or English). Range in Britain, 50°—58°; coast line.
Marshes by the sea. Very rare.

---

* *J. diffusus*, Hoppe; reported as found in Kincardine, is considered as a mere variety of *J. glaucus*.

K.—Marshy places near the sea, at Muchalls, where I have seen several patches of it. First observed by Dr. Murray, author of the "Northern Flora."

7. J. *acutiflorus*, Ehrh. *(Sharp flowered R.)*
Perennial. Flowers, June to August. British type. Range in Britain, 50°—61°; coast line to 1200 feet.
Bogs and marshes. Frequent and general.

8. J. *lamprocarpus*, Ehrh. *(Shining-fruited R.)*
Perennial. Flowers in July and August. British type. Range in Britain, 50°—61; coast line to 2400 feet.
Marshy places. Frequent and general. It occurs on the Callater Rocks at the elevation above mentioned, G. D.

9. J. *uliginosus*, Sibth. *(Lesser Bog R.)*
Perennial. Flowers, June to August. British type. Range in Britain, 50°—61°; coast line to 2400 feet.
Bogs and pools. Frequent and general. It occurs on Morven at the elevation above mentioned, G. D.

10. J. *castaneus*, Smith. *(Clustered Alpine R.)*
Perennial. Flowers in July and August. Highland type. Range in Britain, 56°—57°; 2000 to 2400 feet.
Ledges of dripping rocks. Very rare.
A.—Rocks, head of Glen Callater, near the waterfall, G. D.

11. J. *trifidus*, Linn. *(Trifid R.)*
Perennial. Flowers in July and August. Highland type. Range in Britain, 56°—59°; 2200 to 4300 feet.
Gravelly and stony places. Confined to the higher and inland districts.

A.—By the side of the horse-path—its highest point—on the west shoulder of Mount Keen; Lochnagar, from 2400 feet to the summit; on the Callater Rocks, G. D. Little Craigendall; Ben Avon; summit of Ben-a-Buird, very fine, 9 to 10 inches in length; Braeriach, Mr. R. Mackay. Near the summit of Ben Macdui; and top of the Buck of the Cabrach, (2300 feet,) G. D. I have not found it on Mount Battock nor on Morven.

B.—On Cairngorm, Mr. R. Mackay.

12. J. *compressus*, Jacq. *(Round-fruited R.)*
Perennial. Flowers, June to August. British type. Range in Britain, 50°—61°; coast line.

Marshy places near the sea. Frequent along the coast line only.

K.—Not uncommon from Stonehaven to Aberdeen, G. D.

A.—Old-town Links; banks of the river Ythan, near the sea, G. D.

13. J. *bufonius*, Linn. *(Toad R.)*
Annual. Flowers in July. British type. Range in Britain, 50°—61°; coast line to 1200 feet.

Watery places. Frequent, and generally diffused. Occurs in Corgarff and Mortlach.

14. J. *squarrosus*, Linn. *(Heath R.)*
Perennial. Flowers in June and July. British type. Range in Britain, 50°—61°; coast line to 2300 feet.

Natural pastures. Very frequent, and widely diffused. It grows on Lochnagar at the altitude above mentioned.

15. J. *biglumis*, Linn. *(Two-flowered R.)*
Perennial. Flowers in July and August. Highland type. Range in Britain, 56°—58°; 2400 to ?

Alpine bogs. Very rare and local.

A.—I have gathered only a few specimens on the rocks beside the water-fall, at the head of Glen Callater, G. D.

B.—On Cairngorm, G. and D. Don, ("Flora Scottica.")

16. *J. triglumis*, Linn. *(Three-flowered R.)*
Perennial. Flowers in July and August. Highland type. Range in Britain, 53°—61°; 1200 to 2400 feet.

Alpine bogs. Rather local and rare; confined to the higher and inland parts, but often plentiful in certain places.

A.—In the marsh south-west from the "Invercauld Arms," at Castleton; on the Callater Rocks; and on Ben Macdui, G. D. Little Craigendall and Braeriach, Mr. R. Mackay.

2. LUZULA. WOOD-RUSH.

1. *L. sylvatica*, Bich. *(Great hairy W.)*
Perennial. Flowers in May and June. British type. Range in Britain, 50°—61°; coast line to 2500 feet.

Woods and shady rocks. Frequent and general.

2. *L. pilosa*, Willd. *(Broad-leaved hairy W.)*
Perennial. Flowers in March and April. British type. Range in Britain, 50°—61°; coast line to 1250 feet.

Woods and shady banks. Frequent and general.

3. *L. campestris*, Br. *(Field W.)*
Perennial. Flowers in April and May. British type. Range in Britain, 50°—61°; coast to 3000 feet.

Natural pastures, &c. Common and generally diffused. Is among the few plants on the summit of Morven nearly 3000 feet; and grows on Ben-a-Buird at the same elevation.

4. L. *arcuata*, Hook. *(Curved mountain W.)*
Perennial. Flowers in July. Highland type. Range in Britain, 56°—59°; 3700 to 4320 feet.
Gravelly and stony places at high elevations.

A.—Near the summit of Lochnagar, first observed by Professor Balfour; my former pupil, Mr. R. Mackay, has also gathered it in this locality. Braeriach, Mr. R. Mackay; summit of Ben Avon, but sparingly, Mr. Sutherland; Ben Macdui, rather abundant, and one of the few plants on the summit, G. D.

B.—On Cairngorm, Mr. R. Mackay.

5. L. *spicata*, De Cand. *(Spiked Mountain W.)*
Perennial. Flowers in July. Highland type. Range in Britain, 53°—59°; 1150 to 4300 feet.
Alpine rocks. Confined to the interior, and chiefly on the higher ranges.

A.—Upon the large boulders by the road-side between Bridge of Invercauld and Castleton, G. D.; I believe it was first observed there by Mr. Watson. On Lochnagar; very fine on the Callater Rocks; on Ben Macdui, G. D. Little Craigendall; Ben-a-Buird; Ben Avon; Braeriach, Mr. R. Mackay.

B.—Cairngorm, Mr. R. Mackay; on Belrinnes, "Flora of Moray."

3. NARTHECIUM. BOG-ASPHODEL.

1. N. *ossifragum*, Huds. *(Bog-Asphodel.)*
Perennial. Flowers in July and August. British type. Range in Britain, 50°—61°; coast line to 3200 feet.
Bogs and wet moors. Abundant and general.

ORDER LXVIII.—ALISMACEAE.

1. ALISMA. WATER PLANTAIN.

1. *A. Plantago*, Linn. *(Great W. P.)*

Perennial. Flowers in June and July. British type. Range in Britain, 50°—58°; coast line to 500 feet ?

Ditches, lakes, &c. Frequent in the lower parts of the district, less so in the intermediate, and, so far as I am at present aware, wanting in the more Highland parts, with the exception of Mortlach, where it is very rare.

K.—South Kincardine, Mr. M'Farlane; Arbuthnot, Mr. Chrystall; Mill-dam below Kirk of St. Cyrus, Dr. Stephen; Banchory-Ternan, Rev. J. Brichan; marshes at Maryculter, G. D.

A.—Near Aberdeen, in Dam of Gilcomston; dam north from old Bridge of Don, G. D. Loch of Skene, Mr. Barron; east end of Loch of Park, Dr. Stephen; ditches by the den at Morison's Suspension Bridge, Mr. Sutherland.

B.—In ponds, Deveron-side, Rev. Dr. Todd; rare in Mortlach, Dr. L. Stewart.

2. *A. ranunculoides*, Linn. *(Small W. P.)*

Perennial. Flowers, June to August. British type. Range in Britain, 50°—58°; coast line.

Marshy places. Very rare—only one station known to me.

A.—By the margin of Loch Strathbeg, parish of Crimond, Mr. Cow; I have gathered the plant there, associated with *Anagallis tenella*.

Order LXIX.—JUNCAGINACEAE.

1. TRIGLOCHIN.   ARROW-GRASS.

1. T. *Palustre*, Linn.   *(Marsh A.)*
Perennial. Flowers, June to August. British type. Range in Britain, 50°—61°; coast to 2050 feet.
Wet meadows, &c. Though widely diffused, yet more frequent in the lower districts.

2. T. *maritimum*, Linn.   *(Sea-side A.)*
Perennial. Flowers, June to September. British type. Range in Britain, 50°—61°; coast line only.
Marshes near the sea. Frequent along the whole coast.

Order LXX.—TYPHACEAE.

1. SPARGANIUM.   BUR-REED.

1. S. *ramosum*, Huds.   *(Branched B.)*
Perennial. Flowers in July. British type. Range in Britain, 50°—60°; coast line to 500 feet.
Ditches and pools. Not unfrequent, and rather general in the district.

K.—South Kincardine, Mr. M'Farlane; Arbuthnot, Mr. Chrystall; Banchory-Ternan, Rev. J. Brichan.

A.—Near Aberdeen, abundant in ditches at the brick-work in the Old-town Links, G. D.; Upper Drumnahoy, in Cluny, Mr. Barron; Alford, Rev. J. Farquharson; Auchindoir, Rev. J. Minto; in Cruden, Mr. A. Murray.

B.—In Alvah, Rev. Dr. Todd; Loch Park, in Mortlach, Dr. L. Stewart.

2. S. *simplex*, Huds.   *(Unbranched B.)*
Perennial. Flowers in July. British type. Range in Britain, 50°—58°; 60 to 500 feet.

Ditches and pools. Rather rare and local.

K.—Moss of Arnhall, Mr. Croall; Den of Jackstone, St. Cyrus, Dr. Stephen; ditch in the wood at the north side of the avenue to Maryculter House, Dr. A. Fleming.

A.—Ditches at Braediach moss, in parish of Skene; and at Loch of Skene, G. D. In Alford, Dr. Murray; in parish of Aberdour, Rev. G. Gairdner.

B.—In Alvah, Rev. Dr. Todd.

3. S. *natans*, Linn. *(Floating B.)*

Perennial. Flowers in August. British type. Range in Britain, 50°—60°; coast line to 1600 feet.

In lakes and bog pools. Frequent, and generally diffused.

K. — South Kincardine, Mr. M'Farlane; marsh above Kirk of Garvock, Dr. Stephen; Arbuthnot, Mr. Chrystall; Banchory-Ternan, Rev. J. Brichan.

A.—Near Aberdeen, at Scotston bogs; Braediach moss, in Skene, G. D. In Glen Clunie, at Castleton, Mr. J. T. Syme; in Loch Callater, G. D.; bogs at the base of Ben Macdui, Mr. R. Mackay; in Burn of Cluny, Mr. Barron; in Alford, Dr. Murray; in peat bogs, parish of Clatt, Rev. J. Minto; at Aberdour, Rev. G. Gairdner.

B.—In Alvah, Rev. Dr. Todd.

4. S. *minimum*, Bauh. *(Small B.)*

Perennial. Flowers in July. British type, (or Scottish). Range in Britain? Local at 50 feet.

In bog pools. Very rare?

A.—In the moss at Farm of Fyfe, in Belhelvie, six miles north from Aberdeen, G. D. It is possible that some of the stations for S. *natans* may belong to this species.

ORDER LXXI.—PISTIACEAE.

1. LEMNA. DUCKWEED.

1. *L. minor*, Linn. *(Lesser D.)*
Annual. Flowers in July. British type. Range in Britain, 50°—60°; coast to 500 feet.
Stagnant waters. Frequent, especially in the lower, rare in the intermediate parts, and apparently absent in the most inland, excepting Mortlach, where, however, it is rare.

K.—Arbuthnot; abundant in Nigg, &c. &c.

A.—Not unfrequent at Aberdeen, Alford, Clatt, Cruden.

B.—Alvah; in Mortlach, but rare.

2. *L. trisulca*, Linn. *(Ivy-leaved D.)*
Annual. Flowers in June and July. English type, (or British). Range in Britain, 50°—57°; 150 to 500 feet?
Stagnant waters. Very rare.

K.—Mill-dam at Stone of Morphy, Mr. Croall.

B.—In Mortlach, very rare, Dr. L. Stewart.

ORDER LXXII.—NAIADACEAE.

1. POTAMOGETON. PONDWEED.

1. *P. pectinatus*, Linn. *(Fennel-leaved P.)*
Perennial. Flowers in June and July. British type. Range in Britain, 50°—61°; coast line only.
Lakes and ponds. Very rare and local.

A.—In the small lakes in the Old-town Links, north from the Broadhill, G. D.; at St. Fergus, Stat. Account.

2. P. *pusillus*, Linn. *(Small P.)*
Perennial. Flowers in July. British type. Range in Britain, 50°—60°; coast line to 500 feet.

In pools and ditches. Rather local, and apparently more frequent in the lower districts.

K.—South Kincardine, Mr. M'Farlane. Benholme; Mill-dam, Brotherton; Sooty Wells, near Kirk of Garvock, Dr. Stephen. Banchory-Ternan, Rev. J. Brichan; Maryculter, below ninth mile-stone, Dr. Stephen.

A.—Ditches at Stocket, near Aberdeen; Loch of Park, G. D. Balfluig moss, in Alford, Rev. J. Minto. In parts of Huntly, Drumblade, and Forgue, Rev. J. Abel.

B.—Ponds on Haughs of Clayfolds, Alvah, Rev. Dr. Todd.

3. P. *gramineus*, Linn. *(Grassy P.)*
Perennial. Flowers in July. English type, (or British). Range in Britain, 50°—58°; 200 to 400 feet ?

In lakes. Very rare and local in this district.

K.—Abundant in Loch of Park, twelve miles west from Aberdeen, G. D.

A.—Loch of Auchlossan, in Lumphanan, Dr. Murray.

4. P. *crispus*, Linn. *(Curled P.)*
Perennial. Flowers in June and July. British type, (or English). Range in Britain, 50°—59°; 50 to 200 feet ?

Ditches and rivers, &c. Very local in the district.

K.—South Kincardine, Mr. M'Farlane.

A.—Near Aberdeen, in Gilcomston Dam, and the rivulet running from it; in a mill-dam north from new Bridge of Don, G. D. In the river Ythan, Dr. Murray; in the Buchan district, Mr. Cow; at Laithers, near Turriff, Dr. Shier.

B.—In Deveron, Rev. Dr. Todd.

5. **P. perfoliatus,** Linn. *(Perfoliate P.)*
Perennial. Flowers in July. British type. Range in Britain, 50°—60° ; 50 to 400 feet ?
Ditches and lakes. Rather local.

K.—South parts of Kincardine, Mr. M'Farlane ; parish of Arbuthnot, rare, Mr. Chrystall ; Loch of Park, G. D.

A.—In Corbie Loch, and Loch of Skene, G. D. ; in the river Don, Dr. Murray ; and in the river Philorth, near the bridge, Dr. Murray ; at Laithers, near Turriff, Dr. Shier.

B.—Parish of Alvah, Rev. Dr. Todd ; in the Deveron, at Forglen House, Mr. G. C. Smith ; in Mortlach, Dr. L. Stewart.

6. **P. praelongus,** Wulf. *(Long-stalked P.)*
Perennial. Flowers in July. Scottish type, (or Intermediate). Range in Britain, 51°—58° ; 600 to 1600 feet ?
In lakes. Very rare.

A.—In Loch Cannor, west from Aboyne, Dr. Murray. I believe that it also grows in Loch Callater, but this locality is recorded for the present as rather doubtful, G. D.

7. **P. lucens,** Linn. *(Shining P.)*
Perennial. Flowers in June and July. English type, (or British). Range in Britain, 50°—58° ; 200 to 1100 feet.
In lakes and streams. Rather local.

K.—In parish of Arbuthnot, rare, Mr. Chrystall.

A.—In the river Muick, above the Linn, G. D. ; in the river Don, Dr. Mitchell ; Balfluig moss, Alford, Dr. Murray ; Laithers, near Turriff, Dr. Shier.

B.—In the Deveron, Mr. G. C. Smith.

8. **P. heterophyllus,** Schreb. *(Various leaved P.)*

Perennial. Flowers in June and July. British type, (or English). Range in Britain, 50°—61°; 150 to 1600 feet.

In lakes. Rather local.

K.—Banchory-Ternan, Dr. Adams; Loch of Park, abundant, G. D.

A.—Near Aberdeen, in the Corbie Loch, G. D.; in Lumphanan and at Kincardine O'Neil, Dr. Murray; in Loch Callater, G. D.; in Loch of Skene, Mr. Barron; at St. Fergus, Stat. Account.

9. P. lanceolatus, Smith. *(Lanceolate P.)*

Perennial. Flowers in July. British type, (or English). Range in Britain, 51°—61°? 100 to 300 feet?

Lakes and pools. Very local.

K.—South parts of Kincardine, Mr. M'Farlane; Loch of Leys, Dr. Adams; Loch of Park, G. D.

A.—Formerly in the Aberdeen Canal; Corbie Loch, and Loch of Skene, G. D.

B.—In the Deveron, Rev. Dr. Todd; in parish of Mortlach, Dr. L. Stewart.

10. P. rufescens, Schrad. *(Reddish P.)*

Perennial. Flowers in July. British type. Range in Britain, 50°—59°; 100 to 400 feet?

Lakes and streams. Very local.

A.—Formerly in great profusion in the Aberdeen Canal, G. D.; in different parts of the river Don, and in the Corbie Loch, near Aberdeen, Dr. Murray; in the river Gaddie, at Premnay, Rev. Dr. Smith; Laithers, near Turriff, Dr. Shier.

B.—Rare in Alvah, Rev. Dr. Todd.

11. P. oblongus, Viv. *(Oblong-leaved P.)*

Perennial. Flowers in July. British type. Range in Britain, 50°—60°; coast line to 1900 feet?

In shallow pools. Probably general. This—if it be a good species—is so generally confounded with the next, that perhaps some of the localities for the one may belong to the other. P. *oblongus* I believe to be the one which sometimes occurs at considerable height in the interior, as on the table land above Pannanich, &c.

12. P. *natans*, Linn. *(Sharp-fruited broad-leaved P.)*

Perennial. Flowers in June and July. British type. Range in Britain, 50°—61°; coast line to 400 feet ?

Stagnant waters and slow streams. Probably general. A species under this name is reported from all parts of the district; as already stated, some of the localities may really refer to P. *oblongus*; my own specimens, found at Aberdeen, belong to this species.

2. RUPPIA. RUPPIA.

1. R. *maritima*, Linn. *(Sea R.)*

Perennial. Flowers in July and August. British type. Range in Britain, 50°—61°; coast only.

Salt water pools and ditches. Rare.

Var. β, *rostellata*.

K.—Near Bervie, " Northern Flora." Salt marshes at Torry farm, south side of Aberdeen harbour, this species was discovered here by Rev. J. Minto, in 1849.

B.—At the mouth of the Deveron at Banff, Mr. Thomas Edwards. *

---

* Zostera *marina*, Linn. I have seen cast up on the beach at Aberdeen, but have no record of it in situ. The specimens were doubtless drifted from a distance. The estuary of the Ythan is the place most likely to yield it in this district.

Sub-Class II.—GLUMACEAE.

Order LXXIII.—CYPERACEAE.

1. SCHŒNUS. BOG-RUSH.

1. S. *nigricans*, Linn. *(Black B.)*
Perennial. Flowers in June and July. British type.
Range in Britain, 50°—61°; coast to 1600 feet.
Wet moors and in marshes. Very local.

K.—In a wet hollow at the base of the sea cliffs opposite to Finnan, G. D.

A.—Abundant in the bog opposite to Scotston House, near the north-west corner of the wood at Denmore, G. D. By the side of the Udny road, seven miles north from Aberdeen. In Glen Muick, G. D. Near Ballater, and in Glen Callater, Mr. R. Mackay.

B.—In Mortlach, Dr. L. Stewart.

2. RHYNCOSPORA. BEAK-RUSH.

R. *alba*, Vahl. *(White B.)*
Perennial. Flowers in July and August. British type.
Range in Britain, 50°—61°; 700 to 1500 feet?
Wet pastures and in bogs. Very rare.

K.—Bogs in Strachan, Stat. Account; a large tuft by the road half a-mile south of Bogendreep, Strachan, 1857, Mr. Sutherland.

A.—In Glen Muick, near Ballater; and at the base of Ben-a-Buird and Ben Avon, Mr. R. Mackay. Hill of Clock-farley, parish of King Edward, Mr. Thomas Edwards.

B.—In Mortlach, Dr. L. Stewart.

3. BLYSMUS. BLYSMUS.

1. B. *rufus*, Link. *(Narrow-leaved B.)*

Perennial. Flowers in July. Scottish type. Range in Britain, 53°—61°; coast line.

Marshy spots near the sea. Rather local, but along the whole coast line.

K.—Coast at Brotherton, near Johnshaven, "Northern Flora." Coast north from Stonehaven at Garron Point; and near Portlethen, G. D.

A.—Formerly in the links at Aberdeen, north from the Broadhill, and along with *Carex incurva*, Dr. Murray; Cruden coast, and at Ugie mouth, Mr. A. Murray.

B.—Coast at Banff, Dr. Shier; links at Boyndie, Mr. G. C. Smith.

4. ELEOCHARIS. SPIKE-RUSH.

1. *E. palustris*, Br. *(Creeping S.)*

Perennial. Flowers in June and July. British type. Range in Britain, 50°—61°; coast line to 1200 feet.

By ditches and in marshes. Generally diffused.

Var. β, *uniglumis*, Link. In the links—north from the Broadhill, Aberdeen—by the margin of the south lake, G. D.

2. *E. multicaulis*, Smith. *(Many-stalked S.)*

Perennial. Flowers in July. British type. Range in Britain, 50°—60°; coast to 200 feet ?

In marshy places. Rather local.

K.—St. Cyrus; Bervie, &c. Dr. Stephen. Marshes at Bay of Nigg, G. D.; at Banchory-Ternan, Rev. J. Brichan.

A.—Bog at Smithyhill, Alford; and at Kincardine O'Neil, "Northern Flora." This species is probably often mistaken for *E. palustris;* hence the paucity of stations in this district.

5. ISOLEPIS. MUD-RUSH.

1. I. fluitans, R. Br. *(Floating M.)*
Perennial. Flowers in June and July. British type. Range in Britain, 50°—60°; coast line to 600 feet ?
Lakes and pools. Not very common.

K.—South Kincardine, Mr. M'Farlane; moss of Forth, Garvock, Dr. Stephen; in the marsh above the Bay of Nigg; and at Maryculter, near the house, G. D. Loch of Leys, Dr. Adams.

A.—Marshes at Scotston and Hilton, G. D.; in Belhelvie links, eight miles north from Aberdeen, Dr. A. Fleming; near Aboyne, Stat. Account; on the Hill of Fare, Mr. Barron; Loch of Park, Dr. Stephen.

2. I. setacea, R. Br. *(Bristle-stalked M.)*
Perennial. Flowers in July and August. British type. Range in Britain, 50°—60°; coast line to 1200 feet.
Moist gravelly places. Rather local.

K.—Frequent at St. Cyrus; Garvock, &c. Dr. Stephen. Marshes near new Church of Nigg; and near Mill of Leggart, G. D. Banchory-Ternan, Rev. J. Brichan.

A.—Near Aberdeen, at Stocket moor, and in Belhelvie Links, G. D.; Upper Drumnahoy, Cluny, Mr. Barron; by the west margin of Loch Cannor, and near Ballater, G. D.; in Alford, Rev. Dr. Farquharson; in Corgarff, Mr. Barron; in Clatt, Rev. J. Minto.

B.—In Alvah, Rev. Dr. Todd; banks of the Spey, in Mortlach, Dr. L. Stewart.

6. SCIRPUS. CLUB-RUSH OR BULL-RUSH.

1. S. lacustris, Linn. *(Lake C. or B.)*
Perennial. Flowers in July and August. British type. Range in Britain, 50°—61°; 100 to 600 feet.

Lakes and ponds. Very local.

K.—Lochs of Park and Leys, Dr. Adams.

A.—Corbie Loch, a few miles north from Aberdeen ; and in the river Ythan below Ellon, G. D. Also in the interior at Loch Cannor.

2. S. *maritimus*, Linn. *(Salt-marsh C.)*

Perennial. Flowers in July and August. British type, (or English). Range in Britain, 50°—58° ; coast line.

In salt marshes. Rare in this district.

K.—Mouth of the North Esk, and coast south of Gourdon, Dr. Stephen.

A.—In Old-town Links, a little north-east from the brick-work ; and estuary of the Ythan, near the sea, G. D.

3. S. *sylvaticus*, Linn. *(Wood C.)*

Perennial. Flowers in July. British type, (or English). Range in Britain, 50°—58° ; 50 to 350 feet ?

Moist woods and banks of rivers. Very local.

K.—Banks of the Burn of Beltie, near Glassel, Dr. Adams.

A.—North bank of the Don above the old bridge, Mr. P. Macgillivray ; at Paradise, Monymusk, "Northern Flora ; " banks of the Burn of Tarty, near Newburgh, Dr. A. Fleming ; north bank of the Ythan, above the bridge at Ellon, G. D. ; banks of the Bogie, below Manse of Huntly, "Northern Flora ; " by the river Gaddie, in Premnay, Rev. Dr. Smith ; in Buchan, Mr. A. Murray.

B.—In Alvah, Rev. Dr. Todd.

4. S. *pauciflorus*, Lightf. *(Few-flowered C.)*

Perennial. Flowers in July and August. British type. Range in Britain, 50°—58° ; coast line to 1800 feet.

Wet moors. Not unfrequent throughout the district.

K.—Marshes in Benholme ; Garvock ; Strachan, Dr. Stephen. Banchory-Ternan, Rev. J. Brichan.

A.—Near Aberdeen, in the Old-town Links, and marshy places by the river Dee, G. D. ; on the Hill of Fare, Mr. Barron ; in Alford, Rev. Dr. Farquharson ; in parish of Clatt, not unfrequent, Rev. J. Minto ; at the south base of Morven, and in Glen Muick, two to three miles from Ballater, G. D.

5. S. caespitosus, Linn. *(Scaly-stalked C.)*
Perennial. Flowers in June and July. British type.
Range in Britain, 50°—61° ; coast line to 3500 feet.
Moist moors and heaths. Abundant and general.

7. ERIOPHORUM. COTTON-GRASS.

1. E. vaginatum, Linn. *(Hare-tail C.)*
Perennial. Flowers in March and April. British type.
Range in Britain, 50°—61° ; 100 to 2500 feet.
Bogs and moist moors. Widely diffused, but not a common species.

K.—At Kirk of Garvock, Dr. Stephen ; Banchory-Ternan, Rev. J. Brichan ; Nigg, G. D.

A.—Near Aberdeen, at Corbie Loch ; Braediach moss, parish of Skene, and near Loch of Skene, G. D. In Cluny, Mr. Barron ; on Lochnagar, Ben Macdui, &c. G. D. ; in Clatt and Tullynessle, Rev. J. Minto ; at Cruden, Mr. A. Murray ; in parish of Aberdour, Rev. G. Gairdner.

B.—Marshy places near Moss-town, in Alvah, but rare, Rev. Dr. Todd ; in Mortlach, Dr. L. Stewart.

2. E. angustifolium, Roth. *(Narrow-leaved C.)*
Perennial. Flowers in April and May. British type.
Range in Britain, 50°—61° ; coast line to 3500 feet.
Bogs and moors. Frequent and general.

8. CAREX. CAREX OR SEDGE.

1. C. *dioica*, Linn. *(Diœcious C.)*

Perennial. Flowers in May and June. Scottish type, (or British). Range in Britain, 50°—61°; 200 to 2300 feet?

In spongy bogs. Generally diffused.

K.—Den of Canterland, Mr. Croall; bogs near Church of Nigg, G. D.; Banchory-Ternan, Rev. J. Brichan.

A.—Near Aberdeen, on Stocket moor, and in the Scotston moss, G. D.; Hill of Fare, Mr. Barron; at Castleton, in the bog behind Craig Koynach, Mr. Croall; in Glen Callater, Mr. A. K. Clark; in Alford, Rev. Dr. Farquharson; common in Clatt, Rev. J. Minto.

B.—In Alvah, Rev. Dr. Todd.

2. C. *pulicaris*, Linn. *(Flea C.)*

Perennial. Flowers in May and June. British type. Range in Britain, 50°—61°; coast line to 2000 feet.

In boggy places. Frequent and general.

K.—St. Cyrus; Garvock; Benholme, Dr. Stephen. Bogs near new Church of Nigg; marshes at head of Corbie Den, Maryculter, G. D. Banchory-Ternan, Rev. J. Brichan.

A.—Near Aberdeen, on Stocket moor; at Scotston bog, &c. G. D. Hill of Fare, and Gallowhill, Cluny, Mr. Barron. North bank of Dee below Free Church, Ballater; on the Hill of Khoil; Morven, &c.; and in Glen Callater, G. D. Lochnagar, Mr. R. Mackay; in Alford, Rev. Dr. Farquharson; Clatt, Rev. J. Minto; Corgarff, Mr. Barron.

B.—Alvah, Rev. Dr. Todd; Mortlach, Dr. L. Stewart.

3. **C. rupestris**, All. *(Rock C.)*
Perennial. Flowers in July. Highland type. Range in Britain, 56°—58°; 2000 to 2400 feet?

Moist alpine rocks. Very local, but usually abundant where it grows.

A.—At the waterfall, Glen Callater. On August 2, 1836, this plant was added to the British list, a few specimens having been picked at that date. Some days afterwards, when in company with my friend Dr. Templeton, it was found in great profusion. Little Craigendall, first found there by Professor Balfour.

4. **C. pauciflora**, Lightf. *(Few-flowered C.)*
Perennial. Flowers in June and July. Highland type. Range in Britain, 54°—59°; 800 to 2000 feet.

Alpine moors. Local; chiefly in the interior of the district.

K.—Caerlock Hill, Strachan, and on Cairnmonearn, Durris, Dr. Stephen; east base of Clochnaben, Professor Macgillivray; Banchory-Ternan, Rev. J. Brichan.

A.—North side of Hill of Fare, (800 feet,) above Midmar Castle, Mr. Mackay and G. D.; about Ballater, Mr. R. Mackay; on Morven, Mr. Sutherland; Lochnagar, Dr. Greville; Glen Callater, G. D.; Ben Macdui, Mr. Watson.

5. **C. incurva**, Lightf. *(Curved C.)*
Perennial. Flowers in June. Scottish type. Range in Britain, 56°—61°; coast line only.

Wet places near the sea. Very local and rare.

K.—Coast at Garron Point, north from Stonehaven; and also at Muchalls, G. D.

A.—In the Old-town Links by the side of a road through the sand-hills a little north from the Broadhill, G. D.; links of Strathbeg, Mr. A. Murray.

6. **C. ovalis**, Gooden. *(Oval-spiked C.)*

Perennial. Flowers in June. British type. Range in
Britain, 50°—61°; coast to 1250 feet.
Marshy places. Generally diffused.

K.—St. Cyrus; Durris; Strachan, Dr. Stephen.
Occasionally along the coast from Stonehaven to Aberdeen, G. D.; Banchory-Ternan, Rev. J. Brichan.

A.—Stocket moor; banks of the Dee at the old bridge, &c. &c. G. D. In Cluny, Mr. Barron; Alford, Rev. Dr. Farquharson; Corgarff, Mr. Barron; in Clatt, Rev. J. Minto; Aberdour, Rev. G. Gairdner.

B.—In Mortlach, Dr. L. Stewart.

7. *C. stellulata*, Gooden. *(Prickly-headed C.)*
Perennial. Flowers in June. British type. Range in
Britain, 50°—60°; coast line to 2300 feet.
Marshy places. General in the district.

8. *C. curta*, Gooden. *(White C.)*
Perennial. Flowers in June. British type. Range in
Britain, 50°—58°; coast line to 3500 feet.
Spongy bogs. Rather local.

K.—Arbuthnot, rare, Mr. Chrystall.

A.—Near Aberdeen, formerly in Ferryhill moss; bog at north side of Corsehill, near Scotston; and Braediach moss, in Skene, G. D. Moss at Leggerdale, twelve miles west from Aberdeen, Mr. Barron; Alford, Rev. Dr. Farquharson; abundant in Clatt, Rev. J. Minto; Corgarff, Mr. Barron.

Var. β, *Persoonii*. Upon Lochnagar at 3500 feet, G. D.

B.—Alvah, Rev. Dr. Todd.

9. *C. leporina*, Linn. *(Hare's-foot C.)*
Perennial. Flowers in July. Highland type. Range
in Britain, 56°—58°; 3560 feet.
Moist alpine rocks. Very rare.

A.—This plant was added to the British Flora on 6th August, 1836. Dripping rocks at the south-west corner of the table top of Lochnagar, two to three hundred feet below the top, G. D.; on Cairntoul, Professor Balfour.

10. *C. remota,* Linn. *(Distant-spiked C.)*

Perennial. Flowers in June. British type, (or English). Range in Britain, 50°—58°; local at 100 feet.

Moist shady places. Very rare.

K.—Corbie Den, Kingcausie, Dr. J. Smith.

11. *C. Boenninghausiana,* Weihe. *(Boenninghausen's C.)*

Perennial. Flowers in June. Germanic type? Range in Britain, 50°—58°.

Marshes, &c. Very rare.

B.—Culreach, near Gordon Castle, Mr. Stables.

12. *C. teretiuscula,* Gooden. *(Less panicled C.)*

Perennial. Flowers in June. British type, (or English). Range in Britain, 50°—58°; 100 to 200 feet.

Marshy places. Rare.

A.—Moss on the north side of Corschill, near Scotston; and marsh by the side of the Udny road, seven miles north from Aberdeen, G. D. Scotston moss, Mr. P. Macgillivray.

13. *C. vulpina,* Linn. *(Great C.)*

Perennial. Flowers in June. British type. Range in Britain, 50°—58°; coast only.

Moist shady places. Rare.

K.—Coast between Stonehaven and Aberdeen, at Portlethen; Finnan; and the Cove, G. D.

A.—" In the Old-town Links," Dr. D. Skene.

14. *C. muricata,* Linn. *(Greater prickly C.)*

Perennial. Flowers in May and June. British type.
Range in Britain, 50°—58°; coast to 100 feet.
Gravelly places. Very local.

K.—St. Cyrus, Dr. Stephen; at Thornyhive, south from Stonehaven, and between the latter and Portlethen, to the north, G. D.

A.—North bank of the Dee, below the Manse of Drumoak, G. D.

15. C. *arenaria*, Linn. *(Sea C.)*
Perennial. Flowers in June. British type. Range in Britain, 50°—61°; coast line.
Sandy sea-shore. Abundant in suitable localities along the entire coast.

16. C. *intermedia*, Gooden. *(Soft brown C.)*
Perennial. Flowers in June. English type, (or British). Range in Britain, 50°—57°; coast line.
Marshy places. Very rare.

K.—Coast at St. Cyrus, Stat. Account; at the base of a steep grassy bank, a little south from Mill of Muchalls, and close by the sea. It was first observed here by the late Dr. Murray, where I have also gathered it.

17. C. *Vahlii*, Schkh. *(Close-headed alpine C.)*
Perennial. Flowers in July. Highland type. Range in Britain, 56°—57°; about 2500 to 2700 feet.
Alpine rocks. Very rare.

A.—Head of Glen Callater, first found there by Dr. Greville. I possess the plant as gathered by Mr. R. Mackay upon scarcely accessible ledges of rock above Loch Kander, Glen Callater.

18. C. *atrata*, Linn. *(Black C.)*
Perennial. Flowers in June and July. Highland type.
Range in Britain, 53°—58°; 2500 to 3000 feet.
Alpine rocks. Rare and local.

A.—Rocks west side of Lochnagar; on the Callater cliffs; and from Loch Etichan—on Ben Macdui—upwards, G. D.

19. C. *vulgaris*, Fries. *(Common C.)*
Perennial. Flowers in May and June. British type. Range in Britain, 50°—61°; coast line to 2000 feet?

Wet pastures and moors, &c. Very general and frequent. The height above mentioned—on Morven—is the highest range of which I possess any record; I suspect it rises higher.

20. C. *aquatilis*, Wahl. *(Straight-leaved Water C.)*
Perennial. Flowers in July and August. Highland type. Range in Britain, 56°—58°; 2800 to 3000 feet.

Alpine bogs. Very local.

A.—Table land above Glen Callater, G. D.; frequent in the streams and on the flats round the head of Glen Callater, Mr. Croall; Little Craigendall, Mr. R. Mackay.

21. C. *rigida*, Gooden. *(Rigid C.)*
Perennial. Flowers, June to August. Highland type. Range in Britain, 53°—61°; 2000 to 4320 feet.

Alpine pastures, &c. Confined to the inland and higher parts, but very abundant there.

A.—Summit of Mount Battock; Mount Keen; top of the Khoil, near Ballater; in great profusion on the table land about Loch Muick; Lochnagar; Glen Callater, &c. &c. G. D.

B.—On Belrinnes, Dr. L. Stewart.

22. C. *acuta*, Linn. *(Slender-spiked C.)*
Perennial. Flowers in May and June. British type, (or English). Range in Britain, 50°—58°; 20 to 170 feet.

Margins of rivers, &c. Very local.

K.—At Maryculter, Dr. A. Fleming; by the Dee at Banchory-Ternan, Rev J. Brichan.

A.—Near the old Bridge of Dee, Rev. J. Farquharson; margin of the river Don at Kettock's mill; and at Dyce; by the river Ythan near Ellon, G. D.

23. C. *saxatilis*, Linn. *(Russet C.)*
Perennial. Flowers in June and July. Highland type. Range in Britain, 56°—59; range in altitude ?
Alpine marshes. Very rare.

A.—Cairntoul, Professor Macgillivray in Natural History of Deeside.

24. C. *extensa*, Gooden. *(Long-bracteated C.)*
Perennial. Flowers in June. British type. Range in Britain, 50°—60°; coast line.
Marshes near the sea. Rare.

K.—Coast south of Gourdon, Dr. Stephen; marsh close by the sea near Garron Point, north from Stonehaven, G. D.

B.—Coast at Gamrie, Rev. G. Gairdner.

25. C. *flava*, Linn. *(Yellow C.)*
Perennial. Flowers in May and June. British type. Range in Britain, 50°—61°; coast to 2000 feet.
Marshes and wet pastures. Abundant and general.
Var. β, *Œderi*, Old-town Links, G. D.

26. C. *fulva*, Gooden. *(Tawny C.)*
Perennial. Flowers in June. British type. Range in Britain, 50°—61°; coast line to 600 feet?
Wet meadows. Rather local.

K.—Jackstone, St. Cyrus; Bervie; Benholme, Dr. Stephen. In Arbuthnot, Mr. Chrystall; Banchory-Ternan, Rev. J. Brichan.

A.—Near Aberdeen, Stocket moor, and in the marsh

opposite to the east avenue at Scotston, G. D.; dam at Mill of Clatt, and marsh opposite the quarry at Auchindoir, Rev. J. Minto; in parish of Aberdour, Rev. G. Gairdner.

27. C. *distans*, Linn. *(Loose C.)*
Perennial. Flowers in June. British type. Range in Britain, 50°—59°; coast line.

Marshes near the sea. Very local.

K.—Coast at St. Cyrus, Stat. Account; along the coast from Stonehaven northwards; at the Cove among loose stones close by the sea, G. D.

B.—Coast at Portsoy, " Flora of Moray."

28. C. *binervis*, Smith. *(Green-ribbed C.)*
Perennial. Flowers in June. British type. Range in Britain, 50°—61°; coast line to 3000 feet.

Natural pastures and moors. Very general and abundant.

29. C. *laevigata*, Smith. *(Smooth-stalked C.)*
Perennial. Flowers in June. British type. Range in Britain, 50°—58°; 50 to 280 feet.

Marshy and shady places. Scarce and local.

K.—St. Cyrus, Mr. Cruickshank; Banchory-Ternan, Rev. J. Brichan.

A.—Robslaw Den, Mr. R. Mackay; wood at Countesswells, and at the old Bridge of Don, G. D.; Peter's Braes, Peterculter, Rev. J. Farquharson; Drumoak and Potarch, Mr. P. Macgillivray.

30. C. *vaginata*, Tausch. *(Short brown-spiked C.)*
Perennial. Flowers in July. Highland type. Range in Britain, 56°—59°; 2500 to 3500 feet.

Alpine marshes. Confined to the inland and higher parts, and there rather local.

A.—Rocks west side of Lochnagar, G. D. Little Craigendall; Cairntoul; Braeriach; Ben Macdui; Ben

Avon; Ben-a-Buird, Mr. R. Mackay. Rocks above Loch Kander, head of Glen Callater, Mr. Croall.

31. C. *panicea*, Linn. *(Pink-leaved C.)*
Perennial. Flowers in June. British type. Range in Britain, 50°—61°; coast to 3700 feet.

Marshes and wet pastures. Generally diffused through the district, and very frequent everywhere.

32. C. *pallescens*, Linn. *(Pale C.)*
Perennial. Flowers in June. British type. Range in Britain, 50°—61°; coast line to 1800 feet.

Moist shady places. Generally diffused, but not common.

K.—Upper part of Corbie Den, Kingcausie, G. D.; Banchory-Ternan, Rev. J. Brichan.

A.—Banks of Don, above the old bridge, G. D.; by the Dee in several places, as at Drumoak, Mr. P. Macgillivray; by the road to Pannanich, near Ballater, Mr. Sutherland. North bank of the Dee opposite the Free Church of Ballater; Linn of Muick; Glen Callater, &c. G. D. Throughout the Braemar district among the heath about the bases of the hills, and occasionally in the valleys, Mr. Croall. Near Breda, in Alford, Rev. J. Minto.

33. C. *capillaris*, Linn. *(Dwarf capillary C.)*
Perennial. Flowers in June and July. Highland type. Range in Britain, 54°—61°; 1700 to 2500 feet.

Alpine pastures. Very local, and confined to the inland and higher parts.

A.—Top of Craig Koynach, at Castleton, Braemar, Mr. Gardiner and Mr. Croall; in Glen Callater, near the "break-neck fall," G. D.; on Little Craigendall, Mr. R. Mackay.

34. C. *rariflora*, Smith. *(Loose flowered C.)*
Perennial. Flowers in June. Highland type. Range in Britain, 56°—57°; 2400 to 3500 feet.

o

Alpine marshes. Rare, and confined to the higher ranges.

A.—On Lochnagar, G. D. ; in Glen Callater, on the ascent to Canlochan, Mr. R. Mackay.

B.—Cairngorm, Rev. Mr. Fraser.

35. C. *limosa*, Linn. *(Mud C.)*

Perennial. Flowers in June. Scottish type. Range in Britain, 51°—59° ; 500 to 1000 feet ?

Bogs and marshes. Rare in this district.

A.—In a bog on the farm of Easter Auchmenie, in Clatt, Rev. J. Minto ; it is now probably extirpated, owing to drainage of the locality. In Corgarff, but rare, Mr. Barron.

Var. β, *irrigua*. In a marsh at Loch-an-Yourn, near Loch Builg, Mr. Mackay and G. D.

36. C. *sylvatica*, Huds. *(Pendulous wood C.)*

Perennial. Flowers in May and June. British type, (or English). Range in Britain, 50°—58° ; range in altitude ?

Moist woods. Rare, and as yet only found near the coast line.

A.—Near Aberdeen, in Seaton woods, Dr. A. Fleming.

37. C. *pendula*, Huds. *(Great pendulous C.)*

Perennial. Flowers in May and June. British type, (or English). Range in Britain, 50°—58° ; range in altitude ?

Moist woods. Very rare.

K.—Den Fenella, Mr. Gardiner and Mr. Croall.

A.—At Laithers, near Turriff, Dr. Shier.

B.—Coast at Gamrie, Mr. T. Edwards.

38. C. *glauca*, Scop. *(Glaucous Heath C.)*

Perennial. Flowers in June. British type. Range in Britain, 50°—61° ; coast to 1900 feet.

Moist meadows, &c. Very frequent and general.

39. C. *praecox*, Jacq. *(Vernal C.)*
Perennial. Flowers in May and June. British type.
Range in Britain, 50°—61°; coast to 1800 feet.
Natural pastures. Rather general in the district, but not a common plant.

K.—Kincardineshire coast, Mr. Croall; at Jackstone, St. Cyrus, Dr. Stephen; at Arbuthnot, Mr. Chrystall; in an open grassy hollow at the upper end of Corbie Den, Kingcausie, G. D.

A.—Old Aberdeen Links, Mr. P. Macgillivray; on the glebe at Peterculter, Rev. J. Farquharson; in Robslaw Den, Mr. R. Mackay. At Countesswells; in Glen Muick, on the ascent to Lochnagar, G. D. Craig Koynach, at Castleton; and abundant in grassy pastures, Braemar, Mr. Croall In Alford, Rev. Dr. Farquharson; at manse of Corgarff, Mr. Barron; Laithers, near Turriff, Dr. Shier.

40. C. *pilulifera*, Linn. *(Round-headed C.)*
Perennial. Flowers in June. British type, (or English).
Range in Britain, 50°—59°; coast line to 3300 feet.
Heathy pastures. Very frequent and general.

41. C. *filiformis*, Linn. *(Slender-leaved C.)*
Perennial. Flowers in May. Scottish type, (or British). Range in Britain, 52°—59°; local at 600 feet?
Boggy marshes. Very local and rare.
A.—Loch Cannor, at the east end, (1836,) G. D.

42. C. *hirta*, Linn. *(Hairy C.)*
Perennial. Flowers in May and June. British type Range in Britain, 50°—58°; coast line to 200 feet?

Wet pastures, &c. Rather local, and apparently confined to the coast line chiefly.

K.—Den of Canterland, and bank of the north Esk below stone of Morphy, Mr. Croall; Arbuthnot, Mr. Chrystall; between Dunnottar and Stonehaven, Dr. Stephen. Along the coast from Stonehaven to Aberdeen; at the boat harbour between Finnan and Portlethen, G. D.

A.—In the wood above the old Bridge of Don, Mr. P. Macgillivray; banks of Millden Burn, Belhelvie, near the sea, G. D.

B.—Coast at Gamrie, Rev. G. Gairdner.

43. C. *ampullacea*, Gooden. *(Slender-beaked Bottle C.)*
Perennial. Flowers in June. British type. Range in Britain, 50°—61°; coast line to 500 feet?

Bogs and marshes. Rather general in this district. It probably attains a higher altitude than that—in Alford—above mentioned.

44. C. *vesicaria*, Linn. *(Short-beaked Bladder C.)*
Perennial. Flowers in May and June. British type, (or English). Range in Britain, 50°—58°; 50 to 200 feet.

Marshy places. Apparently very rare.

K.—South bank of the Dee at the bend below Morison's Suspension Bridge, and by a small stream joining the river at the same place, Mr. P. Macgillivray; banks of the Dee at Banchory-Ternan, Dr. Adams.

45. C. *paludosa*, Gooden. *(Lesser common C.)*
Perennial. Flowers in May and June. British type.
Range in Britain, 50°—58°; coast to 400 feet?

Marshy places. Very rare.

K.—Marshes close by the sea, between Muchalls

and Garron Point. I believe it was first observed by Dr. Murray, author of "Northern Flora."

B.—In Mortlach, rare, Dr. L. Stewart.

46. C. *riparia*, Curtis. *(Great common C.)*
Perennial. Flowers in May. British type, (or English). Range in Britain, 50°—58°; coast line to 400 feet.

By rivers, &c. Rare in this district.

K.—At St. Cyrus, Stat. Account.

A.—Ythan river, near Ellon, and Loch of Skene, Dr. Duncan, "M'Gillivray's Aberdeen Flora;" by the Burn of Cluny, Mr. Barron.

B.—Near Birkenbog, Rev. G. Wilson.

ORDER LXXIV.—GRAMINEAE.

1. ANTHOXANTHUM. VERNAL-GRASS.

1. A. *odoratum*, Linn. *(Sweet-scented V.)*
Perennial. Flowers in May and June. British type. Range in Britain, 50°—61°; coast to 3400 feet.

Woods and pastures. Abundant in all parts of the district.

2. NARDUS. MAT-GRASS.

1. N. *stricta*, Linn. *(Common M.)*
Perennial. Flowers in June. British type. Range in Britain, 50°—61°; coast line to 3300 feet.

Natural pastures, &c. Abundant and general.

3. ALOPECURUS. FOX-TAIL-GRASS.

1. A. *pratensis*, Linn. *(Meadow F.)*
Perennial. Flowers in May and June. British type. Range in Britain, 50°—61°; coast line to 1260 feet.

Pastures, &c. Frequent and general. Attains the above elevation in Braemar.

2. A. *alpinus*, Smith. *(Alpine F.)*
Perennial. Flowers in July and August. Highland type. Range in Britain, 56°—58°; 2400 to 3500 feet.

By alpine streams. Rare, and confined to the inland and higher ranges.

A.—Lochnagar, at C. *leporina* station, G. D.; streams by Loch Kander, head of Loch Callater, Professor Macgillivray; Ben Macdui, Mr. R. Mackay; Braeriach, Professor Macgillivray.

3. A. *geniculatus*, Linn. *(Floating F.)*
Perennial. Flowers, May to August. British type. Range in Britain, 50°—61°; coast to 1200 feet.

By pools and in marshes. Frequent and widely diffused.

4. PHALARIS. CANARY-GRASS.

1. P. *arundinacea*, Linn. *Reed C.)*
Perennial. Flowers in July and August. British type. Range in Britain, 50°—61°; coast line to 500 feet.

Sides of lakes and rivers. Frequent along the large rivers of the district in the lower parts of their courses; apparently not so frequent in the interior. Reported as rare in Mortlach.

5. AMMOPHILA. SEA-REED.

1. A. *arundinacea*, Host. *(Common S. R.)*
Perennial. Flowers in July. British type. Range in Britain, 50°—61°; coast line.

Sandy sea-shores. Abundant in suitable localities along the whole coast line.

6. PHLEUM. CAT'S-TAIL-GRASS.

1. P. *pratense*, Linn. *(Common C. or Timothy-grass.)*
Perennial. Flowers, June to September. British type. Range in Britain, 50°—61°; coast to 500 feet.

Pastures, &c. Frequent; reported as in most parts of the three counties, but in some of the more inland probably introduced by cultivation.

2. P. *alpinum*, Linn. *(Alpine C.)*
Perennial. Flowers in July. Highland type. Range in Britain, 56°—58°; 2400 to 3500 feet.

Alpine marshes. Rare, but often abundant where it occurs.

A.—Lochnagar, with C. *leporina* and A. *alpinus*, G. D.; water-course above Loch Kander, head of Loch Callater, Professor Macgillivray; Ben Avon and Ben Macdui, Mr. R. Mackay; south side of Ben-a-Buird, " Northern Flora."

Var. β, *commutatum*. Braeriach and Cairntoul, Mr. R. Mackay.

3. P. *arenarium*, Linn. *(Sea C.)*
Annual. Flowers in May and June. English type, (or British). Range in Britain, 50°—58°; coast line only.

Dry sandy places near the sea. Very rare.

K.—St. Cyrus' sands, Mr. Croall.

A.—Formerly in the Old Aberdeen Links, G. D.; links of St. Fergus, Mr. Brand; Strathbeg, Mr. Cow; links at Rattray-head, Mr. A. Murray.

7. MILIUM. MILLET-GRASS.

1. M. *effusum*, Linn. *(Spreading M.)*
Perennial. Flowers in May and June. British type, (or English). Range in Britain, 50°—58°; 200 to 600 feet?

Moist shady woods. Very rare.

K.—Shady bank below Arbuthnot House, Mr. Chrystall.

A.—On the Barmekin, parish of Echt, Mr. Burnett; in the Buchan district, "Northern Flora."

8. CALAMAGROSTIS. SMALL-REED.

1. C. *Epigejos*, Roth. *(Wood S.)*
Perennial. Flowers in July. English type, (or British). Range in Britain, 50°—58°; 60 to 1000 feet.
Shady banks. Very rare.

A.—Upon a steep bank on the north margin of the Dee, a little east from Manse of Drumoak; I have often gathered it there, it is rather plentiful, and I believe the late Dr. Murray first discovered it. Near Aboyne, Stat. Account; at Loch Cannor, in Cromar, Mr. Sutherland; on a bank by the road-side on the south side of the Dee leading through the forest of Ballachbuie, some miles west from Balmoral. Though not actually measured, data in the vicinity induce me to estimate the height at 1000 feet.

9. AGROSTIS. BENT-GRASS.

1. A. *canina*, Linn. *(Brown B.)*
Perennial. Flowers in June and July. British type. Range in Britain, 50°—61°; coast line to 500 feet ?
Moist pastures and heaths. Abundant and general.

2. A. *vulgaris*, With. *(Fine B.)*
Perennial. Flowers in June and July. British type. Range in Britain, 50°—61°; coast line to 2300 feet.

Natural pastures, &c. Frequent and general. In the form usually of *Var. pumila* it is frequent at high altitudes in the interior, as Mount Keen, Morven,

Lochnagar, Ben Macdui, and Buck of the Cabrach, G. D.

3. A. *alba*, Linn. *(White B.)*
Perennial. Flowers in July and August. British type. Range in Britain, 50°—61°; coast line to 600 feet.

Pastures and wastes. Rather widely diffused, but less so, and not so common as the two preceding species, ceasing also at a lower altitude.

K.—Arbuthnot; Banchory-Ternan.

A.—Frequent about Aberdeen; in Cluny, Alford, Clatt, Aberdour.

B.—Alvah; Mortlach.

10. CATABROSA. WHORL-GRASS.

1. C. *aquatica*, Beauv. *(Water W.)*
Perennial. Flowers in May and June. British type. Range in Britain, 50°—58°; coast line to 500 feet.

Pools and banks of rivers. Rather local.

K.—St. Cyrus, Mr. Kerr; marsh by the sea below West Mathers, St. Cyrus, Dr. Stephen; foot of Brae of Comiston, Mr. Croall.

A.—In a ditch at the west side of Old Aberdeen Links, south from the brick-work, G. D.; ditches in the parish of Echt, Mr. P. Macgillivray; Loch of Skene, Rev. A. Mitchell; banks of the Ythan, Dr. Murray; in Cluny, Mr. Barron; Alford, Rev. Dr. Farquharson; ditch at Ford of Clatt, and marshes at Newton of Clatt, Rev. J. Minto; ditch near Rothmaise, parish of Rayne, Rev. J. Abel; links of St. Fergus, Mr. A. Murray.

B.—In Mortlach, but rare, Dr. L. Stewart.

11. AIRA. HAIR-GRASS.

1. A. *caespitosa*, Linn. *(Tufted H.)*

Perennial. Flowers in June and July. British type. Range in Britain, 50°—61°; coast line to 3500 feet.

Moist pastures and wastes. Common.

2. A. *alpina*, Linn. *(Smooth alpine H.)*
Perennial. Flowers in June and July. Highland type. Range in Britain, 56°—59°; 3000 to 4100 feet.

Moist alpine rocks. Very local, and in the higher parts only.

A.—On Lochnagar, Professor Macgillivray; Ben Avon, Mr. Croall; Ben Macdui, G. D.

B.—Top of Cairngorm, Mr. R. Mackay.

3. A. *flexuosa*, Linn. *(Waved H.)*
Perennial. Flowers in July. British type. Range in Britain, 50°—61°; coast line to 3800 feet.

Natural pastures, heaths, &c. Abundant and general. Frequent at high altitudes. Top of Mount Keen; Ben-a-Buird at 3600, and Lochnagar at 3800 feet.

4. A. *caryophyllea*, Linn. *(Silvery H.)*
Perennial. Flowers in June and July. British type. Range in Britain, 50°—60°; coast line to 1400 feet.

Gravelly pastures, &c. Frequent and widely diffused, occurring in very inland parts, as near Castleton, at 1400 feet; Corgarff, 1300 feet.

5. A. *praecox*, Linn. *(Early H.)*
Annual. Flowers in May and June. British type. Range in Britain, 50°—61°; coast line to 1700 feet.

Sandy pastures, &c. Frequent, and in very inland parts, as Ballater; head of Loch Muick; Corgarff. Occurs on summit of Bennachie.

12. MOLINIA. MOLINIA.

1. M. caerulea, Mœnch. (Purple M.)
Perennial. Flowers in July and August. British type. Range in Britain, 50°—61°; coast to 2500 feet.

Moors and woods, &c. Frequent, but not a common plant.

K.—Benholme; Garvock; Strachan; Durris; coast at Portlethen and Finnan; Banchory-Ternan.

A.—Woods of Hazlehead; Midmar; in Alford; Clatt; Bourtie; Corgarff. Frequent on the higher ranges in the interior, as Ben Macdui, &c.; and inland glens, Garrawalt, Glen Lui, &c.

B.—In Alvah; Mortlach; Binhill, Cullen; Banff parish.

13. MELICA. MELIC-GRASS.

1. M. nutans, Linn. (Mountain M.)
Perennial. Flowers in May and June. Scottish type. Range in Britain, 51°—58°; 100 to 1600 feet.

Woods and shady rocks. Rare in the lower parts of the district, more frequent inland.

K.—Corbie Den, Kingcausie, very rare, G. D.; Banchory-Ternan, Dr. Adams.

A.—North bank of the Dee below the Free Church at Ballater; Craigendarroch; the Garrawalt; Corrymulzie, G. D. The Carr rocks; Glen Candlich and Glen Callater, and frequent in Braemar, Mr. Croall. Near Loch Builg, Mr. Proctor.

B.—Millowood, near Keith, Mr. Craigie; Craighalkie, Tomintoul, "Flora of Moray."

2. M. uniflora, Linn. (Wood M.)
Perennial. Flowers in June and July. English type, (or British). Range in Britain, 50°—58°; 200 to 1100 feet?

Shady woods. Very rare.

K.—Woods of Inchmarlo, Banchory-Ternan, Dr. Adams.

A.—In the Corrymulzie, Braemar, Mr. Gardiner. In this last place I have only seen M. *nutans*, G. D.

14. HOLCUS. SOFT-GRASS.

1. H. *mollis*, Linn. *(Creeping S.)*
Perennial. Flowers in July. British type. Range in Britain, 50°—61°; coast line to 1200 feet.

Pastures and woods. Noted as in all parts of the district as far as Castleton, Corgarff, Mortlach, but not so frequent as the next.

2. H. *lanatus*, Linn. *(Meadow S.)*
Perennial. Flowers in July and August. British type. Range in Britain, 50°—61°; coast to 1400 feet.

Woods and pastures. Common.

15. ARRHENATHERUM. OAT-LIKE GRASS.

1. A. *avenaceum*. Beauv. *(Common O.)*
Perennial. Flowers in June and July. British type. Range in Britain, 50°—61°; coast to 1200 feet.

Pastures and wastes. Common.

16. KOELERIA. KOELERIA

1. K. *cristata*, Pers. *(Crested K.)*
Perennial. Flowers in June and July. British type. Range in Britain, 50°—59°; coast to 2000 feet.

Natural pastures and rocks. Rather local, yet not uncommon.

K.—Along the south parts of the Kincardine coast, Mr. Croall; St. Cyrus, Dr. Stephen; also from Stonehaven to Aberdeen, on the coast, G. D. Banchory-Ternan, Rev. J. Brichan.

A.—Near Aberdeen, by the Dee at Craiglug, &c.; on the Broadhill in the links, G. D. About Ballater;

on the Khoil hill at the elevation above mentioned ; at Castleton, G. D. Drumnahoy, in Cluny, Mr. Barron ; Alford, Rev. Dr. Farquharson ; Clatt and Leslie, Rev. J. Minto ; Hill of Barra, in Bourtie, Rev. J. Abel ; in Buchan, Mr. A. Murray.

B.—In Grange, Stat. Account ; in Alvah, Rev. Dr. Todd ; in Mortlach, Dr. L. Stewart.

17. POA. MEADOW-GRASS.

1. P. *fluitans*, Scop. *(Floating M.)*
Perennial. Flowers in July and August. British type. Range in Britain, 50°—60°; coast line to 2200 feet.

Ditches and pools. Frequent and general. Occurs at Loch Phadrig, near Castleton, at the above elevation.

2. P. *maritima*, Huds. *(Creeping Sea M.)*
Perennial. Flowers in July. British type. Range in Britain, 50°—61°; coast line only.

Marshy places by the sea. Very local.

K.—Coast at Brotherton, Stat. Account ; Benholme, Dr. Stephen ; at the Cove and Girdleness, G. D.

A.—North end of Old Aberdeen Links ; on the Inch at Aberdeen ; at Peterhead, Rev. J. Minto ; general on the Buchan coast, "Northern Flora."

3. P. *pratensis*, Linn. *(Smooth-stalked M.)*
Perennial. Flowers in June and July. British type. Range in Britain, 50°—61° ; coast line to 2900 feet.

Natural pastures, &c. Common and widely diffused. Occurs near the top of Morven at the above altitude.

4. P. *trivialis*, Linn. *(Rough M.)*
Perennial. Flowers in June and July. British type. Range in Britain, 50°—61° ; coast line to 1300 feet.

Meadows and pastures. Frequent throughout the district.

5. **P. alpina**, Linn. *(Alpine M.)*
Perennial. Flowers in June and July. Highland type. Range in Britain, 53°—59°; 2400 to 3700 feet?
Alpine rocks. Rather local; confined to the higher ranges.

A.—Lochnagar, above and below station for Carex *leporina*; Ben Macdui; Callater rocks, G. D. Little Craigendall; Ben Avon; Ben-a-Buird; Cairntoul, and Braeriach, Mr. R. Mackay.

6. **P. laxa**, Haenk. *(Wavy M.)*
Perennial. Flowers in July and August. Highland type. Range in Britain, 56°—58°; 3000 to 3300 feet?
Alpine rocks. Very rare.

A.—Lochnagar. Found originally by Mr. G. Don; since his time by Professor Graham and others.

7. **P. nemoralis**, Linn. *(Wood M.)*
Perennial. Flowers in June and July. British type, (or English). Range in Britain, 50°—58°; 200 to 2500 feet.
Woods and shady rocks. Chiefly in the inland parts.

K.—Dens of Morphy and Fenella, Mr. Croall; Den of Davo, " Northern Flora."

A.—Cliffs at Pannanich; north bank of the Dee below Ballater Free Church; rocks behind the Free manse of Ballater; Bridge of Gairden; Linn of Muick; Linn of Quoich; Corrymulzie and Callater rocks, G. D. In Alford, Rev. Dr. Farquharson; Den of Craig, near Rhynie, Rev. J. Minto; at the fall on Burn of Cachantesin, in Strathdon, G. D.

Var. ε, *Balfourii*. Lochnagar, Mr. R. Mackay;

also on rocks, north base of the Mourne at Castleton, Mr. Croall.

B.—*Var. δ, glauca.* At Tomintoul, "Flora of Moray."

8. P. *annua*, Linn. *(Annual M.)*
Annual. Flowers, April to October. British type. Range in Britain, 50°—61°; coast to 2000 feet ?
Pastures and wastes. Common.

18. TRIODIA. HEATH-GRASS.

1. T. *decumbens*, Beauv. *(Decumbent H.)*
Perennial. Flowers in July. British type. Range in Britain, 50°—61°; coast to 1750 feet.
Heaths and mountain pastures. Very general.

19. BRIZA. QUAKING-GRASS.

1. B. *media*, Linn. *(Common Q.)*
Perennial. Flowers in June. British type, (or English). Range in Britain, 50°—60°; 50 to 1700 feet.
Natural pastures. Widely diffused, but not common.

K.—South parts of Kincardine, Mr. M'Farlane; Arbuthnot, Mr. Chrystall; St. Cyrus; Garvock; Benholme, Dr. Stephen. South bank of the Dee at Morison's Suspension Bridge, Mr. P. Macgillivray; side of the Feugh at Banchory-Ternan, Dr. Adams.

A.—On the glebe at Peterculter, Rev. J. Farquharson; Normandyke, and on a bank at the Church of Drumoak, Dr. Smith; about the base of Morven, "Northern Flora." North bank of the Dee below Ballater Free Church; on the Lin Mui, and in Glen Gairden, at Castleton, G. D. In Alford and Towie, "Northern Flora;" Auchindoir, Rhynie, Rev. J. Minto; in Buchan, Mr. A. Murray.

B.—Parish of Grange, Stat. Account; in Alvah, very rare, Rev. Dr. Todd; Boyndie, near Banff, "Northern Flora;" in Mortlach, Dr. L. Stewart.

20. DACTYLIS. COCK'S-FOOT-GRASS.

1. D. *glomerata,* Linn. *(Rough C.)*
Perennial. Flowers in June and July. British type. Range in Britain, 50°—61°; coast line to 1380 feet.

Pastures and wastes, &c. Frequent in the lower districts, appears to be less so in the more inland parts. Occurs on the Lin Mui, near Ballater, at the above elevation. Grows also at Castleton; Corgarff; Mortlach.

21. CYNOSURUS. DOG'S-TAIL-GRASS.

1. C. *cristatus,* Linn. *(Crested D.)*
Perennial. Flowers in July. British type. Range in Britain, 50°—61°; coast to 1300 feet.

Dry pastures. Frequent and widely diffused.

22. FESTUCA. FESCUE-GRASS.

1. F. *bromoides,* Linn. *(Barren F.)*
Annual. Flowers in June. British type. Range in Britain, 50°—58°; 50 to 1250 feet.

Dry pastures, wastes, and walls. Frequent in the lower parts, less so in the interior; grows, however, in Clatt; Alford; Corgarff.

2. F. *ovina,* Linn. *(Sheep's F.)*
Perennial. Flowers in June and July. British type. Range in Britain, 50°—61°; coast line to 4320 feet.

Pastures and wastes. Common in one or other of its forms; the viviparous variety attaining the summit of Ben Macdui.

Var. a, *vivipara.* Very abundant in the interior; sometimes descending low by rivers and streams; in great profusion about rocks, &c. on the higher ranges.

Var. β, *duriuscula.* Grows in most parts of the

district; coast and inland. Banchory, Ballater, Castleton, Alford, Strathdon, &c.

Var. γ, *rubra.* Is chiefly a coast plant, and is very abundant in suitable places—sandy shores—along the coast line.

3. *F. sylvatica*, Vill. *(Reed F.)* *

Perennial. Flowers in July. Scottish type. Range in Britain, 50°—58°; coast line to 400 feet.

Shady woods. Very local.

K.—Frequent in South Kincardine, Mr. M'Farlane; about Dunnottar, "Northern Flora."

A.—On a steep wooded bank by the Dee, east from Manse of Drumoak; and north bank of the Don above the old Bridge, Dr. Murray. Woods behind Aboyne Castle, Mr. Proctor.

B.—Millowood, near Keith, "Northern Flora."

4. *F. pratensis*, Huds. *(Meadow F.)*

Perennial. Flowers in June and July. British type. Range in Britain, 50°—60°; coast line to 200 feet.

Moist pastures, &c. Very local.

K.—Lower end of the Den of Canterland, and banks of the North Esk, Mr. Croall; on the coast at Portlethen.

A.—Formerly by the river Dee on the Inch at Aberdeen, G. D.

B.—In Alvah, Rev. Dr. Todd.

5. *F. elatior*, Linn. *(Tall F.)*

Perennial. Flowers in June and July. British type. Range in Britain, 50°—60°; coast to 500 feet.

---

* There is some uncertainty respecting the reports received of this and the two following species. I have not seen specimen sfrom all the localities mentioned, and insert the notes as received by me. I have doubts as to the distinctness of these three species.

P

Moist pastures and river banks. Rather local.

K.—Coast at St. Cyrus, Dr. Stephen; Dens of Morphy and Fenella, Stat. Account; at different parts of the coast from Stonehaven to Aberdeen, G. D.; Banchory-Ternan, Dr. Adams.

A.—"In rupes *Don*, prope pontem," Dr. D. Skene; on serpentine rocks near Meadowbank, in Belhelvie, G. D.; at Whitecairns, in Belhelvie, "Northern Flora;" Pondash, by the Don, in Alford, Dr. A. Fleming; banks of the Bogie, half-a-mile south of the Manse of Rhynie, Rev. J. Minto; banks of the Deveron, near Huntly Castle, Rev. J. Abel; by the Burn of Cairney, "Northern Flora."

B.—In Alvah, rare, Rev. Dr. Todd; in Mortlach, Dr. L. Stewart.

6. F. *gigantea*, Vill. *(Tall bearded F.)*
Perennial. Flowers in July and August. British type, (or English). Range in Britain, 50°—58°; 80 to 500 feet?
Shady woods. Rare.

K.—Dens of Morphy and Fenella, Stat. Account; Arbuthnot, Mr. Chrystall; Banchory-Ternan, Dr. Adams; in Strachan, Stat. Account.

A.—In Den of Gight, G. D.; banks of the Don at Pondash, Vale of Alford, Rev. J. Minto.

B.—Den above Mill of Mountblairey, Rev. Dr. Todd; Millowood, near Keith, "Northern Flora;" near the Castle of Boyne, Banff, Mr. T. Edwards.

23. BROMUS. BROME-GRASS.

1. B. *asper*, Linn. *(Hairy, Wood B.)*
Biennial? Flowers in June and July. British type, (or English). Range in Britain, 50°—58°; coast line to 280 feet.
Moist woods. Rare.

K.—Dens of Canterland and Fenella, Mr. Croall; Garvock, Dr. Stephen.

A.—Den of Gight, parish of Methlic, G. D.; by the Don at Monymusk, "Northern Flora;" banks of the Ugie at Peterhead, Rev. J. Minto.

B.—Haugh below Bridge of Alvah, Rev. Dr. Todd; near the Castle of Boyne, Banff, Mr. T. Edwards.

2. B. *sterilis*, Linn. *(Barren B.)*

Annual. Flowers in June. British type, (or English). Range in Britain, 50°—58°; 50 to 460 feet.

Fields and wastes. Rare, and appears to be confined to the lower parts.

K.—St. Cyrus' rocks, Mr. Croall; near Bay of Nigg, at the old Kirk, Mr. P. Macgillivray.

A.—Near Aberdeen, waste places at south end of Crown Street, and the north-east side of Powis' grounds, Old Aberdeen, G. D. Upper Drumnahoy, Cluny, Mr. Barron; in Buchan district, Mr. Murray.

B.—In Alvah, Rev. Dr. Todd; in Mortlach, Dr. L. Stewart.

3. B. *secalinus*, Linn. *(Smooth Rye B.)*

Biennial? Flowers in June and July, British type, (or English). Range in Britain, 50°—58°; 50 to 200 feet?

Dry fields. Very rare. Chiefly in the lower parts of the district.

K.—Frequent in fields in Kincardineshire, Mr. Chrystall.

A.—In a field on the north side of the Dee above Morison's Suspension Bridge, G. D.; on the farm of Mountdurno, in Belhelvie, "Northern Flora."

4. B. *commutatus*, Schrad. *(Tumid Field B.)* *

* Under this name I comprehend B. *racemosus* and B. *arvensis*.

Biennial? Flowers in June and July. British type. Range in Britain, 50°—60°; coast line to 1100 feet.

Fields and wastes. Frequent, and in most parts of the district, coast and inland.

5. B. *mollis*, Linn. *(Soft B.)*
Annual? Flowers in June. British type. Range in Britain, 50°—61°; coast to 1260 feet.

Fields and wastes, &c. &c. Common. In all parts of the district, but never attaining any great altitude.

24. AVENA. OAT.

1. A. *pratensis*, Linn. *(Nar.-leaved perennial O.)*
Perennial. Flowers in June and July. British type. Range in Britain, 50°—58°; coast line to 2000 feet.

Natural pastures, dry banks, &c. Widely diffused, but not common.

K.—Rocks at St. Cyrus, Mr. Croall; Jackstone, St. Cyrus, Dr. Stephen; Arbuthnot, Mr. Chrystall; along the coast from Stonehaven, northwards; at the Cove; on a bank at the north end of Bay of Nigg, G. D. Banchory-Ternan, Rev. J. Brichan.

A.—On serpentine rocks, near Meadowbank, Belhelvie, G. D.; near Seaton House, Old Aberdeen, Professor Macgillivray; abundant on the banks of the Dee at Ballater, G. D.; upon serpentine rocks in Leslie and Clatt, Rev. J. Minto; in Corgarff, Mr. Barron; at Peterhead, Dr. Shier.

B.—In Mortlach, Dr. L. Stewart; at Craighalkie, near Tomintoul, "Flora of Moray."

Var. γ, *alpina*. North bank of the Dee below the Free Church at Ballater; on the Khoil, Glen Muick, G. D. At Aboyne, Stat. Account; rocks at the "Lion's face," Castleton, G. D.; Hill of Barra, Bourtie, Rev. J. Abel; at Inchrory, Mr. Mackay and G. D.

2. A. *pubescens*, Linn. *(Downy O.)*
Perennial. Flowers in June and July. British type. Range in Britain, 50°—60°; coast to 500 feet ?

Dry pastures and banks. Very local. Not so frequent as the last species.

K.— Brae of Comiston, South Kincardine, Mr. Croall. At Thornyhive, near Dunnottar Castle ; and on the coast at Muchalls, G. D.

A.—On serpentine rocks at Meadowbank, with the last species ; and by the side of a field, at the foot-path, east wall of Powis' grounds, Old Aberdeen, G. D.

B.—In Mortlach, Dr. L. Stewart.

3. A. *flavescens*. Linn. *(Yellow O.)*
Perennial. Flowers in July. English type, (or British). Range in Britain, 50°—58°; coast line to 400 feet.

Dry pastures. Very rare.

A.—In the Aberdeen links, south-east from the Broadhill, Rev. J. Farquharson ; I have seen it abundant at this station, it is probably now extirpated. Near Summerhill, two miles west from Aberdeen, Mr. A. Smith ; near Robslaw Den, Mr. R. Mackay ; at Don-mouth, and on the south bank of the same, west from the new bridge, Professor Macgillivray ; at Kebbaty, in a field south from the house, Mr. Barron.

25. PHRAGMITES. REED.

1. P. *communis*, Trin. *(Common R.)*
Perennial. Flowers in July and August. British type. Range in Britain, 50°— 61°; coast line to 500 feet.

Lakes and margins of rivers. Not very common.

K.—In South Kincardine, Mr. M'Farlane ; Arbuthnot, Mr. Chrystall ; Banchory-Ternan, Rev. J. Brichan ; on the coast near Portlethen, G. D.

A.—Banks of the Don near Inverury, Mr. Craig; Corbie Loch, north from Aberdeen, G. D.; in a marsh near Leggerdale, Mr. Barron; in Clatt, Rev. J. Minto; Burn of Forgue, Cobairdy, Rev. J. Abel; banks of the Ythan, near Ellon, G. D.

B.—Deveron-side, but rare, Rev. Dr. Todd.

26. ELYMUS. LYME-GRASS.

1. E. *arenarius*, Linn. *(Upright Sea L.)*

Perennial. Flowers in July. Scottish type, (or British). Range in Britain, 50°—61°; coast line.

Sandy sea-shores. Rather local.

K.—St. Cyrus' sands, abundant, Mr. Croall; near the mouth of Burn of Benholme, Dr. Stephen.

A.—Near Aberdeen, a small patch at the south end of the Fish-town, Footdee; and at the mouth of the Don, on the north side, G. D. Coast at Cruden, Mr. A. Murray; at the village of St. Combes, parish of Lonmay.

27. HORDEUM. BARLEY.

1. H. *murinum*, Linn. *(Wall B.)*

Annual. Flowers in June and July. English type, (or British). Range in Britain, 50°—57°; coast line.

Dry sandy places. Very rare.

K.—Arbuthnot; Johnshaven; Gourdon, "Northern Flora." Between Johnshaven and Brotherton, Mr. Croall.

A.—Near Aberdeen, *Mag. Zool. and Bot.* Vol. I. p. 398.

28. TRITICUM. WHEAT.

1. T. *junceum*, Linn. *(Rushy Sea W.)*

Perennial. Flowers in July and August. British type. Range in Britain, 50°—61°; coast line.

Sandy sea-shores. Frequent in suitable localities along the coast.

2. T. *repens*, Linn. *(Creeping W. or Couch-grass.)*
Annual. Flowers in June and July. British type. Range in Britain, 50°—61°; coast to 1200 feet.

Fields and wastes. Common and generally diffused.

3. T. *caninum*, Huds. *(Fibrous-rooted W.)*
Perennial. Flowers in July. British type. Range in Britain, 50°—58°; coast line to 500 feet.

Woods, banks, &c. Frequent, but apparently less so than the former. Occurs in the lower, and in some of the inland parts of the district. In Alford at the above elevation.

29. BRACHYPODIUM. FALSE BROME-GRASS.

1. B. *sylvaticum*, Beauv. *(Slender F.)*
Perennial. Flowers in June and July. British type. Range in Britain, 50°—60°; coast to 800 feet.

Woods and shady banks. Rather local.

K.—South Kincardine, Mr. M'Farlane. St. Cyrus' cliffs; Dens Fenella and Morphy, Dr. Stephen. Not unfrequent in stony and shady places near the sea from Stonehaven to Aberdeen; plentiful at the Cove, G. D. Banchory-Ternan, Rev. J. Brichan; Corbie Den, Kingcausie, Mr. P. Macgillivray.

A.—In the wood at the old Bridge of Don, G. D.; abundant near Ballater, on the north bank of the Dee below the Free Church, G. D.

B.—Woods in Alvah, Rev. Dr. Todd; in Mortlach, Dr. L. Stewart.

30. LOLIUM. RYE-GRASS.

1. L. *perenne*, Linn. *(Perennial or Beardless R.)*
Perennial. Flowers in June and July. British type. Range in Britain, 50°—61°; coast line to 1250 feet.

Pastures and wastes. Common. Occurs in both lower and inland parts, in the latter it has been probably introduced.

INTRODUCED PLANTS.

The following have been reported from different parts of the three counties, but are not truly indigenous.

EXOGENOUS PLANTS.
RANUNCULACEAE.

Helleborus *fœtidus*, Linn. *(Fœtid H.)*
Alford, Rev. Dr. Farquharson.

H. *viridis*, Linn. *(Greeen H.)*
Den of Robslaw, G. D.

Aquilegia *vulgaris*, Linn. *(Common Columbine.)*
Near House of Culter, Dr. J. Smith; south bank of the Dee, Balbreadie, Durris, Mr. P. Macgillivray; Banchory-Ternan, Rev. J. Brichan; Aboyne, Stat. Account; Den of Morphy, and opposite Stricathro, Dr. Stephen.

PAPAVERACEAE.

Meconopsis *Cambrica*, Vig. *(Welsh Poppy.)*
Banks of the Dee near Church of Banchory-Devenick, Dr. Stephen; wood below Inchline road, half-a-mile above Manse of Marnoch, Rev. Dr. Todd.

Chelidonium *majus*, Linn. *(Celandine.)*
Midmar, Mr. Barron; ruins of Castle of Lismore, in Rhynie, Rev. J. Minto; in Mortlach, Dr. L. Stewart; Castle of Pitfichie, Monymusk, Dr. A. Fleming.

FUMARIACEAE.

Corydalis *lutea*, Lindl. *(Yellow C.)*
Walls near Peterculter House, Mr. Sutherland.

CRUCIFERAE.

Cheiranthus *Cheiri*, Linn. *(Wallflower.)*
Castle of Dunnottar, G. D.; Huntly Castle, Rev. J. Abel.

Koniga *maritima*, Br. *(Sea-side K.)*
Coast near Aberdeen, " British Flora."

Camelina *sativa*, Cr. *(Gold-of-Pleasure.)*
Cluny, Mr. Barron; fields at Old Aberdeen, Dr. A. Fleming; fields in Cromar, rare, Mr. Sutherland.

Brassica *campestris*, L. *(Wild Navew.)*
Ballater, Abergairn.

B. *Rapa*, Linn. *(Turnip.)*
Milton of Kemnay, Mr. Barron.

Sinapis *alba*, Linn. *(White Mustard.)*
Field near Dunnottar Castle, Dr. Stephen; near Aberdeen, G. D.

RESEDACEAE.

Reseda *lutea*, Linn. *(Yellow Mignonette.)*
Formerly on the Inch at Aberdeen, G. D.

CARYOPHYLLACEAE.

Saponaria *officinalis*, Linn. *(Common Soapwort.)*
Hangman's brae, Aberdeen, Dr. D. Skene; Alford, Rev. Dr. Farquharson; road-side half-a-mile west from Strachan Church, Dr. Stephen.

LINACEAE.

Linum *usitatissimum*, Linn. *(Common Flax.)*
Not uncommon in various places, by road-sides, fields, &c.

MALVACEAE.

Malva *sylvestris*, Linn. *(Common Mallow.)*
Johnshaven and St. Cyrus, Dr. Stephen; at the base of the rocks, Dunnottar Castle, Dr. A. Fleming; formerly in Cardenshaugh, Aberdeen, G. D.; Findochty, Clatt, Rev. J. Minto; Mortlach, Dr. L. Stewart.

M. *moschata*, Linn. *(Musk Mallow.)*
Bridge at Burn of Benholme, Dr. Stephen; formerly near Richmond Hill, Aberdeen, G. D.; Alford, Rev. Dr. Farquharson; Alvah, Rev. Dr. Todd.

HYPERICACEAE.

Hypericum *calycinum*, Linn. *(Large-flowered St. John's-wort.)*
Lower side of road west from Church of Banchory-Ternan, Dr. Stephen.

GERANIACEAE.

Geranium *Phaeum*, Linn. *(Dusky Crane's-bill.)*
Wood at Kingcausie, G. D.; road-side between Banchory-Ternan and Loch of Park, Mr. Sutherland.

RHAMNACEAE.

Rhamnus *catharticus*, Linn. *(Com. Buckthorn.)*
In parish of Alvah, Rev. Dr. Todd.

LEGUMINOSAE.

Medicago *denticulata*, Willd. *(Reticulated Medick.)*
Formerly on the Inch at Aberdeen harbour; introduced in ballast, G. D.

Melilotus *officinalis*, Linn. *(Com. yellow Melilot.)*
Inch at Aberdeen, G. D.

ROSACEAE.

Prunus *Avium*, Linn. *(Cherry or Gean.)*

Along the Dee, and several of its tributaries, as far as Castleton, Professor Macgillivray.

P. *Cerasus*, Linn. *(Morello Cherry.)*
Along the course of the Don, in several places, Dr. A. Fleming; Linhead, in Alvah, Rev. Dr. Todd.

Spiraea *Filipendula*, Linn. *(Common Dropwort.)*
South end of St. Cyrus' cliffs, Mr. Sutherland.

Crataegus *Oxyacantha*, Linn. *(Hawthorn.)*
In various parts of the district.

CRASSULACEAE.

Sempervivum *tectorum*, Linn. *(House-leek.)*
Walls at old Bridge of Don, and roofs of houses in various places near Aberdeen, G. D.; Midmar, Mr. Barron.

Sedum *Telephium*, Linn. *(Orpine.)*
Near Morningside, and fields by King Street, &c. G. D.; by stream above Sooty wells, Garvock, Dr. Stephen.

S. *album*, Linn. *(White Stonecrop.)*
On a thatched cottage in the town of Bervie, Mr. Chrystall; roofs of houses in Bervie, east of market cross, Dr. Stephen.

GROSSULACEAE.

Ribes *alpinum*, Linn. *(Mountain Currant.)*
Mortlach, Dr. L. Stewart.

R. *rubrum*, Linn. *(Red Currant.)*
Midmar, Mr. Barron.

R. *Grossularia*, Linn. *(Common Gooseberry.)*
Midmar, Mr. Barron.

SAXIFRAGACEAE.

Saxifraga *umbrosa*, Linn. *(London-Pride.)*

Alford, Rev. Dr. Farquharson; Dunnideer, Mr. M'Donald.

S. *Geum*, Linn. *(Kidney-leaved S.)*
Den of Knockespock, Rev. J. Minto.

UMBELLIFERAE.

Apium *graveolens*, Linn. *(Wild Celery.)*
Craiglug, near Aberdeen, Dr. Murray.

Ægopodium *Podagraria*, Linn. *(Bishop-weed.)*
Reported from various parts of the district, but not a true native.

Carum *Carui*, Linn. *(Common Caraway.)*
Inch at Aberdeen, G. D.; Tillenhilt, Mr. Barron; Alford, Rev. Dr. Farquharson.

Æthusa *Cynapium*, Linn. *(Fool's-Parsley.)*
Inch at Aberdeen; frequent in gardens, as a weed.

Peucedanum *Ostruthium*, Koch. *(Master-wort.)*
Parishes of Skene and Echt, Mr. Burnett.

Coriandrum *sativum*, Linn. *(Coriander.)*
Formerly on the Inch, opposite the dock-yards, Aberdeen.

Smyrnium *Olusatrum*, Linn. *(Alexanders.)*
At the Cove, and Corbie Den, Mr. P. Macgillivray; Cornhill and Skene, Mr. A. Smith; Inverugie Castle, Rev. J. Minto.

Myrrhis *odorata*, Scop. *(Sweet Cicely.)*
Den of Robslaw, &c. G. D; Alford, Rev. Dr. Farquharson; parish of Leslie, Rev. J. Minto. Duff House, Park; Sandlaw, in Alvah, Rev. Dr. Todd.

CAPRIFOLIACEAE.

Sambucus *nigra*, Linn. *(Common Elder.)*
Various parts of the district.

Lonicera *Xylosteum*, Linn. *(Upright Fly Honeysuckle.)*
Bridge of Alvah, Rev. Dr. Todd.

COMPOSITAE.

Hieracium *aurantiacum*, Linn. *(Orange H.)*
Woods of Craigston, near Turriff, Mr. A. Murray. Clova, and Den of Craig, Auchindoir, Mr. Sutherland.

Cichorium *Intybus*, Linn. *(Succory.)*
Banchory-Ternan, in fields, G. D. ; Kemnay, Mr. Burnett ; Alford, Rev. Dr. Farquharson ; farm of Upper Tollo, Inverkeithny, and near Cobairdy House, Rev. J. Abel ; fields in Cushnie, Mr. Sutherland.

Carduus *Marianus*, Linn. *(Milk Thistle.)*
Formerly near Bon-Accord Terrace, Aberdeen, and behind the Boat-house, Kittybrewster, G. D.

Tanacetum *vulgare*, Linn. *(Common Tansy.)*
Road-side, Blackness, Strachan ; Jackstone, and at fishing station, St. Cyrus, Dr. Stephen. Rocks at old Bridge of Don, Dr. D. Skene, where it still grows ; near Kettock's Mill, G. D. ; Alford, Rev. Dr. Farquharson ; at Cruden, Mr. A. Murray ; Pitcaple, Mr. Sutherland ; Forgue and Meldrum, Rev. J. Abel ; Dalphad, in Glen Gairden, at 1200 feet, G. D. ; between farm of Sandlaw and Deveron, Rev. Dr. Todd ; Mortlach, Dr. Stewart.

Senecio *Saracenicus*, Linn. *(Br.-leaved Groundsel.)*
Near Warburton, St. Cyrus, Dr. Stephen ; Den of Robslaw, Mr. A. K. Clark ; Den of Leslie, Mr. M'Donald.

Doronicum *Pardalianches*, Linn. *(Leopard's-bane.)*
Den of Robslaw, and south bank of the Don above Bridge of Dyce, G. D. ; near entrance to Paradise, Monymusk, Rev. A. Beverly.

Matricaria *Parthenium*, Linn. *(Feverfew.)*
By the Dee at Railway Station, Banchory-Ternan, Dr. Stephen ; near Maryculter House, Dr. J. Smith ; Lickley Head, in Premnay, Rev. J. Minto ; Mortlach, Dr. L. Stewart.

Achillaea *tomentosa*, Linn. *(Woolly Yarrow.)*
Auchlunkart, Banffshire, P. Stewart, Esq.

POLEMONIACEAE.

Polemonium *cœruleum*, Linn. *Jacob's Ladder.)*
Near Aberdeen, in an old quarry at Shettocksley, G. D. ; Midmar, Mr. Barron ; Alvah, Rev. Dr. Todd.

CONVOLVULACEAE.

Cuscuta *epilinum*, Weihe. *(Flax Dodder.)*
On flax, in fields ; near Printfield, Dr. Murray.

BORAGINACEAE.

Anchusa *sempervirens*, Linn. *(Evergreen Alkanet.)*
Formerly near old House of Robslaw, and near Powis ; Nether-Banchory ; Banchory-Ternan ; Kildrummy Castle ; Tolquhon Castle ; Clatt ; Rhynie ; Alford ; Cobairdy ; Kirk of Forgue ; Cluny ; Den of Gight ; Mortlach.

Borago *officinalis*, Linn. *(Common Borage.)*
Methlic, Stat. Account ; Binhill, Cullen, Mr. Carmichael.

Symphytum *officinale*, Linn. *(Common Comfrey.)*
In a field by the road-side at Kepplestone, near Robslaw quarry, G. D. ; back of the farm house of Cults, Dr. A. Fleming.

Cynoglossum *officinale*, Linn. *(Hound's-tongue.)*
Castleton, Braemar, Mr. A. K. Clark ; meadow behind Castle Fraser, Dr. D. Skene ; Den of Boyne, Mr. Cowie.

SOLANACEAE.

Solanum *Dulcamara*, Linn. *(Bittersweet.)*

Formerly at Gallowhill, and in Belhelvie, G. D. ; banks of the Carron, at Stonehaven, and by the bridge over a rivulet, east from old Bridge of Dee, Dr. A. Fleming ; woods about Invery, and near Crathes, by the side of the river Dee, Dr. Adams ; Lismore, in Rhynie, Rev. J. Minto ; Tore of Troup, and Den of Auchindoir, "Northern Flora;" walls at Rannes, Mr. Carmichael ; Alvah, Rev. Dr. Todd.

Hyoscyamus *niger*, Linn. *(Henbane.)*

Den of Robslaw, Mr. A. K. Clark. Formerly among ruins of Dunnottar Castle ; coast at St. Cyrus, Stat. Account. Woods of Kemnay, "Northern Flora;" near old Castle of Findlater, Mr. Craigie.

SCROPHULARIACEAE.

Veronica *Buxbaumii*, Ten. *(Buxbauen's Speedwell.)*

Weed in gardens at Rosemount Terrace, Dr. A. Fleming.

Linaria *Cymbalaria*, Mill. *(Ivy-leaved Toad-flax.)*

Den of Robslaw ; Fetteresso, &c.

L. *vulgaris*, Mœnch. *(Yellow Toad-flax.)*

North Esk Bridge ; St. Cyrus, Dr. Stephen ; roadside near Nether-Banchory Church, Dr. A. Fleming ; Banchory-Ternan, Dr. Adams ; Clatt, Rev. J. Minto ; Mortlach, Dr. L. Stewart.

L. *repens*, Ait. *(Creeping T.)*

Near Ballater, and in Auchindoir, Mr. Sutherland ; Alford, Rev. Dr. Farquharson.

Verbascum *Thapsus*, Linn. *(Great Mullein.)*

Banks of the Dee at Aboyne, G. D. ; in Clatt, Rev. J. Minto ; Strathdon, "Northern Flora."

Scrophularia *vernalis*, Linn. *(Yellow Figwort.)*

SCROPHULARIACEAE.

Near Manse of Alford, Rev. Dr. Farquharson.

Mimulus *luteus*, Linn. *(Yellow M.)*

Kincardineshire, Mr. Dickson ; at Pannanich Lodge, G. D. ; Kemnay, Mr. M'Donald. Mill of Hirn, Banchory-Ternan ; and by the river Bervie in Arbuthnot, Dr. Stephen.

LABIATAE.

Mentha *viridis*, Linn. *(Spearmint.)*

Side of a stream at Castle Fraser, Mr. Burnett ; half-a-mile from the gamekeeper's house in Glen Callater, Mr. R. Mackay.

Ballota *nigra*, Linn. *(Horehound.)*

Near Keig ; Castle Forbes, Mr. M'Donald.

CHENOPODIACEAE.

Beta *vulgaris*, Linn. *(Common Beet.)*

A single plant on the Inch at Aberdeen, Rev. J. Minto.

Chenopodium *Bonus Henricus*, Linn. *(Mercury Goose-foot.)*

Not unfrequent in different parts of the district, but in places leading to suspicion of its escape from cultivation. Arbuthnot ; Banchory-Ternan. Near Aberdeen, at Stocket, &c. Alford ; Clatt ; Inverkeithny. Buchan. Alvah. Mortlach.

Atriplex *littoralis*, Linn. *(Grass-leaved Sea O.)*

Formerly on the Inch at Aberdeen, introduced in ballast, G. D.

URTICACEAE.

Parietaria *officinalis*, Linn. *(Pellitory.)*

Walls of Arbuthnot House, Mr. Chrystall ; Castle of Tolquhon, near Ellon, Mr. Thom ; ruins of Inverugie Castle, Rev. J. Minto ; Boyne Castle, Banffshire, Rev. W. Cowie.

SALICACEAE.

Salix *purpurea*, Linn. *(Purple Willow.)*
S. *Helix*, Linn. *(Rose W.)*
S. *fragilis*, Linn. *(Crack W.)*
S. *Russeliana*, Smith. *(Russell's W.)*
S. *alba*, Linn. *(White W.)*
S. *viminalis*, Linn. *(Common Osier.)*

The above reported from different parts of the district; certainly introduced.

ENDOGENOUS PLANTS.

LILIACEAE.

Polygonatum *multiflorum*, All. *(Com. Solomon's Seal.)*

K.—Woods of Ury, near Stonehaven, Dr. Ogilvie; Banchory woods, Dr. A. Fleming; woods by the banks of the Dee, near Morison's Suspension Bridge, Mr. Sutherland; wood at Kingcausie, Mrs. Boswell.

A.—Paradise, at Monymusk, Dr. Ogilvie.

Allium *oleraceum*, Linn. *(Streaked field Garlic.)*
Arbuthnot, Mr. Chrystall.

ARACEAE.

Arum *maculatum*, Linn. *(Spotted Arum.)*

Den of Robslaw, G. D.; by the avenue to Seaton House, Dr. A. Fleming.

GRAMINEAE.

Alopecurus *agrestis*, Linn. *(Slender Fox-tail-grass.)*

On the Inch at Aberdeen, Dr. Murray; beside Kettock's mill, G. D.

Phalaris *Canariensis*, Linn. *(Canary-grass.)*
On the Inch at Aberdeen, &c. &c.

Setaria *viridis*, Beauv. *(Green Bristle-grass.)*
Formerly on the Inch at Aberdeen. Introduced in ballast.

Poa *aquatica*, Linn. *(Reed Meadow-grass.)*
Pond at Breda in Alford, " from which it has escaped into the river Don, and is now naturalized on its banks, several miles below Breda," Rev. J. Minto.

Bromus *arvensis*, Linn. *(Taper Field Brome-grass.)*
In a field by the road near Cardenshaugh, G. D.

Lolium *temulentum*, Linn. *(Darnel.)*
Occasionally in fields, in different parts of the district.

Digitaria *sanguinalis*, Scop. *(Finger-grass.)*
Once found upon the Inch at Aberdeen. Introduced in ballast.

CLASS III.
ACOTYLEDONOUS, OR CELLULAR PLANTS.*

Sub-Class I.—ACROGENAE.
FILICES. FERNS.

I.—POLYPODIACEAE.

1. POLYPODIUM. POLYPODY.

1. P. *vulgare*, Linn. *(Common P.)*
British type. Range in Britain, 50°—61°; coast to 1900 feet. Rocks, walls, &c. Frequent and general.

---

* Generally cellular, excepting Ferns and a few others, which have tubular vessels as well.

2. P. *Phegopteris*, Linn. *(Pale mountain P.)*
Scottish type, (or British). Range in Britain, 50°—61°.
Shady rocks, &c. More frequent in the interior.

K.—Crags of Airlie; Pitready, Strachan; Den of Davo, Garvock, Dr. Stephen. Bank at the water-fall, Corbie Den, Mr. Edgeworth; Banchory-Ternan, Rev. J. Brichan.

A.—In an open part of "College" wood, south shoulder of the Hill of Brimmond, Rev. A. Beverly; by the Burn of Culter, a mile above Culter Mills, Rev. J. Abel; Hill of Fare, Mr. Barron. In the woods between Ballater and Pannanich Lodge; Corrymulzie, and Linn of Quoich, at Castleton, G. D.

B.—Den between Eden and Inverichny, Rev. Dr. Todd.

3. P. *Dryopteris*, Linn. *(Tender three-branched P.)*
Scottish type. Range in Britain, 51°—59°; coast line to ?
Increases in frequency toward the interior of the district.

K.—South Kincardine, Mr. M'Farlane; Arbuthnot, Mr. Chrystall; stony places above marsh south-west from Bay of Nigg, and Corbie Den, Kingcausie, G.D.

A.—Den of Maidencraig, G. D.; rocks at the Burn of Culter, Rev. J. Abel; Hill of Fare, Mr. Barron. Pannanich rocks; banks of Loch Muick; Linns of Corrymulzie and Quoich, at Castleton; Ben Macdui, &c. G. D. Mungo wood, Huntly, Rev. J. Abel; at Laithers, near Turriff, Dr. Shier.

B.—Den at Mountblairy distillery, near the mill-dam, also den at Linhead, Alvah, Rev. Dr. Todd; Mortlach, Dr. L. Stewart.

4. P. *alpestre*, Hoppe. *(Alpine P.)*
Highland type. Range in Britain, 56°—57°; 2200 to 3600 feet.

Fissures of alpine rocks, and under shade of stones. Confined to the higher ranges, there abundant.

A.—On Lochnagar; head of Glen Callater; Corry of Loch Kander, G. D. In sheltered ravines on all the Braemar mountains, Ben Avon, Ben-a-Buird, &c. Very fine round the Wells of Dee, Mr. Croall.

2. ASPIDIUM. SHIELD-FERN.

1. A. *Lonchitis*, Sw. *(Rough alpine S.)*
Highland type. Range in Britain, 53°—59°; 1100 to 2400 feet.
Fissures of moist rocks. Confined to the interior.

A.—Linn of Quoich, south side; Corrymulzie; Callater rocks, G. D.; Craig Koynach, Castleton, Mr. Gardiner; Carr rocks, at Castleton, Mr. Sutherland and Mr. Croall.

2. **A. lobatum,** Sw. *(Close-leaved prickly S.)*
British type. Range in Britain, 50°—58°; 100 to 1000 feet.
Moist woods, &c. Very local in this district.

K.—East side of the river Feugh, below the bridge, near Banchory-Ternan, Dr. Stephen; in the Corbie Den, Kingcausie, G. D.; Durris, in a den two miles west of the house, Rev. A. Beverly.

A.—At the Manganese quarry, north side of the Don at Persley; and Carr Rocks, Castleton, Mr. Sutherland. At Laithers, near Turriff, Dr. Shier; in the Den of Auchmedden, Rev. G. Gairdner.

Var. β, lonchitidoides. In a glen on the ascent to Morven, from Tullich, two miles east from Ballater, Rev. A. Beverly.

3. **A. Oreopteris,** Sw. *(Heath S.)* *
British type. Range in Britain, 50°—61°; 200 to 2000 feet.

Natural pastures, woods, and rocks. Increases in frequency toward the interior, where it occurs often in great profusion.

K.—South Kincardine, Mr. M'Farlane; Arbuthnot, Mr. Chrystall; Banchory-Ternan, Rev. J. Brichan; by the Dye, in Strachan, Dr. Stephen.

A.—Woods west of House of Craibstone, Dr. Ogilvie; sparingly about Drum, Rev. A. Beverly; on Hill of Fare, and in the wood at Midmar Castle, Mr. Barron. In great profusion, and very fine, in the woods between Ballater and Pannanich; on the ascent from Altguisach to Lochnagar; in the woods at Castleton; rocks at the farm of Tomintoul, on the Mourne; rocks near farm of Auchalater, in Glen Clunie, G. D. Tullynessle, Rev. J. Minto; at Cachantesin fall, in Strathdon, G. D.

4. **A. Filix mas,** Sw. *(Blunt S.)*
British type. Range in Britain, 50°—61°; coast to 1747 feet, near the Fall of the Glassilt, head of Loch Muick.

Banks, rocks, &c. &c. Common and generally diffused.

Rev. A. Beverly has furnished the following notes respecting some of its varieties—

Var. incisa. Corbie Den, Maryculter.
Var. crispa. Muick-side, near Ballater.
Var. Borreri, (or paleacea?) Deeside, above Ballater.

---

* A. *Thelypteris,* Sw. Has been reported as found in South Kincardine, and in wood of Midmar, west from Aberdeen. Being doubtful, in the absence of evidence from specimens, I omit it from the list.

Aspidium.]   I. POLYPODIACEAE.   229

5. A. *dilatatum*, Willd. *(Prickly S.)* *
British type. Range in Britain, 50°—60°; coast line to 3500 feet, on Lochnagar.

Very generally diffused throughout the three counties; plentiful along the coast, and also not unfrequent on the higher r ıges, as Lochnagar, Glen Callater, Buck of Cabrach, &c. &c.

3. CYSTOPTERIS.   BLADDER-FERN.

1. C. *fragilis*, Bernh. *(Brittle B.)*
British type, (or Highland?) Range in Britain, 50°—59°; coast to 2000 feet?

Rocks and walls. Widely diffused in the district, but not common.

K.—In Den Fenella, Dr. Stephen. Occasionally along the Kincardineshire coast, as near Garron Point, &c.; Corbie Den, Kingcausie, G. D. On a wall near Fintray House, Professor Macgillivray; Den of Craig, Rev. J. Minto; at Laithers, near Turriff, Dr. Shier.

B.—Coast at Gamrie, Rev. G. Gairdner; rocks below Bridge of Alvah, Rev. Dr. Todd; in Mortlach, Dr. L. Stewart.

Var. β, *dentata*. Muick-side and Gairden-side, Rev. A. Beverly; Linns of Quoich and Corrymulzie, G. D.; Craig Koynach, at Castleton, Mr. Gardiner. North base of the Mourne; Carr Rocks and Glen Callater, Mr. Croall. Mortlach, Dr. L. Stewart.

Var. γ, *Dickieana*. Having been the first to distribute specimens in a living state, among cultivators, my name has been associated with this singular variety. It was, however, no original discovery of mine, the late Professor Knight having been in the habit of showing it to his pupils. It is now completely extirpated from the little cave south from the harbour at the Cove. I have found what appears to be the same variety in the crevices of a moist wall on the north side of the road about two miles west from Dunkeld. About half-a-mile north from the Cove, there is a dripping cave where there is a variety near the last. I have known it there during the last fifteen years.

2. C. *montana*, Link. *(Mountain B.)*
Highland type. Range in Britain, 56°—57°; altitude, 2500 to?
Alpine rocks. Very rare.

A.—Rocks, head of Glen Callater, Mr. Croall.

---

* The true A. *spinulosum*, *(Lastraea spinulosa*, Presl.) has doubtless been generally confounded with the A. *dilatatum*.

4. ASPLENIUM. SPLEENWORT.

1. *A. Septentrionale*, Hull. *(Forked S.)*
Scottish type. Range in Britain, 51°—57°; local at 1400 feet. Alpine rocks. Very rare.

A.—Rocks at the west end of the north side of the Pass of Ballater. This interesting addition to our list was made in 1855, by Dr. Patterson, R. N., from whom I have received living plants.

2. *A. Ruta-muraria*, Linn. *(Wall-rue S.)*
British type. Range in Britain, 50°—59°; 50 to 1500 feet.
Walls and rocks. Very local.

K.—South Kincardine, Mr. M'Farlane; bridge at Den of Brotherton, Dr. Stephen; on an old wall at Kingcausie, Mr. Gammie.

A.—Formerly in the fissures of parapets of the old Bridge of Dee, G. D.; on the old Bridge of Don, Dr. Shier; on a small bridge over a stream half a mile east from old Bridge of Dee, Mr. P. Macgillivray; on the walls of the old Chapel, King's College, Prof. Gregory; on the Old Machar Cathedral, Mr. P. Macgillivray; old walls at Leith-hall, Dr. D. Skene; north and east garden-walls at Drum, Dr. Ogilvie; the garden-wall of Drum, and old Castle of Tillyfour, Monymusk, Rev. A. Beverly; on a shady rock, near the waterfall, in Den of Craig, Auchindoir, Mr. Sutherland; on the very large boulders at the base of the "Lion's face," opposite Invercauld, 1857, G. D.

3. *A. Trichomanes*, Linn. *(Common Wall S.)*
British type. Range in Britain, 50°—60°; 100 to 1600 feet.
Shady rocks. Rather local.

K.—In Den Fenella, with fronds 16 inches long, Dr. Stephen and Rev. A. Beverly; east side of Feugh, below the bridge, at Banchory-Ternan, Dr. Stephen.

A.—Serpentine rocks near Meadowbank, in Belhelvie, G. D.; Den of Craig, Rev. J. Minto; at Towanrieffe, Auchindoir, Mr. Sutherland; serpentine rocks at Knockespock, Dr. A. Fleming. Shady rocks in the wood, south side of the road, a mile west from Bridge of Muick near Ballater; and rocks at the "Lion's face," near Castleton, G. D. Den of Auchmedden, Dr. D. Skene.

B.—Glen Fiddich, Dr. D. Skene; Mortlach, Dr. L. Stewart.

4. *A. viride*, Hudson. *(Green lanceolate S.)*
Highland type. Range in Britain, 51°—59°; 1100 to 2500 feet.

Alpine rocks in the inland and higher parts.

A.—On the craig of Lin Mui, near Ballater; rocks in Corrymulzie, near Castleton ; cliffs of the "Lion's face"; Glen Callater rocks, G.D. Limestone rocks and debris, north base of the Mourne, above Castleton, Mr. Croall. Rocks behind the farm of Tomintoul at Castleton, G.D.

5. A. *marinum*, Linn. *(Sea S.)*

British type, (or Atlantic). Range in Britain, 50°—60° ; coast line only.

Sea rocks. Rather local, but found in suitable localities on the whole coast line.

St. Cyrus' cliffs, Dr. Stephen. About Dunnottar and northwards; at Muchals; Sketrow; Cove; Girdleness; Aberdour; Gamrie.

6. A. *Adiantum nigrum*, Linn. *(Black-stalked S.)*

British type. Range in Britain, 50°—60° ; coast to 1800 feet.

Fissures of rocks. Very local.

K.—Den of Davo, Garvock ; Annie's Den, Benholme ; Den Fenella, above the old bridge, Dr. Stephen. Banchory-Ternan, Rev. J. Brichan. Coast between Stonehaven and Aberdeen, as at Cove, &c., G.D. At Portlethen and Muchalls, 10 to 15 inches long, Rev. A. Beverly.

A.—Rocks near Meadowbank, Belhelvie, G.D. ; in a dyke by a cross-road west of Springhill, near Aberdeen, Rev. A. Beverly ; in Pass of Ballater, sparingly, Mr. Sutherland ; on the Khoil and Craig of Lin Mui, near Ballater, G.D. ; at Leith-hall, Dr. D. Skene ; serpentine rocks, Knockespock, Dr. A. Fleming; Den of Craig and Towanrieffe, Mr. Sutherland.

B.—Coast at Gamrie, Rev. G. Gairdner. Rocks of Alvah; and near Mill of Eden, on rocks, rare, Rev. Dr. Todd. Mortlach, Dr. L. Stewart.

7. A. *Filix fœmina*, Bernh. *(Short-fruited S.)*

British type. Range in Britain, 50°—61° ; coast to 1800 feet.

Moist shady places. Common, and widely diffused in the district. Attains the above elevation in the ravine of the Glassilt, head of Loch Muick.

Var. β, latifolium. Is abundant, growing from the roof of the cave where *var. Dickieana* of *C. fragilis* grew.

5. SCOLOPENDRIUM. HART'S TONGUE.

1. S. *vulgare*, Sym. *(Common H.)*

British type Range in Britain, 50°—61°; coast line only, in this district.

Shady and moist places. Very rare and local.

K.—Den Fenella, abundant, Dr. Stephen. In a cave at north end of Sketrow harbour, Newtonhill station, south from Aberdeen; a few plants only; found first in 1857 by Mr. H. A. Smith.

A.—Among ruins near the House of Frendraught, parish of Forgue, Rev. J. Abel; Den of Auchmedden, Rev. G. Gairdner.

6. PTERIS. BRAKE-FERN.

1. P. *aquilina*, Linn. *(Common B.)*

British type. Range in Britain, 50°—61°; coast to 1900 feet. Woods, pastures, &c. Very common.

7. CRYPTOGRAMMA. ROCK-BRAKE.

1. C. *crispa*, Br. *(Curled R.)*

Highland type. Range in Britain, 51°—59°; 300 to 2600 feet. Stony places in the interior. Very local.

A.—Upon an old wall at Damseat, parish of Echt, Mr. Barron, from whom I have received a specimen. On Cairn William, Monymusk, Rev. A. Beverly, who also states that he has received it from the east slope of a stony brae, two and a-half miles above Ballater. On the east cliffs of Lochnagar, and by the side of the lake at the base of the cliffs, G. D. Ben-a-Buird and Cairntoul, Mr. P. Macgillivray. Corry of Loch Kander, at head of Glen Callater, Prof. Macgillivray.

8. BLECHNUM. HARD-FERN.

1. B. *boreale*, Sw. *(Northern H.)*

British type. Range in Britain, 50°—60°; coast to 2400 feet. Pastures, woods, &c. Very general.

II.—OSMUNDACEAE.

1. OSMUNDA. OSMUND-ROYAL.

1. O. *regalis*, Linn. *(Common O.)*

British type. Range in Britain, 50°—61°; coast to 100 feet. Wet places. Very rare.

K.—On steep rocks, half-a-mile south from the Cove, and by the side of a waterfall, a little north from the Cove, G. D.

A.—On the banks of the rivulet flowing from Loch of Park, first found by the late Mr. P. Grant; reported as now extinct there.

III.—OPHIOGLOSSACEAE.

1. OPHIOGLOSSUM. ADDER'S-TONGUE.

1. O. *vulgatum*, Linn. *(Common A.)*
British type. Range in Britain, 50°—61°; coast line.
Moist pastures and in woods. Very rare.

K.—Den Fenella; north end of Den of Jackstone, St. Cyrus, Dr. Stephen. Arbuthnot, Mr. Chrystall.

2. BOTRYCHIUM. MOONWORT.

1. B. *Lunaria*, Sw. *(Common M.)*
British type. Range in Britain, 50°—61°; coast to 2400 feet.
Natural pastures. Generally diffused.

K.—Sands of St. Cyrus, Mr. Croall. Jackstone, St. Cyrus; Pitready, Strachan, Dr. Stephen. Upper end of Corbie Den, Kingcausie, G. D.; Banchory-Ternan, Rev. J. Brichan.

A.—Near Aberdeen, at Corsehill, Scotston; Links, behind Preventive-station at Don-mouth; bank by the old Stocket road, at the north end of Summerhill, G. D. Hill of Tyrebagger, and at Tartowie, Dr. A. Fleming; at east end of Loch of Drum, Rev. A. Beverly. In Braemar, on Little Craigendall, and Glen Callater, G. D. Green banks in the moss at the foot of the Carr Rocks, Castleton, Mr. Croall; on south face of Morven, G. D.; Tillenhilt and Gallowhill, Cluny, Mr. Barron; Alford, Rev. Dr. Farquharson; Tullynessle, Rev. J. Minto; Corgarff, Mr. Barron; road-side near Tulloch House, Meldrum, Rev. J. Abel; in Cruden, Mr. A. Murray.

B.—Hill of Stoneley, and hilly parts of Rosyburn, Alvah, Rev. Dr. Todd; Mortlach, Dr. L. Stewart.*

IV.—LYCOPODIACEAE.

1. LYCOPODIUM. CLUB-MOSS.

1. L. *clavatum*, Linn. *(Common C.)*

---

* Other three Ferns have been reported as belonging to this district, I have no doubt that some error has arisen regarding them. *Adiantum C. Veneris* is stated to have been found by the river Ury, near Stonehaven, and *Asplenium fontanum* at Garron Point, north from the same place. The other is *Gymnogramma leptophylla*, said to have been found on a wall by the side of the road to Castleton, opposite to Invercauld.

British type. Range in Britain, 50°—60°; coast line to 2200 feet.

Heathy pastures. Frequent and generally diffused. Attains the above elevation on Morven and Lochnagar.

2. L. *annotinum*, Linn. *(Interrupted C.)*

Highland type. Range in Britain, 53°—59°; 1000 ? to 2600 feet.

Mountain heaths. Confined to the interior.

A.—Near the summit of the path on the west shoulder of Mount Keen; abundant on Lochnagar by several ways of ascent; and frequent in Braemar, G. D. On Morven, Mr. Sutherland; plentiful on Ben Avon, covering the hill-side, Mr. Croall; Little Craigendall, Ben-a-Buird, and Ben Macdui, Mr. R. Mackay.

B.—On Cairngorm, Mr. R. Mackay; on Belrinnes, Dr. L. Stewart.

3. L. *selaginoides*, Linn. *(Less Alpine C.)* *

Highland type. Range in Britain, 53°—61°; coast line to 3000 ? feet.

Marshy places. Frequent both in the lower and higher parts of the district.

K.—South Kincardine, Mr. M'Farlane; Banchory-Ternan, Rev. J. Brichan; upper part of Corbie Den, Kingcausie, G. D.

A.—Marsh by the Udny road, seven miles north from Aberdeen; bogs at Deanston; at Scotston and Denmore, G. D. Marsh at Leggerdale, by the Echt road, Mr. Barron; Towanrieffe, Rhynie, Mr. Sutherland. On the Khoil at Ballater; marsh, south base of Morven; Callater Rocks; Glen Gairden, &c. G. D. In Strathdon, at the Fall of Cachantesin, &c. G. D. Ben-a-Buird; Ben Avon; Cairntoul; Braeriach; Ben Macdui, Mr. R. Mackay.

4. L. *alpinum*, Linn. *(Savine-leaved C.)*

Highland type. Range in Britain, 51°—61°; 250 to 3400 feet.

Mountain pastures and heaths. More abundant in the interior; rarer in the lower parts.

K.—Strachan; Benholme, &c. Dr. Stephen. At the base of the cairns on the hills at Nigg, about a mile from the sea, and 250 feet above its level, G. D.; Banchory-Ternan, Rev. J. Brichan.

---

* L. *inundatum* occurs in Moray; I have no record of its presence in this district; it is probably often overlooked.

A.—Top of Brimmanhill, parish of Newhills, G. D. ; Normandyke, at Culter, Dr. J. Smith ; Hill of Fare, Mr. Barron. Near the summit of Mount Battock ; in great profusion on Morven, along with *Sibbaldia* ; on the Khoil at Ballater ; on Lochnagar, &c. &c. G. D. Little Craigendall ; Glen Callater ; Ben Macdui, &c. Mr. R. Mackay. Tullynessle, and abundant at Tullyangus, in Clatt, Rev. J. Minto ; on the Formanhill, in Forgue, Rev. J. Abel ; on the Buck of the Cabrach, G. D. ; in Corgarff, Mr. Barron.

B.—Alvah, Rev. Dr. Todd.

5. L. *Selago*, Linn. *(Fir C.)*

British type, (or Highland). Range in Britain, 50°—61° ; 100 to 4320 feet.

Heathy pastures. Common and generally diffused. One of the few plants which grow on the extreme summits of the higher mountains, as Morven, Lochnagar, Ben Macdui, &c.

V.—MARSILEACEAE.

1. ISOETES. QUILL-WORT.

1. I. *lacustris*, Linn. *(European Q.)*

Highland type. Range in Britain, 52°—59° ; 100 to 2200 feet. Bottoms of lakes. Very local.

A.—At east end of Loch of Park, Dr. A. Fleming ; Loch Cannor and Loch Muick, Prof. Macgillivray ; in Loch Kander, head of Glen Callater, Mr. Croall ; In a small loch, a little to the east of Loch Builg, Mr. Barron.

2. PILULARIA. PILL-WORT.

1. P. *globulifera*, Linn. *(Creeping P.)*

British type. Range in Britain, 50°—59°.

Local at 100 ? feet.

Margins of Lakes. Very rare.

A.—South and east margins of Loch of Park.

VI.—EQUISETACEAE.

EQUISETUM. HORSETAIL.[*]

1. E. *umbrosum*, Willd. *(Blunt topped H.)*

Scottish type. Range in Britain, 53°—58° ; 300 to 700 feet?

---

[*] E *fluviatile*, admitted into "Flora Aberdonensis," 1838, was so by mistake

Moist Shady places. Rare.

K.—Damp shady places near the burn, parish of Fettercairn, rather scarce. Abundant and in fruit on the opposite side of the Esk, Mr. Croall.

A.—Near Ballater by the road to Glen Muick, Mr. R. Mackay.

2. E. *arvense*, Linn. *(Field H.)*
British type. Range in Britain, 50°—61°; coast line to 800 ? feet.
Fields and wastes. Common, chiefly in the lower parts.

3. E. *sylvaticum*, Linn. *(Branched Wood H.)*
British type. Range in Britain, 50°—61°; coast line to 2000 ? feet.
Moist woods and banks. Frequent and general.

4. E. *limosum*, Linn. *(Smooth Naked H.)*
British type. Range in Britain, 50°—61°; 100 to 2200 feet.
Marshes and lakes. Occurs in suitable localities in most parts of the district.

5. E. *palustre*, Linn. *(Marsh H.)*
British type. Range in Britain, 50°—61°; coast line to 2000 ? feet.
Marshes and bogs. Frequent.

6. E. *Mackayi*, Newm. *(Long-stemmed H.)*
Scottish type. Range in Britain, 57°—58°; local at 150 to 170 feet.
Moist shady places. Very rare.

K.—Along the course of the Dee, several miles above and below Banchory-Ternan, Rev. J. Brichan.

7. E. *hyemale*, Linn. *(Rough H.)*
Scottish type, (or British.) Range in Britain, 51°—58°; 150 to 400 feet.
Marshy and shady places. Very local.

K.—Along the course of the Dee at Banchory-Ternan, Rev. J. Brichan ; by a stream below Blackness, Strachan, Dr. Stephen.

A.—Marshy ground on the north-west side of the Farm of Auchmenzie in Clatt; also in Auchindoir on the hill-side opposite the sandstone quarries, Rev. J. Minto ; near the Manse of Cabrach, Rev. W. Gordon.

8. E. *variegatum*, Schleich. *(Variegated rough H.)*
Scottish type. Range in Britain, 50°—58°; 20 to 170 feet. Wet sandy and gravelly places. Very local.

K.—Along the course of the Dee at Banchory-Ternan, Rev. J. Brichan; south bank of the Dee near Aberdeen, between the old bridge and Railway viaduct, Rev. J. Farquharson; links south of Newburgh, and north bank of the Dee at Drumoak, Mr. P. Macgillivray.

MUSCI, MOSSES.*

I.—ANDREAEACEAE.

1. ANDREAEA.

1. A. *alpina*, Dillen. *(Alpine A.)*
On rocks. Rare in the lower, abundant in the higher and inland parts of the district. Hill of Fare, Mr. Mackay and G.D. Plentiful on the higher mountains.

2 A. *rupestris*, Linn. *(Rock A.)*
On rocks and walls. Generally diffused. Clockhill, Benholme; Banchory-Ternan, &c., Dr. Stephen. Near Aberdeen on old walls and boulders, above Bay of Nigg; Tollohill; by the wood west from Pitmedden, G.D. Common in the interior.

3. A. *Rothii*, Web. and Mohr. *(Black falcate-leaved A.)*
On rocks and walls. Generally diffused. Near Aberdeen, on boulders at new Church of Nigg, and on Hill of Fare, G.D. Very abundant in the interior; Pannanich cliffs; Lochnagar; Buck of Cabrach, &c., G.D. Cairngorm.

4. A. *nivalis*, Hooker. *(Tall, slender A.)*
Alpine rocks. Confined to a few of the higher mountains in the interior. Lochnagar; Ben Macdui, Mr. Mackay and G.D. Cairngorm, &c.

II.—SPHAGNACEAE.

1. SPHAGNUM. BOG-MOSS.

1. S. *cymbifolium*, Dill. *(Blunt-leaved B.)*
Bogs and marshes. Common.

* In this Sub-class I have adopted the nomenclature in "Wilson's Bryologia Britannica."

2. S. *compactum*, Bridel. *(Compact B.)*
On dry moors, chiefly inland. On Lochnagar, &c., Mr. Croall.

3. S. *acutifolium*, Ehrh. *(Acute-leaved B.)*
Marshes. Rather local. Loch of Park; Hill of Fare, &c. G.D.

4. S. *molluscum*, Bruch. *(Pale dwarf B.)*
Peat bogs. Moss behind Castleton; Glen Callater, &c., Mr. Croall.

5. S. *cuspidatum*, Dill. *(Wavy-leaved B.)*
Wet bogs. Frequent and general.

6. S. *squarrosum*, Persoon. *(Spreading-leaved B.)*
In peat bogs. Local. Mourne at Castleton, damp places among the heath, north side, Mr. Croall.

III.—BRYACEAE.

1. PHASCUM. EARTH-MOSS.

1. P. *cuspidatum*, Schreb. *(Pointed E.)*
Shady banks, &c. Not unfrequent in old pastures round Aberdeen.

Var γ, *piliferum*. Crevices of rocks at the Girdleness Lighthouse, G.D.

2. P. *subulatum*, Linn. *(Awl-leaved E.)*
Shady banks, &c. Very local. On a steep bank in Den of Leggart, south-west from old Bridge of Dee, G.D. In the moss behind Castleton, Braemar, Mr. Croall.

2. GYMNOSTOMUM. BEARDLESS-MOSS.

1. G. *rupestre*, Schwaeg. *(Rock B.)*
Damp rocks, in lower as well as higher parts of the district. In Den Fenella; at the Burn, &c. &c. Mr. Croall.

2. G. *tenue*, Schrad. *(Slender B.)*
Shady rocks. Rare. North Esk, at the Burn, abundant, Mr. Croall.

3. WEISSIA. WEISSIA.

1. W. *controversa*, Hedw. *(Green-tufted W.)*
Dry banks. Frequent.

2. W. *cirrhata*, Hedw. *(Bent-leaved W.)*

On walls, boulders, &c. Very frequent. Near Aberdeen, at Stocket Moor; Hill of Fare; hills at Nigg, G.D. On ruins of Mar Castle, Mr. Croall.

3. W. *crispula*, Hedw. *(Curly-leaved W.)*
On rocks. Frequent everywhere. Rocks at Girdleness; banks of Dee at Drumoak; Glen Callater rocks, G.D.

4. W. *verticillata*, Bridel. *(Whorled W.)*
Dripping rocks. Rare. Rocks at St. Cyrus, Mr. Croall.

4. RHABDOWEISSIA. STREAK-MOSS.

1. R. *fugax*, Br. and Sch. *(Dwarf S.)*
Crevices of alpine rocks. Rare. At the Linn of the Garrawalt, Mr. Gardiner.

5. SELIGERIA. BRISTLE-MOSS.

1. S. *pusilla*, Br. and Sch. *(Dwarf B.)*
Shady calcareous rocks. Very local. On limestone in the rocky bed of a stream between Loch Builg and Inchrory, Mr. Mackay and G. D.; in crevices of rocks, north base of the Mourne, and Carr Rocks, at Castleton, Mr. Croall.

2. S. *recurvata*, Br. and Sch. *(Curve-necked B.)*
Rare. Rock by the North Esk river, at the Burn, plentiful, Mr. Croall.

6. BLINDIA. BLINDIA.

1. B. *acuta*, Br. and Sch. *(Acute-leaved B.)*
Moist rocks and stones. Generally diffused. Near Aberdeen, at Corsehill, Scotston; Howe of Corrichie, Hill of Fare; common in the interior, G. D.

7. ARCTOA. ARCTOA.

1. A. *fulvella*, Br. and Sch. *(Brownish A.)*
Fissures of alpine rocks. Not unfrequent in the interior. Rocks in Glen Callater, G. D. Top of the cliffs above the Dhuloch; Lochnagar, and on Ben Macdui, Mr. Croall.

8. CYNODONTIUM.

1. C. *Bruntoni*, Br. and Sch. *(Brunton's Fork-moss.)*
Alpine rocks. Frequent in the interior. Pannanich cliffs; Glen Callater Rocks, G. D. Linn of Garrawalt, Mr. Gardiner; rocks in Glen Clunie, north side, Mr. Croall.

9. DICRANUM. FORK-MOSS

1. D. *polycarpum*, Ehrh. *(Many-fruited F.)*

Alpine rocks. Rather local. On Bennachie, Mr. Don, where I have also found it; in Glen Clunie, Mr. Croall.

2. D. *pellucidum*, Hedw. *(Pellucid F.)*

Moist rocks by streams. Very local. Den Fenella, above the old bridge, Dr. Stephen; Den of Robslaw, G. D.; banks of the Dee above Ballater; and Ballochbuie, Mr. Croall.

3. D. *squarrosum*, Schrad. *(Drooping-leaved F.)*

Marshy places. Rather local. Bingley burn, Glen of Dye; south end of the pier at Torry, Dr. Stephen. Bay of Nigg, and Hill of Fare, G. D.

4. D. *varium*, Hedw. *(Variable F.)*

Moist Banks. Not uncommon. Den Fenella; Brae of Comiston, Mr. Croall. Near Aberdeen, steep banks at Torry opposite the new pier; Robslaw quarry, &c. G. D.

5. D. *rufescens*, Turner. *(Reddish F.)*

Moist banks. Rather local. Den Fenella, and Brae of Comiston, Mr. Croall; near Aberdeen, at Robslaw quarry, G. D.

6. D. *cerviculatum*, Hedw. *(Spur-necked F.)*

Turfy and sandy banks. Rather local. Formerly in Ferryhill moss, G. D.; in Den of Midmar, Hill of Fare, &c. Mr. Mackay and G. D.

7. D. *subulatum*, Hedw. *(Awl-leaved F.)*

Moist banks. Sandy braes at Torry, opposite the pier, G. D.; east side of the Mourne at Castleton; and in Glen Callater, Mr. Gardiner.

8. D. *heteromallum*, Hedw. *(Silky-leaved F.)*

Moist banks. Not unfrequent. Near Aberdeen, in Den of Robslaw; Hill of Fare; Bennachie, G. D. In Glen Clunie; road-side west from Castleton, plentiful, Mr. Croall. Glen Callater, Mr. Gardiner.

9. D. *Blyttii*, Br. and Sch. *(Blytt's F.)*

Alpine rocks. Confined to the interior. On Lochnagar, &c. Mr. Croall.

10. D. *Starkii*, Web. and Mohr. *(Starke's F.)*

Alpine rocks. On the higher mountains. In Glen Callater, G. D.; top of Ben-a-Buird, Mr. Gardiner.

Var. β, *molle*. North side of Lochnagar, among boulders, abundant in fruit, Mr. Croall.

11. D. *falcatum*, Hedw. *(Sickle-leaved F.)*
Alpine rocks. Abundant in the higher parts. Hill of Fare ; Glen Callater, &c. Mr. Mackay and G. D. Top of Ben-a-Buird, Mr. Gardiner.

12. D. *fuscescens*, Turner. *(Dusky F.)*
Shady rocks, &c. Generally diffused. Near Aberdeen, in Den of Maidencraig; Den of Midmar, G. D. Lochnagar and Ben Avon, Mr. Croall; Garrawalt and Glen Callater, Mr. Gardiner.

13. D. *scoparium*, Hedw. *(Broom F.)*
Shady banks, rocks, &c. Very common.

14. D. *circinatum*, Wilson. *(Circinate F.)*
Not unfrequent in the higher valleys, mixed with other mosses, &c.; never by itself. Among *J. Doniana*, head of Loch Avon, &c. Mr. Croall.

15. D. *palustre*, Bridel. *(Marsh F.)*
Marshy places and moist banks. Rather local. Wet places among the sand-hills in Belhelvie links, as at Black Dog, &c. G. D.

16. D. *spurium*, Hedw. *(Wide-leaved F.)*
On moors in the interior. Very local. South side of the river Muick near the saw-mill, G. D.; among the heath on the ascent from Little Craigendall to Ben Avon, Mr. Croall.

17. D. *majus*, Turner. *(Tall F.)*
Shady banks and rocks. Rather local. In Corrymulzie and Glen Clunie, &c. Mr. Croall.

10. LEUCOBRYUM. FORK-MOSS.

1. L. *glaucum*, Hampe. *(White-leaved F.)*
Moist places on moors. Generally diffused. Near Aberdeen, on Scotston moor; hills at Nigg; Hill of Fare; Bennachie, &c. G. D.

11. CERATODON. FORK-MOSS.

1. C. *purpureus*, Bridel. *(Purple F.)*
On banks, &c. &c. Very common everywhere.

12. CAMPYLOPUS. SWAN-NECK MOSS.

1. C. *flexuosus*, Dill. *(Rusty S.)*
Moist rocks. Chiefly in upland parts. Den of Midmar.

and Hill of Fare; at Loch of Park; on Lochnagar, &c. Mr. Mackay and G. D. Glen Callater, Mr. Croall; Cairn-a-Drochet, Braemar, Mr. Gardiner.

2. C. *longipilus*, Bridel. *(Bristly S.)*
Dripping rocks in the interior. Ben Macdui; Dhuloch; Glen Callater, &c. Mr. Croall.

13. POTTIA. POTTIA.

1. P. *truncata*, Br. and Sch. *(Common P.)*
On moist soil, old pastures, &c. Common.

2. P. *crinita*, Wilson. *(Bristly P.)*
Moist spots among rocks near the sea. Rare. On a rocky point opposite Girdleness Lighthouse, G. D.

3. P. *Heimii*, Br. and Sch. *(Lance-leaved P.)*
Moist banks near the sea. Rather local. Along with last, and in the Old Aberdeen links, G. D.

14. ANACALYPTA. ANACALYPTA.

1. A. *latifolia*, Nees. *(Bulb-leaved A.)*
Crevices of alpine rocks. Very local. Rocks, north base of the Mourne, above Castleton, plentiful, Mr. Croall.

15. DISTICHIUM. DISTICHIUM.

1. D. *capillaceum*, Br. and Sch. *(Fine-leaved D.)*
Shady alpine rocks. Frequent in the interior. Callater rocks, Mr. Mackay and G. D.; Craig Koynach, at Castleton, Mr. Gardiner. Carr rocks; Glen Clunie, &c. Mr. Croall.

16. DIDYMODON. DIDYMODON.

1. D. *rubellus*, Br. and Sch. *(Reddish D.)*
Shady walls, rocks, &c. Frequent. Rocks at the Burn, parish of Fettercairn, Mr. Croall; on walls at Denmore, near Aberdeen, G. D.; on the bridge in Glen Clunie, Mr. Croall; Corrymulzie and Glen Callater, Mr. Gardiner.

17. TRICHOSTOMUM. TRICHOSTOMUM.

1. T. *rigidulum*, Smith. *(Rigid-leaved T.)*
Moist walls, banks, &c. Rather local. Den of Canterland; rocks of the Burn, Mr. Croall. Near Aberdeen, at Robslaw quarry, &c. G. D. East side of the Mourne at Castleton, Mr. Gardiner.

2. T. *flexicaule*, Br. and Sch. *(Wavy-stemmed T.)*
On shady rocks. Local. Rocks at the Burn; frequent in Braemar; Glen Callater; Carr rocks, &c.; always barren, Mr. Croall.

3. T. *homomallum*, Br. and Sch. *(Curve-leaved T.)*
Sandy banks. Not unfrequent. Near Aberdeen, at Robslaw quarry, G. D.; Moist banks in Glen Clunie, Mr. Croall; on the east side of the Mourne, Mr. Gardiner.

18. TORTULA. SCREW-MOSS

1. T. *unguiculata*, Hedw. *(Bird's-claw S.)*
Moist banks, &c. Very frequent. Rocks at St. Cyrus, Mr. Croall. Near Aberdeen, south bank of the Don between the two bridges, G. D.

2. T. *fallax*, Hedw. *(Fallacious S.)*
Moist banks, &c. Not uncommon. Den Fenella, &c. Mr. Croall. Near Aberdeen, on the banks of the Don, and in the dry den, Countesswells, G. D.

3. T. *tortuosa*, Web. and Mohr. *(Curly-leaved S.)*
On rocks. Not frequent. Usually barren. On the Kincardineshire coast, G. D.; rocks at the Burn, Mr. Croall; Glen Muick and Craig Koynach, Mr. Gardiner; Carr rocks, among the debris, abundant in fruit, Mr. Croall.

4. T. *muralis*, Timm. *(Wall S.)*
Tops of walls, &c. Very common.

5. T. *subulata*, Bridel. *(Awl-leaved S.)*
Moist banks, &c. Very frequent.

6. T. *ruralis*, Hedw. *(Great hairy S.)*
Walls, dry banks, &c. Frequent. Abundant on St. Cyrus' sands, Mr. Croall; plentiful in fruit among the sand-hills in Old Aberdeen links, G. D.; roofs of houses at Castleton, Mr. Croall.

19. CINCLIDOTUS. WATER SCREW-MOSS.

1. C. *fontinaloides*, P. Beauv. *(Smaller W.)*
On stones in streams. Very local. Den Fenella, at the old Bridge, Mr. Croall; Den of Leggart, near Aberdeen, Dr. Stephen.

20. ENCALYPTA. EXTINGUISHER-MOSS.

1. E. *commutata*, Nees. *(Sharp-leaved E.)*

Alpine rocks. Very local and rare. Glen Callater rocks, Mr. Mackay and G. D.

2. E. *vulgaris*, Hedw. *(Common E.)*

Walls, banks, &c. Very local. Old walls on the hill north from Den Fenella, Mr. Croall; wall by the old road at Brigton, St. Cyrus, Dr. Stephen. Near Aberdeen, on an old wall, east side of the road from old Bridge of Don to Scotston and Denmore, G. D.; on the Carr rocks, at Castleton, Mr. Croall.

3. E. *ciliata*, Hedw. *(Fringed E.)*

Shady rocks. Very local. Only in the interior. Abundant upon rocks in a wood on the south side of the road to Glen Muick, about two miles west from Ballater, G. D. In Corrymulzie; Glen Callater, &c. Mr. Croall.

4. E. *streptocarpa*, Hedw. *(Spiral-fruited E.)*

Walls and rocks. Very rare and local. Old walls at the Burn, Mr. Croall; on the bridge at Auchallater, near Castleton, Mr. Gardiner; on the old Bridge of Dee at Invercauld, Mr. Gardiner and Mr. Croall.

21. HEDWIGIA. BEARDLESS-MOSS.

1. H. *ciliata*, Hedw. *(Hoary, branched B.)*

On rocks and stones. Very abundant and general. St. Cyrus, Dr. Stephen. A common species on the numerous boulders upon moors round Aberdeen, and in the interior, G. D.

22. SCHISTIDIUM.

1. S. *apocarpum*, Br. and Sch. *(Sessile S.)*

On rocks and walls. Very frequent and general.

Var. γ, *rivulare.* On stones in streams. Den of Robslaw, &c. &c.

2. S. *maritimum*, Br. and Sch. *(Sea-side S.)*

Maritime rocks. Very abundant along the coast.

23. GRIMMIA.

1. G. *pulvinata*, Smith. *(Grey-cushioned G.)*

On walls, roofs, and rocks. Common everywhere.

2. G. *spiralis*, Hook. and Tayl. *(Spiral-leaved G.)*

Alpine rocks. Confined to the interior, and local. Pannanich cliffs, and Khoil hill, near Ballater, G. D. Ben Avon, Mr. Gardiner; Callater rocks, Mr. Mackay and G. D.

3. G. *torta*, Hornsch. *(Twisted-leaved G.)*
Alpine rocks. Confined to the interior. Craig Koynach, at Castleton, Mr. Gardiner; Callater rocks, Mr. Mackay and G. D.

4. G. *tricophylla*, Greville. *(Hair-pointed G.)*
On stones and walls. Apparently rare. Near Aberdeen, on blocks of gneiss, west from Gilcomston Dam, near the former site of the spade-mill, G. D.

5. G. *patens*, Br. and Sch. *(Tall alpine G.)*
Shady alpine rocks. Local in the interior. Glen Callater and Lochnagar, Mr. Croall; rocks of the Dhuloch, Mr. Mackay and G. D.

6. G. *Doniana*, Smith. *(Don's G.)*
Rocks and walls. Chiefly in the interior. On stones, &c. by the road leading from Midmar Castle to the moss on the Hill of Fare, Mr. Mackay and G. D.; Pannanich cliffs, G. D.; old walls about Invercauld, Mr. Croall; Craig Koynach and Ben Avon, Mr. Gardiner; Cairngorm, Mr. Drummond.

7. G. *ovata*, Web. and Mohr. *(Oval-fruited G.)*
Alpine rocks. Rather local. On the summit of Bennachie; Pannanich cliffs, and on the walls of the vitrified fort, top of Noth, G. D.

8. G. *atrata*, Mielich. *(Black-tufted G.)*
Alpine rocks. In the interior, and very rare. Glen Callater, Dr. Greville; rocks above Loch Kander, Mr. Croall.

24. RACOMITRIUM. FRINGE-MOSS.

1. R. *aciculare*, Bridel. *(Dark, Mountain F.)*
Moist rocks. In different parts of the district. Den Fenella, and Bridge of Feugh, Dr. Stephen; rocks at the Burn, Mr. Croall. Near Aberdeen, in Den of Leggart, G. D.; abundant in Braemar, Mr. Croall; Pannanich cliffs, and Glen Muick, G. D.

2. R. *protensum*, Al. Braun. *(Narrow-leaved F.)*
Moist alpine rocks. Higher parts of the interior. Glen Callater, and base of Ben Macdui, Mr. Croall.

3. R. *sudeticum*, Br. and Sch. *(Slender Mountain F.)*
Alpine rocks. Higher parts of the interior. Glen Callater and Dhuloch rocks, Mr. Mackay and G. D.

4. R. *fasciculare*, Bridel. *(Green Mountain F.)*

On rocks and stones. Generally diffused. Hill of Woodston, Mr. Croall. Near Aberdeen, at Tollohill, Hill of Fare. &c. G. D. Near Ballater, and old walls at Invercauld, Mr. Croall.

5. R. *heterostichum*, Bridel. *(Bristly Mountain F.)*
On rocks and boulders. Very frequent and general.

6. R. *lanuginosum*, Bridel. *(Woolly F.)*
On walls, rocks, and the bare soil. Common everywhere; forming a carpet of vegetation on the tops of the higher mountains.

7. R. *canescens*, Bridel. *(Hoary F.)*
Heaths, and sandy and gravelly places. Frequent. St. Cyrus' sands, Mr. Croall. Near Aberdeen, at Middleton; on Hill of Fare; in Glen Callater, &c. G. D.

25. PTYCHOMITRIUM.

1. P. *polyphyllum*, Br. and Sch. *(Many-leaved P.)*
On walls and rocks. Apparently local. Near Aberdeen, in the wood at Middleton, &c. G. D.

26. ORTHOTRICHUM. BRISTLE-MOSS.

1. O. *cupulatum*, Hoffm. *(Single-fringed, sessile B.)*
Rocks and walls. Rather local. Den Fenella, Dr. Stephen; St. Cyrus, Mr. Croall.

2. O. *anomalum*, Hedw. *(Anomalous B.)*
On rocks and walls. Rather local. St. Cyrus' rocks; rocks and old walls, north base of the Mourne at Castleton, Mr. Croall. Serpentine rocks near Meadowbank, Belhelvie; Ballater; Corrymulzie, G. D.

3. O. *affine*, Schrad. *(Common Wood B.)*
Rocks; walls; usually on trees. Very general. Trees, Den Fenella, Mr. Croall. Near Aberdeen, at Drum; Hill of Fare; Kinmundy of Skene; Corrymulzie; Craigendarroch, G. D.

4. O. *speciosum*, Nees. ab Es. *(Showy B.)*
On trees. Apparently rare, and confined to the interior. Corrymulzie, Braemar, Mr. Adamson.

5. O. *diaphanum*, Schrader. *(White-tipped B.)*
Trees, &c. Apparently rather local. Near Aberdeen, on trees at Hildon-tree, and Hermitage at Powis, G. D.

6. O. *leiocarpum*, Br. and Sch. *(Smooth-fruited B.)*
Usually on trees. Apparently local. Beside House of Kinmundy, parish of Skene, G. D.

7. O. *pulchellum*, Smith. *(Elegant B.)*
Usually on trees. Local, but usually abundant. Near Aberdeen, on trees in Dens of Leggart and Maidencraig; and in the dry Den, Countesswells, G. D.

8. O. *crispum*, Hedw. *(Curled B.)*
On trees. Very frequent, especially in the lower parts of this district. Hill of Woodston, and at the Burn, Mr. Croall. Den Fenella, Dr. Stephen. Hill of Fare; Maidencraig; about Ballater, G. D.

9. O. *Bruchii*, Bridel. *(Tawny-fruited B.)*
On trees. Apparently confined to the interior. At the Burn, parish of Fettercairn; trees west from Castleton, and on Craig Koynach, Mr. Croall.

10. O. *Drummondii*, Hook. and Grev. *(Drummond's B.)*
Chiefly on Birch trees. In the upper districts. About Castleton, Mr. Croall; Ben Beck, at Castleton, Mr. Gardiner; Corrymulzie, G. D.

11. O. *Hutchinsiae*, Smith. *(Miss Hutchin's B.)*
On rocks. Chiefly in the inland and higher parts. Rare. Rocks at the Burn, Mr. Croall; Callater rocks, and rocks of the Dhuloch, Mr. Mackay and G. D.

27. ZYGODON. YOKE-MOSS.

1. Z. *Lapponicus*, Br. and Sch. *(Lapland Y.)*
Crevices of alpine rocks. In the interior. Rather local. Khoil at Ballater; Glen Callater, Mr. Mackay and G. D.

2. Z. *Mougeotii*, Br. and Sch. *(Mougeot's Y.)*
On moist shady rocks. Confined to the interior. Glen Callater; Corrymulzie, Mr. Croall.

28. TETRAPHIS. FOUR-TOOTHED MOSS.

1. T. *pellucida*, Hedw. *(Pellucid F.)*
Moist shady banks. Rather local. By the footpath near the Queen's Well, at Midmar Castle, Mr. Mackay and G. D.; in Ballachbuie and Glen Callater, Mr. Croall; near Pannanich Wells, G. D.; Linns of Garrawalt and Quoich, Mr. Gardiner.

29. BUXBAUMIA.

1. B. *aphylla*, Haller. *(Leafless B.)*

On stones in woods, and on heaths. Apparently rare. Near Aberdeen, Mr. Jackson; on a moss-covered granite block on the south side of the road about half-way between Pannanich Lodge and Ballater, Mr. A. Cruickshank, from whom I received a specimen. I have often searched, but in vain, for this fine species, yet I cannot doubt that it must be frequent in such a district as this.

30. DIPHYSCIUM.

1. D. *foliosum*, Web. and Mohr. *(Leafy D.)*

Usually on peat, in hollows on heaths. Very local. On the hill one mile south-east of Pannanich Lodge, Mr. A. Cruickshank; Mr. C. conducted me to this spot, where the plant grew in great profusion. Glen Callater, Mr. Croall; Ben Beck, Castleton, Mr. Gardiner. It is often associated with *Buxbaumia*, and both will doubtless be found in other localities.

31. ATRICHUM. HAIR-MOSS.

1. A. *undulatum*, P. Beauv. *(Wavy-leaved H.)*

On shady gravelly places. Generally diffused. Hills of Woodston; at the Burn, &c. Mr. Croall. Near Aberdeen, at Robslaw quarry, &c. G. D.

32. OLIGOTRICHUM. HAIR-MOSS.

1. O. *hercynicum*, De Cand. *(Hercynian H.)*

On gravelly soil. Rare in the lower parts; abundant on the higher ranges in the interior. Near Aberdeen, upon banks by the side of an old road between Bieldside and the river Dee, G. D.; Hill of Fare, Mr. Mackay and G. D.; abundant in the interior, on Lochnagar, in Glen Callater, &c. &c.

33. POGONATUM. HAIR-MOSS.

1. P. *nanum*, Bridel. *(Dwarf H.)*

Moist gravelly banks. Rather local. At Robslaw quarry, &c. G. D.

2. P. *aloides*, Bridel. *(Aloe-like H.)*

Moist banks, Frequent, and probably general. At the Burn; Den Fenella; Hill of Woodston, &c. Mr. Croall. Near Aberdeen, at Robslaw quarry; Hill of Fare, &c. G. D. In the interior, on Craig Koynach and in Glen Clunie, Mr. Croall.

3. P. *urnigerum*, Bridel. *(Urn-fruited H.)*
On moist shady banks. Frequent. At the Burn; on Hill of Woodston, Mr. Croall. Robslaw quarry; Nigg, &c. G. D. In the interior, in Glen Clunie; and road-side to Corrymulzie, Mr. Croall.

4. P. *alpinum*, Bridel. *(Alpine H.)*
On rocks, &c. Chiefly in the interior; very abundant. Hill of Fare and top of Bennachie; Morven; Lochnagar; Glen Callater, &c. &c. G. D.

34. POLYTRICHUM. HAIR-MOSS.

1. P. *sexangulare*, Hoppe. *(Northern H.)*
On rocks and on the ground. Confined to the higher ranges. Ben Macdui, Mr. Mackay and G. D. Ben-a-Buird, in fruit 1856; Ben-a-Main, in fruit 1857, Mr. Croall. Upon Lochnagar, bnt rather scarce, G. D.

2. P. *commune*, Linn. *(Common H.)*
In woods; on moors; and in bogs. Common.

3. P. *juniperinum*, Hedw. *(Juniper-leaved H.)*
On heaths, &c. Very frequent; probably general. Moors of Garvock, &c. Mr. Croall. Stocket and Scotston moors; Den of Midmar; top of Ben Newe, &c. G. D.

4. P. *piliferum*, Schreb. *(Bristle-pointed H.)*
On moors, wall tops, &c. Frequent. Garvock; Hill of Bandra; St. Cyrus. In the interior, in Glen Clunie, Mr. Croall. Top of Bennachie; frequent on turf-capped walls round Aberdeen, G. D.

35. AULACOMNION. THREAD-MOSS.

1. A. *palustre*, Schwaeg. *(Marsh T.)*
Bogs and marshes. Frequent. Near Aberdeen, at Corsehill; Nigg; Hill of Fare, &c. G. D. About Castleton, Glen Eye; the Mourne, &c. Mr. Croall.

2. A. *androgynum*, Schwaeg. *(Bud-headed T.)*
Crevices of dry rocks. Very local. Den of Maidencraig, near Aberdeen; by the footpath half way up Craigendarroch, and in Glen Muick, G. D. Linn of the Garrawalt, Mr. Gardiner; about roots of birches, by the stream running into the moss behind Castleton, Mr. Croall.

36. LEPTOBRYUM. THREAD-MOSS.

1. L. *pyriforme*, Br. and Sch. *(Golden T.)*

Rocks and banks. Apparently very rare in this district. Among the rubbish of Robslaw quarry, north side, I have only once seen it, G. D.

37. BRYUM. THREAD-MOSS.

1. B. *polymorphum*, Br. and Sch. (*Variable T.*)
On alpine rocks, &c. Apparently rare; in the higher parts only. Damp banks, Lochnagar, &c. Mr. Croall.

2. B. *elongatum*, Dicks. (*Long-fruited T.*)
Crevices of rocks. In the higher parts only. Glen Callater and Lochnagar, Mr. Croall and G. D.

3. B. *crudum*, Schreb. (*Alpine glaucous T.*)
Rocks and banks. In the lower and higher parts of the district. Near Aberdeen, in Den of Cults; Den of Midmar; Pannanich cliffs, G. D. Old walls at Castleton; Glen Callater; Craig Koynach, Mr. Croall. Linn of the Garrawalt, Mr. Gardiner.

4. B. *nutans*, Schreb. (*Pendulous T.*)
Heaths and banks. Apparently of general occurrence. Near Aberdeen, in the wood at Pitmedden; Hill of Fare; Lochnagar and Glen Callater, G. D.

5. B. *Wahlenbergii*, Schwaeg. (*Wahlenberg's T.*)
Wet banks and dripping rocks. Not unfrequent. Den Fenella, and Den of Canterland. Mr. Croall Howe of Corrichie, on Hill of Fare, and Glen Callater, Mr. Mackay and G. D. Falls of the Garrawalt, Mr. Croall.

6. B. *Ludwigii*, Sprengel. (*Ludwig's T.*)
On moist alpine banks and slopes. Very local. Head of Glen Callater, on the ascent to Canlochan, Mr. Mackay and G. D.; Ben-a-Buird, Mr. Gardiner; Lochnagar, Mr. Croall; Ben Macdui, from Loch Etichan upwards, G. D.

7. B. *pseudotriquetrum*, Schwaeg. (*Alpine-bog T.*)
Bogs, wet banks, &c. Frequent, especially inland. Near Aberdeen, in the bog of Scotston, G. D.; sides of streams, Glen Callater, &c. Mr. Croall.

8. B. *alpinum*, Linn. (*Alpine, purple T.*)
Moist stones and banks. Most frequent inland. Near Aberdeen, at Scotston and Stocket moors, always barren; Hill of Fare, about Ballater, &c. &c. G. D.; Craig Koynach, Mr. Croall; in fruit on Ben-a-Buird, Mr. Gardiner.

9. B. *pallens*, Swartz. *(Pale-leaved T.)*
Moist places near springs, &c. In the lower parts and inland. Den of Canterland; Glen Clunie, road-side to Corrymulzie, Mr. Croall; near Aberdeen, at Robslaw quarry, G. D.

10. B. *uliginosum*, Br. and Sch. *(Bog T.)*
Wet banks, &c. Apparently local. Road-side to Corrymulzie, Mr. Croall.

11. B. *inclinatum*, Br. and Sch. *(Small-mouthed T.)*
On walls, banks, &c. Local? St. Cyrus' sands, Mr. Croall.

12. B. *intermedium*, Bridel. *(Intermediate T.)*
Walls, rocks, banks, &c. Probably often overlooked. Den of Canterland, Mr. Croall

13. *bimum*, Schreb. *(Lowland-bog T.)*
Marshes, bogs, and wet rocks. Rocks at the Burn, Mr. Croall; Hill of Fare, Mr. Mackay and G. D.

14. B. *capillare*, Hedw. *(Greater-matted T.)*
Walls, rocks, &c. Very frequent.

15. B. *cæspiticium*, Linn. *(Lesser-matted T.)*
Walls, roofs, rocks, &c. Very common.

16. B. *sanguineum*, Ludwig. *(Bloody T.)*
Heaths, walls, banks, &c. At the Glassilt, head of Loch Muick, Mr. Croall.

17. B. *julaceum*, Smith. *(Slender-branched T.)*
Wet gravelly places. Not unfrequent. Gravelly banks of the Dee near Aberdeen; Corbie Den, Kingcausie; Hill of Fare; abundant by the Dee at Ballater, Mr. Mackay and G. D. Glen Callater and Lochnagar, Mr. Croall.

18. B. *argenteum*, Linn. *(Silvery T.)*
On banks, walls, roofs, &c. Common everywhere.

19. B. *Zierii*, Dickson. *(Zierian T.)*
Crevices of alpine rocks. Interior only, very rare. Glen Callater rocks, Mr. Mackay and G. D.; Lochnagar, Mr. Croall; Corry of Loch Kander. Mr. Gardiner.

20. B. *roseum*, Schreb. *(Rosaceous T.)*
Shady Banks. Rare in this district. Woods of the Burn, Mr. Croall; Corbie Den, Kingcausie, G. D.

38. MNIUM. THYME, THREAD-MOSS.

1. M. *affine*, Bland. *(Many-fruited T.)*
Shady banks, rocks, &c. Rare. St. Cyrus' rocks, Mr. Croall.

2, M. *cuspidatum*, Hedw. *(Pointed T.)*
Shady banks and rocks. very local. Den of Robslaw; and wood at Pitmedden, G. D.

3. M. *rostratum*, Schwaeg. *(Beaked T.)*
Moist shady rocks. Probably local. Abundant in Den Fenella, about the old bridge, Dr. Stephen; Corrymulzie, Mr. Croall.

4. M. *serratum*, Bridel. *(Serrated T.)*
Shady rocks and banks. Local. Den Fenella and Corrymulzie, Mr. Croall; Den of Midmar, Mr. Mackay and G. D.

5. M. *hornum*, Linn. *(Swan-neck T.)*
Shady banks and woods. Very frequent. Burn of Bingley, Glen Dye; Den Fenella; hill of Woodston, St. Cyrus, Dr. Stephen. Den of Robslaw; summit of Bennachie; Den of Midmar, G. D. Corrymulzie; Craig Koynach, Mr. Croall.

6. M. *undulatum*, Hedw. *(Wavy-leaved T.)*
Shady banks and in woods. Frequent. In fruit at the bottom of the stair in Den Fenella; Den of Davo, Garvock, Dr. Stephen; Hill of Woodston, in fruit, Mr. Croall. Den of Robslaw, in fruit; Den of Midmar, G. D.

7. M. *cinclidioides*, Huebener. *(Large-leaved T.)*
Wet alpine rocks and marshes. Very rare. Along with *Carex leporina*, on Lochnagar, G. D.

8. M. *punctatum*, Hedw. *(Dotted T.)*
Wet shady places. Very frequent. Den Fenella, Mr. Croall. Near the Railway bridge at Nigg, Dr. Stephen. Den of Robslaw; Den of Midmar; and frequent on the coast between Stonehaven and Aberdeen, G. D.

9. M. *subglobosum*, Br. and Sch. *(Round-fruited T.)*
Bogs and marshes, &c. Perhaps frequent, often mistaken for the last. Hill of Woodston; Glen Callater, &c. Mr. Croall.

39. MIELICHHOFERIA.

1. M. *nitida*, Hornsch. *(Mielichhofer's Thread-moss.)*

Moist alpine rocks. Very rare. Head of Glen Callater, 1830, Dr. Greville; in 1856, Dr. A. O. Black.

40. MEESIA.

M. *uliginosa*, Hedw. *(Long-stalked M.)*

By springs; in marshes and bogs. Rather local. Near Aberdeen, on Hill of Fare; at Pannanich, G. D. Glen Callater; Ben Votran, Mr. Croall.

41. AMBLYODON.

1. A. *dealbatus*, P. Beauv. *(Lesser, pale A.)*

Wet places in the higher districts. Very local. In Glen Callater, Mr. Croall.

42. FUNARIA. CORD-MOSS.

1. F. *hygrometrica*, Hedw. *(Common C.)*

Banks, walls, &c. Common in the lower parts and inland.

43. PHYSCOMITRIUM. BLADDER-MOSS.

1. P. *ericetorum*, De Notaris. *(Heath B.)*

Moist spots, among heath, &c. Rather local North side of Hill of Fare, opposite Mill of Midmar, Mrs. Mackay. Roadside between Ballater and Bridge of Muick, G. D. Glen Clunie, Castleton, Mr. Croall.

44. BARTRAMIA. APPLE-MOSS.

1. B. *fontana*, Bridel. *(Fountain A.)*

Wet places, near springs, &c. A common species in the lower districts, and often at high altitudes in the interior, as at C. *leporina* station on Lochnagar.

2. B. *calcarea*, Br. and Sch. *(Thick-nerved A.)*

Wet places. In the interior chiefly, and rare. Rocks at the Burn, Glen Callater, Mr. Croall.

3. B. *pomiformis*, Hedw. *(Common A.)*

Dry shady banks. Very frequent. Garvock; St. Cyrus, &c. Dr. Stephen. Den Fenella; Rocks at the Burn, Mr. Croall. Near Aberdeen, Den of Maidencraig, &c.; Hill of Fare; Pannanich; Glen Callater, &c. G. D. Craig Koynach; Corrymulzie, Mr. Croall.

4. B. *Halleriana*, Hedw. *(Haller's A.)*

Alpine rocks. In the interior only, and rare. Glen Callater, Mr. Edmonston.

5. B. *ithyphylla*, Bridel. *(Straight-leaved A.)*
Shady banks and rocks. Rather general. Near Aberdeen, at Robslaw quarry; Bieldside; Den of Maidencraig; on Bennachie; Pannanich Cliffs; Glen Callater, G. D.

6. B. *arcuata*, Bridel. *(Arched A.)*
On moist rocks and banks. Very local. Banks at the burn; Hill of Woodston, Mr. Croall. Shevock, Durris, Dr. Stephen; north side of Hill of Fare, near Mill of Midmar, Mr. Mackay and G. D. Glen Callater; Glen Eye, &c. Mr. Croall.

45. CONOSTOMUM. CONE-FRINGE MOSS.

1. C. *boreale*, Swartz. *(Northern C.)*
Gravelly places; on the higher mountains only. Abundant on Mount Keen; Lochnagar; Ben Macdui, &c. &c.

46. SPLACHNUM. COLLAR-MOSS.

1. S. *vasculosum*, Linn. *(Large-fruited C.)*
About Alpine springs. Rather local. On the Mourne at Castleton, Mr. Gardiner. Head of Glen Callater, Mr. Croall.

2. S. *ampullaceum*, Linn. *(Flagon-fruited C.)*
In bogs on droppings of cattle. Very local. In the bog below Affrosh, Banchory-Ternan, Dr. Stephen. Near Aberdeen, in the bog at south side of Corsehill, at Scotston, G. D. In a boggy place, south side of Glen Muick road, near the saw-mill, Mrs. Mackay.

3. S. *sphaericum*, Hedw. *(Round-fruited C.)*
Alpine bogs on decaying animal matter. Frequent. On different parts of the Hill of Fare. Very fine and abundant on the table land above Glen Callater, Mr. Mackay and G. D. On Ben Avon, Mr. Croall.

47. TETRAPLODON. COLLAR-MOSS.

1. T. *mnioides*, Br. & Sch. *(Brown Tapering C.)*
On decaying animal matter, as bones, &c. Very frequent. Glen of Dye, Mr. Kerr. North side of the Hill of Fare, near Mill of Midmar, Mr. Mackay and G. D. Abundant in the interior; on Lochnagar; in Glen Callater; Glen Derry, &c. G. D. Glen Dee; on the Mourne; on Ben Macdui, Mr. Croall.

2. T. *angustatus*, Br. and Sch. *(Narrow-leaved C.)*
On decaying animal matter. In the higher parts. Rare. Glen Dee; Glen Derry; Lochnagar; the Mourne, Mr. Croall.

48. TAYLORIA. COLLAR-MOSS.

1. T. *serrata*, Br. and Sch. *(Serrated C.)*
On peat soil. On the higher mountains only. Rare. *Var.* γ. *tenuis*. On the east shoulder of Mount Battock, at a cairn by the side of the footpath, G. D. In Glens Derry and Callater, Mr. Mackay and G. D. Moist ground by the side of Callater Burn, at the head of the Loch, Mr. Gardiner.

50. DISSODON. COLLAR-MOSS.

1. D. *Froelichianus*, Grev. and Arnott. *(Froelich's C.)*
On Ben High, Aberdeenshire, Mr. Dickson. Believing that the mountain so named is Bennachie (which is sometimes called Ben High), I may state my belief that no such species grows there. Mr. Wilson thinks the specimen in Mr. Turner's Herbarium is but a starved state of D. *splachnoides*. This statement induces me to believe that the specimen was from some other part of Scotland, since I have no note of D. *splachnoides* in this district.

51. ŒDIPODIUM. COLLAR-MOSS.

1. Œ. *Griffithianum*, Schwaeg. *(Griffith's alpine C.)*
Crevices of alpine rocks. Very rare; in the interior only. Steep rocks above the head of Loch Callater, on the west side, by the ascent to Canlochan, Mr. Mackay and G. D.; Mr. Croall and others have also gathered it in Glen Callater.

52. FISSIDENS. FLAT FORK-MOSS.

1. F. *bryoides*, Hedw. *(Common F.)*
Moist shady banks. Very frequent. Jackstone, St. Cyrus, Dr. Stephen; Dens Fenella and Canterland, Mr. Croall. Near Aberdeen, in Dens of Leggart and Robslaw; on Pannanich cliffs, &c. G. D.

2. F. *adiantoides*, Hedw. *(Marsh F.)*
Marshes, wet rocks, &c. Frequent. Dens Fenella and Canterland, Mr. Croall. Near Aberdeen, at Corsehill moss; Corbie Den; Den of Midmar; on Pannanich cliffs; Corrymulzie, G. D. At Linn of Dee, Mr. Croall.

3. F. *taxifolius*, Hedw. *(Yew-leaved F.)*
Moist shady clay banks. Apparently local. North bank of the Don above the old bridge, in a steep ravine, G. D.

53. ANŒCTANGIUM. BEARDLESS-MOSS.

1. A. *compactum*, Schwaeg. *(Compact B.)*
Crevices of alpine rocks. In the interior, and rare. Rocks in Glen Callater, Mr. T. Edmonston.

54. ANTITRICHIA. WING-MOSS.

1. A. *curtipendula*, Bridel. *(Pendulous W.)*
Shady rocks; and on trees. Rather local. Hill of Woodston, Mr. Croall. At Linn of Muick plentiful, and in fruit (1840), Mr. Mackay and G. D. Corrymulzie, Mr. Gardiner; Craig Koynach, Mr. Croall.

55. ANOMODON.

1. A. *viticulosus*, Hook. and Tayl. *(Tall A.)*
Shady rocks and trees. Apparently very local. Den Fenella, Mr. Croall.

56. PTEROGONIUM. THREAD-MOSS.

1. P. *filiforme*, Hedw. *(Thread-like T.)*
Rocks and trees. Apparently very local. Linn of Muick, Mr. Mackay and G. D.; at the Lion's Face, Castleton, Mr. Gardiner.

2. P. *gracile*, Sw. *(Slender W.)*
Shady rocks; and on trees. Chiefly in the interior; and local. Den of Midmar; Khoil, at Ballater, Mr. Mackay and G. D. In Glen Callater, Mr. Croall.

56. ISOTHECIUM. FROND MOSS.

1. I. *myurum*, Dillen. *(Blunt-leaved F.)*
On rocks and trees. Coast line and interior. Den Fenella; Corriemulzie, Mr. Croall.

2. I. *myosuroides*, Dill. *(Acute-leaved F.)*
Trunks of trees and on rocks. Rather local. Den Fenella, Mr. Kerr. Rocks at Girdleness, and Robslaw Den, G. D.

3. I. *alopecurum*, Dill. *(Foxtail F.)*
In shady places. Coast line and interior. Dens Fenella and Davo, Dr. Stephen. Dens of Cults, Midmar, &c. G. D. Corrymulzie, at Castleton, Mr. Croall.

57. CLIMACIUM. TREE MOSS.

1. C. *dendroides*, Web. and Mohr. *(Marsh T.)*

Shady and marshy places. Frequent. St. Cyrus' sands, Dr. Stephen. Abundant in Old-town Links, and east end of Loch of Park, &c. G. D. Linn of Dee, &c. Mr. Croall.

58. LESKEA.

1. L. *sericea*, Dillen. *(Silky L.)*

Walls, rocks, &c. Frequent. St. Cyrus' rocks, Mr. Croall. Bridge of Muick, and Khoil near Ballater, Mr. Mackay and G. D. Glen Callater and Craig Koynach, Mr. Croall.

2. L. *rufescens*, Smith. *(Reddish L.)*

Alpine rocks. Frequent at high altitudes in the interior. Lochnagar; Glen Callater, &c. &c.

3. L. *subrufa*, Wilson. *(Fine-leaved L.)*

Alpine rocks. Apparently local, and confined to the interior. Glen Callater rocks, Mr. Mackay and G. D. Mr. Croall has also found it there.

59. HYPNUM. FEATHER-MOSS.

1. H. *albicans*, Dillen. *(Whitish F.)*

Shady places. Apparently local. St. Cyrus' sands Mr. Croall; Hill of Fare, Mr. Mackay and G. D.

2. H. *salebrosum*, Hoffm. *(Smooth-stalked F.)*

On banks and trees. Falls of the Garrawalt, Dr. A. O. Black.

3. H. *populeum*, Hedw. *(Matted F.)*

Rocks and trees. Coast at Muchalls; Den of Leggart, &c., G. D.

4. H. *velutinum*, Dillen. *(Velvet F.)*

Banks and trees. Probably frequent. Den Fenella; woods of the Burn, Mr. Croall. Den of Leggart, G. D.; Ballater and Castleton, Mr. Croall.

5. H. *rutabulum*, Dillen. *(Common rough-stalked F.)*

Banks, walls, trees. Common.

6. H. *rivulare*, Bruch. *(River F.)*

On rocks and stones by streams; and sometimes under water. Rocks at the Burn, and in Den Fenella, Mr. Croall.

7. H. *praelongum*, Linn. *(Long F.)*

Moist shady banks. Frequent; coast line and inland. Den Fenella, Mr. Croall; Dens of Leggart, Robslaw, &c. &c. G. D. Corrymulzie, Mr. Croall.

8. **H. striatum**, Hedw. *(Common striated F.)*

Shady banks and in woods. Woods of the Burn, and Den Fenella, Mr. Croall; Den of Robslaw, G. D.; Corrymulzie and Ballachbuie, Mr. Croall.

9. **H. ruscifolium**, Dillen. *(Long-beaked water F.)*

On rocks and stones in rivulets. Very frequent. Den Fenella, Dr. Stephen. Rocks of the Burn; Corrymulzie; Glen Callater, Mr. Croall. Common in streams near Aberdeen.

10. **H. catenulatum**, Schwaeg. *(Catenulate F.)*

Rocks and stones. Apparently local. On the moor at Kirkhill, near new Church of Nigg, G. D.

11. **H. serpens**, Linn. *(Creeping F.)*

Shady walls, banks, and trees. Den Fenella, Dr. Stephen. Woods of the Burn; Hill of Woodston; and in the interior at Corrymulzie, Mr. Croall. Rocks at the old Bridge of Don, Mr. P. Grant. Abundant in Den of Midmar, Mr. Mackay and G. D.

12. **H. stellatum**, Schreb. *(Yellow starry F.)*

Bogs and marshes. Probably frequent. Corsehill bog, near Scotston; Glen Muick, &c. Mr. Mackay and G. D.

13. **H. palustre**, Dillen. *(Marsh F.)*

Stones and rocks in streams. Coast line and inland. Rocks at the Burn, Mr. Croall; Dens of Robslaw and Midmar, G. D. Corrymulzie, above the bridge, Mr. Croall.

14. **H. molle**, Dickson. *(Soft, water F.)*

Alpine rivulets. In the interior only, and rare. Aberdeenshire, Mr. G. Don; Lochnagar, Mr. Mackay and G. D.

15. **H. arcticum**, Sommerfelt. *(Arctic F.)*

Alpine rivulets. In the interior only, and local. Lochnagar, Mr. Mackay and G. D.; head of Glen Callater, Mr. Croall.

16. **H. stramineum**, Dickson. *(Straw-like F.)*

In marshes. On the hills round the head of Glen Callater, Mr. Croall; at the top of the waterfall, Glen Callater, Mr. Gardiner.

17. **H. sarmentosum**, Wahlenberg. *(Twiggy F.)*

Moist alpine rocks. Confined to the interior. Ben-a-Main, in fruit, Mr. Croall.

18. **H. cordifolium**, Swartz. *(Heart-leaved F.)*

Marshes, &c. Very frequent. Annie's Dam, St. Cyrus, Dr. Stephen. Near Aberdeen, at Corsehill; Hill of Fare, &c. G. D. Glen Callater, &c. Mr. Croall.

19. H. *cuspidatum*, Dillen. *(Pointed F.)*

In marshes. Coast line and interior. Corsehill marsh, &c. near Aberdeen, G. D. Marshes above the river, Glen Clunie, Castleton, Mr. Croall.

20. H. *Schreberi*, Dillen. *(Schreber's F.)*

Woods and shady banks. Glen Quoich, &c. Mr. Croall.

21. H. *purum*, Linn. *(Neat F.)*

Shady banks, &c. Very frequent.

22. H. *tamariscinum*, Hedw. *(Tamarisk F.)*

Woods and shady banks. Very frequent.

23. H. *splendens*, Dillen. *(Glittering F.)*

In woods; on heaths, &c. Common. On Bennachie; Den of Midmar, in fruit.

24. H. *umbratum*, Ehrhart. *(Shady-rock F.)*

In alpine districts only; generally on stones. Glen Callater, Dr. A. O. Black.

25. H. *triquetrum*, Linn. *(Triangular-leaved F.)*

Woods and banks. Very frequent. Coast line and interior. Top of Bennachie; summit of Lochnagar, &c. G. D.

26. H. *loreum*, Linn. *(Trailing mountain F.)*

In woods, &c. Very frequent.

27. H. *squarrosum*, Linn. *(Drooping-leaved F.)*

Banks and woods. Frequent. Hill of Woodston; woods of the Burn, Mr. Croall. Near Aberdeen, at Bieldside; Maidencraig, &c. &c. G. D.

28. H. *fluitans*, Linn. *(Floating F.)*

Marshes and bogs. Frequent. Garvock; Glen Callater, Mr. Croall. Hill of Fare, &c. &c. G. D.

29. H. *revolvens*, Swartz. *(Circinate F.)*

Bogs and marshes. Probably local. Black-dog burn. Belhelvie, G. D. Glen Clunie; Glen Callater, &c. Mr. Croall.

30. H. *aduncum*, Linn. *(Claw-leaved F.)*

Marshes and wet moors, &c. Frequent. Dripping rocks on the coast south from Aberdeen; Corsehill; Hill of Fare, G. D. Den Fenella; Glen Callater, Mr. Croall.

31. H. *rugosum*, Hedw. *(Rugose F.)*

Alpine rocks. Rare. In the interior only. Rocks, Glen Callater, Mr. T. Edmonston.

32. H. *filicinum*, Linn. *(Lesser Fern F.)*

Dripping rocks, &c. Local. Den of Jackstone, St. Cyrus; Den Fenella; rocks at the Burn, Mr. Croall.

33. H. *commutatum*, Hedw. *(Curled Fern F.)*

Dripping rocks. Coast and interior. Den of Morphy, Dr. Stephen. Rocks at the Burn; Den of Canterland, Mr. Croall. Abundant on moist rocks at Muchalls, G. D. Corrymulzie; Glen Clunie, &c. Mr. Croall.

34. H. *uncinatum*, Hedw. *(Sickle-leaved F.)*

Walls and rocks. Coast line and interior. St. Cyrus, Dr. Stephen; Den Fenella, Mr. Croall. Robslaw Den; Loch of Park; banks of the Dee at Ballater, G. D. Corrymulzie, Mr. Croall.

35. H. *Crista-Castrensis*, Linn. *(Ostrich-plume F.)*

Woods and banks. Chiefly in the interior. Woods in Den of Midmar, Mr. Mackay and Mr. Barron; wood near Bridge of Muick, at Ballater, Mrs. Mackay. At Loch Muick, in fruit; Craig Koynach, and in the wood west from Castleton, Mr. Croall.

36. H. *cupressiforme*, Linn. *(Cypress-like F.)*

Walls, rocks, roofs, trees, &c. Very frequent.

37. H. *molluscum*, Dillen. *(Plume-crested F.)*

On moist banks; on the ground, &c. Frequent.

38. H. *ochraceum*, Turner. *(Yellow mountain F.)*

On stones in and near alpine rivulets. Lochnagar, 1807, Mr. G. Don; bogs, head of Glen Callater, Mr. Gardiner; head of Loch Avon, Mr. Croall.

39. H. *scorpioides*, Linn. *(Scorpion F.)*

In bogs. Rather local. Moor of Benholme; Glen Dye, Strachan, Dr. Stephen. Corsehill bog, G. D.; moss behind Castleton, Mr. Croall; Ben-a-Buird, Mr. Gardiner.

40. H. *pulchellum*, Dickson. *(Neat, Mountain F.)*

Shady rocks. Chiefly in the interior. Den of Midmar, Mr. Mackay. Carr Linn; Corrymulzie; Craig Koynach, Mr. Gardiner. Glen Callater, Mr. Croall.

41. H. *Muhlenbeckii*, Br. and Sch. *(Muhlenbeck's F.)*

Alpine rocks. Apparently in the interior only. Near the top of the Mourne, at Castleton, G. D.; Glen Callater, &c. Mr. Croall.

42. H. *undulatum*, Dillen. *(Waved F.)*
In woods; on dry moors, &c. Very frequent.

43. H. *sylvaticum*, Linn. *(Wood F.)*
Woods and rocks. Local. Lochnagar and Glen Callater, Mr. Mackay and G. D.

44. H. *denticulatum*, Dillen. *(Denticulate F.)*
Woods and moist rocks. Coast line and interior. Den Fenella; Den of Davo, Garvock, Dr. Stephen. Woods of the Burn, Mr. Croall. Robslaw Den; Bennachie, G. D.

Var. β, *obtusifolium*. On the Mourne at Castleton, Mr. Gardiner.

60. OMALIA. FEATHER-MOSS.

1. O. *trichomanoides*, Schreber. *(Fern-like F.)*
On trees and shady rocks. Near Aberdeen, in Den of Cults, upon trees; north bank of the Dee below Ballater Free Church, G. D.

61. NECKERA.

1. N. *complanata*, Br. and Sch. *(Flat-leaved N.)*
Trunks of trees, walls, &c. Rather local. Den Fenella, Mr. Croall; Corbie Den, Kingcausie, on trees, G. D.; Den of Midmar, Mr. Mackay; Glen Callater, Mr. Croall.

2. N. *crispa*, Hedwig. *(Crisped Neckera.)*
On rocks and trees. Chiefly in the interior. Linn of Muick, and Khoil hill, near Ballater; and rocky bed of a stream between Loch Builg and Inchrory, Mr. Mackay and G. D.

62. HOOKERIA.

1. H. *lucens*, Linn. *(Shining H.)*
Moist banks and fissures of rocks. Generally diffused. Near the stair in Den Fenella; lower part of the Burn of Bingley, Glen Dye, Dr. Stephen. On the coast at the Cove; Corbie Den, Kingcausie; north bank of the Don above the old Bridge. In the interior, on the Glen Callater rocks, G. D. By a stream below the Carr rocks at Castleton, Mr. Croall.

63. FONTINALIS. WATER-MOSS.

1. F. *antipyretica*, Linn. *(Greater W.)*
On stones and rocks; in lakes and streams. Very frequent.

2. F. *squamosa*, Linn. *(Alpine W.)*
Mountain rivulets. Apparently confined to the interior. Hill of Fare, Dr. Stephen. Upon Lochnagar, G. D. Glassilt burn, in fruit; Glen Callater, Mr. Croall.

HEPATICAE. LIVERWORTS.

I.—RICCIACEAE.

1. RICCIA.

1. R. *crystallina*, Linn. *(Crystalline R.)*
On moist banks. Very rare. Rocks at Grip, a quarter of a mile west of Johnshaven, and on the borders of St. Cyrus, Dr. Stephen.

II.—MARCHANTIACEAE.

1. MARCHANTIA.

1. M. *polymorpha*, Linn. *(Polymorphous M.)*
Moist shady places and marshes. Frequent. Dens Fenella and Laurieston, Mr. Croall. Near Newtonhill Station, north from Stonehaven; Hill of Brigton, St. Cyrus, Dr. Stephen. Near Aberdeen, in a little marsh close by a wall at the bridge on the road west from Summerhill; and Braediach moss, Skene, in fruit at both places, G. D. Corrymulzie, and Falls of the Garrawalt, Mr. Croall.

2. FEGATELLA.

1. F. *conica*, Linn. *(Conical F.)*
Moist shady places. Rather local. Den Fenella and Den of Davo, Dr. Stephen. On the Kincardineshire coast, cave at the Cove, &c. G. D.

2. F. *hemispherica*, Linn. *(Hemispherical F.)*
Shady moist places. Frequent. Den Fenella, Dr. Stephen. Near Aberdeen, in Den of Robslaw, &c. G. D. Common in Braemar, Mr. Croall.

III.—JUNGERMANNIACEAE. *

JUNGERMANNIA.

1. J. *asplenioides*, Linn. *(Spleenwort J.)* [*Plagiochila*.]

---

* In compiling, from my own collection, &c. the species of this family, I have followed the arrangement in *Hooker's British Flora*, Vol. II. The new genera of "Synopsis Hepaticarum" of Gottsche, &c. are in brackets.

Woods, shady banks, &c. Very general. Den Fenella; rocks at the Burn, Mr. Croall. At Corbie Den; Robslaw Den; Dens of Leggart and Midmar; Pannanich cliffs; Corrymulzie and Glen Callater, G. D.

2. J. *spinulosa*, Dickson. (*Prickly-leaved J.*)
Shady alpine rocks. Local. Glen Callater rocks, Mr. Mackay and G. D.

3. J. *Doniana*, Hooker. (*Don's J.*)
Alpine districts. Rare. Head of Loch Avon, Mr. Lyon.

4. J. *pumila*, With. (*Dwarf, simple J.*)
Beds of alpine streams. Rare. Rocky bed of a stream west from Loch Builg, Mr. Mackay and G. D.

5. J. *cordifolia*, Hooker. (*Heart-leaved J.*)
Alpine bogs and springs. In the interior only. Lochnagar; Ben Macdui; Dhuloch, Mr. Mackay and G. D.

6. J. *Sphagni*, Dickson. (*Bog-moss J.*) [*Sphagnocetis*, Nees ab E.]
Boggy places. Rather local. At the Dhuloch and in Glen Callater, Mr. Mackay and G. D.

7. J. *crenulata*, Smith.
Moist heaths and banks. Not unfrequent. South bank of Don above the new bridge; wood at Pitmedden; Brimman hill; and Hill of Fare, G. D.

8. J. *compressa*, Hooker. (*Compressed J.*) [*Alicularia.*]
Mountain rivulets. Local. Hill of Fare, Mr. Mackay and G. D.; Glen Avon, Mr. Croall.

9. J. *emarginata*, Ehrh. (*Notched J.*) [*Sarcoscyphus.*]
Wet alpine rocks. Chiefly in the higher parts. Dhuloch, Mr. Mackay and G. D.; Callater rocks, Mr. Croall; Cairngorm, Mr. Don.

10. J. *concinnata*, Lightf. (*Braided J.*) [*Gymnomitrium.*]
Moist alpine rocks. In the interior only. Lochnagar, Mr. Mackay and G. D.; at the same place, in fruit, Mr. Croall; Cairngorm, Mr. Don.

11. J. *Orcadensis*, Hooker. (*Orkney J.*)
Among mosses, &c. in alpine parts of the district. Rocks of Dhuloch, Mr. Mackay and G. D.; top of the Mourne at Castleton, Mr. Gardiner.

12. J. *inflata*, Hudson. (*Inflated J.*)

Moist heaths. On the hills at Nigg, G. D.; Craig Koynach and Ben Macdui, Mr. Gardiner.

13. J. *excisa*, Dickson. *(Small notch-leaved J.)*
Moist banks in heaths and in woods. Corbie Den, Kingcausie; and Glen Callater, G. D.

14. J. *ventricosa*, Dickson. *(Tumid J.)*
Shady woods and banks. Robslaw quarry, and wood at Pitmedden, G. D.

15. J. *bicuspidata*, Linn. *(Forked J.)*
Moist banks and heaths. Frequent. Corbie Den; Den of Maidencraig; Pitmedden wood; Hill of Fare; Brimman hill, G. D. Glen Gairden; Loch Builg, Mr. Mackay and G. D.

16. J. *connivens*, Dickson. *(Forcipate J.)*
Edges of bogs and marshes. About Aberdeen, and on Hill of Fare.

17. J. *byssacea*, Roth. *(Byssus-like J.)*
Dry heaths. Probably frequent. Among Polytrichum, Mill of Finnan; Hill of Ardo, near Aberdeen; Robslaw quarry; among *Hypnum*, in Den of Cults, G. D.

18. J. *nemorosa*, Linn. *(Wood J.)* [*Scapania Nees ab E.*]
Woods and rocks. Very frequent. Bay of Nigg; Corbie Den; Den of Maidencraig; Hill of Fare, G. D.

Var. β, *purpurascens*. Dhuloch; Ben Macdui; Pannanich, Mr. Mackay and G. D. Ben-a-Buird, Mr. Gardiner.

19. J. *planifolia*, Hooker. *(Flat-leaved J.)* [*Scapania.*]
Moist alpine rocks. Rare. Head of Loch Avon, Mr. Croall; Ben-a-Buird and Ben Macdui, Mr. Don.

20. J. *umbrosa*, Schrad. *(Shady J.)* [*Scapania.*]
Alpine rocks. Apparently rare. On the Khoil at Ballater, Mr. Mackay and G. D.

21. J. *undulata*, Linn. *(Wavy-leaved J.)* [*Scapania.*]
Wet places among rocks and by streams. Frequent. Moist rocks on the Kincardineshire coast, as at the Cove, &c. Hill of Fare; Loch Muick; Lochnagar, &c. G. D.

22. J. *albicans*, Linn. *(Whitish J.)*
Moist banks. Frequent. Mud fences at the Burn; dry banks near Corrymulzie, Mr. Croall. Nigg; wood at Tullis; top of Bennachie, G. D. Hill of Fare; Glen Callater, Mr. Mackay and G. D. At Castleton, Mr. Gardiner.

23. J. *minuta*, Crantz. *(Small J.)*
Alpine rocks. In the interior only. Craig Koynach, Mr. Croall; Ben Beck, Mr. Gardiner; Glen Callater rocks, G. D.

24. J. *cochleariformis*, Weis. *(Hollow-leaved J.)* [*Physiotium.*]
Moist alpine moors and among rocks. Very local. Base of Ben Macdui; in Glen Dee; Glen Avon, Mr. Croall.

25. J. *complanata*, Linn. *(Flat J.)* [*Radula.*]
Trunks of trees. Common in most parts of the district.

26. J. *Taylori*, Hooker. *(Taylor's J.)*
Moist rocks and bogs in alpine districts. Local. Glen Callater and Corrymulzie, Mr. Croall; Lochnagar and Dhuloch, Mr. Mackay and G. D.

27. J. *scalaris*, Schrad. *(Ladder J.)* [*Alicularia.*]
Banks, &c. Ben-a-Buird, Mr. Gardiner.

28. J. *polyanthos*, Linn. *(Many flowered J.)* [*Chiloscyphus.*]
Marshy places. Rather local. About Ballater, Mr. Croall.

29. J. *Trichomanis*, Dickson. *(Fern J.)* [*Calypogeia.*]
Moist ground in woods, &c. Local. Near Aberdeen, in Den of Leggart, G. D.

30. J. *bidentata*, Linn. *(Two-toothed J.)* [*Lophocolea.*]
Moist banks by roads and in woods. Common.

31. J. *barbata*, Schreb. *(Toothed J.)*
Rocks, woods, and heaths. Frequent. Rocks at the Burn; Den Fenella, Mr. Croall. Maidencraig; Robslaw Den; Den of Midmar; Hill of Fare, G. D.

32. J. *reptans*, Linn. *(Creeping J.)* [*Lepidozia.*]
Woods and shady places. Rather local. Den of Midmar, on decaying stumps of trees, Mr. Mackay and G. D.

33. J. *trilobata*, Linn. *(Three-lobed J.)* [*Mastigobryum.*]
Moist alpine places. Interior chiefly. Den of Midmar and Hill of Fare, Mr. Mackay and G. D.

Var. β, *minor*. Ben Beck, Mr. Gardiner; Glen Callater, G. D.

34. J. *juniperina*, Sw. *(Juniper-leaved J.)* [*Sendtnera.*]
Alpine heaths and rocks. Very local. Glen Callater, Dr. Black; Ben Macdui, Mr. Mackay and G. D.

35. J. *julacea*, Linn. *(Silvery alpine J.)*
On stones in alpine rivulets and marshes. Very abundant. On all the higher mountains in the interior—Mount Keen; Lochnagar; Glen Callater; Ben Macdui, &c. G. D. In fruit on Ben Avon, Mr. Croall.

36. J. *tricophylla*, Linn. *(Hair-leaved J.)*
Turfy heaths. At high altitudes in the interior. Rare. Glen Callater.

37. J. *setiformis*, Ehrh. *(Bristle-like J.)*
Alpine rocks. Rather local. Lochnagar, Mr. Croall; Glen Callater, Mr. Gardiner; craigs of Pannanich, G. D.; rocks of the Dhuloch, Mr. Mackay and G. D.

38. J. *platyphylla*, Linn. *(Flat-leaved J.)* [*Madotheca.*]
Walls, rocks, and trunks of trees. Very frequent and general.

39. J. *ciliaris*, Linn. *(Ciliate J.)* [*Ptilidium.*]
Heaths and rocks. Coast line and interior. Hill at Nigg; Brimman hill; Hill of Fare, G. D. Top of Mount Battock, and frequent on all the higher mountains.

40. J. *tomentella*, Ehrh. *(Spongy J.)* [*Trichocolea.*]
Moist shady places. Very rare. Hill of Fenella, Kincardineshire, Mr. Cruickshank.

41. J. *serpyllifolia*, Dickson. *(Thyme-leaved J.)* [*Lejeunia.*]
Trees and rocks in sub-alpine districts. Coast line and interior; local. Near Aberdeen, on trees, Pitmedden, G. D. Glen Clunie, &c. Mr. Croall. With *Grimmia torta*, Callater rocks, Mr. Mackay and G. D.

42. J. *dilatata*, Linn. *(Dilated J.)* [*Frullania.*]
Trunks of trees. Common.

43. J. *Tamarisci*, Linn. *(Tamarisk J.)* [*Frullania.*]
On the ground, &c. Very frequent.

44. J. *pinguis*, Linn. *(Slippery J.)* [*Aneura.*]
Bogs and watery places. Rather local. Hill of Fare; Glen Muick; Glen Callater, Mr. Mackay and G. D.

45. J. *multifida*, Linn. *(Many-cleft J.)* [*Aneura.*]
Moist shady places. Frequent. Near Aberdeen, at Robslaw; Den of Maidencraig, &c. G. D.

46. J. *Blasia*, Hooker. *(Flask-bearing J.)* [*Blasia.*]

Sides of rills and pools. Rather local. Usually in a barren state. Abundant in fruit by the margin of a dam at the south end of Den of Leggart, near Aberdeen, 1840, G. D. Roadside to Corrymulzie, Mr. Croall.

47. J. *epiphylla*, Linn. *(Broad-leaved J.)* [*Pellia.*]
Moist banks by road-sides; in woods and waste places. Very common.

48. J. *furcata*, Linn. *(Forked J.)* [*Metzgeria.*]
On trees, rocks, &c. Coast line and interior. Near Aberdeen, north bank of Don at the old bridge; Dens of Cults and Maidencraig; Callater rocks, G. D.

Var. β, *elongata.* Corrymulzie, G. D.

49. J. *pubescens*, Schrank. *(Downy J.)* [*Metzgeria.*]
Moist rocks. Inland parts only. Corrymulzie; Loch Builg; Ben Macdui, Mr. Mackay and G. D.

CHARAE.*

ORDER I.—CHARACEAE.

1. NITELLA.

1. *N. flexilis*, Linn.
In pools and ditches. In several places in the vicinity of Aberdeen; marshes, &c. west from the Ruthrieston station, Deeside line; by the side of the Stocket road, west from Summerhill; very abundant in pools by the side of the Dee near Murtle, and in various similar localities, but uncertain in its appearance, G. D.

2. *N. translucens*, Pers.
This fine species formerly existed in Ferryhill moss; a variety of it is very abundant in Loch of Park, G. D.

2. CHARA.

1. *C. vulgaris*, Linn.
Near Aberdeen, in pools on the moor at Scotston and Denmore; near Summerhill, along with *N. flexilis;* in ditches, west side of Old-town Links, G. D.

2. *C. aspera*, Willd.

---

* These singular plants, usually placed among *Algae*, ought certainly to occupy a higher place, for reasons which it would be irrelevant to discuss here.

This beautiful species is abundant in the Loch of Park, G. D. In Loch Strathbeg, parish of Crimond, Dr. Templeton and G. D.

3. C. *fragilis*, Desv.

In various places at Aberdeen, near Scotston and Denmore; Stocket, &c. G. D. In the parish of Clatt, Rev. J. Minto.

LICHENES. LICHENS.*

I. GYMNOCARPI.

I.—USNEACEAE.

1. USNEA.

1. U. *barbata*, Acharius.

This well known species is plentiful on trees in various parts of the district, as well as its forms, *Var. florida; Var. plicata*.

II.—CORNICULARIACEAE.

2. CORNICULARIA.

1. C. *jubata*, Acharius.

A very abundant species, generally on old fir trees.

Var. a, bicolor. Plentiful, especially in the interior; usually prostrate among mosses, &c.

2. C. *ochroleuca*, Ach.

On Cairngorm, where it was first observed by Sir W. J. Hooker and Mr. Borrer.

3. RAMALINA.

1. R. *farinacea*, Ach.

Common on old trees. Near Aberdeen, in Tollohill wood, &c. &c. and also in the interior.

2. R. *fraxinea*, Ach.

Common upon old trees. In the woods of Countesswells, near Aberdeen, abundant, and often in fruit.

3. R. *scopulorum*, Ach.

In great profusion along the coast, growing on rocks.

---

* In compiling the *Lichens* from my own collection, and notes by others, I have followed "Schaerer's Enumeratio critica, Lichenum Europaeorum." The old names are, however, usually added.

4. PHYSCIA.

1. P. *furfuracea*, Ach.
Rather local in the lower parts of the district. On the Hill of Ardo, near Aberdeen, parish of Nether-Banchory, G. D. Craig Koynach, Mr. Gardiner.

2. P. *ciliaris*, Ach.
Frequent on trees. Very fine in the woods at Midmar Castle, Mr. Mackay and G. D.

3. P. *tenella*, Ach.
On trees. Near Aberdeen, as at Den of Leggart, &c.; also in the interior, on rocks, summit of the Khoil at Ballater, &c.

4. P. *prunastri*, Ach.
Plentiful on trees. Den of Robslaw, &c.

III.—CETRARIACEAE.

5. CETRARIA.

1. *C. glauca*, Ach.
On rocks and trees. Not uncommon. Near Aberdeen, in the wood west of Pitmedden; Bennachie, &c. Abundant in Glen Muick, G. D.; Craig Koynach, Mr. Gardiner.

2. *C. nivalis*, Ach.
Confined to the higher ranges in the interior, but there it is very abundant, Lochnagar, Ben Macdui, &c. &c.

3. *C. sepincola*, Ach.
Woods at Pitmedden, &c. but not common.

4. *C. Islandica*, Ach.
Upon the ground at the cairns on the hills at Nigg, near Aberdeen, about a mile from the sea, and 200 to 300 feet above its level. Very generally diffused in the interior. Rare in fruit, but found many years ago with *apothecia* by the late Professor Graham, on the Mourne at Castleton.

5. *C. aculeata*, Ach.
Very abundant, both in the lower and higher parts of the district. Near Aberdeen, along the coast; in fructification upon the Hill of Ardo, Nether-Banchory. Very general in the interior, and often along with *C. Islandica*.

IV.—PELTIDEACEAE.

6. NEPHROMA.

1. *N. resupinatum*, Ach.

Rather local. Chiefly in the interior. Jackstone, St. Cyrus, Dr. Stephen; on old trees, Glenmuick, and rocks of the Dhuloch, Mr. Mackay and G. D.; Craig Koynach, Mr. Gardiner.

7. PELTIGERA.

1. P. *venosa*, Ach.

In crevices of rocks in the interior. Rocks of the Dhuloch, Mr. Mackay and G. D.

2. P. *aphthosa*, Ach.

Moist rocks among mosses. Rather local. Clockhill, Benholme, and at St. Cyrus, Dr. Stephen. Abundant in fruit, upon Craig Clunie, and the "Lion's face," Mr. Gardiner. Craigs of Pannanich, G. D.

3. P. *rubiginosa*, Ach.

On trees in sub-alpine districts.

Var. a, affinis. The "Lion's face" at Castleton, Mr. Gardiner.

4. P. *canina*, Ach.

Very common among mosses, &c. in different parts of the district.

5. P. *polydactyla*, Ach.

Rather scarce, Den Fenella, Dr. Stephen. Near Aberdeen it occurs on the Brimman hill; beside the wood west from Pitmedden; and at the Stocket moor, near Summerhill.

Var. scutata. Upon Ben Beck at Castleton, Braemar, Mr. Gardiner.

8. SOLORINA.

1. S. *crocea*, Ach.

Confined to the more inland and higher districts. In crevices of rocks on Lochnagar and Mona-rua range, Professor Macgillivray. Rocks of the Dhuloch, Mr. Mackay and G. D.

2. S. *saccata*, Ach.

Confined to the interior, and rare. In shady crevices of rocks on Craig Koynach, near Castleton, Mr. Gardiner.

Var. laetevirens, (Endocarpon laetevirens). On peat, near the base of the north-east slope of Cairnmanearn, Durris, Mr. Sutherland.

V.—UMBILICARIACEAE.

9. UMBILICARIA.

1. U. *polymorpha*, Schrad.

Very generally diffused in one or other of its forms from some of the lower districts to the higher points in the interior.

Var. 1, *cylindrica.* On the Hill of Fare ; summit of the Buck of the Cabrach, and other parts of the interior, G. D. Upon Ben Beck, Castleton, Mr. Gardiner.

Var. 2, *deusta.* (U. *proboscidea*, Ach.) Common on rocks and stones in the interior. Buck of the Cabrach, G. D. ; Ben Beck, Castleton, Mr. Gardiner.

2. U. *polyphylla*, Ach.
Chiefly in the interior. Ben Beck, Castleton, Mr. Gardiner.

3. U. *erosa*, Ach.
Grows with other species of this genus ; is confined to the interior, and rare. Ben Beck, Castleton, Mr. Gardiner.

4. U. *polyrhizos*, Linn. *(Gyrophora pellita.)*
Not uncommon. Near Aberdeen, on Corsehill, at Scotston, upon boulders. In the interior, Ben Beck, Castleton, &c.

VI.—PARMELIACEAE.
10. STICTA.

1. S. *pulmonaria*, Ach.
·Very local. Grip, west of Johnshaven ; and Dunnottar Castle, Dr. Stephen. Abundant and fine upon old willows at the head of Loch Muick, Mr. Mackay and G. D.

2. S. *scrobiculata*, Ach.
Along with the last, and also on the Dhuloch rocks, Mr. Mackay and G D. Craig Koynach, Mr. Gardiner.

3. S. *sylvatica*, Ach.
Rare. Trunks and roots of trees, Upper Braemar, Professor Macgillivray.

4. S. *limbata*, Ach.
On rocks. At Annie's Dam, Kincardineshire, Dr. Stephen.

11. PARMELIA.

1. P. *amplissima*, Schaerer. *(P. glomulifera*, Ach.*)*
Trees and rocks. Rocks at Annie's Den, Kincardineshire, Dr. Stephen.

2. P. *caperata*, Ach.
On trees and rocks. On a tree upon the hill above Brigton, St. Cyrus, Dr. Stephen.

3. P. *conspersa*, Ach.

On rocks and stones. Pier at Loch of Park, and at Bridge of Feuch, Dr. Stephen.

4. P. *saxatilis*, Ach.

Very abundant on trees and rocks in all parts of the district. Fertile on trees at Scotston, near Aberdeen; and Glen Muick, &c.

Var. 1, *omphalodes*. Plentiful everywhere. Near Aberdeen, upon the Hill of Ardo, in fruit. Common in the interior. A very remarkable form occurs on the top of the Buck of the Cabrach, in general appearance resembling P. *sinuosa*, which at first I supposed it to be.

5. P. *stellaris*, Ach.

Not uncommon on trees, coast line and interior. At Kinmundy of Skene; Den of Leggart, &c. At Ballater, G. D.

6. P. *Mougeotii*, Schaerer. (Considered by some to be a variety of P. *conspersa*.)

On rocks and boulders. Local. Upon Gneiss boulders at Stocket moor, and in fruit, G. D.

7. P. *ceratophylla*, Wallr. [P. *physodes*, Ach.]

On trees, &c. General.

Var. physodes. Very frequent.

8. P. *olivacea*, Ach.

Not uncommon on trees. At Bieldside, near Aberdeen, &c. G. D.

9. P. *Fahlunensis*, Ach.

Abundant on stones in the interior.

Var. 1, *stygia*. Upon the hills at Nigg, near Aberdeen, and also in the interior.

Var. 2, *tristis*. Abundant at the north top of Bennachie. Very common on the higher mountains in the interior.

Var. 3, *lanata*. Plentiful on Morven, and general on the higher ranges.

10. P. *aquila*, Ach.

Very abundant on the rocks at Girdleness lighthouse, G. D. Benholme; Hill of Grip, &c. Dr. Stephen.

11. P. *parietina*, Ach.

On trees and walls. Common.

Var. candelaria. On trees, &c. Frequent.

12. P. *elegans*, Ach.

On the Khoil at Ballater; at the head of Loch Muick; Ben Macdui, &c. G. D.

13. P. *hypnorum*, Ach.

On the ground upon peat, and on various species of moss. Very general in the interior. Pannanich cliffs; Glen Muick, &c. &c.

VII.—LECANORIACEAE.

12. LECANORA.

1 L. *murorum*, Ach.

On walls and rocks. Frequent. About Aberdeen, at Stocket and Robslaw; on the Khoil at Ballater, &c. &c.

2. L. *atra*, Ach.

Common. Upon trees and rocks in different parts of the district.

3. L. *subfusca*, Ach.

Generally on the bark of trees; sometimes on rocks and stones. Abundant and general.

Var. hypnorum. Creeping over decayed roots of plants in crevices of rocks at Girdleness, G. D.

4. L. *muralis*, Schaerer. *(Squamaria saxicola.)*

Var. saxicola, Ach. Rocks and stones. Frequent. Very fine upon serpentine rocks, on the Khoil at Ballater, G. D.

5. L. *pallescens*, Linn.

On trees, rocks, and boulders.

Var. 1. *parella.* Is one of our most common species.

Var. 2. *Upsaliensis.* In the interior, encrusting mosses, stems of heath, &c. Pannanich cliffs; Buck of Cabrach, &c.

6. L. *tartarea*, Ach.

In great profusion on rocks and boulders in the interior. Very fine at Spital of Muick.

7. L. *vitellina*, Ach.

On trees and rocks. Very frequent. Coast line and interior.

8. L. *varia*, Ach.

Not uncommon on wooden palings, &c. On dead trees in the wood west of Pitmedden House.

Var. maculaeformis. On walls, Bay of Nigg; on shady rocks in Glen Ey, and opposite Invercauld, Prof. Macgillivray.

T

9. L. *Haematomma*, Ach.
Rare. On rocks about Ballater, Professor Macgillivray.

10. L. *ventosa*, Ach.
This beautiful species is abundant on the boulders at Aberdeen; on Stocket moor, &c. Very fine on the rocks of the north summit of Bennachie. Plentiful in the interior.

13. URCEOLARIA.

1. U. *calcarea*, Ach.
On rocks and stones. Bridge of Feugh, Prof. Macgillivray. Jackstone, St. Cyrus; Benholme, Dr. Stephen.

2. U. *scruposa*, Ach.
On rocks and stones, and on the ground on moors. Common, Professor Macgillivray.

14. GYALECTA.

1. G. *Acharii*, Schaerer. (*Urceolaria Acharii.*)
On rocks and stones. By the Burn, east of Hill of Woodston; St. Cyrus, Dr. Stephen.

VIII.—LECIDEACEAE.
15. LECIDEA.

1. L. *triptophylla*, Acharius.
On turfy heaths. Local.
Var. β, *coronata*. Head of Glen Callater, Mr. Gardiner.

2. L. *lugubris*, Sommf.
On rocks and stones. Rare. On weathered gneissic boulders, moor immediately to the west of the Free Church Schoolhouse of Castleton, Braemar, half-a-mile from the village, and south side of the road to Linn of Dee, Dr. Lindsay.

3. L. *canescens*, Ach. (*Placodium canescens.*)
On trees and rocks. St. Cyrus; Benholme; Muchalls, Dr. Stephen. Deeside, Professor Macgillivray.

4. L. *geographica*, Linn.
On rocks and stones. Common. Very fine on some of the higher mountains, as the Mourne at Castleton, &c.
Var. *atro-virens*. Very frequent in different parts of the district.

5. L. *fumosa*, Ach. (*L. cechumena.*)
Var. *nitida.* On rocks and stones. Frequent.

6. L. *rivulosa*, Ach.

"On rocks and stones of various kinds," Professor Macgillivray.

7. L. *verruculosa*, Schaerer.

Var. atro-alba. Frequent on rocks and stones, Professor Macgillivray.

8. L. *confervoides*, De Cand.

On rocks and stones.

Var. concreta. Glen Clunie; Glen Callater, and other parts of Braemar, Professor Macgillivray.

9. L. *confluens*, Ach.

Abundant on rocks and stones. Very fine upon rocks at Girdleness; also in the interior, as Glen Callater, &c.

10. L. *albo-caerulescens*, Wulf.

On rocks and stones.

Var. flavo-caerulescens. Aberdeenshire, Professor Macgillivray.

11. L. *flavo-virescens*, Ach.

Var. scabrosa. On tiles near Aberdeen, Professor Macgillivray.

12. L. *punctata*, Hoffm.

On trees. Frequent.

Var. parasema. Aberdeen, Professor Macgillivray.
Var. pinicola. On bark of the Scotch fir.

13. L. *sanguinaria*, Ach.

On rocks and trees. Frequent about Braemar. Ben Beck; and "Lion's face," Castleton, Mr. Gardiner.

14. L. *sabuletorum*, Flk.

Var. muscorum. On moors in Nigg, Durris, and Banchory-Ternan, Professor Macgillivray.

15. L. *granulosa*, Ach.

Var. decolorans. Probably of general occurrence in the district; the finest examples I possess are from peat soil, a little to the south of the north top of Bennachie, where it is plentiful.

16. L. *aeruginosa*, Schaerer. *(L. icmadophila.)*

This beautiful species is plentiful on peat in the higher parts of the district. Very fine on the hill above Pannanich, near Ballater, G. D. Hill of Fare; and in Strachan, Dr. Stephen.

17. L. *ferruginea*, Schaerer.

St. Cyrus; Johnshaven, Dr. Stephen. Khoil at Ballater, G. D.

Var. festiva. On granite at Nigg, &c., Prof. Macgillivray.

18. L. *aurantiaca*, Schaerer.

Var. flavo-virescens. On rocks and stones in the upper parts, Professor Macgillivray.

19. L. *cerina*, Schaerer.

On bark of trees. Rather scarce. Slievanachie, Ballater, G. D.

IX.—GRAPHIDIACEAE.

16. OPEGRAPHA.

1. O. *scripta*, Ach.

On the smooth bark of trees. On the bark of the Hazel, Professor Macgillivray. Hill of Fare, Dr. Stephen.

2. O. *atra*, Pers.

In its various forms on the bark of trees.

Var. radiata. On the Beech, Mountain Ash, and other trees.

Var. epipasta. On the bark of trees, Deeside, Professor Macgillivray.

Var. vulgata. On the bark of Elms in Den of Robslaw.

Var. Swartziana. On trees, Deeside, Professor Macgillivray.

3. O. *herpetica*, Ach.

Var. siderella. On the bark of trees, Deeside, Professor Macgillivray.

4. O. *saxatilis*, De Cand.

On rocks and stones. On the wall by the sea at Brotherton, near Johnshaven, Dr. Stephen. Mica slate in Glen Ey; on Hornblende slate upon Morven, Professor Macgillivray, (Under the name *Lecidea simplex.*)

17. ARTHONIA.

1. A. *impolita*, Borrer.

On the bark of trees. Not unfrequent near Aberdeen. Den of Robslaw, G. D. On Ash, foot of Den of Leggart, Dr. Stephen.

X.—CALICIACEAE.
18 CALICIUM.
1. *C. turbinatum*, Pers.

On *Pertusaria communis*, Deeside, Professor Macgillivray.

XI.—CLADONIACEAE.
19. STEREOCAULON.
1. *S. condensatum*, Hoffm.

On peat soil, Hill of Ardo, near Aberdeen.

2. *S. paschale*, Ach.

Hill of Ardo; abundant in the interior, very fine on the summit of Morven.

Var. denudatum. Cairn-a-Drochet, Castleton, Mr. Gardiner.

20. BAEOMYCES.
1. *B. roseus*, Pers.

Jackstone, St. Cyrus; Benholme; Hill of Fare, Dr. Stephen. In the wood at Denmore, and in Den of Leggart, near Aberdeen, G. D.

2. *B. byssoides*, Schaerer. *(B. rufus Wahl.)*

On rocks and on the ground, Deeside, Professor Macgillivray. Brigton, St. Cyrus; Nigg; Corrichie on Hill of Fare, Dr. Stephen.

3. *B. placophyllus*, Ach.

On the ground and on the wall tops, Deeside, Professor Macgillivray.

21. CLADONIA.
1. *C. extensa*, Schaerer. *(C. coccifera.)*

On moors, abundant everywhere.

2. *C. deformis*, Hoffm.

On moors; not very frequent. At Hazelhead; Hill of Fare, &c.

3. *C. bellidiflora*, Schaerer.

On rocks and on the ground. Generally diffused, but finer and more abundant in the interior. Lochnagar, &c. &c.

4. *C. fimbriata*, Fries.

On heaths, walls, &c. Not uncommon. Very large on the Hill of Fare.

5. C. *pyxidata*, Schaerer.
On heaths, walls, &c. Common.

6. C. *alcicornis*, Flk.
On heaths. Hill of Ardo near Aberdeen; crevices of moist rocks; Pannanich, &c.

7. C. *cervicornis*, Schaerer.
On the ground and moist rocks. Deeside, Professor Macgillivray.

8. C. *gracilis*, Flk.
On moors. Hill of Fare, &c.

9. C. *stellata*, Schaerer.
On peat soil.

Var. uncialis. On moors near Aberdeen; Hill of Fare; Pannanich, &c. &c.

10. C. *squamosa*, Hoffm.
On dead trees, &c. Fine and abundant in the wood, a little west from the House of Pitmedden.

11. C. *furcata*, Schaerer.
On moors, &c. Stocket Moor, &c.

12. C *rangiferina*, Hoffm.
Very abundant. Coast line and interior.

13. C. *papillaria*, Hoffm.
Moors on Benholme and Strachan, Dr. Stephen; on Ben Macdui, Dr. Lindsay; Hill of Ardo, near Aberdeen, G. D.

22. THAMNOLIA.*

1. T. *vermicularis*, Ach.
On alpine moors. Local. Hill of Fare. Braemar, &c.

XII.—COLLEMACEAE.
23. COLLEMA.

1. C. *nigrescens*, Ach.
On moist shady rocks, and on trees. In Den of Robslaw, G. D.; Den Fenella, above the old bridge, in fruit, Dr. Stephen.

2. C. *spongiosum*, Ach.

---

* The position of this genus is still rather doubtful; some would place it near *Baeomyces*.

On the ground among mosses. Deeside, Professor Macgillivray.

3. *C. muscicola,* Ach.

On rocks, among mosses. North-west side of Clockhill, Benholme; and westward, in St. Cyrus, Dr. Stephen.

4. *C. atro-caeruleum,* Schaerer.

Var. lacerum, among mosses in shady places. Lower part of Den Fenella, Dr. Stephen; Deeside, Prof. Macgillivray.

24. LICHINA.

1. *L confinis,* Agardh.

Marine rocks, near high water mark. Abundant along the Kincardineshire coast.

II.—ANGIOCARPI.

XIII.—SPHAEROPHORACEAE.

25. SPHAEROPHORON.

1. *S. coralloides,* Pers.

On the ground, &c. Sometimes plentiful—especially in the inland and higher parts. Glen Callater; Buck of Cabrach, &c.

2. *S. fragile,* Pers.

On rocks, &c. Generally diffused, and sometimes with the last species.

XIV.—ENDOCARPACEAE.

26. ENDOCARPON.

1. *E. miniatum,* Ach.

On rocks, dry or moist. Rather local. Near Cove Hill, Johnshaven; burn east of Biddrie, St. Cyrus, Dr. Stephen. On stones at the outlet of Gilcomston dam; and very abundant on boulders at Loch of Loirston, G. D.

2. *E. smaragdulum,* Ach. *(Lecanora cervina, var smaragdulum,* Sch.)

On rocks and walls. Rather local. Upon stones of a wall opposite Robslaw quarry, south side; and boulders, Stocket moor, G. D.

3. *E. pusillum,* Hedw. (*E. Hedwigii,* Ach.)

On barren heaths. St. Cyrus; Muchalls; Nigg, &c. Dr. Stephen.

27. PERTUSARIA.

1. *P. communis*, De Cand.
On trees. Frequent. Den Fenella, Dr. Stephen. Abundant in Den of Robslaw, &c. &c. G. D.

2. *P. sulphurea*, Schaerer.
Upon trees. Rather local. On the Beech, Corby Den, Maryculter, Professor Macgillivray.

28. THELOTREMA.

1. *T. lepadinum*, Ach.
On the trunks of trees. Deeside, Professor Macgillivray.

XV.—VERRUCARIACEAE.

29. PYRENULA.

1. *P. submersa*, Schaerer. (*Verrucaria submersa*,)
On wet stones. Very local. In the wood at Tullis, Nigg; in a rivulet on Little Craigendall, G. D.

2. *P. Maura*, Flk. (*Verrucaria Maura.*)
On rocks. Very abundant on the Kincardineshire coast.

3. *P. nigrescens*, Ach. (*Verrucaria nigrescens*, Pers.)
On rocks and walls. Deeside, Professor Macgillivray.

4. *P. nitida*, Ach. (*Verrucaria nitida.*)
On bark of trees. Hill of Fare; by the burn of Hatton, on Alders, Dr. Stephen,

30. VERRUCARIA.

1. *V. epipolaea*, Ach.
On rocks. At Abergairn, near Ballater, Professor Macgillivray.

2. *V. epidermidis*, Ach.
On bark of trees. On birches, Hill of Fare, Dr. Stephen; in Corbie Den, G. D,

3. *V. laevata*, Ach.
Rocky beds of streams. Rocks by the burn in Den Fenella; and east from Hill of Woodston, St. Cyrus, Dr. Stephen.

ALGAE. SEA-WEEDS, &c.

Sub-Class I.—MELANOSPERMEAE.

I.—FUCACEAE.

1. HALIDRYS.

1. H. *siliquosa*, Lyngb. *(Podded H.)*
Common on all rocky parts of the coast; in pools between tide-marks, and at greater depths.

2. FUCUS.

1. F. *vesiculosus*, L. *(Twin-bladdered F.)*
Common on all parts of the coast.

2. F. *ceranoides*, L. *(Horn-like F.)*
Abundant near mouths of rivers.

3. F. *serratus*, L. *(Serrated F.)*
Common between tide-marks.

4. F. *nodosus*, L. *(Nobbed F.)*
Common between tide-marks.

5. F. *canaliculatus*, L. *(Channeled F.)*
Common from half-tide level to high-water mark, and beyond on rocks moistened by spray.

3. HIMANTHALIA.

1. H. *Lorea*, Lyngb. *(Thong-like H.)*
Abundant about low-water mark.

II.—SPOROCHNACEAE.

4. DESMARESTIA.

1. D. *ligulata*, Lamour. *(Tapering D.)*
Rather rare; generally in deep water on our coast.

2. D. *aculeata*, Lamour. *(Prickly D.)*
Common in pools about low-water mark, and in deep water.

3. D. *viridis*, Lamour. *(Green D.)*
Rare; usually cast up from deep water.

III.—LAMINARIACEAE.
5. ALARIA.
1. A. *esculenta*, Greville. *(Edible A.)*
Common about low-water mark.

6. LAMINARIA.
1. L. *digitata*, Lamour. *(Fingered L.)*
Common; usually from deep water to low-water mark.

Var. *stenophylla.* Distinguished from the last by its more slender proportions, and darker colour. Occasionally cast up in Bay of Nigg and elsewhere.

2. L. *longicruris*, De la Pyl. *(Long-stalked L.)*
Cast up at Cruden, Mr. Dawson; and at Peterhead, Mr. Peach. I possess a specimen of this remarkable species, found by Rev. G. Harris in May, 1850, on the beach at Gamrie, Banffshire; it had evidently been drifted from some distant locality. Specimens have been found, under like circumstances, at Orkney, also on Ayrshire coast, and in the North of Ireland. It is a well-known plant on the coast of Greenland and northern shores of America.

3. L. *saccharina*, Lamour. *(Saccharine L.)*
Abundant in deep water, and about low-water mark.

4. L. *Phyllitis*, Lamour. *(Hart's-tongue L.)*
Coast at Peterhead, Rev. J. Yuill, and Mr. Bell. Rather scarce on the Kincardineshire coast; at Cove, G. D. Coast at Macduff, Rev. W. Grigor.

5. L. *Fascia*, Ag. *(Band L.)*
About Stonehaven, Miss Smith. At Peterhead, Rev. J. Yuill, and Mr. Bell. Bay of Nigg, &c.; upon *Rhodymenia palmata*, G. D.

7. CHORDA.
1. C. *Filum*, Lamour. *(Thread C.)*
General on the coast; in pools between tide-marks and in deeper water.

2. C. *lomentaria*, Lyngb. *(Jointed C.)*
Common in pools between high and low-water marks.

IV.—DICTYOTACEAE.
8. DICTYOSIPHON.
1. D. *fœniculaceus*, Greville. *(Fennel D.)*
Common between tide-marks.

9. PUNCTARIA.

1. P. *latifolia*, Greville. *(Broad-leaved P.)*
Coast at Peterhead, Rev. J. Yuill and Mr. Bell.

2. P. *plantaginea*, Greville. *(Plantain P.)*
Common between tide-marks.

10. ASPEROCOCCUS.

1. A. *echinatus*, Greville. *(Prickly A.)*
Common between tide-marks.

11. LITOSIPHON.

1. L. *pusillus*, Harvey. *(Small L.)*
Upon other *Algae*, but not common.

2. L. *Laminariae*, Harvey. *(Laminaria L.)*
Not uncommon; growing upon *Alaria esculenta*.

V.—CHORDARIACEAE.

12. CHORDARIA.

1. C. *flagelliformis*, Agardh. *(Whip-like C.)*
Common between tide-marks.

13. MESOGLOIA.

1. M. *vermicularis*, Agardh.* *(Worm-like M.)*
Between tide-marks. Rather local. At Peterhead, Rev. J. Yuill and Mr. Bell; at Gamrie, Rev. G. Harris and G. D.

2. M. *virescens*, Carmichael. *(Pale-green M.)*
Of general occurrence between tide-marks.

14. LEATHESIA.

1. L. *tuberiformis*, S. F. Gray. *(Tuber-like L.)*
Common on rocks and *Algae* between tide-marks.

15. RALFSIA.

1. R. *verrucosa*, Berkeley. *(Warty R.)*
Abundant on the Kincardineshire coast, south of Aberdeen. Usually encrusting the bottom of rocky pools, near high-water mark. I have found the fructification on specimens gathered at Girdleness.

---

* Rev. J. Yuill writes—"M. *vermicularis* and M. *virescens* seem to be the same plant, *virescens* in its spring state, and *vermicularis* when older." My own observations induce me to consider them distinct, G. D.

16. ELACHISTA.

1. E. *fucicola*, Fries. *(Fucus E.)*
On various species of *Fucus*. Occasionally along our coasts.

2. E. *velutina*, Fries. *(Velvety E.)*
Upon *Himanthalia Lorea* ; at the Cove, four miles south from Aberdeen, G. D.

17. MYRIONEMA.

1. M. *strangulans*, Greville. *(Choking M.)*
At the Cove, upon *Entoromorpha compressa*.

2. M. *punctiforme*, Harvey. *(Dot-like M.)*
Not uncommon upon *Ceramium rubrum*.

VI.—ECTOCARPACEAE.

18. CLADOSTEPHUS.

1. C. *verticillatus*, Agardh. *(Whorled C.)*
Rather rare. Coast south of Aberdeen, G. D. At Peterhead, Rev. J. Yuill and Mr. Bell.

2. C. *spongiosus*, Agardh. *(Spongy C.)*
Not uncommon about low-water mark.

19. SPHACELARIA.

1. S. *plumosa*, Lyngbye. *(Feathery S.)*
Rare. Coast at Stonehaven, Miss Smith; at low-water mark, south side of the Bay of Nigg, G. D.; at Peterhead, Rev. J. Yuill and Mr. Bell; at Macduff, Rev. W. Grigor.

2. S. *cirrhosa*, Agardh. *(Hair-like S.)*
Not uncommon, between tide-marks, in small tufts upon other *Algae*.

3. S. *radicans*, Harvey. *(Rooting S.)*
I have only seen this species in one locality, viz. at a little cove opposite to the Girdleness lighthouse, on perpendicular faces of rocks between tide-marks.

20. ECTOCARPUS.

1. E. *siliculosus*, Lyngbye. *(Pod-fruited E.)*
Common on other *Algae* between tide-marks.

2. E. *fasciculatus*, Harvey. *(Fasciculate E.)*
Between tide-marks on other *Algae*. At Peterhead, Rev. J. Yuill and Mr. Bell.

3. **E. Hincksiae**, Harvey. *(Hinck's E.)*
Abundant on the fronds of *Laminaria digitata* at Bay of Nigg and other places, G. D. At Peterhead, Rev. J. Yuill and Mr. Bell.

4. **E. tomentosus**, Lyngbye. *(Woolly E.)*
Very abundant on *Algae* and on rocks between tide-marks.

5. **E. crinitus**, Carmichael. *(Hairy E.)*
Muddy shores. Rare. At Peterhead, Rev. J. Yuill and Mr. Bell.

6. **E. littoralis**, Lyngbye. *(Shore E.)*
Very common at various depths along the coast, and often in estuaries.

7. **E. granulosus**, Agardh. *(Granulous E.)*
In rock pools at Torry, opposite the pier-head, G. D. At Peterhead, Rev. J. Yuill and Mr. Bell.

8. **E. sphaerophorus**, Carm. *(Warty E.)*
Between tide marks. Upon *Callithamnion Arbuscula, Polysiphonia nigrescens*, &c. at Girdleness; Bay of Nigg, &c. G. D. At Peterhead, Rev. J. Yuill and Mr. Bell.

9. **E. Mertensii**, Agardh. *(Mertens' E.)*
Rare. On the walls of the north harbour at Peterhead, Mr. Peach, from whom I have received specimens.

10. **E. brachiatus**, Harvey. *(Cross-branched E.)*
Very rare. A few specimens cast on shore at Peterhead, Rev. J. Yuill.

21. MYRIOTRICHIA.

1. **M. clavaeformis**, Harvey. *(Club-shaped M.)*
Rare. Upon *Mesogloia virescens* at Girdleness, &c.

2. **M. filiformis**, Harvey. *(Thread-like M.)*
Not uncommon. Usually upon *Chorda lomentaria*, at Nigg, &c. At Peterhead, Rev. J. Yuill and Mr. Bell.

Sub-Class II.—RHODOSPERMEAE.

VII.—RHODOMELACEAE.

22. ODONTHALIA.

1. **O. dentata**, Lyngbye. *(Toothed O.)*

About low-water mark, and in deep water. Very abundant along our shores, as, indeed, it generally is in Scotland; confined to north of England and north of Ireland.

23. RHODOMELA.

1. R. *lycopodioides*, Agardh. *((Lycopodium R.)*
Abundant on rocks and on *Algae* at Girdleness; Cove; Peterhead, &c.

2. R. *subfusca*, Agardh. *(Brownish R.)*
Occasionally along the Kincardineshire coast, G. D. At Peterhead, Rev. J. Yuill and Mr. Bell.

24. POLYSIPHONIA.

1. P. *urceolata*, Greville. *(Pitchered P.)*
Common on rocks and *Algae* about low-water mark.

2. P. *fibrata*, Harvey. *(Fibred P.)*
Occasionally on the coast south of Aberdeen, about low-water mark, G. D.; at Peterhead, Rev. J. Yuill and Mr. Bell.

3. P. *elongella*, Harvey. *(Divaricate P.)*
Occasionally cast up on the coast south of Aberdeen, G. D.; at Peterhead, Rev. J. Yuill and Mr. Bell.

4. P. *elongata*, Greville. *(Elongated P.)*
At Peterhead, Rev. J. Yuill and Mr. Bell.

5. P. *violacea*, Greville. *(Violet P.)*
About low-water mark. Not uncommon on the coast south from Aberdeen, G. D.; Peterhead, Rev. J. Yuill and Mr. Bell.

6. P. *fibrillosa*, Greville. *(Fibrillose P.)*
Pools between tide-marks. Frequent. At Peterhead, Rev. J. Yuill and Mr. Bell; Kincardineshire coast, G. D.

7. P. *Brodiaei*, Greville. *(Brodie's P.)*
About low-water mark. Abundant.

8. P. *nigrescens*, Greville. *(Blackish P.)*
Common on rocks, &c. between tide-marks.

9. P. *atro-rubescens*, Greville. *(Dark-red P.)*
Local. In pools on the scaly rocks at Black-dog, Belhelvie, G. D.; Peterhead, Rev. J. Yuill and Mr. Bell.

10. P. *fastigiata*, Greville. *(Tufted P.)*
Generally between tide-marks. Very common on *Fucus*.

11. P. *parasitica*, Greville. (*Parasitic P.*)
About low-water mark. Rare. In the small cove at Dunnottar Castle, Miss Smith; Peterhead, Rev. J. Yuill and Mr. Bell; Macduff, Rev. W. Grigor.

12. P. *byssoides*, Greville. (*Byssoid P.*)
Occasionally cast up at Aberdeen, G. D.; Peterhead, Rev. J. Yuill and Mr. Bell.

25. DASYA.

1. D. *coccinea*, Ag. (*Scarlet D.*)
Rare. Near Stonehaven, Miss Smith; at Peterhead, Rev. J. Yuill and Mr. Bell; Macduff, Rev. W. Grigor.

VIII.—LAURENCIACEAE.

26. BONNEMAISONIA.

1. B. *asparagoides*, Ag. (*Asparagus-like B.*)
Rare. Peterhead, Mr. Peach.

27. LAURENCIA.

1. L. *pinnatifida*, Lamour. (*Pinnatifid L.*)
Between tide-marks, and in deeper water. Very common, and exceedingly variable in habit.

2. L. *dasyphylla*, Greville. (*Thick-leaved D.*)
Rare. Peterhead, Rev. J. Yuill and Mr. Bell.

28. CHRYSYMENIA.

1. C. *clavellosa*, J. Agardh. (*Clubbed C.*)
Frequently cast up from deep water.

29. CHYLOCLADIA.

1. C. *articulata*, Greville. (*Jointed C.*)
Between tide-marks. Very common.

2. C. *kaliformis*, Greville. (*Whorled K.*)
Deep water. Rare. Buchan coast, Prof. Macgillivray.

IX.—CORALLINACEAE.

30. CORALLINA.

1. C. *officinalis*, Linn. (*Medicinal C.*)
Abundant on all our rocky coast between tide-marks.

31. JANIA.

1. J. *rubens*, Lamour. *(Red J.)*
Parasitical upon small *Algae* in rock pools. Rare. Peterhead, Rev. J. Yuill and Mr. Bell.

32. MELOBESIA.

1. M. *polymorpha*, Linn. *(Many-shaped M.)*
Forming a crust upon rocks. Common.

2. M. *farinosa*, Lamour. *(Mealy M.)*
Not uncommon upon various *Algae*.

3. M. *verrucata*, Lamour. *(Warty M.)*
Upon *Phyllophora rubens*.

33. HILDENBRANTIA.

1. H. *rubra*, Meneghini. *(Red H.)*
In the form of a red film upon stones and rocks at the Cove, &c.

34. HAPALIDIUM.

1. H. *Phyllactidium*, Kützing. *(Fan-like P.)* *(Lithocystis Allmanni.)*
Upon smaller *Algae*. Peterhead, Mr. Peach.

X.—DELESSERIACEAE.

35. DELESSERIA.

1. D. *sanguinea*, Lamour. *(Blood-red D.)*
Common in rock pools between tide-marks, and in deeper water.

2. D. *sinuosa*, Lamour. *(Sinuous D.)*
Occasionally with the last; more frequently upon *Laminaria digitata*.

3. D. *alata*, Lamour. *(Winged D.)*
Very common at various depths, often on stems of *Laminaria*.

4. D. *angustissima*, Griffiths. *(Narrow D.)*
Abundant with the last, of which it may be a variety.

36. NITOPHYLLUM.

1. N. *punctatum*, Greville. *(Dotted N.)*
Rare. Coast at Stonehaven, Miss Smith. At Peterhead, Rev. J. Yuill and Mr. Bell.

2. N. *Bonnemaisoni*, Greville. *(Bonnemaison's N.)*
Rare. Peterhead, Mr. Peach.

3. N. *laceratum*, Greville. *(Torn N.)*
Not uncommon. Generally found cast up from deep water.

37. PLOCAMIUM.

1. P. *coccineum*, Lyngb. *(Scarlet P.)*
Very common.

XI.—RHODYMENIACEAE.
38. RHODYMENIA.

1. R. *laciniata*, Greville. *(Jagged R.)*
Not uncommon. Generally cast up from deep water.

2. R. *jubata*, Greville. *(Cirrhose R.)*
Rare. Kincardineshire coast, Miss Smith.

3. R. *palmata*, Greville. *(Palmate R.)*
Common everywhere.

39. CYSTOCLONIUM. (HYPNEA.)

1. C. *purpurascens*, Harvey. *(Purple C.)*
Common on rocks and stones between tide marks.

XII.—CRYPTONEMIACEAE.
40. GELIDIUM.

1. G. *corneum*, Lamour. *(Horny G.)*
Rare. Peterhead, Rev. J. Yuill and Mr. Bell.

41. GIGARTINA.

1. G. *mamillosa*, J. Agardh. *(Mamillose G.)*
Common on rocks about low-water mark.

42. CHONDRUS.

1. C. *crispus*, Lyngb. *(Curled C.)*
Common on rocky parts of the coast.

43. PHYLLOPHORA.

1. P. *rubens*, Greville. *(Red P.)*
In pools about low-water mark; occasionally along our coast. At Cove, Bay of Nigg, Girdleness, &c. G. D. Peterhead, Rev. J. Yuill and Mr. Bell.

2. P. *membranifolia*, J. Agardh. *(Thin-leaved P.)*
In pools between tide-marks. At Cove, Bay of Nigg, &c. G. D. Peterhead, Rev. J. Yuill and Mr. Bell.

44. GYMNOGONGRUS.

1. G. *plicatus*, Kützing. *(Entangled G.)*
Very common at various depths.

45. POLYIDES.

1. P. *rotundus*, Greville. *(Round P.)*
In pools near low-water mark. Rather rare. Bay of Nigg, &c. G. D. Peterhead, Rev. J. Yuill and Mr. Bell.

46. FURCELLARIA.

1. F. *fastigiata*, Lamour. *(Pointed F.)*
Very common in rock pools.

47. DUMONTIA.

1. D. *filiformis*, Greville. *(Thread-like D.)*
Not uncommon between tide-marks.

48. HALYMENIA.

1. H. *ligulata*, Agardh. *(Strap-shaped H.)*
Usually in deep water. Very rare. Peterhead, Mr. Bell. Coast at Macduff, Rev. W. Grigor.

49. IRIDAEA.

1. I. *edulis*, Bory. *(Edible I.)*
Common about low-water mark.

50. CATENELLA.

1. C. *Opuntia*, Greville. *(Fig-like C.)*
On rocks near high-water mark. Very local. Abundant at the west end of the "needle e'e," an arch of rock a mile south from Bay of Nigg.

51. GLOIOSIPHONIA.

1. G. *capillaris*, Carmichael. *(Hair-like G.)*
Rare; about low-water mark. Sometimes cast up from deep water. At the Cove, south from Aberdeen, Miss Smith. Peterhead, Mr. Peach.

52. DUDRESNAIA.

1. D. *divaricata*, J. Agardh. *(Divaricate D.)*

Rare. About low-water mark, and also in deep water.
Bay of Nigg, G. D. ; Peterhead, Rev. J. Yuill and Mr. Bell.
Very fine in the little bay at Gamrie, Rev. G. Harris and
G. D.

XIII.—CERAMIACEAE.
53. PTILOTA.

1. P. *plumosa*, Agardh. *(Feathery P.)*
Common on stems of *Laminaria digitata*.

2. P. *sericea*, Gmelin. *(Silken P.)*
Very common on faces of rocks between tide-marks.

54. CERAMIUM.

1. C. *rubrum*, Agardh. *(Red C.)*
Very common at various depths.

2. C. *Deslongchampsii*, Chauvin. *(Deslongchamp's C.)*
Between tide-marks. Probably local. Peterhead, Rev. J. Yuill and Mr. Bell. Girdleness, G. D.

3. C. *diaphanum*, Roth. *(Diaphanous C.)*
Between tide-marks. Not uncommon.

4. C. *acanthonotum*, Carm. *(One-spined C.)*
On rocks, &c. between tide-marks. Abundant on Kincardineshire coast, and on the pier at Aberdeen, G. D. Peterhead, Rev. J. Yuill and Mr. Bell.

5. C. *ciliatum*, Ducluz. *(Ciliated C.)*
On rocks, &c. between tide-marks. Not uncommon.

55. GRIFFITHSIA.

1. G. *setacea*, Agardh. *(Bristly G.)*
Rare. Peterhead, Rev. J. Yuill and Mr. Bell.

56. CALLITHAMNION.

1. C. *Plumula*, Lyngb. *(Feathered C.)*
Rare. Peterhead, Rev. J. Yuill and Mr. Bell.

2. C. *floccosum*, Agardh. *(Floccose C.)*
On rocks about low-water mark ; rare. On rocks opposite the arched cave a little south of the harbour at the Cove, G. D. On the wall of the north harbour at Peterhead, Mr. Peach.

3. C. *Turneri*, Agardh. *(Turner's C.)*

On other *Algae* between tide-marks. Kincardineshire coast, abundant, G. D. Peterhead, Rev. J. Yuill and Mr. Bell.

4. C. *Arbuscula*, Lyngb. (*Bush C.*)

On rocks and shells between tide-marks. Common. Abundant on the Kincardineshire coast.

5. C. *Brodiaei*, Harvey. (*Brodie's C.*)

On *Algae*, at low-water mark. Rare. Peterhead, Rev. J. Yuill and Mr. Bell. On the pier at Aberdeen, G. D.

6. C. *tetragonum*, Agardh. (*Four-angled C.*)

Rare. Usually on larger *Algae*. Peterhead, Rev. J. Yuill and Mr. Bell.

7. C. *Hookeri*, Agardh. (*Hooker's C.*)

On rocks, &c. between tide-marks, and in deeper water. Not common in this district. Kincardineshire coast, Miss Smith. Peterhead, Rev. J. Yuill and Mr. Bell.

8. C. *roseum*, Lyngb. (*Rosy C.*)

On rocks and larger *Algae* at low-water mark. Kincardineshire coast, Miss Smith; at Girdleness, G. D.; Peterhead, Rev. J. Yuill and Mr. Bell.

9. C. *polyspermum*, Agardh. (*Many-seeded C.*)

On *Algae*, &c. between tide-marks. Common.

10. C. *corymbosum*, Agardh. (*Corymbose C.*)

On rocks and *Algae* about low-water mark. Peterhead, Rev. J. Yuill and Mr. Bell.

11. C. *Rothii*, Lyngb. (*Roth's C.*)

Forming a velvet-like crust in the shallow rock pools at Muchalls harbour, ten miles south from Aberdeen, G. D.

Var. β, *purpurea.* On rocks above ordinary high-water mark under the arch at Muchalls, G. D.

12. C. *sparsum*, Harvey. (*Scattered C.*)

A plant agreeing with the characters of this species occurs occasionally on the stems of *Laminaria digitata*, at Bay of Nigg, &c. G. D.

13. C. *Daviesii*, Lyngb. (*Davies's C.*)

Occasionally in Bay of Nigg and other parts of the Kincardineshire coast, along with *Ectocarpus Hincksiae* upon *L. digitata*, and sometimes upon *Porphyra vulgaris*, G. D.

57. TRENTEPOHLIA.

1. T. *pulchella*, Agardh. *(Neat T.)*

In streams upon *Lemania fluviatilis*. Not uncommon. Usually very plentiful in the stream—Denburn—at the north side of Robslaw quarry, G. D.

Sub-Class III.—CHLOROSPERMEAE.

XIV.—LEMANIEAE.

58. LEMANIA. *

1. L. *fluviatilis*, Agardh.

A common plant in most of our rapid streams along the coast line and in the interior. Burn of Robslaw; Burn of Cults; Hill of Fare, &c. &c. G. D.

XV.—BATRACHOSPERMACEAE.

59. BATRACHOSPERMUM.

1. B. *vagum*, Agardh.

In bog-pools and lakes, chiefly inland. Howe of Corrichie, on Hill of Fare, and in Loch Phadrig, near Castleton, Braemar, about 2000 feet, G. D.

2. B. *moniliforme*, Agardh.

In slow streams and spring wells. Not uncommon. In the burn at the Stocket; in the well in the wood on north bank of Don, at the old bridge; in the well by the road-side at west end of Summerhill; in pools at Robslaw quarry, &c. G. D.

3. B. *atrum*, Harvey.

Upon stones in the Corbie Loch, Mr. P. Grant.

XVI.—CHAETOPHOROIDEAE.

60. BULBOCHAETE.

1. B. *setigera*, Agardh.

Forming fleece-like tufts upon water plants. Not uncommon. Corbie Loch, north from Aberdeen, Mr. P. Grant. Loch of Skene; in a spring well at the south end of the old Bridge of Dee, &c. G. D.

---

* The reader is referred to a paper on the structure and affinities of this plant—*(Trans. Edinburgh Bot. Soc.* VI. p. 243)—by Dr. W. J. Thomson, who thinks it ought to be placed high in the series, in the order *Sporochnaceae*.

61. COLEOCHAETE.

1. *C. scutata*, Brebisson.

Abundant on the stems and leaves of *Poa fluitans* in a ditch at the west side of the Old-town Links, south from the brick-work, G. D.

62. DRAPARNALDIA.

1. *D. plumosa*, Agardh.

Common in streams and wells at Aberdeen, G. D.

2. *D. glomerata*, Agardh.

Often with the last species. Near Ballater, at 1800 feet, G. D.

3. *D. tenuis*, Agardh.

Along with *Batrachospermum atrum* in Corbie Loch, September, 1847, Mr. P. Grant.

63. CHAETOPHORA.

1. *C. elegans*, Agardh.

Upon sticks, &c. &c. in stagnant waters. At Stocket; Robslaw quarry; Hill of Fare, &c. G. D

2. *C. tuberculosa*, Hooker.

Fresh water pools in the Old-town Links, G. D.

3. *C. pisiformis*, Agardh.

In Loch of Skene, July, 1843, G. D.

XVII.—SIPHONACEAE.

64. CODIUM.

1. *C. tomentosum*, Stack.

In pools near low-water mark. Apparently rare in this district. Coast at Peterhead. I have only seen one specimen in the possession of the late Professor Macgillivray.

65. BRYOPSIS.

1. *B. plumosa*, Agardh.

In pools between tide-marks. Very rare, and dwarf on our coasts. At the Cove, a little south from the boat harbour, G. D. Peterhead, Rev. J. Yuill and Mr. Bell.

66. VAUCHERIA.

1. *V. velutina*, Agardh.

On muddy shores between tide-marks. At the north end

of the Old-town Links; shore between Torry farm at Nigg and the river Dee, G. D.

2. *V. dichotoma*, Agardh.

In ponds and ditches. In the stream at Gilcomston dam, and in Old-town Links, &c. G. D.

3. *V. terrestris*, Vaucher.

On the ground in shady places about Aberdeen, G. D. Doubtless other species of this genus occur in the district: the above are all I can vouch for at present.

67. BOTRYDIUM.

1. *B. granulatum*, Greville.

On damp soil in gardens, &c. It is probably common, but I have only a single record of its occurrence; Cherryvale. near Aberdeen.

XVIII.—CONFERVACEAE.

68. CLADOPHORA.

1. *C. rupestris*, Kützing.

On rocks between tide-marks. Very abundant on all rocky parts of the coast.

2. *C. lanosa*, Kützing.

On other *Algae* and rocks. Frequent.

3. *C. arcta*, Kützing.

On rocks between tide-marks. Very general on our coast.

4. *C. laetevirens*, Kützing.

Between tide-marks. Occasionally along the coast, as at Girdleness, &c. Peterhead, Rev. J. Yuill and Mr. Bell.

5. *C. gracilis*, Griffiths.

Rare. Peterhead, Rev. J. Yuill and Mr. Bell.

6. *C. glomerata*, Linn.

Common in fresh water streams and pools.

69. CONFERVA.

1. *C. tortuosa*, Dillwyn.

In rock pools at Nigg; opposite the pier at Aberdeen; and at the Cove, G. D.

2. *C. implexa*, Dillwyn.

Rock pools between tide-marks at Girdleness, &c. G. D.

3. *C. Melagonium*, Web. and Mohr.

In rock pools near low-water mark, at Muchalls, the Cove, &c. G. D. Peterhead, Rev. J. Yuill and Mr. Bell; Macduff, Rev. W. Grigor.

XIX.—CONJUGATAE.*
70. ZYGNEMA.

1. *Z. quininum*, Agardh.

Fresh water ditches. Ditch by the road-side south from the quarry at Hilton, G. D.

2. *Z. nitidum*, Agardh.

In ditches at Bieldside, Deeside road, G. D.

71. TYNDARIDEA.

1. *T. lutescens*, Hassal.

In bog-pools on the moor near Scotston, G. D.

72. MOUGEOTIA.

1. *M. genuflexa*, Agardh.

In pools at Stocket moor, G. D.

73. ZYGOGONIUM.

1. *Z. ericetorum*, Kützing.

Moist places on moors, &c. Common; often at high altitudes, G. D.

XX.—DESMIDIACEAE.

The species of this order, found in this district, are recorded in Mr. Ralfs's admirable monograph of "British *Desmideae*;" living specimens of nearly all were transmitted to him. It is impossible to give exact localities of each species; it may be sufficient to state that in the neighbourhood of Aberdeen the most productive places are pools on the Stocket and Scotston moors, and similar localities elsewhere, many species being usually associated.

74. HYALOTHECA.

1. *H. dissiliens*, Smith.

In pools at Stocket and Scotston, Mr. P. Grant and G. D.

2. *H. mucosa*, Mertens.

Bog-pools at Scotston, Mr. P. Grant.

* Several species of *Vesiculifera* occur in the district; such confusion exists regarding them that I omit them for the present.

75. DIDYMOPRIUM.

1. D. *Grevillii*, Kützing.
At Stocket and elsewhere, in pools, Mr. P. Grant and G. D.

2. D. *Borreri*, Ralfs.
In Glen Lui, Braemar, G. D. Near Aberdeen, and Moss Hagg, Banffshire, Mr. P. Grant.

76. DESMIDIUM.

1. D. *Swartzii*, Agardh.
In pools at Stocket and Scotston moors, Mr. P. Grant and G. D.

2. D. *quadrangulatum*, Ralfs.
Scotston moss, Mr. P. Grant and G. D.

77. MICRASTERIAS.

1. M. *denticulata*, Brebisson.
Near Aberdeen, Mr. P. Grant and G. D.

2. M. *rotata*, Greville.
Near Aberdeen, Mr. P. Grant. Hill of Fare, and at Loch Etichan, 3400 feet; Lochnagar, 3600 feet, G. D.

3. M. *papillifera*, Brebisson.
Near Aberdeen, Mr. P. Grant and G. D.

4. M. *truncata*, Corda.
Aberdeen, Mr. P. Grant and G. D.

5. M. *oscitans*, Ralfs.
Aberdeen, Mr. P. Grant.

78. EUASTRUM.

1. E. *vernicosum*, Ehrenberg.
Aberdeenshire and Banffshire, Mr. P. Grant.

2. E. *oblongum*, Greville.
Marshes round Aberdeen, Mr. P. Grant and G. D.

3. E. *crassum*, Brebisson.
Near Aberdeen, and also in the interior at high elevations, Ben Macdui, &c., G. D.

4. E. *affine*, Ralfs.
At Aberdeen, Mr. P. Grant. Also in the interior, Little Craigendall, &c. G. D.

5. E. *insigne*, Hassall.

Banffshire, at 3000 feet (Cairngorm.), Mr. P. Grant.

6. E. *Didelta*, Turpin.

Hill of Fare, Mr. P. Grant. In the interior at high elevations, G. D.

7. E. *ansatum*, Ehrenberg.

Aberdeenshire and Banffshire, at high elevations, Mr P. Grant and G. D.

8. E. *pectinatum*, Brebisson.

Aberdeen, and east side of Hill of Fare, Mr. P. Grant. Glen Derry, Braemar, G. D. Moss hagg, Banffshire, Mr. P. Grant.

9. E. *gemmatum*, Brebisson.

Aberdeen, Mr. P. Grant and G. D.

10. E. *rostratum*, Ralfs.

Aberdeen, Mr. P. Grant and G. D. Moss Hagg, between Tomintoul and Loch Avon, Mr. P. Grant.

11. E. *elegans*, Brebisson.

Aberdeenshire and Banffshire, coast line to 3000 feet, Mr. P. Grant.

12. E. *binale*, Turpin.

Aberdeen, Mr. P. Grant. Hill of Khoil, at Ballater, G. D.

13. E. *cuneatum*, Jenner.

Aberdeen, G. D.

79. COSMARIUM.

1. C. *quadratum*, Ralfs.

Aberdeen, Mr. P. Grant. Not uncommon in the interior at high altitudes.

2. C. *Cucumis*, Corda.

Coast line and inland, G. D. In Banffshire, Mr. P. Grant.

3. C. *Ralfsii*, Brebisson.

About Aberdeen, Mr. P. Grant. Also in the Braemar district, G. D.

4. C. *pyramidatum*, Brebisson.

At Aberdeen, Mr. P. Grant. The Khoil, at Ballater, G. D.

5. C. *bioculatum*, Ralfs.

Aberdeen, Mr. P. Grant.

6. *C. crenatum*, Ralfs.
Hill of Fare, &c., Mr. P. Grant. On the Khoil, at Ballater, G. D. Head of Banffshire, Mr. P. Grant.

7. *C. tetraophthalmum*, Kützing.
At Aberdeen, Mr. P. Grant.

8. *C. Botrytis*, Bory.
Aberdeen, Mr. P. Grant. On the Khoil, at Ballater, G. D. Interior of Banffshire, Mr. P. Grant.

9. *C. margaritiferum*, Turpin.
Aberdeen, Mr. P. Grant. Frequent in the interior at high altitudes, G. D.

10. *C. ornatum*, Ralfs.
Aberdeen, and frequent at high altitudes, G. D.

80. XANTHIDIUM.

1. *X. armatum*, Brebisson.
At Aberdeen, Mr. P. Grant. About Ballater and elsewhere inland, G. D. Upper part of Banffshire, Mr. P. Grant.

2. *X. fasciculatum*, Ehrenberg.
At Aberdeen, Mr. P. Grant. On Craigendarroch and the Khoil, near Ballater, G. D.

3. *X. cristatum*, Brebisson.
Aberdeen, Mr. P. Grant.

81. ARTHRODESMUS.

1. *A. convergens*, Ehrenberg.
Aberdeen, Mr. P. Grant and G. D.

2. *A. Incus*, Brebisson.
Aberdeen, Mr. P. Grant.

82. STAURASTRUM.

1. *S. dejectum*, Brebisson.
Aberdeen, Mr. P. Grant and G. D. I have found this species bearing *Sporangia*.

2. *S. Dickiei*, Ralfs.
Aberdeen, G. D.

3. *S. orbiculare*, Ehrenberg.
Ben Macdui at 3480 feet, G. D. In the higher parts of Banffshire, Mr. P. Grant,

4. S. *hirsutum*, Ehrenberg.
Aberdeenshire, Mr. P. Grant.

5. S. *brachiatum*, Ralfs.
Craigendarroch and Glen Lui, G. D.

6. S. *alternans*, Brebisson.
Glen Lui at 1300 feet, G. D.   Near Aberdeen, Mr. P. Grant.

7. S. *margaritaceum*, Ehrenberg.
Aberdeenshire, Mr. P. Grant.

8. S. *Arachne*, Ralfs.
Aberdeen, Mr. P. Grant.

9. S. *tetracerum*, Kützing.
Aberdeen, Mr. P. Grant.

10. S. *paradoxum*, Meyen.
Aberdeen and Banffshires, Mr. P. Grant.

83. TETMEMORUS.

1. T. *Brebissonii*, Meneghini.
Common from coast line to 3500 feet, G. D. It is generally very abundant in pools at Robslaw quarry. Banffshire, Mr. P. Grant.

2. T. *laevis*, Kützing.
Aberdeen, G. D.

3. T. *granulosus*, Brebisson.
Aberdeenshire, 1600 to 2455 feet, G. D. Banffshire, 1600 feet, Mr. P. Grant.

84. PENIUM.

1. P. *margaritaceum*, Ehrenberg.
At Aberdeen, Mr. P. Grant.

2. P. *Digitus*, Ehrenberg.
At Aberdeen, G. D. Banffshire, Mr. P. Grant.

3. P. *Brebissonii*, Meneghini.
Aberdeen, G. D. Banffshire, Mr. P. Grant.

85. DOCIDIUM.

1. D. *nodulosum*, Brebisson.
Aberdeen, Mr. P. Grant.

2. D. *Ehrenbergii*, Ralfs.
Aberdeen, Mr. P. Grant.

3. D. *Baculum*, Brebisson.
Aberdeenshire, Mr. P. Grant and G. D.

86. CLOSTERIUM.

1. C. *Lunula*, Müller.
A common species in pools. Aberdeen and inland, Mr. P. Grant and G. D.

2. C. *acerosum*, Schrank.
At Aberdeen and head of Banffshire, Mr. P. Grant.

3. C. *turgidum*, Ehrenberg.
Aberdeen, Mr. P. Grant.

4. C. *Ehrenbergii*, Meneghini.
Aberdeen and head of Banffshire, Mr. P. Grant.

5. C. *moniliferum*, Bory.
Aberdeen, G. D. Banffshire, Mr. P. Grant.

6. C. *Leibleinii*, Kützing.
Aberdeen, Mr. P. Grant.

7. C. *Dianae*, Ehrenberg.
Aberdeen, Mr. P. Grant and G. D.

8. C. *didymotocum*, Corda.
Aberdeen, Mr. P. Grant.

9. C. *costatum*, Corda.
Aberdeen, Mr. P. Grant and G. D.

10. C. *striolatum*, Ehrenberg.
Aberdeen, Mr. P. Grant.

11. C. *juncidum*, Ralfs.
Aberdeen, Mr. P. Grant and G. D.

12. C. *lineatum*, Ehrenberg.
Aberdeen and Banffshires, Mr. P. Grant.

13. C *Ralfsii*, Brebisson.
Aberdeen, G. D.

14. C. *rostratum*, Ehrenberg.
Aberdeen, Mr. P. Grant.

15. C. *setaceum*, Ehrenberg.
Aberdeen, Mr. P. Grant.

87. SPIROTAENIA.
1. S. *condensata*, Brebisson.
Aberdeen, Mr. P. Grant and G. D.

88. PEDIASTRUM.
1. P. *Tetras*, Ehrenberg.
Near Aberdeen, Mr. P. Grant.

2. P. *Heptactis*, Ehrenberg.
Aberdeen, Mr. P. Grant.

3. P. *simplex*, Meyen.
Near Aberdeen, Mr. P. Grant.

4. P. *pertusum*, Kützing.
Aberdeen, Mr. P. Grant.

5. P. *Napoleonis*, Turpin.
At Aberdeen, Mr. P. Grant.

6. P. *angulosum*, Ehrenberg.
Aberdeen, Mr. P. Grant.

7. P. *ellipticum*, Ehrenberg.
Aberdeen and Banffshires, Mr. P. Grant.

89. SCENEDESMUS.
1. S. *quadricauda*, Turpin.
Aberdeen and Banffshires, Mr. P. Grant.

2. S. *dimorphus*, Turpin.
Aberdeen, Mr. P. Grant.

3. S. *obliquus*, Turpin.
Near Aberdeen, Mr. P. Grant and G. D.

4. S. *obtusus*, Meyen.
Aberdeen, Mr. P. Grant.

The following notes will give an idea of the altitudinal distribution of the DESMIDEAE *in this district.*

1.—Hill of Fare, fourteen miles west from Aberdeen, at 450 feet, found by Mr. P. Grant.
Closterium *Dianae*, C. *lineatum*, C. *moniliferum*.

Cosmarium *Botrytis*, C. *crenatum*, C. *quadratum*, C. *margariti-ferum*.
Euastrum *affine*, E. *Didelta*, E. *gemmatum*, E. *oblongum*, E. *crassum*, E. *rostratum*.
Micrasterias *rotata*.
Penium *Digitus*.
Staurastrum *dejectum*, S. *orbiculare*, S. *tetracerum*.
Tetmemorus *Brebissonii*.

II.—Pannanich cliffs, forty miles inland, 1000 to 1100 feet, G.D.

Cosmarium *quadratum*, C. *margaritiferum*.
Docidium *Ehrenbergii*.
Penium *Digitus*, P. *margaritaceum*, P. *Brebissonii*.
Staurastrum *muricatum*, S. *tricorne*.
Tetmemorus *Brebissonii*, T. *granulatus*.
Euastrum *Didelta*.
Micrasterias *rotata*.
Penium *Digitus*, P. *Brebissonii*.

III.—Near Linn of Dee, sixty-seven miles inland, at 1190 feet.

Closterium *Dianae*, C. *turgidum*.
Cosmarium *margaritiferum*, C. *ornatum*.
Docidium *Ehrenbergii*.
Tetmemorus *Brebissonii*.

IV.—Glen Lui, about seventy miles inland, at 1300 feet.

Didymoprium *Borreri*.
Euastrum *affine*, E. *Didelta*, E. *crassum*.
Staurastrum *bifidum*, S. *margaritaceum*, S. *dejectum*, S. *alternans*.

V.—Hill of Craigendarroch, forty-two miles inland, at 1340 feet.

Arthrodesmus *Incus*.
Closterium *striolatum*.
Cosmarium *crenatum*, C. *Cucurbita*, C. *margaritiferum*, C. *quadratum*, C. *connatum*.
Docidium *Ehrenbergii*.
Euastrum *Didelta*.
Penium *Digitus*.
Staurastrum *bifidum*, S. *margaritaceum*.
Xanthidium *fasciculatum*.

VI.—Face of the Khoil, forty-three miles inland, at 1600 feet.

Closterium *Dianae*, C. *striolatum*.
Cosmarium *Botrytis*, C. *Ralfsii*, C. *margaritiferum*, C. *orbiculatum*, C. *ovale*, C. *quadratum*.
Docidium *Ehrenbergii*.
Euastrum *binale*, E. *Didelta*.
Scenedesmus *obliquus*.
Tetmemorus *granulatus*.
Xanthidium *fasciculatum*, X. *armatum*.

VII.—Glen Derry, about seventy miles inland, at 1600 feet.
Closterium *acerosum*, C. *Cornu*, C. *Dianae*, C. *Lunula*, C. *moniliferum*.
Cosmarium *Ralfsii*, C. *margaritiferum*, C. *ornatum*.
Didymoprium *Borreri*.
Euastrum *affine*, E. *binale*, E. *Didelta*, E. *gemmatum*, E. *oblongum*.

VIII.—Little Craigendall, Braemar, at 2450 feet.
Closterium *Dianae*.
Cosmarium *Cucurbita*, C. *margaritiferum*, C. *ornatum*, C. *quadratum*.
Euastrum *affine*.
Pediastrum *ellipticum*.
Penium *Digitus*.
Staurastrum *margaritaceum*.
Tetmemorus *granulatus*.

IX.—Lochnagar, at 2600 feet.
Arthrodesmus *convergens*.
Closterium *Lunula*.
Cosmarium *margaritiferum*.
Docidium *Trabecula*.
Euastrum *Didelta*.
Penium *Digitus*, P. *Brebissonii*.
Tetmemorus *Brebissonii*.

X.—Loch Etichan, east side of Ben Macdui, at 2800 feet.
Cosmarium *margaritiferum*, C. *ornatum*.
Euastrum *affine*.
Penium *Brebissonii*.
Tetmemorus *Brebissonii*.
(These five species were found in a black mud beneath snow, which also contained a profusion of *Diatomaceae*.)

XI.—In a marsh supplied by melting snow, above Loch Etichan, at 3480 feet.
Cosmarium *Cucurbita*.
Euastrum *affine*, E. *crassum*.
Micrasterias *rotata*.
Penium *Digitus*.
Staurastrum *orbiculare*.
Tetmemorus *Brebissonii*.

XII.—Lochnagar, at 3600 feet.
Closterium *Lunula*.
Cosmarium *Cucurbita*, C. *margaritiferum*, C. *quadratum*.

XIII.—Lochnagar, at 3700 feet, in a spring well.
Arthrodesmus *convergens*.
Closterium *Dianae*.
Penium *Brebissonii*.

The following table indicates the number of British species in each genus found at various altitudes in Aberdeenshire.

	No. of species from 1000 to 2000 feet.	No. of species from 2000 to 3000 feet.	No. of species 3000 feet and upwards.
Arthrodesmus,	1	..	1
Closterium,	7	2	2
Cosmarium,	11	4	3
Didymoprium,	1	..	..
Docidium,	1	..	..
Euastrum,	5	2	2
Micrasterias,	..	1	1
Pediastrum,	..	1	..
Penium,	3	2	2
Scenedesmus,	1	..	..
Staurastrum,	7	2	2
Tetmemorus,	2	2	2
Xanthidium,	2	..	..
	41	16	15

To the late Mr. P. Grant I am indebted for the following list of species, collected in the interior of Banffshire and on its borders.

I.—Near Loch Builg.

Closterium *Ehrenbergii*, C. *moniliferum*, C. *striolatum*.
Cosmarium *Botrytis*, C. *crenatum*.
Euastrum *affine*, E. *gemmatum*.
Scenedesmus *quadricauda*.
Staurastrum *orbiculare*.
Tetmemorus *granulatus*.

II.—Glenlivat, altitude unknown.

Closterium *acerosum*, C. *Lunula*, C. *lineatum*.
Cosmarium *Botrytis*, C. *margaritiferum*.
Penium *Digitus*.
Scenedesmus *quadricaudatus*.
Tetmemorus *granulatus*.
Xanthidium *furcatum*.

III.—Source of the Alyniach, at 3000 feet, more or less.

Closterium *Dianae*, C. *Lunula*, C. *moniliferum*.
Cosmarium *Botrytis*, C. *Cucurbita*, C. *quadratum*.
Desmidium *Swartzii*.
Didymoprium *Borreri*.
Euastrum *Didelta*, E. *pectinatum*, E. *affine*, E. *oblongum*, E. *crassum*, E. *rostratum*, E. *elegans*, E. *verrucosum*.
Micrasterias *rotata*.
Pediastrum *angulosum*, P. *ellipticum*.

Penium *Digitus*, P. *Brebissonii*.
Scenedesmus *quadriseriatus*.
Staurastrum *paradoxum*.
Tetmemorus *Brebissonii*.

XXI.—ULVACEAE.

90. ENTEROMORPHA.

1. E. *intestinalis*, Link.

Common along the coast between tide-marks, and also in the estuaries of the different rivers.

2. E. *compressa*, Greville.

Common along with the last species.

3. E. *erecta*, Hooker.

Occasionally between high and low-water marks.

Var. ramulosa. At Peterhead, Rev. J. Yuill and Mr. Bell.

91. ULVA.

1. U. *latissima*, Linn.

Common at various depths along the whole coast.

2. U. *Lactuca*, Linn.

Rather local. Peterhead, Rev. J. Yuill and Mr. Bell.

3. U. *Linza*, Linn.

Occasionally along the coast between tide-marks.

4. U. *bullosa*, Roth.

Fresh water pools in the links, north from the Broadhill, May, 1840, and July, 1843, G. D.

5. U. *crispa*, Lightfoot.

Frequent on damp ground by the sides of walls, &c. Abundant by the side of a wall at Carden's well, near Aberdeen, G. D.

Var. furfuracea. On damp rocks, south bank of the Don, east from the old bridge, G. D.

6. U. *calophylla*, Sprengel.

Abundant on stones, where the water issues from Gilcomston dam; April, 1842, and March, 1845, G. D.

92. TETRASPORA.

1. T. *lubrica*, Agardh.

Pools in the Old-town Links; in the Denburn at Cardens, &c. G. D. In Braediach moss, parish of Skene. On the Hill of Fare I have found a variety of it, which may, perhaps, be the T. *gelatinosa* of authors, G. D.

93. PORPHYRA.

1. P. *laciniata*, Agardh.
Very common everywhere on the coast.

2. P. *vulgaris*, Agardh.
Abundant between tide-marks.
Var. linearis, is plentiful on boulders in the bay of Nigg.

94. BANGIA.

1. B. *fusco-purpurea*, Lyngb.
Abundant on boulders, near high-water mark in bay of Nigg, G. D.; Peterhead, Rev. J. Yuill and Mr. Bell; Macduff, Rev. W. Grigor.

2. B. *ceramicola*, Chauvin.
On smaller *Algae*, between tide-marks. Rare. Peterhead, Rev. J. Yuill and Mr. Bell.

XXII.—RIVULARIACEAE.

95. RIVULARIA.

1. R. *atra*, Roth.
On *Corallina officinalis*, *Cladophora rupestris*, and sometimes on *Ralfsia deusta*; at the Cove, and other parts of the same coast, G. D.

2. R. *viridis*, Hassall.
In pools, Robslaw quarry. Probably the same species occurs in the interior at high altitudes; Craigendall and Glen Derry, G. D.

3. R. *echinulata*, Berkeley?
This beautiful species I found abundantly in the Corbie Loch, some miles north from Aberdeen, in July, 1847. It was in such profusion, along with *Trichormus Flos-aquae*, as to tinge the waters of the Lake.

96. STIGONEMA.

1. S. *atro-virens*, Agardh.
Abundant on dripping rocks at Pannanich, near Ballater; and near farm of Achallater, Glen Clunie, Castleton, G. D.

2. S. *mammillosum*, Agardh.

Moist rocks on the Hill of Fare, and near Achallater, Braemar, G. D.

97. SCYTONEMA.

1. *S. ocellatum*, Harvey.

Upon mosses, &c. ; at Loch Etichan, on Ben Macdui, G. D.

2. *S. myochrous*, Agardh.

Abundant in wet places on the Hill of Fare, G. D.

98. PETALONEMA.

1. *P. alatum*, Berkeley.

Wet cliffs on the coast, south from Aberdeen, G. D.

99. CALOTHRIX.

1. *C. scopulorum*, Agardh.

Rocks, near high-water mark. Bay of Gamrie, Rev. G. Harris and G. D.

2. *C. confervicola*, Agardh.

Upon various of the smaller *Algae*, between tide-marks; at the Cove and elsewhere, G. D.

3. *C. mirabilis*, Agardh.

Wet rocks at the fall, Corbie Den, Kingcausie, G. D.

100. TOLYPOTHRIX.

1. *T. distorta*, Kützing.

Upon sticks, &c. at the water-fall in Corbie Den, Kingcausie ; in the dripping cave, a little south from the harbour at the Cove, G. D. Pools on summit of Craigendarroch, at Ballater ; in the lake, east side of Lochnagar, G. D.

101. LYNGBYA.

1. *L. copulata*, Hassall.

Abundant in a spring-well by the sheep-path, north side of Glen Callater, opposite the gamekeeper's house ; also on the table land above Glen Callater, at an elevation of 3000 feet, August, 1846, G. D.

2. *L. ferruginea*, Agardh.

In shallow pools at high-water mark, near the lighthouse at Girdleness, and at the Altons, two miles south from Bay of Nigg.

3. *L. Carmichaelii*, Harvey,

On sea weeds between tide-marks, at Girdleness, Bay of Nigg, &c. G. D.

4. L. *speciosa*, Carmichael.
On rocks, &c. between tide-marks, Girdleness, &c. G. D.

5. L. *zonata*, Hassall.
On wet rocks. Probably general. Coast at the Cove ; at Linn of Dee ; on Lochnagar.

6. L. *floccosa*, Hassall.
In rivulets. Kinmundy, parish of Skene ; Hill of Fare, upon Lemania *fluviatilis*.

XXIII.—OSCILLATORIACEAE.

102. OSCILLATORIA.

1. O. *aerugescens*, Agardh.
Bottom of pools by the road-side at Stocket moor, G. D.

2. O. *autumnalis*, Agardh.
Abundant in rivulets near Aberdeen, G. D.

3. O. *rupestris*, Agardh.
On dripping rocks near Ballater ; on Pannanich cliffs and Lochnagar, G. D.

4. O. *terebriformis*, Agardh.
In marshes near Aberdeen, G. D.

5. O. *Dickieii*, Hassall.
In pools of fresh water at the bottom of the cliffs, and near the sea, a little south from the harbour at the Cove, G. D.

6. O. *nigra*, Carmichael.
Loch Etichan, on ascent to Ben Macdui, G. D.

103. MICROCOLEUS.

1. M. *gracilis*, Hassall.
In salt marshes at Aberdeen, 1844. The exact locality was not recorded, but it was probably at north end of the Old-town Links, G. D.

104. SPIRULINA.

1. S. *tenuissima*, Kützing.
Upon mud at Don-mouth, July, 1843 ; also at low-water mark upon the Inch at Aberdeen, July, 1845. Very fine and plentiful in a cave upon the coast, a little north from the salmon fishing station at the Altons, south from Bay of Nigg, Mr. P. Grant ; where I have repeatedly gathered this very singular plant.

XXIV.—NOSTOCHINEAE.
105. NOSTOC.

1. *N. commune*, Vaucher.

Lin Mui near Ballater, at 1700 feet; and at Dunnottar, G. D.

2. *N. foliaceum*, Agardh.

On damp ground at Robslaw quarry; also on Lochnagar, about 3000 feet, G. D.

3. *N. sphaericum*, Vaucher.

On stones in a rivulet, Craigendall, at 2000 feet, G. D.

4. *verrucosum*, Vaucher.

On stones in rivulets, Aberdeen and inland, G. D.

106. SPHAEROZYGA.

1. *S. Jacobi*, Agardh.

In wet places by the Stocket road, west from Summerhill, G. D.

107. TRICHORMUS.

1. *T. Flos-aquae*, Lyngb.

Observed in Corbie Loch, in 1846, 1847, and 1848.

For some years excursions were made with the students of my botanical class to a loch on the estate of Parkhill, about four miles north-west from Aberdeen. The sheet of water in question is about a quarter of a mile in its greatest length; on almost all sides it is surrounded by extensive deposits of peat, with the soluble matter of which a great proportion of the water passing into the loch is impregnated. The loch abounds in *Scirpus lacustris, Arundo Phragmites, Nuphar lutea, Nymphaea alba*, and various species of *Potamogeton*, &c. The locality was generally visited in the beginning of July; nothing peculiar had ever been observed till the summer of 1846, when my attention was arrested by a peculiar appearance of the water, especially near the edge, but extending also some distance into the loch. Numerous minute bodies with a spherical outline, and varying in size from 1-24th to 1-12th of an inch in diameter, were seen floating at different depths, and giving the water a peculiar appearance. In some places they were very densely congregated, especially in small creeks at the edge of the loch. A quantity was collected by filtration through a piece of cloth, and, on examination by the microscope, there could be no doubt that the production was of a vegetable nature and a species of *Rivularia*; one, however, unknown to me, and not agreeing with the description of any species described in works to which I had access. Specimens were sent to the Rev. M. J. Berkeley; he informed me that the plant belonged to the genus mentioned, and stated it to be *Rivularia echinulata*, E. B. Along with it, but in very small quantity, I also found another plant, the *Trichormus Flos-aquae*, Bory.

In the first week of July, 1847, the same species were observed similarly associated, but the *Trichormus* was now more plentiful, without, however, any apparent corresponding diminution in the quantity of the *Rivularia*.

In July, 1848, it was observed that the *Rivularia* was as rare as the *Trichormus* had been in 1846; to the latter consequently the water of the loch now owed its colour, which was a very dull green; the colour, however, becomes brighter when the plant is dried. In neither of the seasons mentioned was it in my power to make any observations on the colour of the loch earlier or later than the date above-mentioned, consequently nothing can be added respecting the comparative development of the two plants at other periods of the season. Other two lochs in the vicinity did not contain the plants alluded to.

108. CYLINDROSPERMUM.

1. *C. catenatum*, Ralfs.

Wet places, side of the road at south-end of Stocket moor, September, 1852, G. D.

109. DOLICHOSPERMUM.

1. *D. Ralfsii*, Kützing.

Bottom of pools at the Stocket moor, September, 1852, G. D.

XXV.—PALMELLACEAE.

110. PALMELLA.

1. *P. cruenta*, Agardh.

In the form of a red crust on damp walls and on the ground. Beneath the portico in King's College, and elsewhere near Aberdeen.

111. SOROSPORA.

1. *S. montana*, Hassall.

On dripping rocks, a little west from the farm of Achallater, in Glen Clunie, Castleton; and on Little Craigendall.

112. COCCOCHLORIS.

1. *C. protuberans*, Sprengel.

Among damp mosses, &c., in Den of Maidencraig; on Pannanich cliffs, and rocks at Achallater, G. D.

2. *C. muscicola*, Meneghini.

On wet mosses, Den of Maidencraig, G. D.

XXVI.—PROTOCOCCEAE.
113. HAEMATOCOCCUS.

1. H. *murorum*, Hassall.
On damp walls, Aberdeen, G. D.

2. H. *rupestris*, Hassall.
Moist rocks on the coast at the Cove, G. D.

3. H. *granosus*, Harvey.
Moist rocks at the Cove, G. D.

4. H. *lividus*, Hassall.
Very abundant in a dripping cave half-a-mile north from the Cove.

5. H. *binalis*, Hassall.
Very abundant everywhere, in pools, &c. mixed with other *Algae*. Found also at high altitudes in the interior; top of Craigendarroch; Ben Macdui, at 2800 feet, G. D.

6. H. *furfuraceus*, Hassall.
Along with H. *frustulosus*, G. D.

114. PROTOCOCCUS.

1. P. *nivalis*, Agardh.
Upon snow, near the summit of Ben Macdui, in 1846. This is the Red Snow Plant, so plentiful in the Arctic Zone; it seems very rare in this quarter, I have only seen it in the locality and in the year above mentioned.

The following notes of some of the preceding ALGAE *observed at different altitudes in the interior, appear worthy of a place here.*

I.—Pannanich cliffs, at about 1100 feet.
  Coccochloris *protuberans*, Hæmatococcus *murorum*, Oscillatoria *rupestris?* Stigonema *atrovirens*.

II.—Craigendarroch, about 1300 feet.
  Hassallia *ocellata*, Hæmatococcus *binalis*, Tetraspora *lubrica*, Tolypothrix *distorta*, Zygogonium *ericetorum*.

III.—Khoil, at 1600 feet.
  Draparnaldia *glomerata*, Hæmatococcus *binalis*, Nostoc *commune*, N. *sphæricum*, Oscillatoria ———?

IV.—Lochnagar, at 2000 feet
  Hassallia *ocellata*, Hæmatococcus *binalis*, Lyngbya *zonata*.

V.—Lake of Lochnagar, 2563 feet.
Bulbochæte *setigera*, Hassallia *ocellata*, Tolypothrix *distorta* ; in boggy places near the lake, Hæmatococcus *binalis*.

VI.—Lochnagar, at 2600 feet.
Hæmatococcus *binalis*, and Zygnema ———?

VII.—Lochnagar, at 3600 feet
Hæmatococcus *binalis*, Lyngbya *zonata*, Nostoc *commune*, and Oscillatoria ———?

VIII.—Near Loch Etichan, at 2800 feet.
Hassallia *ocellata*, Hæmatococcus *binalis*, Stigonema *mammillosum*, Tetraspora *lubrica* ; in the loch, Conferva *ericetorum*, Oscillatoria *nigra*, and Scytonema *Myochrous*, the latter, along with Jungermannia *emarginata*, was in great profusion, covering the stones in the bottom.

IX.—Near Linn of Dee, about 1190 feet.
Draparnaldia *glomerata* and Lyngbya *zonata*.

X.—Near Castleton of Braemar, about 1100 feet.
Coccochloris *protuberans*, Sorospora *montana*, Stigonema *atrovirens*.

XI.—On the table-land, north side of Loch Callater, in a spring, was found abundantly Lyngbya *copulata* ; the altitude was not measured, but estimated as about 3000 feet.

XII.—Little Craigendall, at about 2064 feet.
Nostoc *sphaericum*.

XIII.—Little Craigendall, at 2400 feet.
Bulbochæte *setigera*, Hassallia *ocellata*, Hæmatococcus *binalis*. H. *rupestris*, Raphidia *viridis*, Sorospora *montana*.

XXVII.—DIATOMACEAE.

The following species have been found in different parts of the district, and many others may yet be expected to occur. The names are adopted from the late Professor Smith's monograph of the British species. Many are usually associated in suitable habitats, and therefore the special localities of a few have alone been indicated, the supplemental list in some degree compensates for this. Dripping rocks, marshes, &c. on the coast and everywhere in the district will be found rich in species. With a few exceptions they are widely diffused ; those of the genus *Eunotia* are, however, mainly confined to the higher inland parts.

115. EPITHEMIA.

E. turgida, E. Argus, E. rupestris, E. gibba, E. ventricosa, E. Zebra, E. longicornis, E. Westermanni, E. granulata, E. alpestris.

116. EUNOTIA.

E. monodon, E. diodon, E. triodon, E. tetraodon, E. Arcus, E. bidentula, E. tridentula, E. quaternaria, E. incisa, E. gracilis, E. Camelus.

117. CYMBELLA.

C. Ehrenbergii, C. cuspidata, C. maculata, C. Helvetica, C. Scotica, C. ventricosa, C. aequalis, C. lunata, C. affinis.

118. AMPHORA.

A. ovalis, A. membranacea, A. affinis, A. hyalina.

119. COCCONEIS.

C. Pediculus, C. Placentula, C. Thwaitesii, C. Scutellum.

120. COSCINODISCUS.

C. minor, C. radiatus, C. eccentricus.

121. ACTINOCYCLUS.

A. undulatus.

122. CYCLOTELLA.

C. antiqua, C. Kutzingiana, C. operculata.

123. CAMPYLODISCUS.

C. costatus, C. spiralis.

124. SURIRELLA.

S. biseriata, S. linearis, S. splendida, S. constricta, S. Gemma, S. ovata, S. salina.

125. CYMATOPLEURA.

C. elliptica, C. apiculata, C. solea.

126. NITZSCHIA.

N. sigmoidea, N. sigma, N. linearis, N. acicularis, N. curvula.

127. AMPHIPRORA.

A. alata.

128. AMPHIPLEURA.

A. pellucida, forming large sheets, with a metallic lustre, in fresh-water ditches, at Kinmundy, parish of Skene.

129. NAVICULA.

N. rhomboides, N. crassinervia, N. serians, N. cuspidata, N. firma, N. ovalis, N. semen, N. liber, N. inflata, N. gibberula, N. amphirhyncus, N. elliptica, N. elegans, N. patula, N. punctulata, N. didyma, N. cocconeiformis, N. angustata, N. cryptocephala.

130. PINNULARIA.

P. nobilis, P. major, P. viridis, P. acuminata, P. oblonga, P. lata, P. alpina, P. acuta, P. radiosa, P. divergens, P. stauroneiformis, P. gibba, P. mesolepta, P. interrupta, P. borealis, P. gracillima, P. nodosa, P. hemiptera, P. late-striata, P. tenuis, P. gracilis, P. peregrina.

131. STAURONEIS.

S. Phoenicenteron, S. acuta, S. dilatata, S. anceps, S. linearis, S. punctata, S. gracilis.

132. PLEUROSIGMA.

P. angulatum, P. attenuatum, P. lacustre.

133. SYNEDRA.

S. lunaris, S. pulchella, S. radians, S. Ulna, S. capitata, S. affinis.

134. COCCONEMA.

C. lanceolatum, C. cymbiforme, C. cistula.

135. DORYPHORA.

D. Amphiceros.

136. GOMPHONEMA.

G. geminatum, G. constrictum, G. acuminatum, G. dichotomum, G. vibrio, G. curvatum, G. marinum, G. capitatum, G. ventricosum, G. insigne, G. tenellum, G. olivaceum, G. intricatum.

137. RHIPIDOPHORA.

R. paradoxa, R. Dalmatica, R. elongata.

138. LICMOPHORA.

L. flabellata.

139. MERIDION.

M. circulare. Very abundant in the ditches and pools in the Old Aberdeen Links.

M. constrictum. With the last. Both occur in Braemar also.

140. HIMANTIDIUM.
H. *pectinale*, H. *undulatum*, H. *Arcus*, H. *gracile*, H. *majus*.

141. ODONTIDIUM.
O. *hyemale*, O. *mesodon*, O. *anomalum*, O. *mutabile*, O. *Tabellaria*, O. *Harrisonii*.

142. DENTICULA.
D. *obtusa*, D. *tenuis*, D. *sinuata*.

143. FRAGILARIA.
F. *capucina*, F. *virescens*.

144. ACHNANTHES.
A. *longipes*, A. *brevipes*, A. *exilis*, A. *subsessilis*.

145. ACHNANTHIDIUM.
A. *lanceolatum*, A. *microcephalum*, A. *flexellum*.

146. RHABDONEMA.
R. *arcuatum*, R. *minutum*.

147. DIATOMA.
D. *vulgare*, D. *elongatum*. D. *tenue*.

148. ASTERIONELLA.
A. *formosa*. In a spring well near Walker's dam, at Robslaw.

149. GRAMMATOPHORA.
G. *marina*.

150. DIATOMELLA.
D. *Balfouriana*. Alpine marshes.

151. TABELLARIA.
T. *flocculosa*, T. *fenestrata*.

152. PODOSIRA.
P. *Montagnei*.

153. MELOSIRA.
M. *nummuloides*, M. *Borreri*, M. *subflexilis*, M. *varians*, M. *nivalis*, M. *distans*.

154. ORTHOSIRA.
O. *arenaria*, O. *marina*, O. *orichalcea*.
O. *Dickieii*. Very abundant, in the form of a greenish

pulpy mud, on dripping rocks in a small cave a little south from the boat-harbour at the Cove, near Aberdeen. The only locality known.

O. *spinosa*. Along with the last. Very abundant, and unmixed, on dripping rocks in a cave a little north from the harbour at Skaterow, near Newtonhill station, Scottish North Eastern line. It occurs also in Braemar.

155. DICKIEIA.

D. *ulvoides*, Ralfs.

Very rare. In shallow rock pools about low-water mark, opposite the cave where O. *Dickieii* occurs. In April and May only.

D. *pinnata*, Ralfs.

Along with the last, and more abundant than it.

156. SCHIZONEMA.

1. S. *helmintosum*, Chauv.

In pools at low-water mark, opposite the small cave at the Cove, and in other similar places. Abundant.

2. S. *comoides*, Agardh.

Very common in rock pools between tide-marks, at Bay of Nigg, &c. &c.

3. S. *confertum*, Smith.

At Cove, along with S. *helmintosum* ; also at high-water mark opposite the hut at north end of Bay of Nigg.

4. S. *Grevillii*, Agardh.

Very rare. At Girdleness, once only a few fragments.

5. S. *molle*, Smith.

Coast south from Aberdeen,

6. S. *Dilwynii*, Agardh.

Very abundant at Girdleness, Cove, &c. G. D. Peterhead, Rev. J. Yuill.

7. S. *parasiticum*, Harvey.

Upon Corallina *officinalis*, &c. at Bay of Nigg, Cove, &c.

SUPPLEMENTAL LISTS.

Cave at north end of Skaterow harbour.

Epithemia *rupestris*, Denticula *obtusa*, Odontidium *mutabile*. Cocconeis *Thwaitesii*, Navicula *elliptica*, N. *Smithii*, Pinnularia *gracilis*, Orthosira *spinosa*. Mr. P. Gray, Mr. H. A. Smith, and G. D.

Cave at the Cove.
> Achnanthidium *microcephalum*, Fragilaria *virescens*, Orthosira *Dickieii*, O. *spinosa*.

Dripping rocks at the Cove.
> Cocconema *cistula*, Cymbella *ventricosa*, Denticula *obtusa*.

In a slightly brackish pool close by the sea, and half-a-mile north from Girdleness lighthouse.
> Epithemia *granulata*, Nitzschia *acicularis*, N. *gracilis*, Melosira *subflexilis*, Fragilaria *virescens*.

In a spring-well a little north from the last.
> Achnanthidium *lanceolatum*, Diatoma *elongatum*, Fragilaria *virescens*, Odontidium *mesodon*, O. *mutabile*, Orthosira *orichalcea*.

The following are given on the authority of the late Dr. Stephen.

Den Fenella, St. Cyrus.
> Cocconeis *pediculus*, Diatoma *vulgare*, Cocconema *cymbiforme*, C. *lanceolatum*, Surirella *ovata*, Synedra *radians*, Nitzschia *linearis*, N. *sigmoidea*, Cymatopleura *apiculata*, Melosira *varians*, Fragilaria *capucina*, Gomphonema *constrictum*, G. *curvatum*, G. *acuminatum*.

Glen of Dye, Strachan.
> Himantidium *gracile*, H. *Arcus*, H. *undulatum*, Navicula *rhomboides*, N. *serians*, Pinnularia *viridis*, Eunotia *tetraodon*, Melosira *varians*, Pinnularia *acuta*, P. *peregrina*, Tabellaria *flocculosa*.

At Girdleness, (marine.)
> Rhabdonema *arcuatum*, R. *minutum*, Rhipidophora *elongata*, Licmophora *flabellata*, Cocconeis *scutellum*, Gomphonema *marinum*, Grammatophora *marina*, Orthosira *marina*, Podosira *Montagnei*.

Mud from the south side of the Dee, at Aberdeen, near Wellington bridge.
> Orthosira *marina*, Actinocyclus *undulatus*, Surirella *ovata*, S. *salina*, S. *Gemma*, Pleurosigma *attenuatum*, Achnanthes *brevipes*, Navicula *elegans*, N. *didyma*, Pinnularia *peregrina*, P. *gracilis*, Amphora *affinis*, Doryphora *amphiceros*, Amphiprora *alata*, Coscinodiscus *minor*, C. *eccentricus*, C. *radiatus*, Surirella *constricta*.

XXVIII.—VOLVOCINEAE.

The singular and beautiful objects of this family, formerly ranked as animals, are now removed to the vegetable kingdom.

157. VOLVOX.

1. V. *globator*, Ehr.
In pools by the side of the new Stocket road, near the rivulet and bridge, half-a-mile west from Summerhill. In the months of June, July, and August, the late Mr. P. Grant and G. D.

FUNGI, MUSHROOMS.*

I.—HYMENOMYCETES.

1. AGARICUS.

1. A. *vaginatus*, Bull. *(Sheathed A.)*
Very local. In the woods by the Skene road, half-a-mile west from Robslaw quarry. August to October?

2. A. *nivalis*, Grev. *(Alpine A.)*
In alpine places. Autumn. On Ben Macdui, G. D. ; on Lochnagar, Professor Macgillivray.

3. A. *muscarius*, Linn. *(Fly A.)*
In woods. August to November. Very frequent and abundant in woods near Aberdeen, as Hazelhead, Denmore. August and September.

4. A. *excelsus*, Fries. *(Tall fly A.)*
In woods. August to September. Rather local. In the wood south-west from Banchory House.

5. A. *granulosus*, Batsch. *(Granulose A.)*
Frequent in woods near Aberdeen, Hazelhead, &c. In Autumn.

6. A. *olivaceo-albus*, Fries. *(Olive and white A.)*
Woods by the Skene road, west from Robslaw qurry. September and October?

7. A. *hypothejus*, Fries. *(Yellow, slimy A.)*
Woods, along with the last. October and November?

---

* The following notes of *Fungi* are founded on specimens in my own collection. Doubtless many other species grow in the district; and indeed not a few have been omitted, because not satisfactorily authenticated. The nomenclature and arrangement are adopted from the volume by Rev. M. J. Berkeley, forming vol. V. part 2, of the "English Flora," by Sir W. J. Hooker.

8. A. *rutilans*, Schoeff. *(Crimson-red, downy A.)*
In woods upon dead stumps. September and October. Wood at Pitfodels.

9. A. *luteus*, Huds. *(Yellow A.)*
In woods. Autumn. Den of Robslaw.

10. A. *emeticus*, Schoeff. *(Simple-gilled A.)*
Frequent in woods. Hazelhead, Den of Leggart, Denmore, &c.

11. A. *deliciosus*, Linn. *(Orange-milked A.)*
Fir woods at Hazelhead.

12. A. *quietus*, Fries. *(Mild rufous A.)*
In woods. Autumn. Hazelhead and other places. Frequent.

13. A. *glyciosmus*, Fries. *(Sweet-scented A.)*
In Fir woods. September and October. Hazelhead woods.

14. A. *infundibuliformis*, Bull. *(Variable, wood A.)*
In woods among grass, &c. August to October. Den of Leggart.

15. A. *nebulosus*, Batsch. *(New-cheese A.)*
Rather local. Den of Leggart, under Fir trees.

16. A. *dealbatus*, Sowerby. *(Dirty-white A.)*
In pastures, &c. Autumn. About old whin stumps in Old-town Links.

17. A. *pratensis*, Pers. *(Reddish, field A.)*
Grassy pastures. Belhelvie links.

18. A. *psittacinus*, Schoeff. *(Parroquet A.)*
Pastures. September to November. Links at Aberdeen and Belhelvie.

19. A. *ceraceus*, Wulf. *(Wax-like A.)*
Pastures. July to November. Old-town Links.

20. A. *conicus*, Schoeff. *(Conic, black-stained A.)*
Pastures, &c. September to November. Den of Leggart.

21. A. *miniatus*, Fries. *(Dry, scarlet A.)*
Moist woods, &c. July to August. Old-town Links.

22. A. *laccatus*, Scop. *(Lake A.)*
In woods. June to November. Hazelhead woods.

23. A. *sulphureus*, Bull. *(Brimstone A.)*
In woods. September to November. Very local. In the wood at Middleton, near Aberdeen

24. A. *fusipes*, Bull. *(Spindle-stemmed A.)*
On stumps of trees. July to August. Very frequent.

25. A. *confluens*, Pers. *(Confluent, hoary A.)*
Woods. August to October. Den of Maidencraig.

26. A. *dryophilus*, Bull. *(Oak-leaf A.)*
Among fallen leaves. May to October. Common in woods.

27. A. *peronatus*, Bolt. *(Spatterdash A.)*
Among rotten leaves. July to November. Abundant at Hazelhead, Den of Leggart, &c.

28. A. *oreades*, Bolt. *(Fairy-ring A.)*
Pastures. Growing in circles. May to November. Links at Aberdeen; Belhelvie, &c. &c.

29. A. *conigenus*, Pers. *(Fir-cone A.)*
On dead fir cones. October to November. Hazelhead woods.

30. A. *ramealis*, Bull. *(Stick A.)*
On decaying branches of Hazel, &c. &c. All the year.

31. A. *Rotula*, Scop. *(Wheel A.)*
On dead leaves, &c. in woods. All the year. Very common near Aberdeen.

32. A. *alliaceus*, Jacq. *(Garlic A.)*
Among sticks and leaves in woods. In Autumn. Frequent. Hazelhead, &c.

33. A. *atro-albus*, Bolt. *(Black and white A.)*
In pastures, &c. August to November. Den of Robslaw.

34. A. *sanguinolentus*, Alb. and Schw. *(Bloody-juiced A.)*
In woods on sticks, &c. August to November. Hazelhead woods.

35. A. *Adonis*, Bull. *(Beautiful A.)*
In woods. Autumn. Den of Leggart.

36. A. *lacteus*, Pers. *(Milk-white A.)*
Among sticks and leaves in woods. October to December. Den of Leggart, Den of Robslaw.

37. A. *tenerrimus*, Berk. *(Very tender A.)*
On dead cones, sticks, &c. August to December. Cherryvale, &c.

38. A. *corticola*, Bull. *(Bark A.)*
On dead bark of trees, &c. October to February. Hazelhead woods.

39. A. *capillaris*, Schum. *(Hair A.)*
On beech leaves. October. Den of Leggart; and wood at the old Bridge of Don.

40. A. *Fibula*, Bull. *(Small orange A.)*
Amongst moss. September to May. Den of Leggart.

41. A. *umbelliferus*, Linn. *(Variable, Heath A.)*
In heathy pastures. May to November. Old-town Links.

42. A. *septicus*, Fries. *(Small shell A.)*
On dead trunks of trees. October to April. Den of Robslaw.

43. A. *stypticus*, Bull. *(Styptic A.)*
On dead trees. October to April. Very local. Den of Leggart.

44. A. *mitis*, Pers. *(Larch A.)*
On dead wood. October. Dead larches, Den of Leggart,

45 A. *striatulus*. Pers. *(Minutely striate A.)*
On dead wood. May to December. Rare. Cherryvale.

46. A. *torvus*, Fries. *(Hosed A.)*
In woods. September and October.

47. A. *cinnamomeus*, Linn. *(Cinnamon A.)*
In woods. Autumn. Hazelhead.

48. A. *raphanoides*, Pers. *(Reddish, scented A.)*
In fir woods, &c. July to October. Wood near new Church of Nigg.

49. A. *squarrosus*, Mull. *(Squarrox A.)*
On trees. August to December. Very local. In woods at Middleton near Aberdeen.

50. A. *collinitus*, Sowerby. *(Slime-coated A.)*
In woods. July to November. Very local. In a small wood, due west from Robslaw quarry.

51. A. *flavidus*, Schoeff. (*Dirty-yellow A.*)
On pine trunks. August to November. Den of Robslaw.

52. A. *pyriodorus*, Pers. (*Pear-scented A.*)
In woods and gardens. September to October. In a small wood, side of the road, west from Denmore.

53. A. *furfuraceus*, Pers. (*Branny A.*)
On dead twigs, &c. All the year. On mossy stumps of trees in Den of Maidencraig.

54. A. *hypnorum*, Schrank. (*Moss A.*)
Among moss in woods. July to November. Old-town Links.

55. A. *involutus*, Batsch. (*Involute A.*)
Woods. July to November. Den of Leggart.

56. A. *campestris*, Linn. (*Common Mushroom.*)
Dry grassy pastures. May to October. Coast at Girdleness, &c. Old-town Links.

57. A. *praecox*, Pers. (*Early A.*)
Grassy places, &c. Spring chiefly. Road-side, on wall tops, near old house of Robslaw.

58. A. *semiglobatus*, Batsch. (*Hemispherical H.*)
In pastures, on droppings of animals. May to November. Very frequent near Aberdeen.

59. A. *aeruginosus*, Curtis. (*Verdigris A.*)
In meadows and gardens. August to November. Rather scarce. Uncertain in appearance.

60. A. *lateritius*, Schoeff. (*Large fasciculate A.*)
Stumps of trees, &c. May to October. Hazelhead.

61. A. *fascicularis*, Hudson. (*fasciculate A.*)
Roots of trees, &c. April to November. Hazelhead woods, &c.

62. A. *callosus*, Fries. (*Conic dung A.*)
Upon droppings of animals. Frequent. Hazelhead, &c.

63. A. *cernuus*, Mull. (*Nodding A.*)
Waste places. August to November. Common.

64. A. *atomatus*, Fries. (*Spangled A.*)
Among grass, wastes, &c. August to September. Old-town Links.

65. A. *comatus*, Mull. *(Cylindric A.)*
Meadows and wastes. April to October. Old-town Links.

66. A. *cinereus*, Bull. *(Cinereous A.)*
Meadows, gardens, &c. July to October. In Den of Leggart.

67. A. *rutilus*, Schoeff. *(Purplish-red A.)*
In fir woods. August to October. Hazelhead, &c.

2. CANTHARELLUS.

1. C. *cibarius*, Fries. *(Common Chantarelle.)*
Woods. July to October. In the wood at Banchory House. Frequent in the interior of Aberdeenshire.

2. C. *lobatus*, Pers. *(Lobed C.)*
Marshy places on different species of moss. In bog at Scotston and Denmore.

3. MERULIUS.

1. M. *corium*, Grev. *(Coriaceous M.)*
On timber, in moist shady places. Winter. Frequent.

2. M. *lachrymans*, Wulf. *(Dry-rot.)*
On wood in buildings, where ventilation is imperfect. Very frequent.

3. M. *Carmichaelianus*, Grev. *(Carmichael's M.)*
On bark, dead leaves, &c. December. Very local. In the Dry Den, near Countesswells.

4. DAEDALEA.

1. D. *unicolor*, Bull. *(Self-coloured D.)*
Trunks of trees, &c. Autumn and Spring. Dead fir branches, in the Dry Den.

2. D. *biennis*, Bull. *(Biennial D.)*
Stumps of trees. July to January. In same locality as the last.

5. POLYPORUS.

1. P. *perennis*, Linn. *(Perennial, cinnamon P.)*
On the ground in sandy places, &c. &c. Autumn and Winter. Woods of Paradise, Monymusk. In Glen Dee at the base of Ben Macdui.

2. P. *varius*, Pers. *(Variable P.)*
On trees, &c. All the year. Dry Den near Countesswells.

3. P. *hispidus*, Bull. (*Hispid P.*)
On ash, elm, &c. Summer. Very local. In the interior at Castle Newe, Strathdon.

4. P. *adustus*, Willd. (*Scorched P.*)
Trunks of trees. All the year. Tollohill woods near Aberdeen.

5. P. *velutinus*, Pers. (*Velvety P.*)
On stumps of trees. April to October. In the wood near new Church of Nigg.

6. P. *versicolor*, Linn. (*Party-coloured P.*)
On trees, posts, &c. All the year. Very frequent at Aberdeen.

7. P. *abietinus*, Pers. (*Violet P.*)
On dead firs. All the year. Common.

8. P. *incarnatus*, Pers. (*Orange-flesh P.*)
On fir trunks. Summer and Autumn. In the wood at Middleton near Aberdeen.

9. P. *molluscus*, Pers. (*Soft, prostrate P.*)
Forming a thin soft coating on dead twigs. Wood by the Skene road, west from Robslaw quarry.

6. BOLETUS.

1. B. *luteus*, Linn, (*Yellow B.*)
In fir woods. Autumn. Common everywhere.

2. B. *Grevillei*, Klotsch. (*Greville's B.*)
Woods, heaths, &c. May to October. Frequent about Aberdeen.

3. B. *piperatus*, Bull. (*Pepper B.*)
In woods. In Autumn. Hazelhead; Den of Leggart, &c.

4. B. *subtomentosus*, Linn. (*Subtomentose B.*)
In woods. Summer and Autumn. Very frequent near Aberdeen, and in the interior.

5. B. *pachypus*, Fries. (*Thick-stemmed B.*)
In fir woods. July to September? Hazelhead, Denmore, &c.

6. B. *luridus*, Schoeff. (*Poisonous B.*)
In woods. Summer and Autumn. Very frequent near Aberdeen.

7. B. *edulis*, Bull. *(Esculent C.)*
Woods and pastures. July to October. Rather local. Denmore; Den of Leggart.

7. HYDNUM.

1. H. *repandum*, *(Common H.)*
In woods. Autumn. Rather local. By the Skene road, west from Robslaw quarry.

2. H. *auriscalpium*. Linn *(Hairy-stalked H.)*
On cones of Scotch fir. All the year. Very local. In Den of Leggart, near the south-west end.

3. H. *farinaceum*, Pers. *(Mealy H.)*
On decayed trees. November? and December. Rare. In the wood, a little east of new Church of Nigg.

8. RADULUM.

1. R. *orbiculare*, Fries. *(Circular R.)*
On dead birches. May to January. Den of Midmar, Mr. Mackay and G. D.

9. THELEPHORA.

1. T. *laciniata*, Pers. *(Fringed T.)*
On the ground in fir woods. November. Hazelhead woods, abundant.

2. T. *rubiginosa*, Schrad. *(Rusty T.)*
On dead trees. All the year. Frequent. At Middleton and other places near Aberdeen.

3. T. *rugosa*, Pers. *(Coarse T.)*
On stumps of trees. Summer and Autumn. Frequent near Aberdeen.

4. T. *hirsuta*, Willd. *(Hairy T.)*
On dead wood. Perennial. Frequent. Near Craigiebuckler; at Hazelhead, &c.

5. T. *sanguinolenta*, Alb. and Schw. *(Silky blood-stained T.)*
On fir stumps. Perennial. Frequent. In the Dry Den, near Countesswells, &c. &c.

6. T. *quercina*. Pers. *(Oak T.)*
On fallen branches of oak, beech, &c. All the year. Frequent near Aberdeen.

7. T. *byssoides*, Pers. *(Byssoid T.)*

On the ground in fir woods. Autumn and Winter. In the Dry Den and other places. Frequent.

8. T. caerulea, Schrad. *(Blue T.)*
On decaying wood. Frequent. Autumn and Winter. On fir branches at Middleton and other places.

9. T. miniata, Berkeley. *(Scarlet T.)*
On dead wood. Autumn. This beautiful species seems very local; only once have I found it. Woods at Middleton.

10. T. granulosa, Pers. *(Granulose T.)*
On dead wood. Winter. Dry Den, near Aberdeen.

11. T. incarnata Pers. *(Bright coloured T.)*
On fallen branches of different trees and shrubs. Winter. On dead whins in Belhelvie links.

10. CLAVARIA.

1. C. abietina, Pers. *(Fir-grove C.)*
On the ground in fir woods. August and September. At Craibston, Hazelhead, Den of Robslaw.

2. C. pratensis, Pers. *(Meadow C.)*
In pastures. October to December. In Belhelvie links, near the coast-guard station at Don-mouth; generally plentiful.

3. C. corniculata, Schoeff. *(Yellow-horned C.)*
In pastures and woods. October. Den of Robslaw and Craibstone.

4. C. rugosa, Bull. *(Wrinkled C.)*
Grassy places and woods. August to November. In Den of Leggart, and wood at old Bridge of Don.

11. CALOCERA.

1. C. cornea, Batsch. *(Horny C.)*
On stumps of trees. Autumn and Winter. Hazelhead, &c. &c. Frequent.

12. GEOGLOSSUM.

1. G. glabrum, Pers. *(Smooth G.)*
In dry pastures. Autumn. Rare. Among the sand-hills at Black-dog, Belhelvie.

13. SPATHULARIA.

1. S. flavida Pers. *(Common S.)*

On the ground in fir woods. July to October. This beautiful species is generally abundant in Den of Leggart, near old Bridge of Dee.

14. TYPHULA.

1. *T. erythropus*, Pers. *(Red-stemmed T.)*
On dead plants. Autumn. On dead fern stems, Dry Den, Countesswells.

15. MORCHELLA.

1. *M. esculenta*, Linn. *(Common M.)*
In woods, pastures, &c. Rare in this district. Near Aberdeen, Dr. A. Fleming; in the interior in Glen Dee, G. D.

16. LEOTIA.

1. *L. lubrica*, Scop. *(Slimy A.)*
In woods on the ground. Autumn. Rare. Craibstone, Dr. Ogilvie; Den of Leggart, G. D.

17. VIBRISSEA.

1. *V. truncorum*, A. & S. *(Golden V.)*
On branches in wet places. Summer. Very rare. This singular species I have only met with once, upon sticks buried under moist leaves in the wood at Middleton.

18. PEZIZA.

1. *P. cochleata*, Bull. *(Cochleate P.)*
In woods. Summer and Autumn. Local. Den of Maidencraig, near Aberdeen.

2. *P. tuberosa*, Bull. *(Tuberous P.)*
In woods. Spring. Very local. Den of Maidencraig, G. D.; Den of Midmar, Mr. Mackay.

3. *P. cupularis*, Linn. *(Scolloped P.)*
On the ground in woods. December. Rare. In Den of Leggart.

4. *P. rutilans*, Fries. *(Orange-red P.)*
On the ground among mosses. Autumn. On the Inch at Aberdeen.

5. *P. humosa*, Fries. *(Ground P.)*
On the ground among mosses. Autumn. Tops of walls among *Polytrichum*; at Denmore, near Aberdeen.

6. *P. stercorea*, Pers. *(Dung P.)*
On droppings of animals. Common.

7. P. *virginea*, Batsch. (*Virgin-white P.*)
On dead stumps, &c. Autumn. Tollohill wood.

8. P. *calycina*, Schum. (*White and orange P.*)
On bark of dead firs. Frequent.

9. P. *cerinea*, Pers. (*Wax-like P.*)
Upon dead stumps of trees. Frequent.

10. P. *villosa*, Pers. (*Villous P.*)
On dead twigs, &c. Common.

11. P. *Grevillii*, Berkeley. (*Greville's P.*)
On stems of herbaceous plants. Autumn. On dead raspberry stems at Aberdeen.

12. P. *anomala*, Pers. (*Anomalous P.*)
On dead trees. Autumn. Not unfrequent at Aberdeen.

13. P. *caerulea*, Bolt. (*Blue P.*)
On dead wood. October to December. Rare. Tollohill and Denmore.

19. TYMPANIS.

1. T. *conspersa*, Fries. (*Common T.*)
On dead raspberry branches. Frequent.

20. STICTIS.

1. S. *pallida*, Pers. (*Pale S.*)
On dead plants. Dry Den, near Aberdeen.

21. CRYPTOMYCES.

1. C. *versicolor*, Fries. (*Various-coloured C.*)
On dead branches of different kinds. Frequent. In Den of Leggart.

22. TREMELLA.

1. T. *foliacea*, Pers. (*Leaf-like T.*)
On stumps of trees. Rather local. In Glen Muick.

2. T. *mesenterica*, Retz. (*Orange T.*)
On dead branches, all the year. Frequent near Aberdeen.

3. T. *albida*, Smith. (*Dull-white T.*)
On fallen trees, palings, &c. Winter and Spring. Frequent near Aberdeen.

4. T. *sarcoides*, With. (*Flesh-like T.*)

On stumps of trees, &c. Winter. On whin, Den of Leggart.

23. EXIDIA.

1. E. *glandulosa*, Bull. *(Witches' Butter.)*
On dead trunks and branches. Autumn and Winter. On dead whins, Den of Leggart.

II.—GASTEROMYCETES.

24. PHALLUS.

1. P. *impudicus*, Linn. *(Common Stinkhorn.)*
In woods and thickets. Summer and Autumn. Local. Den of Midmar, Mr. Mackay; banks of the Dee at Banchory-Ternan, Dr. Adams.

25. RHIZOPOGON.

1. R. *albus*, Bull. *(White Truffle.)*
On the ground in woods. Very rare. At Craibstone, Dr. Ogilvie.

26. NIDULARIA.

1. P. *campanulata*, With. *(Bell-shaped B.)*
On the ground. In gardens and wet places not uncommon.

27. SPHAERIA.

1. S. *Hypoxylon*, Linn. *(Flat-horned S.)*
On sticks, stumps of trees, &c. Very common.

2. S. *fragiformis*, Pers. *(Strawberry S.)*
On beech bark. Common.

3. S. *stigma*, Hoffm. *(Black-dotted S.)*
On dead wood. Frequent about Aberdeen.

4. S. *verrucaeformis*, Ehr. *(Wart-like S.)*
On dead trees. Corbie Den, &c.

5. S. *lata*, Pers. *(Broad S.)*
On dead wood. Very frequent at Aberdeen.

6. S. *hispida*, Tode. *(Hispid S.)*
On dead whins at Tullis, in Nigg.

7. S. *spermoides*, Hoffm. *(Seed-like S.)*
On dead stems. On dead cabbage stems at Aberdeen.

8. S. *rudis*, Moug. *(Dingy-black S.)*
On dead branches of laburnum. About Aberdeen.

9. S. *leioplaca*, Fries. *(Patchy S.)*
On dead trees. Near Aberdeen, in the Dry Den on branches.

10. S. *byssiseda*, Tode. *(Greyish Lyssoid S.)*
On dead branches, &c. On dead raspberry branches in gardens and elsewhere at Aberdeen.

28. CYTISPORA.

1. C. *leucosperma*, Pers. *(White-seeded C.)*
On dead trees. Aberdeen.

29. RHYTISMA.

1. R. *Acerinum*, Pers. *(Sycamore R.)*
On leaves of maple. Very common.

30. HYSTERIUM.

1. H. *Fraxini*, Pers. *(Ash-twig H.)*
On dead branches of Ash. Winter and Spring. Common.

2. H. *lineare*, Fries. *(Linear H.)*
On dead plants of different kinds. Frequent.

31. BOVISTA.

1. B. *nigrescens*, Pers. *(Blackish Puff-ball.)*
Heaths and dry pastures. Frequent.

2. B. *plumbea*, Pers. *(Lead-coloured P. B.)*
Heaths and dry pastures. Frequent.

32. LYCOPERDON.

1. L. *giganteum*, Batsch. *(Giant Puff-ball.)*
In fields and pastures. Rather local. Autumn. In Old Aberdeen links, and in Belhelvie links.

2. L. *cœlatum*, Bull. *(Embossed P. B.)*
Meadows and pastures, &c. Rather local. Den of Leggart, &c.

3. L. *gemmatum*, Batsch. *(Studded P. B.)*
Fields and woods. Very frequent.

4. L. *pusillum*, Batsch. *(Dwarf P. B.)*
In pastures. Rather local. Old Aberdeen Links.

33. ELAPHOMYCES.

1. E. *muricatus*, Fries. *(Sharp-warted E.)*

About roots of trees. Autumn and winter. In the wood south side of Skene road, west from Robslaw quarry.

34. LYCOGALA.

1. L. *epidendrum*, Linn. *(Scarlet L.)*
On rotten stumps, pales, &c. Spring to autumn. Common.

35. PHYSARUM.

1. P. *album*, Nees. *(Flat, white P.)*
On various decaying substances. Frequent. Dead wood, Tullis, parish of Nigg.

36. STEMONITIS.

1. S. *fusca*, Roth. *(Brown S.)*
On rotten wood. Summer and winter. Wood at the old Bridge of Don; and in the Dry Den, near Countesswells.

37. DICTIDIUM.

1. D. *umbilicatum*, Schrad. *(Umbilicate D.)*
On rotten wood. Very local. In the wood at Tullis.

38. RETICULARIA.

1. R. *atra*, A. and S. *(Black R.)*
On wood and bark of dead pines. Frequent. In the Dry Den, Countesswells, in July.

39. ÆTHALIUM.

1. Æ. *septicum*, Linn. *(Common Æ.)*
On mosses in woods, &c. Common.

40. SPUMARIA.

1. S. *alba*, Bull. *(White S.)*
On stems of grass. Very frequent.

41. ARCYRIA.

1. A. *nutans*, Bull. *(Flaccid A.)*
On rotten wood. Autumn. Very local. Wood at Tullis; and Cherryvale.

42. LASIOBOTRYS.

1. L. *Linnææ*, Berk. *(Linnaea L.)*
On the leaves of *Linnaea borealis*. Frequent upon *Linnaea*, at Aberdeen.

43. ERYSIPHE.

1. E. *communis*, Schl. *(Common E.)*
On herbaceous plants. Common. Frequent on the cultivated pea, &c.

III.—HYPHOMYCETES.

44. ASCOPHORA.

1. A. *Mucedo*, Tode. *(Common H.)*
On various matters in damp places. Common.

45. DACTYLIUM.

1. D. *dendroides*, Fries. *(Tree-like D.)*
On decaying *Agarics*. Frequent. In the woods of Countesswells, &c.

46. OIDIUM.

1. O. *erysiphoides*, Fries. *(Mildew O.)*
On various cultivated plants. Frequent.

2. O. *leucoconium*, Desm. *(Small Mildew O.)*
On leaves of various plants, as apple trees, &c. &c.

47. SEPEDONIUM.

1. S. *chrysospermum*, Lk. *(Golden-seeded S.)*
On decaying *Fungi*. Frequent. In woods of Countesswells, &c.

IV.—CONIOMYCETES.

48. NAEMASPORA.

1. N. *crocea*, Pers. *(Saffron-yellow N.)*
On beech trees. Frequent. Hazelhead woods, &c.

49. AREGMA.

1. A. *bulbosum*, Fries. *(Bramble A.)*
On leaves of different species of *Rubus*. Frequent.

50. HYDROPHORA.

1. H. *stercorea*, Tode. *(Common H.)*
On droppings of animals after rain. Frequent.

51. MUCOR.

1. M. *Mucedo*, Linn. *(Common Mould.)*
On fruit preserves, &c. &c. Common.

52. PACHNOCYBE.

1. P. *subulata*, Berk. (*Subulate P.*)
On decaying plants. On dead fir cones in the wood at Tullis.

53. HELMINTHOSPORIUM.

1. H. *macrocarpum*, Grev. (*Large-seeded H.*)
On decaying wood. Frequent. On dead whins in the wood at Tullis.

54. ASPERGILLUS.

1. A. *candidus*, Lk. (*White A.*)
On decaying matters of different kinds. Common.

2. A. *glaucus*, Lk. (*Blue Mould.*)
On various matters, as bread, &c. Common.

55. BOTRYTIS.

1. B. *parasitica*, Pers. (*Parasitic B.*)
On *Capsella B. Pastoris*, &c. Frequent.

56. PODISOMA.

1. P. *Juniperi communis*, Fries. (*Common Juniper P.*)
On living branches of Juniper. Rather local. On the high ground at Banchory-Ternan, north from the village.

57. PUCCINIA.

1. P. *Polygonorum*, Lk. (*Polygonum P.*)
On Polygonum *viviparum*, in Corbie Den.

58. ÆCIDIUM.

1. Æ. *leucospermum*, De C. (*White-seeded Æ.*)
On leaves of wood Anemone. Corbie Den, &c.

2. Æ. *Epilobii*, De C.
On Epilobium *montanum*. Common.

3. Æ. *Pini*, Pers. (*Pine Æ.*)
On dead branches of Scotch fir. Dry Den, Countesswells.

59. UREDO.

1. U. *Anthyllidis*, Grev. (*Kidney-vetch U.*)
On Anthyllis *vulneraria*. Frequent.

2. U. *apiculosa* Lk. (*Apiculate U.*)
On leaves of Lapsana *communis*. Frequent.

3. U. *Epilobii*, De C.   (*Willow-herb U.*)
On leaves of E. *montanum*.   Aberdeen.

4. U. *Campanulae*, Pers.   (*Bell-flower U.*)
On leaves of Campanula *rotundifolia*.   Aberdeen.

5. U. *caprearum*, De C.   (*Sallow U.*)
On leaves of Salix *caprea*.   Aberdeen.

6. U. *intrusa*, Grev.   (*Lady's-mantle U.*)
On leaves of Alchemilla *vulgaris*.   Aberdeen.

7. U. *Polygonorum*, De. C.   (*Polygonum U.*)
On leaves of Polygonum *aviculare*, &c.   Frequent.

8. U. *Potentillarum*, De C.   (*Potentilla U.*)
On leaves of Alchemilla, &c.   Aberdeen.

9. U. *Rosae*, De C.   (*Rose U.*)
On Rose leaves.   Common.

10. U. *Ruborum*, De C.   (*Bramble U.*)
On Bramble leaves.   Common.

11. U. *Saliceti*, Schl.   (*Willow U.*)
On Willow leaves.   Common.

12. U. *Senecionis*, Schl.   (*Grounsel U.*)
On leaves of common Grounsel.   Common.

ADDENDA.

P. 24.—After *Lychnis*, add

 Agrostemma *Githago*. Frequent in cultivated fields throughout the district.

P. 67.—Saxifraga *hypnoides*, add

 K.—Coast at the Cove, where, I am informed, it was discovered by a lady, in 1859.

P. 78.—Linnaea *borealis*, add

 Fir wood, west side of road, a little east of Midmar Castle, and Tomanide wood opposite Manse of Midmar, Mr. Charles Mackay. Wood a little west of the farm of Hillhead, Midmar, Mrs. Donald.

P. 106.—Vaccinium *Oxycoccos*, add

 Boggy ground west of Greenhill, in Strathdon, Mr. Mackay and G. D.

P. 226.—Et seq, add

 In Den of Dunnottar, near Stonehaven, Asplenium *Adiantum nigrum*, Aspidium *lobatum*, and its *var.* β, Mr. James Collie. Braes of Gight, Asplenium *Trichomanes*, Aspidium *Adiantum nigrum*, Aspidium *oreopteris*, Cystopteris *fragilis*, *var.* *dentata*, Mr. James Collie. Mill of Laithers, Scolopendrium *vulgate*, Mr. Hislop. Asplenium *septentrionale*, on cliffs two miles west from Inver, Braemar, Mr. James Collie, August 22, 1860.

INTRODUCED PLANTS.
DICOTYLEDONS.
COMPOSITAE.

 Anthemis *arvensis*, occasionally in fields near Aberdeen, Professor Macgillivray.

MONOCOTYLEDONS.
HYDROCHARIDACEAE.

 Anacharis *alsinastrum*, Bab. Introduced into pools by the road-side west from Summerhill, near Aberdeen; and into the small lake in the Old-town Links.

TYPHACEAE.

 Typha *latifolia*, L. Introduced into Loch of Park, where it is now very abundant.

CORRIGENDA.

Page 13.—For Thalianun, *read*, Thalianum.

Page 28.—Cerastium *semidecandrum*.

For K.—Coast at St. Cyrus, &c. &c. *read*,

K.—Coast at St. Cyrus, Dr. Stephen; near Aberdeen, at south pier, G. D.

A.—Inch, &c. G. D.; in Buchan, Mr. Murray; Aberdour, Rev. G. Gairdner; Clatt, Rev. J. Minto.

Page 49.—For 6. R. Chamaemorus, *read*, 7. &c.

Pages 54 and 55.—For 1, 3, 4, 5, 6, 7, 8, *read*, 1, 2, 3, 4, 5, 6, 7.

Page 98.—For 1382 to 4250 feet, *read*, 1350 to 4250.

Page 188, top,—For Curex, *read*, Carex.

Page 223.—For Buxbauen's, *read*, Buxbaum's.

Page 278.—For Collernaceae, *read*, Collemaceae.

INDEX.

FLOWERING PLANTS, FERNS, AND ALLIES.

	Page.		Page.		Page.
Achillea,	103	Arrhenatherum,	204	Caltha,	4
Adoxa,	74	Artemisia,	96	Camelina,	217
Ægopodium,	220	Arum,	225	Campanula,	103
Æthusa,	220	Asperula,	82	Capsella,	15
Agraphis,	165	Aspidium,	227	Cardamine,	10
Agrimonia,	53	Asplenium,	230	Carduus,	93
Agrostemma,	336	Aster,	100	Carex,	185
Agrostis,	200	Astragalus,	41	Carlina,	94
Aira,	201	Atriplex,	138	Carum,	220
Ajuga,	126	Avena,	212	Catabrosa,	201
Alchemilla,	52	Azalea,	107	Centaurea,	95
Alisma,	172			Cerastium,	27
Alliaria,	14	Ballota,	224	Chaerophyllum,	73
Allium,	165	Barbarea,	9	Cheiranthus,	217
Alnus,	150	Bartsia,	121	Chelidonium,	216
Alopecurus,	197	Bellis,	102	Chenopodium,	138
Ammophila,	198	Beta,	224	Chrysanthemum	102
Anacharis,	336	Betula,	149	Chrysosplenium,	67
Anagallis,	134	Bidens,	95	Cichorium,	221
Anchusa,	222	Blechnum,	232	Cicuta,	69
Anemone,	2	Blysmus,	180	Circaea,	59
Angelica,	71	Borago,	222	Cnicus,	94
Antennaria,	96	Botrychium,	233	Cochlearia,	10
Anthemis,	336	Brachypodium,	215	Comarum,	50
Anthoxanthum,	197	Brassica,	217	Conium,	72
Anthriscus,	72	Briza,	207	Convolvulus,	114
Anthyllis,	38	Bromus,	210	Coriandrum,	220
Apargia,	84	Bunium,	69	Cornus,	75
Aquilegia,	216			Corydalis,	8
Arabis,	9	Cakile,	13	Corylus,	156
Arctium,	92	Calamagrostis,	200	Crataegus,	219
Arctostaphylos,	108	Calamintha,	129	Crepis,	86
Arenaria,	26	Callitriche,	148	Cryptogramma,	232
Armeria,	135	Calluna,	107	Cuscuta,	222

INDEX.

	Page.		Page.		Page.
Cynoglossum,	222	Habenaria,	. 162	Lycopus,	. 124
Cynosurus,	. 208	Hedera, .	. 75	Lysimachia,	. 134
Cystopteris,	. 229	Helianthemum,	17		
		Helleborus,	. 216	Malaxis, .	. 158
Dactylis,	. 208	Helosciadium,	69	Malva, .	. 31
Daucus, .	. 73	Heracleum,	. 71	Matricaria,	. 102
Dianthus,	. 21	Hieracium,	. 87	Meconopsis,	. 216
Digitalis,	. 123	Hippuris,	. 60	Medicago,	. 38
Digitaria,	. 226	Honckenya,	. 25	Melampyrum,	122
Doronicum,	. 221	Holcus, .	. 204	Melica, .	. 203
Draba, .	. 10	Hordeum,	. 214	Melilotus,	. 218
Drosera, .	. 19	Hydrocotyle, .	68	Mentha, .	. 124
Dryas, .	. 46	Hyoscyamus,	. 223	Menyanthes,	. 113
		Hypericum,	. 31	Mercurialis,	. 146
Echium,	. 114	Hypochaeris, .	85	Mertensia,	. 115
Elatine, .	. 21			Meum, .	. 71
Eleocharis,	. 181	Ilex,	. 111	Milium, .	. 199
Elymus, .	. 214	Iris,	. 164	Molinia, .	. 203
Empetrum,	. 146	Isoetes, .	. 235	Monesis, .	. 108
Epilobium,	. 56	Isolepis, .	. 182	Montia, .	. 61
Epipactis,	. 159			Mulgedium,	. 85
Equisetum,	. 235	Jasione, .	. 104	Myosotis,	. 116
Erica, .	. 106	Juncus, .	. 166	Myrica, .	. 149
Erigeron,	. 100	Juniperus,	. 158	Myriophyllum,	60
Eriophorum,	. 184			Myrrhis,	. 220
Erodium,	. 35	Knautia,	. 83		
Eryngium,	. 69	Koeleria,	. 204	Nardus, .	. 197
Erysimum,		Koniga, .	. 217	Narthecium,	. 171
Erythraea,	. 112			Nasturtium,	. 10
Eupatorium,	. 96	Lamium,	. 127	Nepeta, .	. 129
Euphorbia,	. 147	Lapsana,	. 91	Nuphar, .	. 6
Euphrasia,	. 121	Lathyrus,	. 44	Nymphaea,	. 5
		Lemna, .	. 175		
		Leontodon,	. 87	Œnanthe,	. 70
Fedia, .	. 83	Lepidium,	. 15	Ononis, .	. 37
Festuca, .	. 209	Ligusticum,	. 71	Ophioglossum,	233
Filago, .	. 98	Limosella,	. 124	Orchis, .	. 161
Fragaria,	. 49	Linaria, .	. 223	Origanum,	. 125
Fumaria,	. 8	Linnaea,	. 77	Ornithopus,	. 43
		Linum, .	. 30	Orobus, .	. 44
Galeopsis,	. 126	Listera, .	. 159	Osmunda,	. 232
Galium, .	. 79	Lithospermum,	115	Oxalis, .	. 36
Genista, .	. 36	Littorella,	. 137	Oxyria, .	. 145
Gentiana,	. 113	Lobelia, .	. 104		
Geranium,	. 33	Lolium, .	. 215	Papaver,	. 7
Geum, .	. 46	Lonicera,	. 77	Parietaria,	. 224
Glaucium,	. 7	Lotus, .	. 40	Paris, .	. 164
Glaux, .	. 133	Luzula, .	. 170	Parnassia,	. 20
Gnaphalium,	. 97	Lychnis,	. 23	Pedicularis,	. 123
Goodyera,	. 160	Lycopodium, .	233	Peplis, .	. 61
Gymnadenia, .	162	Lycopsis,	. 117	Petasites,	. 99

INDEX. 341

	Page.		Page.		Page.
Phalaris,	198	Sagina,	24	Stachys,	128
Phleum,	199	Salicornia,	139	Stellaria,	27
Phragmites,	213	Salix,	151	Suaeda,	139
Pilularia,	235	Salsola,	139	Subularia,	14
Pimpinella,	70	Sambucus,	76	Symphytum,	117
Pinguicula,	130	Sanicula,	68		
Pinus,	156	Saponaria,	217	Tanacetum,	221
Plantago,	136	Saussurea,	93	Teesdalia,	12
Poa,	205	Saxifraga,	64	Teucrium,	125
Polemonium,	222	Scabiosa,	83	Thalictrum,	1
Polygala,	21	Scandix,	72	Thlaspi,	12
Polygonatum,	225	Schoenus,	180	Thymus,	125
Polygonum,	140	Scilla,	165	Tofieldia,	166
Polypodium,	226	Scirpus,	182	Torilis,	74
Populus,	155	Scleranthus,	140	Tragopogon,	84
Potamogeton,	175	Scolopendrium,	231	Trientalis,	133
Potentilla,	50	Scrophularia,	123	Trifolium,	38
Primula,	132	Scutellaria,	130	Triglochin,	173
Prunella,	130	Sedum,	63	Triodia,	207
Prunus,	44	Sempervivum,	219	Triticum,	214
Pteris,	232	Senebiera,	16	Trollius,	5
Pyrola,	109	Senecio,	101	Tussilago,	99
Pyrus,	56	Setaria,	226	Typha,	336
		Sherardia,	81		
Quercus,	155	Sibbaldia,	51	Ulex,	36
		Silene,	22	Urtica,	149
Radiola,	30	Sinapis,	16	Utricularia,	131
Ranunculus,	2	Sisymbrium,	13		
Raphanus,	15	Smyrnium,	220	Vaccinium,	105
Reseda,	16	Solanum,	223	Valeriana,	82
Rhamnus,	218	Solidago,	100	Verbascum,	223
Rhinanthus,	121	Sonchus,	85	Veronica,	118
Rhyncospora,	180	Sparganium,	173	Viburnum,	76
Ribes,	219	Spartium,	37	Vicia,	42
Rosa,	54	Spergula,	62	Viola,	18
Rubus,	47	Spergularia,	62		
Rumex,	143	Spiraea,	45	Zostera,	179
Ruppia,	179				

ACOTYLEDONOUS PLANTS,

Excepting FERNS *and their* ALLIES.

	Page.		Page.		Page.
Achnanthes,	316	Calicium,	277	Cynodontium,	239
Achnanthidium,	316	Callithamnion,	291	Cystoclonium,	289
Actinocyclus,	314	Calocera,	327	Cytispora,	331
Æcidium,	334	Calothrix,	308		
Æthalium,	332	Campylodiscus,	314	Dactylium,	333
Agaricus,	319	Campylopus	241	Daedalea,	324
Alaria,	282	Cantharellus,	324	Dasya,	287
Amblyodon,	253	Catenella,	290	Dellesseria,	288
Amphipleura,	314	Ceramium,	291	Denticula,	316
Amphiprora,	314	Ceratodon,	241	Desmarestia,	281
Amphora,	314	Cetraria,	269	Desmidium,	297
Anacalypta,	242	Chaetophora,	294	Diatoma,	316
Andreaea,	237	Chara,	267	Diatomella,	316
Anoectangium,	256	Chondrus,	289	Dickieia,	317
Anomodon,	256	Chorda,	282	Dicranum,	239
Antitrichia,	256	Chordaria,	283	Dictidium,	332
Arctoa,	239	Chrysymenia,	287	Dictyosiphon,	282
Arcyria,	332	Chylocladia,	287	Didymodon,	242
Aregma,	333	Cinclidotus,	243	Didymoprium,	297
Arthonia,	276	Cladonia,	277	Diphyscium,	248
Arthrodesmus,	299	Cladostephus,	284	Dissodon,	255
Ascophora,	333	Cladophora,	295	Distichium,	242
Aspergillus,	334	Clavaria,	327	Docidium,	300
Asperococcus,	283	Climacium,	256	Dolichosper- }	311
Asterionella,	316	Closterium,	301	mum,	
Atricum,	248	Coccochloris,	311	Doryphora,	315
Aulacomnion,	249	Cocconeis,	314	Draparnaldia,	294
		Cocconema,	315	Dudresnaia,	290
Baeomyces,	277	Codium,	294	Dumontia,	290
Bangia,	307	Coleochaete,	294		
Bartramia,	253	Collema,	278		
Batrachosper- }	293	Conferva,	295	Ectocarpus,	284
mum,		Conostomum,	254	Elachista,	284
Blindia,	239	Corallina,	287	Elaphomyces,	331
Boletus,	325	Cornicularia,	268	Encalypta,	243
Bonnemaisonia,	287	Coscinodiscus,	314	Endocarpon,	279
Botrydium,	295	Cosmarium,	298	Enteromorpha,	306
Botrytis,	334	Cryptomyces,	329	Epithemia,	314
Bovista,	331	Cyclotella,	314	Erysiphe,	333
Bryopsis,	294	Cylindrosper- }	311	Euastrum,	297
Bryum,	250	mum,		Eucampia,	
Bulbochaete,	293	Cymatopleura,	314	Eunotia,	314
Buxbaumia,	248	Cymbella,	314	Exidia,	330

INDEX.

	Page.		Page.		Page.
Fegatella,	262	Leskea,	257	Pediastrum,	302
Fissidens,	255	Leucobryum,	241	Peltigera,	270
Fontinalis,	261	Lichina,	279	Penium,	300
Fragilaria,	316	Licmophora,	315	Pertusaria,	280
Fucus,	281	Litosiphon,	283	Petalonema,	308
Funaria,	253	Lycogala,	332	Peziza,	328
Furcellaria,	290	Lycoperdon,	331	Phallus,	330
		Lyngbya,	308	Phascum,	238
Gelidium,	289			Phyllophora,	289
Geoglossum,	327	Marchantia,	262	Physarum,	332
Gigartina,	289	Mastogloia,		Physcia,	269
Gloiosiphonia,	290	Meesia,	253	Physcomitrium,	253
Gomphonema,	315	Melobesia,	288	Pinnularia,	315
Grammatophora	316	Melosira,	316	Pleurosigma,	315
Griffithsia,	291	Meridion,	315	Plocamium,	289
Grimmia,	244	Merulius,	324	Podisoma,	334
Gyalecta,	274	Mesogloia,	283	Podosira,	316
Gymnogongrus,	290	Micrasterias,	297	Pogonatum,	248
Gymnostomum,	238	Microcoleus,	309	Polyides,	290
		Mielichhoferia,	252	Polyporus,	324
Haematococcus,	312	Mnium,	252	Polysiphonia,	286
Halidrys,	281	Morchella,	328	Polytrichum,	249
Halymenia,	290	Mougeotia,	296	Porphyra,	307
Hapalidium,	288	Myrionema,	284	Pottia,	242
Hedwigia,	244	Myriotrichia,	285	Protococcus,	312
Helminthos- porium,	} 334	Mucor,	333	Pterogonium,	256
				Ptilota,	291
Hildenbrantia,	288	Naemaspora,	333	Ptychomitrium,	246
Himanthalia,	281	Navicula,	315	Puccinia,	334
Himantidium,	316	Neckera,	261	Punctaria,	283
Hookeria,	261	Nephroma,	269	Pyrenula,	280
Hyalotheca,	296	Nidularia,	330		
Hydnum,	326	Nitella,	267	Racomitrium,	245
Hydrophora,	333	Nitophyllum,	288	Radulum,	326
Hypnum,	257	Nitzschia,	314	Ralfsia,	283
Hysterium,	331	Nostoc,	310	Ramalina,	268
				Reticularia,	332
Iridaea,	290	Odonthalia,	285	Rhabdonema,	316
Isothecium,	256	Odontidium,	316	Rhabdoweissia,	239
		Œdipodum,	255	Rhipidophora,	315
Jania,	288	Oidium,	333	Rhizopogon,	330
Jungermannia,	263	Oligotrichum,	248	Rhodomela,	286
Laminaria,	282	Omalia,	261	Rhodymenia,	289
Lasiobotrys,	332	Opegrapha	276	Rhytisma,	331
Laurencia,	287	Orthosira,	316	Riccia,	262
Leathesia,	283	Orthotrichum,	246	Rivularia,	307
Lecanora,	273	Oscillatoria,	309		
Lecidea,	274			Scenedesmus,	302
Lemania,	293	Pachnocybe,	334	Schistidium,	244
Leotia,	328	Palmella,	311	Schizonema,	317
Leptobryum,	249	Parmelia,	271	Scytonema,	308

	Page		Page		Page
Seligeria,	239	Surirella,	314	Ulva,	306
Sepedonium,	333	Synedra,	315	Umbilicaria,	270
Solorina,	270			Urceolaria,	274
Sorospora,	311	Tabellaria,	316	Uredo,	334
Spathularia,	327	Tayloria,	255	Usnea,	268
Sphacelaria,	284	Tetmemorus,	300		
Sphaerphoron,	279	Tetraphis,	247	Vaucheria,	294
Sphaeria,	330	Tetraplodon,	254	Verrucaria,	280
Sphaerozyga,	310	Tetraspora,	306	Vibrissea,	328
Sphagnum,	237	Thamnolia,	278	Volvox,	319
Spirotaenia,	302	Thelephora,	326		
Spirulina,	309	Thelotrema,	280	Weissia,	238
Splachnum,	254	Tolypothrix,	308		
Spumaria,	332	Tortula,	243	Zygnema,	296
Staurastrum,	299	Tremella,	329	Zygodon,	247
Stauroneis,	315	Trentepohlia,	293	Zygogonium,	296
Stemonitis,	332	Trichormus,	310		
Stereocaulon,	277	Trichostomum,	242	Xanthidium,	299
Sticta,	271	Tympanis,	329		
Stictis,	329	Tyndaridea,	296		
Stigonema,	307	Typhula,	328		

G. CORNWALL & SONS, PRINTERS, ABERDEEN.

www.ingramcontent.com/pod-product-compliance
Lightning Source LLC
Chambersburg PA
CBHW030407230426
43664CB00007BB/782